PERSPECTIVES ON
COGNITIVE DISSONANCE

COMPLEX HUMAN BEHAVIOR

A series of volumes edited by
Leon Festinger and **Stanley Schachter**

PERSPECTIVES ON COGNITIVE DISSONANCE

Robert A. Wicklund

UNIVERSITY OF TEXAS AT AUSTIN

Jack W. Brehm

UNIVERSITY OF KANSAS

 LAWRENCE ERLBAUM ASSOCIATES, PUBLISHERS

1976   Hillsdale, New Jersey

DISTRIBUTED BY THE HALSTED PRESS DIVISION OF

JOHN WILEY & SONS

New York   Toronto   London   Sydney

Lawrence Erlbaum Associates, Inc., Publishers
62 Maria Drive
Hillsdale, New Jersey 07642

Distributed solely by Halsted Press Division
John Wiley & Sons, Inc., New York

Library of Congress Cataloging in Publication Data
Wicklund, Robert A
   Perspectives on cognitive dissonance.

   (Complex human behavior)
   "A Halsted Press book."
   Includes indexes.
   1. Dissonance (Psychology) I. Brehm, Jack
Williams, joint author. II. Title. [DNLM: 1. Cognitive dissonance. 2. Decision making. BF335
W637p]
BF311.W575 1976 153.4 75-43699
ISBN 0-470-15008-4

Printed in the United States of America

Contents

Foreword

The research reported in this book spans a period of roughly 18 years, years which have marked the emergence of social psychology as a vital experimental discipline. The stimulus of dissonance theory had much to do with this emergence. Not only has dissonance theory provided a substantive focus for researchers in the field, but much of the research partakes of a style that provides a paradigm for other research efforts as well. Without great strain one can see in this research style the fruition of the kind of theory-based experimentation envisaged, but never really realized, by Kurt Lewin. In particular, the idea of a highly general theory being tested in a variety of socially interesting domains exemplifies Lewin's proposed paradigm: the conceptual replication of an abstract functional relation in different concrete life spaces.

Leon Festinger's 1957 book presented a simple theoretical notion that many thought was implicit in the writings of Heider, Lecky, and others. There was nothing very new about the idea that cognitive inconsistency was unpleasant, and it was not a great step to suggest that it was motivating. The presentation of the theory was neither rhetorically compelling nor convincingly buttressed with experimental data generated by the theory. And yet, the fuller implications of this new presentation of a consistency theory were tantalizing indeed. This modest book crept up on the reader and eventually enthralled him in sets of intriguing and testable paradoxes.

Further construction on Festinger's scaffold required the intricate interplay of experimental data and theory. First there was a reaching out process—into those different life spaces Lewin wrote about. Jack Brehm and his Yale colleagues began exploring the implications of dissonance theory for attitude change. Judson Mills brought the power of the theory to focus on value internalization. Elliot Aronson attacked the principle of effort leading to attraction. Festinger himself moved with Lawrence into the area of animal behavior in an attempt to explain a number of learning phenomena in dissonance terms.

As the evidence from these early stake outs accumulated, research effort began to focus more and more on theoretical issues and their development. *Explorations in Cognitive Dissonance,* by Jack Brehm and the late Bob Cohen, was the pivot of this transition. By this time enough of the toes of tradition had been bruised to inspire critical rebuttal. After all, here was a theory that proferred an explanation for resistance to extinction, moral fervor, attentional selectivity, object preferences, proselytizing, and attitude change. It is not surprising that as dissonance research bounced from one traditional domain to another, alternative explanations followed in its wake.

In fact, while the applications of dissonance theory to different psychological problems continued, along with attempts to give the theory more precision, a skeptical countermovement of some proportions was developing. At times, in the late sixties, it appeared that dissonance theorists and reinforcement theorists were engaged in a holy war. But the important thing was that finally social psychology had come to a point where there were identifiable theoretical battlegrounds, and issues could in fact be joined and resolved without irreconcilable polemics.

The methodological style of the dissonance proponents also fed the flames of controversy. Those who fashioned the dissonance literature were, by and large, uncommonly bright and inventive. But their inventiveness was usually coupled with the use of deceptive scenarios and a procedural complexity that made precise replication difficult. Those bred in the tradition of cumulative research in experimental psychology thought they saw serious vulnerability in this complexity and in the apparent disregard of standardized dependent-variable measurement.

Instead, and this was difficult to realize at any given moment, there was developing a body of literature that was *conceptually* cumulative and therefore more impressive than permutations on a measuring device or a statistical inference rule. No one can read this book without appreciating the development of a solid research consensus on a number of important and once controversial issues. No one can any more claim that dissonance effects are artifacts or that dissonance is at most a contrived laboratory experience. Undoubtedly many readers of this volume will have reservations about specific interpretations and prefer their own alternatives. Nonetheless, the cumulative reach of dissonance research is remarkable. We may now have reached a less flamboyant stage of tidying of loose ends and charting out the relations between dissonance theory and other psychological conceptions, but whatever the future holds, the dissonance research "movement" has been the most important development in social psychology to date.

EDWARD E. JONES

A Special Dedication

The publication in 1962 of *Explorations in cognitive dissonance* was the culmination of five years of joint research between Arthur R. Cohen and myself, and it was an attempt to assess the status of dissonance theory after the initial research results were in. We felt that the theory had considerable potential for the understanding of behavior, and we wanted to stimulate further work. *Explorations* did, no doubt, act as such a stimulus, but there was no way for us to foresee the almost incredible amount of research that was to be generated by dissonance theory during the ensuing dozen years. A revision of *Explorations* would have been appropriate within a few years of its publication. Unfortunately, however, there was no chance for us to do a normal revision because of Bob Cohen's untimely death in 1963.

Had he lived, Bob would certainly have been the prime mover of this latest attempt to assess dissonance theory, and the evaluation would have benefitted greatly from his insight and scholarship. It stands as a tribute to his brilliance that his research on dissonance theory remains an important part of the literature and continues to be widely referenced. Though much has happened since his death, his contributions live on both through the research that he did and through his part in the writing of *Explorations,* from which we have borrowed freely in the present volume. In recognition of those contributions, both explicit and implicit, and in recognition of Bob's place as one of the outstanding social psychologists of his time, my coauthor, Robert Wicklund, joins me in dedicating this book to the memory of Arthur R. Cohen.

JACK W. BREHM

Preface

Since its publication by Leon Festinger in 1957, the theory of cognitive dissonance has generated an enormous amount of research and considerable theoretical discussion. It has been supported by the bulk of the published research, but some research and, more importantly, some of the theoretical discussion has called into question one or another aspect of the theory. Because of the amount and variety of accumulated research, and because of the disparate nature of the questions raised, an evaluation of dissonance theory has become increasingly difficult for the involved scholar as well as the interested observer. Have some derivations been supported while others have been disconfirmed? Have there been telling theoretical or methodological criticisms? Has dissonance theory been replaced or subsumed by alternative theories? In short, after hundreds of empirical tests by innumerable researchers, after numerous criticisms of the theory and the methods used to test it, and after various alternative theories have been proposed, what is the status of dissonance theory? Answering this question has been our primary intent in writing the present volume.

As implied by the above questions, there are various dimensions on which dissonance theory might be evaluated, and we have selected those that serve our particular purposes. We are primarily concerned with what dissonance theory can tell us about human behavior that other theory or knowledge does not tell us. This concern leads in turn to two kinds of evaluation: (a) the extent to which the basic propositions of the theory have been supported, and (b) the extent to which dissonance phenomena are interpretable in terms of alternative theories. In addition, we have tried to show the degree to which dissonance theory has been useful in the understanding of a variety of behavioral phenomena.

Given our intentions, it will come as no surprise that we have devoted little attention to metatheoretical or epistemological issues. Perhaps less obvious will be the fact that we have not attempted to be exhaustive in our report of the literature. The term *cognitive dissonance* has been widely and sometimes loosely used, and a report on all uses of the term would include a great deal of material that is irrelevant to our purposes. In addition, in order to avoid overburdening the reader with unimportant detail, we have omitted studies that had serious ambiguities or that provided weak evidence that was consistent with other, stronger evidence.

In an attempt to ensure that we located all material of importance, we enlisted the help of various foreign scholars in the search for information about work that is relevant to the theory. For their help and for making special papers available to us, we would like to thank Drs. Dieter Frey, Charles Greenbaum, Stefan Hormuth, Martin Irle, Jaromir Janousek, Hanna Malewska-Peyre, Serge Moscovici, Jacob Rabbie, Peter Schönbach, and Ina Spiegel-Rösing.

Once we had completed a first draft, we asked many people to read one or more chapters that were in their areas of expertise, and we wish to thank the following for their helpful comments: J. Stacy Adams, Abram Amsel, Richard Archer, Elliot Aronson, Daryl Bem, Joel Cooper, David Glass, Bettina Götz-Marchand, Robert Helmreich, Martin Irle, Charles Kiesler, Gerald Leventhal, Darwyn Linder, David Mettee, Judson Mills, Jozef Nuttin, Jr., Lee Sechrest, David Shaffer, Steven Sherman, Suzanne Sogin, James Tedeschi, Stephen West, Stephen Worchel, Mark Zanna, and Philip Zimbardo.

We are particularly grateful to the late Nickolas Cottrell for helping us to write the chapter on the energizing effects of dissonance. We are also especially grateful to Sharon Brehm and to Dieter Frey, both of whom read the entire first draft and made many helpful suggestions. Our greatest indebtedness is to Edward E. Jones, who gave us the benefit of his editorial, scholarly, and conceptual skills on the entire revised manuscript.

Needless to say, Leon Festinger's encouragement and comments have also been helpful, as have those of our editor-publisher, Lawrence Erlbaum.

We are highly appreciative of the able and rapid typing of the manuscript, carried out in Austin by Brenda Romines, Claudia Cates, Pat Childers, Faye Gibson, and Jan Seriff, and in Durham by Wilma Long.

For permission to include tabular material from various articles we would like to thank the various authors involved as well as the following publishers: Academic Press, the American Psychological Association, Mouton and Company, Stanford University Press, and the University of California Press.

Finally, for permission to borrow freely from *Explorations in cognitive dissonance,* we wish to give special thanks to Barbara Cohen Green.

PERSPECTIVES ON
COGNITIVE DISSONANCE

1
Introduction to the Theory

Imagine a fearful person who cannot find an adequate cause for his fear. His knowledge, on the one hand, that he is fearful is quite inconsistent with his knowledge, on the other, that there is nothing to fear. Such an inconsistency in knowledge, according to Festinger (1957), gives rise to a psychological state which he called "cognitive dissonance." Cognitive dissonance was defined as a motivational state that impels the individual to attempt to reduce and eliminate it. Because dissonance arises from inconsistent knowledge, it can be reduced by decreasing or eliminating the inconsistency. Thus, according to Festinger's analysis, a fearful person who could find nothing to fear is motivated by cognitive dissonance either to reduce his fear or to find some fear-provoking event. Accomplishment of either of these possibilities eliminates the state of cognitive dissonance.

While the example of a fearful person who has nothing to fear contains the central idea of dissonance theory, it omits those aspects of Festinger's (1957) theoretical statement that distinguished it from other theories of cognitive balance (e.g., Heider, 1958; Newcomb, 1953). Most notably, the original statement of dissonance theory included propositions about the resistance-to-change of cognitions and about the proportion of cognitions that are dissonant, both of which allowed powerful and innovative analyses of psychological situations. It was the inclusion of these latter propositions that not only distinguished dissonance theory from other theories of cognitive balance, but also made dissonance theory a fertile source of research.

The theory we shall present here is an evolved version of Festinger's (1957) original statement. The only significant change from the original has to do with the concept of personal responsibility, to be described later.

SPELLING OUT THE THEORY

Cognitions, Consonance, Dissonance, and Importance

Any bit of knowledge that a person has about himself or the environment is a "cognition," or "cognitive element." Cognitions about the self would include such components as knowledge of one's weight, awareness of hunger, the memory of a previous visit at the dentist's office, and the intention to go to the bank tomorrow. Cognitions about the environment would perhaps include knowledge of the distance between London and Paris, knowing which candidate for political office is a Democrat, perceiving that grass is green, recalling that one's car is in need of repair, and expecting the sun to rise tomorrow. Cognitions may be very specific bits of information or they may be general concepts and relations, and they may be quite firm and clear or they may be vague.

The relationship between two cognitive elements is *consonant* if one implies the other in some psychological sense. Psychological implication can arise from cultural mores, pressure to be logical, behavioral commitment, past experience, and so on. What is meant by implication is that having cognition A implies having cognition B. Knowing that steak is a tasty food is consonant with knowing that one is eating steak. Similarly, a person's knowledge that he has voted for John Smith to be mayor is consonant with his belief that Smith has the qualities of a good mayor. The detection of psychological implication is frequently possible by measurement of what else a person expects when he holds a given cognition.

If having cognition A implies having cognition B, a dissonant relationship exists when the person has cognitions A and the obverse or opposite of B. If, for example, a person knows that he voted for candidate A and he also believes that candidate A is unworthy of public office, he has two cognitions that are in a dissonant relationship. Whenever a person has two or more cognitions that are dissonant with regard to each other, he experiences cognitive dissonance, a motivational tension.

Many cognitions that a person has will be neither consonant nor dissonant— that is, these cognitions will have nothing to do with one another. Such cognitions are said to be *irrelevant.*

When a person holds two cognitions that are in a dissonant relationship, the amount of dissonance he experiences is a direct function of how important those cognitions are to him. For example, a person about to fight a guerilla war who also has knowledge of the personal dangers of such wars possesses two dissonant cognitive elements, and the relatively great importance of these elements would give rise to a considerable amount of cognitive dissonance. In contrast, the knowledge that it is raining coupled with the dissonant knowledge of having forgotten the umbrella would create less dissonance because these cognitive elements are not as important as those in the life-or-death guerilla warfare example.

Our description of dissonance theory thus far depicts the idea as little more than a notion about cognitive conflict or cognitive imbalance. And aside from the effect of importance, we have mentioned no way to calculate different degrees of dissonance. The factor to be introduced next, "resistance to change of cognitions," has a direct bearing on both of these issues. Through an analysis of the malleability, or "fixedness" of relevant cognitions it becomes possible to speak about degrees of dissonance, and we also are enabled to derive a distinct class of phenomena that are nowhere implied in other statements of cognitive consistency.

In the above examples used to illustrate the arousal of cognitive dissonance no mention was made of how dissonance would actually be reduced. Given the definition of a dissonant relationship, all that could be said about dissonance reduction is that there will be some attempt to eliminate the dissonant relationship by changing one element or the other in order to render the two either consonant or irrelevant. In addition to making possible statements about the degree of dissonance, the concept of resistance to change allows statements about the directions to be taken by the dissonance-reducing individual.

Resistance to Change of Cognitive Elements

Cognitions—elements of knowledge—vary in the extent to which they are resistant to change. A person's perception of the greenness of grass is highly resistant to change; for people with normal vision it would be exceedingly difficult to see grass as being any color other than green. In contrast, judgments about which college basketball team is best, about the pallatibility of steak *au poivre*, or about the amount of money that should go into the nation's defense budget, may not be completely firm and in many cases can be quite unstable. Compared to the perception of green in grass, the latter cognitions have relatively little resistance to change.

In general, there are two distinguishable sources to resistance to change. The first is the clarity of the "reality" represented by the cognition. What normally are referred to as "facts"—that is, that grass is green—are aspects of the world that give rise to clear and firm cognitions. At the other end of this dimension are events that are highly ambiguous—what the quality of life will be like a century from now, or how many grains of sand there are on the outer banks of North Carolina. Cognitions about the latter kind of event will, of course, have relatively low resistance to change.

The second source of resistance to change comes from the difficulty of changing the event that is cognized. Historical events, for example, cannot be changed and cognitions concerning them will therefore be highly resistant to change. Contemporaneous events, on the other hand, will sometimes be easy to change and when they are, the cognitions representing them have low resistance to change. If a person finds, for example, that his air conditioner is making too much noise to allow sleep, the air conditioner can be turned off.

The Magnitude of Dissonance

When there are both consonant and dissonant relationships among the elements of a set of relevant cognitions, the calculation of the magnitude of dissonance is carried out using the most resistant cognition as a focal point, or point of orientation. The magnitude of dissonance with regard to the most resistant element is a direct function of the proportion of relevant elements that is dissonant with it. In other words, given the most highly resistant cognition, the magnitude of dissonance is increased with regard to that cognition as the number of dissonant cognitions increases; the magnitude of dissonance with regard to that cognition decreases as the number of consonant cognitions increases. This formulation can be schematically represented as follows:

$$\begin{array}{l} \text{dissonance associated} \\ \text{with most resistant} \\ \text{cognition} \end{array} = \frac{[\text{dissonant cognition} \times \text{importance of cognition}]}{[\text{consonant cognition} \times \text{importance of cognition}]}$$

Note that each consonant or dissonant cognition is weighted for its importance to the individual.

The schematic representation helps to make clear an interesting aspect of the theory, namely, that with the number and importance of dissonant cognitions held constant, the magnitude of dissonance decreases as the number or importance of consonant cognitions increases. Let us suppose, for example, that a person has voted for John Smith to be mayor despite also believing that Smith is not very bright, and let us assume that the cognition about voting is the more resistant element. The magnitude of dissonance that our voter experiences from this dissonant relationship is an inverse function of the number of cognitions that are consonant with the knowledge that he voted for Smith. If he voted for Smith because he believes Smith to be honest and he also believes that Smith endorses the right side on all important election issues, then these consonant cognitions in addition to the dissonant one will add up to only negligible dissonance. However, if the only reason he had for supporting Smith was his belief in Smith's honesty, then the consonant cognitions do not clearly outweigh the dissonant (that Smith is stupid), and the magnitude of dissonance experienced is relatively great.

Dissonance Reduction

As the schematic representation indicates, dissonance can be reduced in several ways. Dissonant cognitions can be eliminated, or their importance can be reduced. Consonant cognitions can be added, or the importance of preexistent consonant cognitions can be increased. In the above example of voting for Smith as mayor, the voter could reduce dissonance by convincing himself that Smith was really not so dumb, or by thinking that brightness is not a necessary characteristic for being a good mayor. In addition, or instead, he could magnify the importance of having an honest mayor, or he could find additional reasons for thinking that Smith would be a good mayor.

This delineation of ways in which dissonance can be reduced does not indicate what a person who is experiencing dissonance will actually do. First of all, the theory does not assert that a person will be successful in reducing dissonance, but rather that the existence of dissonance will motivate a person to *attempt* to reduce it. Second, the way in which a person attempts dissonance reduction will depend in part on the resistance to change of the relevant cognitions. In general, we may expect that attempts to reduce dissonance, and successful dissonance reduction, will involve cognitive operations on those cognitions that are least resistant to change. Opinions (i.e., cognitions about somewhat ambiguous events) and cognitions about easily changed aspects of reality will tend to be the locus of dissonance reduction efforts.

While the cognition of a recent behavior or behavioral commitment, such as a decision, is usually assumed to be the element most resistant to change, this cognition will occasionally be less resistant to change than one or more of the cognitions with which it is dissonant. Consider, for example, a case in which a person has bought a sports car and has found that those characteristics of the car about which he had predecisional misgivings indeed make driving the car unpleasant. If the individual is unable to convince himself that he really likes to drive the car, then his dissonance will persist and indeed will be salient every time the car is driven. Under these conditions, dissonance reduction may more easily be accomplished by changing the cognition about the behavior. While it would be difficult to deny that the car had been purchased, it may not be so difficult to change the reality—to come to believe that buying it was a mistake, and to sell it. In this case, the resistance to change of the behavioral cognitive element is less than that of the cognitions with which it is dissonant, and dissonance reduction is accomplished by changing the behavioral element. The way dissonance is reduced here also illustrates an important theoretical point, namely, that dissonance reduction is organized around the cognition that is most resistant to change, whether or not that cognition has its basis in a behavioral commitment.

Many of the analyses to come later involve cognitive dissonance between a recently performed behavior and an attitude. For example, a person first holds a particular political belief, and then is asked to take a contrary position in some overt fashion. It may be naive to say that one cognition (recent behavior) is firmly rooted in behavior, while the other (prior attitude) is not. If for example the attitude is a political belief, there is every likelihood that some sort of belief-consistent action has been taken previously. Perhaps the person has voted consistently with his beliefs in earlier elections, or he may have campaigned on behalf of candidates representing these beliefs. This being the case, are we not dealing with two opposing cognitions that should both be highly resistant to change? And if so, which cognition is the stronger? Around which cognition will dissonance be reduced?

Since it is generally true, in experimentation, that attitudes do in fact shift in the direction of the more recent commitment, it becomes necessary to make an extratheoretical assumption having to do with the recency of behaviorally based cognitions. In general, if two cognitions are in opposition, both of which represent behaviors or other events that are in close touch with the constraints of reality, it is the more recently acquired cognition that possesses the higher resistance to change. There are at least two plausible reasons for this:

1. Taking an overt position at variance with an earlier one is a form of conversion. It may generally be true that a conversion is difficult to reconvert. There are barriers of having to admit to hypocrisy, indecisiveness, and uncertainty; and

2. The recent behavior is bound to be more salient in the individual's consciousness. If previous behaviors are relatively out of mind, they provide less basis for a highly resistant-to-change cognitive element.

One additional point must be made in regard to behavioral commitment. *Explorations in Cognitive Dissonance* (Brehm & Cohen, 1962) emphasized behavioral commitment not only as an anchor around which dissonance is reduced, but also as a condition possibly necessary for the arousal of cognitive dissonance. Subsequently, Festinger (1964) and his associates reaffirmed the importance of commitment in the dissonance reduction process. They held that dissonance reduction processes ensue only when a commitment implies consequences that are dissonant with it. However, they did not say whether or not commitment was a necessary condition for the arousal of dissonance.

As the present emphasis on resistance to change implies, we find Festinger's (1957) original statement of the theory to be superior to the more restrictive views. We believe that the notion of resistance to change not only incorporates the important aspect of behavioral commitment, but it also guides the researcher in thinking about the resistance of other relevant cognitions. In our above discussion of the role of resistance to change we have tried to show that a careful analysis of resistance must be made for all relevant cognitions in order to know around which cognition dissonance will be reduced, and in order to specify which of the logically possible ways dissonance is likely to be reduced.

Foreseeability and the Broader Concept of Responsibility

In addition to emphasizing the role of commitment in the arousal and reduction of dissonance, Brehm and Cohen (1962) raised questions about the capability of unforeseen consequences to arouse dissonance. On the basis of evidence then available, they theorized that prior choice and commitment were sufficient conditions for subsequent unforeseen (negative) events to arouse dissonance. They supposed that if a person freely committed himself to a course of action, unforeseen negative consequences of that action would result in dissonance arousal and normal dissonance reduction processes. As will be seen in Chapter 4, subsequent research has failed to support their reasoning.

Under what conditions do events subsequent to a behavioral commitment affect the magnitude of dissonance? Imagine, for example, that a person has bought a house and is becoming familiar with the consequences of that purchase. He might discover that the roof leaks, that taxes on the house are high, and that water running through the pipes is excessively noisy. Would these discoveries arouse dissonance? Suppose also that after the purchase was made, and completely unexpectedly, all of the wooded land around his house was donated as a natural wild life preserve, thus increasing his property value substantially. Would knowledge of that reduce the dissonance associated with his purchase?

When an individual has no foresight, or hint, that his commitments might have discrepant implications, he is thereby not a causal agent in the cognitive inconsistency. This is a theoretical point that was not explicit in the original theory (Festinger, 1957), but recent research (Chapter 4) has made it abundantly clear that dissonance reduction as we know it takes place only when the dissonant elements have been brought together through the personal responsibility of the individual who experiences dissonance. A feeling of personal responsibility can arise in various ways, but generally the elements of foreseeability and choice are necessary. If the person understands the possibility that his actions might bring together dissonant cognitions, and if he acts freely without the imposition of external constraint, there is then engendered a feeling of being personally responsible for juxtaposing the dissonant cognitions. Without personal responsibility the dissonant elements are *psychologically* irrelevant for the individual.

Thus the answers to the above questions about the purchaser of a house are as follows. A leaky roof, high taxes, and noisy pipes are all foreseeable characteristics of a house, and they can be expected to arouse dissonance even though they were not known explicitly at the time of the purchase. On the other hand, the completely unexpected increase in property value was not foreseeable and it should not provide a consonant cognition, that is, it would not reduce any dissonance associated with purchase of the house. By the same token, if the house suddenly began to sink and nothing of that sort had happened to any other houses in the vicinity, knowledge of the sinking would not be dissonant with purchase of the house even though such knowledge would no doubt be unpleasant.

Various consequences may seem to be logically related to or caused by a prior behavioral commitment, but if the person had no responsibility for the consistent or inconsistent relationships between those consequences and his commitment, there is then effectively no psychological connection between them. On the one hand the individual has behaved, and on the other hand later events are inconsistent (or consistent) with that behavior. But this "dissonance" (or "consonance") is simply in the eye of the observer. If a consequence is forced on an individual because the behavior was performed under constraint, or if a consequence comes as a complete surprise, the individual's dissonance reduction efforts will not reflect the existence of that consequence.

The sole exception to these *choice* and *foreseeability* criteria of responsibility is noted in Chapter 4, and for the most part consists of the individual's performance as a direct source of personal responsibility. That is, when poor performance brings forth an undesired consequence that is unchosen and unexpected, dissonance reduction appears to ensue anyway. Thus, responsibility evidently arises when a potentially dissonance-arousing event is a direct consequence of some central aspect of the person, or when the event is chosen and foreseeable.

The Major Theoretical Paradigms

In his original statement of the theory, Festinger (1957) outlined three major ways in which dissonance is created: (a) a choice between alternatives, (b) induction of behavior that would normally be avoided, and (c) exposure to information. Nearly all of the research on dissonance theory can be subsumed by these three categories.

A choice between alternatives creates dissonance to the extent that the alternatives are about equal in attractiveness, and to the extent that the alternatives involve different sets of consequences. When an alternative is chosen, the positive aspects of the chosen alternative and the negative aspects of the rejected alternative are consonant with the cognition of choice; the negative aspects of the chosen alternative and the positive aspects of the rejected alternative are dissonant with the cognition of choice. Since the resulting dissonance can be reduced by enhancing the consonant cognitions and minimizing the dissonant, it may be expected that the perceived attractiveness of the chosen alternative will increase, and the perceived attractiveness of the rejected will decrease.

The induction of a behavior that would normally be avoided, called "forced compliance" by Festinger (1957), involves the use of a force such as the promise of a reward to induce a person to engage in the behavior. A person's prior (negative) evaluation of the behavior is dissonant with the knowledge that he has engaged in it or will engage in it, while knowledge of the reward to be received (or the punishment to be avoided) is consonant with knowledge of the behavioral commitment. It follows that the magnitude of dissonance created by induction of the behavior increases as the reward (or threatened punishment) decreases. This is by far the most widely tested paradigm in dissonance research. Much of the early research on this and on the choice paradigm, described above, is reported in Chapter 5, Evidence on Fundamental Propositions.

The third major paradigm that Festinger described for the creation of dissonance, exposure to information, has been well researched but has fared less well than the first two. The notion is that a person who is experiencing dissonance will be motivated to expose himself to consonant information and to avoid exposure to dissonant information. Because these derivations are not seen as fundamental to the theory, and because the testing of these derivations has turned out to be rather complicated, a separate chapter (Chapter 12, Selective Exposure) has been devoted to this mode of handling dissonance.

In the chapters immediately following this theoretical introduction, the major theoretical dimensions are discussed and the relevant research reported. These chapters discuss the concepts of commitment, choice, and foreseeability and responsibility, in order to lay the groundwork for the analyses and understanding of all further work that is reported.

A Note on the Methodology

When dissonance theory was first evolving in Festinger's mind and in discussions with his associates at the University of Minnesota, the problems inherent in testing the theory loomed large indeed. Most baffling was how to test the forced-compliance paradigm. It should be recalled that at the time, around 1954 and 1955, there was no tradition of study of postdecisional behavior. Experimental laboratory studies of conflict had been carried out, but the purpose of these studies had been to examine the phenomena leading up to and including the decision rather than to look at postdecisional effects. What was called for to test the forced-compliance hypothesis was a method of inducing subjects to engage in a behavior they would normally avoid while simultaneously giving them the impression that they were free not to comply. Those conditions had not previously been attempted in an experimental test, and it seemed that it would be exceedingly difficult to create them. To give subjects the impression that they had complete freedom not to comply, and yet to get them all to comply appeared as an impossible task. Indeed, some clever attempts were made and abandoned, and it was evident that a new methodology had to be worked out in order to test many implications from dissonance theory.

Now, twenty years later, the methods of giving subjects high or low choice and still getting most or all of them to comply have been well established. While Brehm and Cohen (1962) discussed at length the problems and weaknesses of dissonance research, and others (e.g., Chapanis & Chapanis, 1964) were critical to the point of rejecting all support for the theory, today there is no longer any serious methodological problem to discuss. This is not to say that all or even any dissonance experiments rule out all alternative theoretical interpretations. It is only to say that the early methodological weaknesses such as subject self-selection, which sometimes weakened a dissonance interpretation of results, do not seem to have led to false conclusions and have by now been essentially eliminated altogether by increased methodological sophistication.

THE THEORY SUMMARIZED

Cognitive dissonance is a motivational state brought about when a person has cognitive elements that imply the opposite of one another. As a tension state, it may be said to persist until cognitive work lowers the relative number or importance of relevant cognitions discrepant with the elements that are most resistant to change. This cognitive work can consist of adding consonant cognitions, increasing the importance of consonant cognitions, subtracting dissonant cognitions and decreasing the importance of dissonant cognitions. The resistance-to-change concept is the hallmark of the theory, for without it the unique predictions of the theory would be impossible; it provides an organizing point for determining the magnitude of dissonance and how dissonance will most likely be reduced. Finally, the evolved theory which we discuss here is also a theory about personal responsibility. Dissonance reduction may be observed only to the degree that the individual sees himself as responsible for bringing cognitions into an inconsistent relationship.

2
Commitment

An individual's behavior frequently affects the course of events. A person might sell his house, and at some point in the transaction, it may become impossible for him to reacquire the house at any price. A general in the Army may decide to concentrate his defensive forces at point A rather that at point B, and it might take days to reshift his forces should his opponent decide to attack at point B. A candidate for office may publically refer to some people as "Polacks," and this information is spread by the news media so that potential voters become informed of the slur. In each of these cases an individual has behaved in a way that has significance in regard to subsequent events, and it would be difficult for the individual to deny the meaningfulness of his behavior or to change what he had done. These instances in which the cognition about one's own behavior is relatively resistant to change may be called behavioral commitments.

It is behavioral commitment that gives many dissonance reduction processes their irrational tone. Once a person has made a commitment he closes himself off to information that would have led him to alternative types of commitments, and it is this "closedness" in the face of new considerations that leads to the apparent irrationality.

The rational man is one who alters his opinion or behavior in proportion to the evidence implied in each bit of incoming information. He is a computer, or processer, who serves as almost a mathematical link between evidence, evaluation, and behavior. Assuming momentarily that the world can be characterized objectively in terms of whether any particular event is "positive" or "negative" for a specified person, this person will process each incoming piece of information into an overall evaluation of the event. If the price of shaving lotion skyrockets, he will develop an aversion (but a rational aversion) to shaving lotion, if his neighbor shoots his dog he will come to dislike the neighbor, and if the sun should not shine during his visit to Hawaii, Hawaii will fall in his evaluative hierarchy.

11

But these seemingly obvious and presumably universal rational evaluations run into trouble once behavioral commitment is inserted into the information-processing sequence. The clear and predictable linear relationship between goodness of information and positivity of evaluation can, in fact, be turned around by the existence of a commitment. This reversal can even lead the person to evaluate an event more positively as the incoming information becomes "objectively" more negative.

We should note that dissonance reduction processes are not set in motion by an ambiguous commitment. For example, when an alternative is selected for consumption, but there is some question about whether or not other options are thereby ruled out, systematic reevaluation of alternatives is no greater than prior to the commitment. The onset of the irrational processes of dissonance reduction requires that the person have a definite understanding of the implications of his commitment. This point is elaborated by Festinger (1964), especially in the context of research by Jecker (1964).

Before proceeding with the experimental examples, a short overview of the types of situations we have in mind will be helpful for clarification. Assume that a person is involved in a weight-guessing contest at a county fair. He has been called upon to guess the total weight of a series of 15 goats, and the procedure works as follows. The first goat is trotted out, the contestant guesses its weight, and he also estimates the total weight of the 15 goats, 14 of which he has not seen. This procedure is repeated through 15 animals. What would be the strategy of the rational weight guesser? Undoubtedly his estimate for the summed 15 animals would be adjusted, depending on the weights of successive goats. If they gradually increased in size, his estimate for the grand total would also increase gradually. So far dissonance theory has not entered the picture. Now, a second contestant undergoes a slightly altered procedure. After the 10th goat has been presented, the guesser is told that his estimate for the sum of 15 goats at that point will be taken as his final estimate, and that he will not have a chance, after seeing the last five goats, to revise his estimate for the grand total. In terms of dissonance theory, the grand estimate after Goat 10 is a definite behavioral commitment. The guesser would have to hope that Goats 11 to 15 do not differ radically from the average of the first 10. As it happens, Goat 11 is quite a substantial animal, a good 30 lb heavier than its predecessors. The incoming information is quite dissonant with the previous commitment, and how is the dissonance to be reduced? One clear possibility is for dissonant cognitions to be subtracted, and this can be done by refusing to admit that the heavy goat implies any change in the grand total weight of all animals. Therefore, the total estimate should not change much between the 10th and 11th animals, even though rationality would call for an increased estimate. No doubt this kind of rationality would be found in the first weight guesser, who is not bound by a commitment, and who would not experience dissonance when the decidedly heavy 11th goat appears.

For a second example, consider a college freshman who has pledged a fraternity, and to his consternation, has been unable to impress his fraternity brothers. In fact, he has noticed that they have gradually become less enthused about him over the course of several weeks. If this fraternity pledge is the rational man, how much influence should his fraternity have on him? Common sense would dictate that they would gradually be losing influence. Certainly a fraternity should be attractive if one feels welcomed by the members, and it seems almost folklore that the attractive group has more influence over the individual member. (Going beyond folklore, Hare, 1962, cites a number of research findings supporting this conclusion.) This common sense dictate would probably hold provided the pledge felt free to depledge once the group became sufficiently unattractive to him. In other words, if he has no long-term commitment to the group, its negative actions toward him will be directly reflected in his distaste for the members, a decreased influence power of the group over him, and eventually, in his leaving the group.

What if he had formally committed himself to the fraternity through the remaining four years? Here we have a case of dissonance arousal, for the group's relative nonacceptance of him is highly dissonant with the cognition of having committed himself. To reduce the number of dissonant elements he can convince himself of the members' virtues, and further, that they are worth listening to. Ironically then, the worse the group treats him, the more it will tend to win his dedication and respect.

The following pieces of research are examples of these two themes carried into practice in the laboratory. In each case it should be evident that effects often taken for granted can be altered in important ways by the introduction of behavioral commitment. Before each line of research is presented, some rationale will be provided regarding the "common sense" process that receives interference as a result of the commitment—dissonance sequence.

JUDGMENTAL PROCESSES AND DISSONANCE

Brehm and Leventhal

The preceding weight-guessing example was taken directly from the present experiment (Brehm & Leventhal, 1962). The idea was to confront subjects sequentially with a series of weights and to ask for an estimate of all weights (including those not yet presented) after each weight guess was registered. From a description of the low- and high-commitment conditions it will be evident that considerable dissonance was aroused in the high-commitment condition upon presentation of the eleventh, and highly discrepant weight. Further, it will be evident that the subject must abandon a rational judgmental approach to the overall weight estimate if he is to minimize dissonance. Finally, it was proposed by Brehm and Leventhal that such dissonance processes would be enhanced if the importance of the experimental task were experimentally heightened.

The subjects were students from introductory psychology classes, and were run individually. When a subject arrived for the experimental session, he was seated at a table facing a black curtain that prevented his seeing what was at the experimenter's side of the table. The experimenter reminded him that the study was concerned with judging weights. The manipulation of importance was then introduced.

Low importance was created by the experimenter's making the following points: (1) that he was not concerned with how well the subject performed but only with how people in general behaved; (2) that the task was not very interesting; (3) that he was conducting the experiment simply as practice for a course he was taking; and (4) that the experiment was not working, and the present subject's results would therefore not be useful in any way.

High importance was created by indicating that the study was a regular scientific experiment and by stressing that it would determine how well the subject would do on the task. Thus, instead of reducing the subject's natural ego involvement, the experimenter stressed it, and, in addition, instead of saying that the study was for practice, he said that it was a regular scientific experiment.

After the instructions for the importance manipulation, the description of the weight-judgment task was given. The task involved the subject's sitting at a desk, putting his hand under a curtain, lifting a small weight, assigning a value to that weight, and then predicting the average weight of a series of 15 weights. This routine was followed for each of 11 trials. The weights were identical in size and appearance and had the following gram values: 80, 90, 101, 113.7, 127.5, 144, and 291.6. The weights were given to the subject in the following order: 113.7, 80, 127.5, 90, 144, 101, 113.7, 80, 127.5, 90, and 291.6. It will be noted that the weights alternated between light and heavy. Subjects were told that there was a simple system that might help them in estimating the weights and the series average. Almost all subjects later reported having noted that the eleventh weight was much heavier than the subject was likely to expect. Thus, the eleventh weight served as the inconsistent information.

Prior to lifting any weights, the subject was told how to assign numbers and what was meant by an average. He was then told that to keep subjects interested and on their toes, a prize consisting of a $5 ($1 for some subjects) gift certificate would be given to anyone who reached a certain level of accuracy in his prediction of the average. (The monetary variation was originally intended as a second importance manipulation. However, it was ineffective and will not be discussed here.) To make the prize seem within reach, the experimenter said that between one third and one half of the participants were expected to win one. He explained that near the end of the series of weights, the subject would be given one critical judgment that would determine whether or not he would win a prize.

The experimenter explained the weight value scale in the following way. He told the subject that any value between 0 and 200 could be assigned to each weight. He also said that the values of the first two weights would be given to the subject and that, subsequently, it would be up to the subject to assign the values. The first two weights were then placed under the subject's hand, and the subject was instructed to lift them alternately. The subject was told that the value of the first and heavier weight was 50, while the value of the second and lighter weight was 38. The subject was then given each of the other weights in the series, one by one.

The commitment condition was inserted after the tenth weight and just prior to presentation of the discrepant weight. In the low-commitment condition, the weight value and estimate of the series average were obtained in the same way as for all other weights. (There was a slight variation of this in the low-importance condition in that subjects were instructed to consider this estimate of the average very carefully even though it would not be the estimate determining whether or not they won a prize. This was instituted to control for attention and care in making this particular estimate. Its effect should be to maximize the subject's motivation to be accurate, although it may also have raised the degree of commitment somewhat.)

High commitment was obtained by telling the subject, after he assigned a value to the tenth weight, that his estimate of the average at that point was the crucial guess which would determine whether or not he would win a prize and, hence, how well he performed on the task.

Subjects in the low-commitment conditions were oriented toward making an accurate estimate of the average weight for the series. Their concern with being accurate would be greater under the high-importance conditions than under the low. Hence we might expect subjects in the high-importance condition, compared with those in the low, to try harder to take the discrepant weight into account in making their estimates of the average. Thus the high-importance subjects should show more shift of their estimated average from before to after exposure to the discrepant weight than low-importance subjects.

If it is true that commitment provides the condition necessary for inconsistent information to arouse dissonance, then subjects in the high-commitment conditions should behave differently from those in the low-commitment conditions. Furthermore, since dissonance is also a direct function of the importance of the inconsistent cognitions, the effect of high commitment should be greater in the high- than in the low-importance condition. The dissonance aroused in conjunction with the commitment might conceivably be reduced in a number of different ways. It could result in perceptual distortion that minimizes the inconsistency, selective exposure to further relevant information, and so on. However, perceptual distortion would, in this case, be difficult, for the inconsistency is large and clear and would thus require tremendous distortion for the elimination of dissonance. Exposure to further information was not a plausible response, since the inconsistent weight indicated that the remaining weights in the series might also be different from the preceding weights. However, the subject could quite easily engage in judgmental distortion. He could simply convince himself that the inconsistent weight was not representative of the series and that it was therefore not as important toward estimation of the average as were the previous ten weights. The result of such distortion would be a relatively small shift in the estimated average due to exposure to the inconsistent weight. Thus we would expect subjects in the high-commitment condition to show relatively little shift in their estimate of the average, and we would further expect this shift to be smaller as the importance of being accurate increased.

Since we are primarily interested in shifts in the estimated average, and such shifts are presumably a function of the perceived inconsistency, an appropriate measure is the ratio of the change in estimated average from before to after the inconsistent weight, over the discrepancy between the perceived value of the critical weight and the prior estimated average. We will call this measure the *corrected shift score.* It has been multiplied by 100 to make it more comparable with the figures from which it was derived.

As may be seen from Table 1, the shift scores show that subjects in the low-commitment condition, presumably in an attempt to be more accurate, change their estimates of the average more under the high-importance condition than under low (significant by F test at the 5% level). And, as we would expect, subjects in the high-commitment condition tend to show less shift in their average in the high- than in the low-importance condition. Although this latter tendency is not statistically significant, it is significantly different from the opposing tendency in the low-commitment condition (interaction F significant at 5% level). Thus the effect of commitment is to reverse the rational, judgmental process. That is, when a person is exposed to information inconsistent with a judgment he has made, the direct effect of the inconsistent information will increase with its importance so long as the individual is not committed. However, when the individual is committed prior to exposure to the inconsistent information, dissonance is created, and the pressure to reduce the dissonance may lead the individual to minimize the significance of the inconsistent information.

TABLE 1
Subjects' Adjustment in Mean Estimate
(Corrected Shift Scores)

	Low importance	High importance
Low commitment	18.5	28.1
High commitment	19.8	14.0

Thibaut and Ross

When an array of stimuli is presented in gradually increasing intensity, the individual members of that array are perceived as more intense than when the stimuli are presented in gradually decreasing intensity. Thibaut and Ross (1969) document this point by citing research on judgments of weight (Nash, 1950), judgments of loudness and brightness (Stevens, 1957), and judgments of another person based on that person's positive or negative reactions to the subject (Aronson & Linder, 1965). Based on discussions by Helson (1964) and Jones and Gerard (1967, p. 14), Thibaut and Ross offer what appears to be a commonly accepted explanation for the difference between judgments of stimuli presented in ascending and descending order.

The explanation is a totally judgmental one, and certainly could be classified as rational. The idea is that an adaptation level builds up early in presentation of the stimuli. If the first few stimuli are small, the person adapts to "smallness" and reacts to subsequent stimuli against this background of smallness. The converse is true when large stimuli are presented first: The subsequent and smaller stimuli are evaluated against a reference point of large size. Now, if a person's reference point is small, larger stimuli will create a contrast, and it is this contrast that is the basis of the subject's exaggeration of size when stimuli come in ascending order of weight. Similarly, when moving from large to small there is also a contrast. Subsequent small stimuli appear as especially small when judged against the initial reference point of substantial size.

Thibaut and Ross showed subjects two separate series of 20 slides each. Each slide had 256 elements on it, the elements being either "1"s or "0"s, and the proportion of "1"s was varied between a small and large percentage. Subjects were presented with the slides in either ascending or descending order. In the ascending order the first slide contained 3/16 "1"s, and the final (twentieth) slide had 13/16 "1"s.

A rather complex meaning was attached to the proportion of "1"s in each slide, and it will suffice to say that subjects were led to believe that "1"s meant that a certain artist was of high calibre, whereas "0"s meant that the artist was untalented. After each series of 20 slides the subject rated the artist. This might be a useful place to review the predictions made by the contrast explanation given above.

If the 20 slides are presented in ascending order the subject will infer from the first few slides that the artist is poor. This means that later slides will contrast with the initial impression, and because of the contrast, the final evaluation of the artist will be relatively high. Exactly the same reasoning is used in the descending order condition, leading to the conclusion that the final evaluation will be rather low.

These predictions are for uncommitted subjects. However, half of the subjects were given a commitment induction, predisposing them to expect a certain pattern of slides. Specifically, before the commitment condition subjects received the ascending order they were given an expectation that the artist was poor; and prior to receiving the descending order they were led to expect the artist to be good. It can be seen that these initial commitment instructions should counter the contrast effects.

Here we might note the analogy to Brehm and Leventhal. The rational, or judgmental process would consist of the subject's exaggerating the goodness of the artist (given the ascending order). But the commitment–condition subject has a preconception that the artist is of low quality, and we may assume that this preconception is a cognition highly resistant to change, due to the way it was introduced. Since the preconception is not likely to bend during the ascending presentation, dissonance can be reduced by evaluating the artist in a manner consistent with the preconception.

The results showed a tendency toward the characteristic contrast effect for uncommitted subjects. Ratings were slightly higher in the ascending case. But there was a strong reversal of this effect within the commitment condition. The ratings here were very much in line with subjects' preconceptions. In other words, instead of showing the contrast effect, commitment subjects assimilated the information contained in the slides to their preconceived ideas about the artist. Again, the judgmental process is negated by the intrusion of commitment.

One final study was conducted by Wilson and Russell (1966). Subjects were instructed to lift both heavy and light weights, and dissonance was varied in the following way. Some subjects received payment in proportion to the magnitude of the weight lifted, and it was argued by Wilson and Russell that such a procedure should arouse little dissonance. The subject performs a relatively difficult task (lifting a heavy weight) and is rewarded appropriately. A high dissonance group was created by reversing this payment schedule, giving the greater payment for the smaller weight. Here the subject is performing the more onerous task for the least justification, and can reduce his dissonance by coming to minimize the estimated distance he has lifted the heavier weight. The results took exactly this form.

Summary

These three experiments demonstrate how irrationality can interfere with psychophysical judgments when cognitive dissonance enters due to commitment. In the initial effort by Brehm and Leventhal, subjects who were prematurely committed to a guess about the weight of the overall array became reluctant to change their estimates when inconsistent information entered the scene. Their estimate for average weight occurred following the tenth weight stimulus, and although the final (eleventh) weight was of considerable magnitude, they were hesitant to alter their overall estimates in light of it. The Thibaut and Ross experiment adds another important qualification to historically precedented psychophysical relationships. Prior to their experiment the accepted finding was a contrast effect, whereby the overall magnitude of an array is judged greater if the stimuli occur in ascending order of intensity, as opposed to descending order. This common finding was turned completely around when subjects were committed to stimuli occurring early in the array. It might be noted that these experiments have made use of the most basic dissonance principles (commitment and importance of cognitions). Presumably psychophysical judgments could be further altered by somewhat more elaborate procedures incorporating variations in choice, justification, foreseeability, and other variables.

GROUP ATTRACTIVENESS AND DISSONANCE

Kiesler and his associates have generated an impressive number of studies congruent with the preceding fraternity example. The "common sense" idea against which dissonance processes operate is a widely accepted notion that attractive groups have more influence power (Hare, 1962). Given that a person is not committed to a group, that group should have more potential to influence the individual's attitudes when he is accepted by it, or when any other prevailing conditions make group membership desirable for him. Even more obvious or at least commonly accepted, is that an individual should be attracted only to groups that accept him. Certainly a monotonic relationship should normally be found between the group's desire to have the person and the person's subsequent devotion to the group. Surprisingly, these two accepted and nearly obvious effects of group acceptance of the individual can be negated when the person is highly committed to group membership.

Kiesler and Corbin (1965)

Subjects were recruited in groups of approximately six for the purpose of evaluating paintings. Once a group had met and interacted for part of the session, there was a manipulation of the degree to which each participant felt accepted by his fellow group members. This feedback gave the subject an impression of how much he was liked by the others and how much they thought he contributed to the discussion. There were three levels of acceptance, which we may label *high, moderate,* and *low,* departing slightly from the labels of Kiesler and Corbin.

Subsequent to that manipulation, all subjects were led to discover a discrepancy between their own rankings of the paintings and the rankings of the remainder of the group. Subjects then had an opportunity to change their rankings, providing the conformity measure. The authors went out of their way to insure that this measure was one of private change, and not mere public conformity. So far the conformity measure should directly reflect the acceptance manipulation: more conformity with more acceptance. However, there was also a variation in commitment, consisting of whether or not subjects had a strong expectation of continuing in the same group for three additional hours. The authors expected commitment to alter the acceptance—conformity relationship in the following way: At some fairly strong level of nonacceptance, the subject who is stuck with the group is in need of finding a method of dissonance reduction, and he can best do this by becoming more like the other group members.

The results indicated that Kiesler and Corbin were right. Within both the "committed" and "uncommitted" conditions there was decreasing conformity when prior acceptance was lowered from "high" to "moderate," and this decrease continued among uncommitted subjects as acceptance was lowered to "low." However, this latter result was exactly the opposite among committed subjects, indicating that the combination of commitment and virtual rejection generated dissonance-reducing private-opinion change toward the group.

Subjects' attraction to the group paralleled the conformity finding almost exactly, meaning that within the committed condition, subjects who were not accepted at all were more attracted to the group than those who were accepted moderately. It should be noted, however, that these attraction results are not entirely independent of the opinion change effects, and in fact Kiesler and Corbin provide evidence that opinion change preceded and generated the attraction results.

Kiesler, Zanna, and De Salvo (1966)

Although the present experiment emphasized variables different from those of Kiesler and Corbin, Kiesler *et al.* (1966) again obtained the effect for commitment when subjects were not accepted by the group. In short, conformity was greater among subjects committed to the group for future sessions than among subjects not committed. This study also showed that the subject's solution to his cognitive dilemma was resistant in the face of future attack.

Kiesler and De Salvo (1967)

This experiment is in keeping theoretically with the previous two, the major difference being the dependent measure. Attraction to a task chosen by the group was the primary measure, rather than conformity.

The subject and three (sometimes two) others were formed into a group. The experimenter described two tasks, one of which the group was to choose to pursue, then a premeasure of task attractiveness was taken from each subject. The "dull" task consisted of collating papers, while the "interesting" task entailed reconstructing the biography of a famous contemporary person. As in previous research, "group attractiveness" was then manipulated, although instead of manipulating the group's apparent acceptance, the experimenter simply gave each subject a strong expectancy about whether or not the group would be likable.

All subjects then found that the other members of their group preferred the collating task, and immediately after introducing this information the experimenter went on to vary whether or not the subject was committed to complete that task. Uncommitted subjects were assured that the group's preference to work on the collating task was not final. The experimenter also suggested that he would take part of the responsibility for assigning a task later. The purpose of these instructions was, of course, to convince uncommitted subjects that the selection of the task was still an open matter. On the other hand, committed subjects were told that the group's decision was final.

A second measure of task attractiveness was then taken, enabling the use of attractiveness change as the measure of dissonance reduction. The measure of dissonance reduction consisted of the amount of increased attractiveness in the dull task plus the amount of decreased attractiveness in the interesting task. Since those respective increases and decreases should both reflect dissonance reduction, the authors simply added them.

Among uncommitted subjects the tendency to like the dull task was a positive function of group attractiveness, but exactly the opposite held among committed subjects. Again, it seems clear that commitment to a group can have a powerful reversal effect on the "usual" relationship between group attractiveness and desire to please the group or appreciate its various facets.

Gerard (1965)

In an experiment antedating some of Kiesler's work, Gerard (1965) designed a highly unique procedure in which the commitment consisted of whether or not the subject thought he conformed. Subjects were asked to perform a simple discrimination procedure. For each of several pairs of stars they were to determine which had the greater number of points, and during the first stage of the experiment subjects were led to think that their ability at this discrimination task was either high or low. Then, prior to a series of discriminations the subject was wired up to some "electromyographic equipment," with the excuse that his "first impulse" to choose one star or the other could be detected through the device. Just before each discrimination of the series the subject saw the discriminations of two other subjects, which meant that his "first impulse" could be classified as conforming or nonconforming. As the series proceeded the subject found himself to be a conformer or nonconformer. In summary, the study has four basic conditions: two levels of ability crosscut by two levels of conformity.

What does this design mean vis-a-vis dissonance theory? One route to a clear understanding is to draw a parallel to Kiesler's research. Kiesler's commitment versus noncommitment to the group has a perfect counterpart here in the subject's conformity versus nonconformity. By the end of the series of discrimination, Gerard's Commitment subjects should have felt that they were conforming to the group, for they found inevitably that their first impulse led them to agree with the other two subjects.

What difference should the subject's ability make? In the low-ability condition subjects were probably not surprised by either conformity or deviance. Neither behavior would have aroused much dissonance, for their ability level would not have led them necessarily to expect to be different from or similar to the group. In contrast, high-ability subjects who find themselves to be conformers should experience considerable dissonance. Their ability level should have led them to expect a certain amount of independence, and the commitment to conformity should have brought forth dissonance arousal. By the same reasoning dissonance would have been minimal for high-ability deviates.

How can the subject reduce his dissonance? Again using Kiesler and Corbin as a parallel, consonant cognitions can be added by coming to like the group. The reasoning is simple. The high-ability conformer has made a commitment to a group, he has good reason to be uncomfortable about his conforming commitment, and one cognition that would support his conformity is liking for the two group members. The results were entirely in keeping with this line of thought. Among high-ability subjects there was more liking for the others when subjects conformed than when they were deviant, while the opposite relationship held among low-ability subjects. This opposite effect among low-ability subjects might have resulted from their desire to improve their standing with the group (i.e., move close to it) when they found themselves to be deviate.

COMMITMENT TO ONE'S OWN BELIEF

In a work devoted entirely to the concept of commitment, Kiesler (1971) has elaborated the commitment notion in directions that enable us to talk about the relationship between the impact of "freezing" someone to a behavior and the person's subsequent likelihood of behaving otherwise. In Chapter 15 we will discuss his developments in detail, including one experiment by Kiesler, Pallak, and Kanouse (1968) that separates the effects of commitment from those of dissonance arousal. For the present we will summarize that experiment briefly, for it provides an interesting contrast to the research we have just reviewed.

Subjects were first asked to commit themselves to an attitudinally consonant position. This was done either under conditions of high or low commitment, meaning that the attitude-consistent speech was either to be played publicly and with the subject's name associated, or else anonymously.

At this point an important distinction should be drawn which is central to Kiesler's thesis. To test the effects of commitment independently of dissonance, one must create a situation wherein the consonant act does not arouse dissonance. It is therefore important to insure that subjects are not asked to take a more (or less) extreme position than that which they actually hold preexperimentally.

Subsequent to the initial commitment manipulation subjects were placed in a dissonance-arousing counterattitudinal essay-writing paradigm, under either high- or low-choice conditions. The issue involved was closely related to that used in the commitment phase.

On a postmeasure of attitude on the relevant issue (tuition increases) the high-choice subjects showed more agreement with the position of the essay than did low-choice subjects, which should be expected from dissonance theory. However, this was the case only among subjects who had been in the low commitment and no-commitment variations. For subjects who had been highly committed experimentally to their preexisting attitudes, the choice manipulation had no impact on dissonance reduction. The point is simply that a predissonance-arousal commitment to a prior belief can interfere directly with potentially dissonance-reducing attitude change.

Kiesler argues that the attitude-consistent behavior in this instance was not dissonance arousing, and he provides evidence for this point. That is, Kiesler and his colleagues showed that high versus low commitment in and of itself had no effect on subsequent attitudes. But such would not always be the case. For example, Jellison and Mills (1969) found that a consonant commitment to one's own position results in taking a more extreme position. Although they did not offer a dissonance-theory interpretation of this result, there is no reason why one should necessarily be ruled out. To the degree that an attitudinally consonant behavior has undesired consequences, dissonance should most certainly be aroused as long as there is a sufficient element of responsibility. There is no shortage of negative consequences that might accrue from an attitude-consistent commitment, and Kiesler (1971, pp. 11–12) lists a number of such consequences.

But Kiesler's new model proposes that commitment has "freezing" effects even though commitment may not be dissonance arousing, and in the context of the Kiesler *et al.* (1968) study this is an important precondition for Kiesler's model. It might be noted that the commitment could have aroused dissonance that was reduced in unmeasured ways. But since the investigation used a common method of assessing dissonance reduction, we offer this as no more than a possibility that is present in every experiment.

SUMMARY

The notion of commitment has been broadened to include acts that do not create dissonance. Whether commitment affects dissonance or not, it has become evident that cognitions relevant to recent commitments are often brought into line with those commitments. The research of Kiesler *et al.* (1968) demonstrates that prior commitment can interfere with the dissonance-reduction effects that would ordinarily be expected from a subsequent commitment, while the earlier research has examined dissonance arousal as a function of a single commitment. The central lesson of the earlier research is quite clear: When dissonance is created through a commitment, subsequent shifts of attitude in a commitment-consistent direction will be in proportion to the dissonance created. Perhaps the most extreme example of this was in the conformity research by Kiesler and colleagues, in which commitment mediated the paradoxical effect of a group becoming influential and likable in proportion to its rejecting qualities.

3
Choice

The notion of choice as a mediator of dissonance processes has come to be treated as virtual magic among dissonance researchers. Quite reliably, it has been a uniquely instrumental variable in the creation of dissonance-reduction effects, especially within the sometimes perplexing forced-compliance procedure. But the discovery of choice as a crucial manipulation should in no way imply that choice bears no qualitative similarity to other variables affecting dissonance arousal. In fact, the empirical notion of "choice," which stands for certain operations and nothing more, is directly implied by the ratio formula for dissonance arousal. This point was touched upon earlier and might be elaborated briefly.

It is normally assumed in this analysis that the behavioral commitment, the focal point of a dissonance analysis, is by definition the primary consonant cognition. Any cognitive elements consistent with it are labeled "consonant" and serve to reduce dissonance, while elements inconsistent are labeled "dissonant" and serve to raise dissonance. For the sake of example assume that a highly intellectual student from a prestige school is asked to compose an essay favoring compulsory religious courses at his school. He privately believes the opposite, thus the commitment to defend religion should be dissonance provoking as long as there are few cognitions consistent with his commitment. Now to the choice variable.

In order to simplify the situation, assume the existence of just three relevant cognitions: the preexisting anticompulsory-religion attitude (the only dissonant cognition), the commitment to write (consonant by definition), and some degree of coercion to write (a consonant cognition):

$$\text{amount of dissonance} = \frac{\text{preexisting antireligious attitude}}{\text{a degree of coercion}}$$

Two of these elements are easy to effect experimentally. To commit a person to defending a position requires no unusual considerations, and it is also a simple matter to insure that the person initially disagrees with the stance implied by his commitment. Methodologically the third factor is one that must be treated with sensitivity. As the presence of coercive elements increases, dissonance can quickly be reduced to near zero. In inducing someone to perform counterattitudinal actions it is all too easy to create strong forces toward compliance, for a common method of requesting is to issue an order, or to request in such a way that it is unthinkable to refuse. Normally it is viewed as hostile to refuse a request or favor, especially when an experimenter is asking that favor for supposed scientific purposes. It would seem then, that a typical request would carry with it so many forces to perform the behavior that the denominator of the above equation would be heavily laden with dissonance-minimizing cognitive elements. Accordingly, care must be taken to place the subject into a genuine conflict state, such that his primary identifiable basis for action is his own free will. This strategy is exemplified well in the following experiment, which serves as a prototype for the subsequent research of this chapter.

The "forced-compliance" experiment by Arthur R. Cohen and Bibb Latané (1962) utilized a direct verbal manipulation of choice and examined the effect on attitude change of differences in perceived choice in taking a discrepant stand. Yale undergraduates were chosen at random from four residential colleges and were seen individually in their rooms. The experimenter introduced himself to each subject as a student taking a survey as "part of a research course" and asked the subject to indicate his opinion on 10 issues pertaining to student life at Yale. Embedded in the questionnaire was the relevant attitude dimension: an item concerning the institution of a compulsory religion course at Yale.

Three weeks later another experimenter interviewed all subjects in their rooms. He approached only those subjects opposed to the institution of a compulsory religion course as measured by the preliminary questionnaire. (Most subjects were strongly opposed to the idea: Only nine students were dropped from the experiment prior to the second session because of being initially neutral or favorable.) The experimenter introduced himself as a student working for the Yale News Bureau who had been given the subject's name by the bureau. Subjects were told that the "Chicago Yale Alumni Board" was very much interested in the question of a compulsory religion course at Yale, but before going ahead with any action, they wanted to get some ideas on the issue. Subjects were then asked if they would help by tape recording a statement giving their views. They were told that a program was to be put together which would represent a collection of ideas on the proposal rather than an opinion poll. The taped statements would be edited and a final program of ideas made up on both sides of the issue.

The subjects were then told: "We have many statements against the compulsory religion course, and now we need some ideas on the other side of the issue—a strong, convincing argument in favor of the compulsory religion course at Yale."

However, before speaking into the microphone, which was ostensibly to record the speeches to be presented to the Chicago Alumni Board, subjects were given the choice manipulation. Half the subjects (those assigned to the low-choice condition) were simply asked to make the discrepant speech. The microphone was practically pushed into their hands, and they were given no chance to decline or to have any say in the matter. The other half of the subjects, assigned to the high-choice condition, were told, "We need some people to speak in favor of the proposal, but, of course, the matter is entirely up to you." In effect, the experimenter attempted to create the illusion that the subject was entirely free to refuse. At this same time the experimenter reopened the issue (of the subject's giving the speech) every time the subject appeared to be vacillating and on the edge of refusal. In this manner the experimenter and subject sometimes "argued" back and forth as much as three times, but in all cases agreement was finally reached. Furthermore, after agreement was reached, the experimenter emphasized that he did not want to force the subject into anything he did not want to do, and he made certain the decision was again seen by the subject as his own.

The subject was again told that it was necessary to take a strong stand for compulsory religion at Yale; he gave his name, address, and class at Yale; he spoke into a tape recorder which was apparently taking down everything he said; and he assumed that his speech, identified as his statement, would be played before an important group of Yale alumni. Thus, subjects in this experiment who varied in the amount of choice given them took a strong public stand on an issue they opposed, producing a situation in which differential dissonance and attitude change could be expected.

After finishing his speech, the subject filled out the postquestionnaire, which included the relevant opinion measure and a check on the choice manipulation. When subjects had completed the postmeasures, they were told about the experiment and cautioned not to speak about it for an appropriate time. This concluded the experiment.

The check on the choice manipulation indicated that it was effective in creating differing perceptions of choice in taking the discrepant stand. The data also show that all subjects were extremely and almost identically opposed to the compulsory religion course at Yale at the outset.

The change in subjects' attitudes toward acceptance of the compulsory religion course from before to after taking the discrepant stand constitutes the main measure. The mean change for the low-choice condition was 1.8, whereas for the high-choice condition it was 2.7, though this difference did not reach statistical significance. Upon inspection of the distribution of change scores within each of the two choice conditions, it was found that a few extreme change scores in the low-choice condition were responsible for the reduced significance of the difference between conditions. Thus, when a chi-square test was performed on the data after splitting change at the median, the choice groups were significantly different in the predicted direction ($p < .01$).

This study is an excellent illustration of a method by which coercive forces on the subject can be minimized. As indicated by the experimenter's alternately pushing and pulling subjects with respect to the experimental task, a considerable effort may be required to insure that the person's discrepant commitment cannot be attributed by him to exigencies of the scientific setting. Subjects typically are set to make such attributions, and the high-choice manipulation is an effort to convince subjects to shift the attribution of causality toward themselves.

Should choice, one of many antecedents of dissonance, be more important than other variables? Theoretically this would be a foolish question, since the answer depends on the strength or salience of those other variables. But empirically, that is, with reference to accomplished research, choice has a profound influence. The reason is that experimental situations, particularly of the forced compliance variety, lend themselves all too easily to a complete minimization of choice—hence minimization of dissonance arousal. What this means is that the introduction of choice, if carried out in a potent manner, facilitates the arousal of dissonance. The induction of choice may therefore be a vital consideration if the "natural state" of laboratory provides the subject with adequate justification (consonant elements) for attitude-discrepant behaviors.

The implication is that extreme caution must be taken in experiments where subjects are expected to decide in a preordained way. Choice is especially likely to be minimal in such procedures, and this is one possible reason for some of the "negative" results to be examined later in this chapter.

With these considerations as a background, the existing literature on choice will be examined briefly. In so doing it will be possible to address directly some of the empirical criticism reviewed later in this chapter, and at the same time illustrate the workings of a consistently powerful variable.

EXPERIMENTS INVOLVING ONLY CHOICE

In addition to the Cohen and Latané experiment there have been two other fairly simple experiments involving only the dimension of choice.

The direct manipulation of choice was first used in an "exposure" experiment by Cohen, Terry, and Jones (1959). Subsequent to an initial attitude measurement, college students were given high or low choice about whether or not to listen to a communication characterized as upholding a position counter to their own. All subjects were then exposed to the communication, and, finally, their attitudes on the issue were measured again. Analysis of attitude-change scores according to the subject's initial position on the issue revealed that choice had little or no effect on those who were initially moderate, but had a great effect on those who were extreme in their opposition to the position of the communication. Among extreme subjects, high choice produced greater change toward the position of the communication than did low choice. Thus, these data support the notion that dissonance is a direct function of choice and degree of discrepancy between one's own position and the counterattitudinal act.

A "forced-compliance" experiment by Brock (1962) provides further evidence on the effect of choice on dissonance. Giving nonCatholic college students either high or low choice in whether or not to comply, he induced them to write an essay on "Why I would like to become a Catholic." Change in attitudes toward Catholicism, as measured by pre- and postexperimental questionnaires, supported the expectation that dissonance and consequent attitude change toward the position of the essay would increase as choice increased. These results, in addition to supporting the hypothesized effect of choice on dissonance, show that dissonance can affect attitudes on an important social issue.

A Brock and Buss (1962) shock experiment also provides some supporting evidence for the assertion that the direct manipulation of choice in agreeing to engage in discrepant behavior affects dissonance and consequent attitude change. In their experiment, for subjects confronting male victims, those given a high degree of choice in whether or not they would participate in the shock-deliverance task changed their attitudes so as to evaluate the shock as *less* painful after delivering it than before. But subjects in the no-choice condition, having experienced little dissonance, tended to perceive the shock as *more* painful than before.

One final experiment in this category is reported by Brock (1968). The experiment included a justification variable, but since that was ineffective this can be treated as one-variable experiment. Brock asked subjects to perform a tedious task, varying choice over three levels. Low-choice subjects found that they were required to perform the task, medium-choice subjects were told that performance was not absolutely necessary, and the high-choice group found that whether or not to perform was entirely their choice. Subjects then engaged in the tedious task and finally indicated their enjoyment of the task. Consistent with the theory there was a monotonic relationship between choice and enjoyment, such that the greatest enjoyment was evidenced among high-choice subjects.

INCENTIVE OR SECONDARY REINFORCEMENT EFFECTS

Much of the literature on choice still to be discussed bears directly upon the disconfirmability of the theory. Because this literature serves as a direct response to a number of results that have been viewed as contrary to the theory, we find this an opportune time to summarize the negative findings. Most of these negative findings consist of what is popularly called the "incentive effect," or "secondary reinforcement effect." By this is meant that a person develops an aversion to a situation or event that is paired with something unpleasant, and similarly, a situation paired with a favorable or pleasant stimulus should come to be enjoyed, liked, or approached. Our purpose is to comb these negative results to discover why they are indeed negative, and then to proceed to a number of more recent dissonance experiments that vary both incentive level and choice. It will be seen later that choice, which is one of the components of personal responsibility, is an invaluable tool for clarifying the impact of other dissonance-related and incentive-related variables.

Negative Evidence (Secondary Reinforcement Effects) from Experiments Not Designed to Test Dissonance Theory

In an experiment by Wicklund, Cooper, and Linder (1967) subjects were asked to undergo a small period of unpleasant delay before hearing a taperecorded speech that ran contrary to their views. On the basis of the theory it was argued that the delay operated as a cognition dissonant with subjects' commitment to hear the message, and that dissonance reduction could be served by coming to agree more with the communicator. The results took exactly this form, although there is reason to think that delay might sometimes produce opposite effects. For example, we might consider a study by Lott, Aponte, Lott, and McGinley (1969). Children were asked to perform a task repeatedly while being led to expect to receive a prize (a dried bean) for successful performance. When sufficient beans were accumulated the subject could trade them in for a toy. Each child worked alternately for two experimenters: One of these always delivered the bean immediately upon successful performance, while the other always produced a bean following a 10-sec delay. After a number of trials the subject's liking for these two experimenters was assessed, and consistent with the authors' expectations the experimenter who rewarded immediately was better liked.

Given the dissonance-theory findings of Wicklund et al. (1967) the results of the present experiment with children might be viewed as surprising. Should not subjects have justified their wait (however short) by coming to like something about the situation better? Just as the Wicklund et al. (1967) subjects justified their effort by coming to agree with the communication, the subjects of Lott et al. (1969) might have been expected to develop a liking for the experimenter who was associated with delay of gratification.

However many parallels might be seen between these two lines of research, a crucial similarity is lacking. Lott et al. (1969) did not intend to arouse cognitive dissonance in their subjects, and accordingly, they did not set up the necessary conditions to do so. Most particularly, we emphasized earlier that subjects must be given a minimum of force in the direction of the commitment, or else the person's knowledge of that force will provide a ready means of minimization of dissonance. Lott *et al.* (1969) did not undertake the sensitive procedure of carefully cajoling subjects into performing the task.

Not only were the sufficient conditions for dissonance arousal lacking, but the procedure contained a factor working against possible dissonance-reduction effects, namely, that which the experimenters meant to demonstrate. Thus, if dissonance were a factor it would have had to work against a disposition of subjects to show their preference for the immediately rewarding experimenter.

Mischel, Grusec, and Masters (1969) also investigated delay, independently of dissonance-theory considerations. The subject was shown several rewards, one of which he expected to receive later. Before discovering which reward he was to receive the subject was asked to rate all of the rewards. Each reward (such as $.50) was described as available "now" or else after a considerable waiting period. The results from four quite similar experiments were consistent: rewards described as available "now" were more attractive than rewards associated with a delay.

Again, this result appears at least superficially contrary to the evidence of Wicklund *et al.* (1967) and other similar effort-justification experiments, but as in the case of Lott *et al.* (1969) the authors were not attempting to shed light on dissonance theory. This being the case, they did not create even the most fundamental conditions necessary for a test of the theory—this being a behavioral commitment. At the time of the ratings, subjects were by no means committed to any of the potential rewards, meaning there is no basis for analyzing the situation is terms of cognitions most and least resistant to change.

Janis, Kaye, and Kirschner (1965) asked subjects to read four persuasive communications, each advocating an unpopular view, and as the subject undertook his task he was offered some peanuts and Pepsi-Cola by the experimenter. The results generally supported a secondary reinforcement view-point. Harking back to the research on insufficient justification, it might be thought that subjects not offered these refreshments would experience more dissonance than would subjects given the justification of peanuts and Pepsi. At the very least, subjects were committed to reading an essay with which they disagreed, which often would be a dissonance-arousing procedure. But two questions need to be asked in light of previous considerations:

1. Were subjects forced to read the essays such that dissonance would not be aroused to any great degree? There is no indication in the procedure that subjects were induced lightly into reading the essays, suggesting that the obligatory nature of the task provided a ready justification of their performing it.

2. Were the food and drink necessary as justification for reading, or did subjects already think they had adequate reason for performing the task? There was apparently no concerted effort in this research to request special efforts or unpleasant experiences from the subjects.

Given that they expected to take part in some research they may well have viewed the task as consonant with their expectations about the desirability of the task. The important point is that the effort justification research (Chapter 5) typically contains unusually noxious or onerous elements that subjects would prefer to avoid.

These studies have been cited to demonstrate that testing dissonance theory is not just a matter of designing research in which reward, effort, or similar variables are manipulated. There are numerous ways in which to employ reward and effort that have no bearing on dissonance processes, for the arousal of dissonance involves crucial ingredients that happened to be lacking in the above research. At a minimum, the subject must have committed himself to an act he normally would avoid, and his commitment must be largely his own doing, not attributable to external pressures.

It should now be apparent that the most convincing negative evidence would be that found where researchers have specifically set out to put the theory to a test. Even in those direct tests it is still important to ask whether or not the appropriate conditions have been created, since it is easy to "disprove" the theory by neglecting a single necessary condition. Moreover, as in all research, it is easy to include accidental artifacts, as will be demonstrated vividly by the research on selective exposure (Chapter 12).

Negative Evidence (Secondary Reinforcement Effects) from Experiments Designed to Test Dissonance Theory

The foregoing sample of studies was included merely to illustrate how easily the preconditions for dissonance arousal can be lacking when the investigator's purpose is other than evaluating the tenets of the theory. The negative evidence pursued in this section is in sharp contrast to the above sample, for the present investigators had in mind precisely to evaluate the theory. Of course, just because someone says he tests the theory does not guarantee his developing conditions suitable for dissonance arousal. This is a matter to be taken up in the context of each experiment.

Within the realm of "conditions suitable for dissonance arousal" there is a more general point, one which will facilitate our transition to the more recent literature on choice presented in the next section. Throughout the dissonance research presented thus far there has been a continuous assumption that one of the crucial antecedent conditions is sufficient volition. But what is "sufficient volition?" Are certain skills necessary in order to understand the intricacies of the manifold pressures a subject might experience, and is the person sympathetic with dissonance theory likely to attend to these nuances more than a critic of the theory? There is a way to avert such problems. If the factor of volition is varied together with manipulation of other theoretical variables, such as monetary incentive, the ambiguity of "sufficient volition" is reduced considerably.

The reason is simple. No matter what the impact of variations in effort, pain, or external justification on measures of dissonance reduction, such variables should operate more in accordance with the theory if volition is increased. But this is a topic for the next section. The present experiments are relatively simple, in the sense of including no choice manipulation. Thus it is necessary to look at them from the standpoint of whether or not too much pressure was placed on subjects to embark on the dissonance-producing task.

Negative evidence of Janis.   Janis and Gilmore (1965) begin by proposing an "incentive theory." The idea is that various kinds of incentives can help motivate a person to think up arguments. In a dissonance-theory paradigm where subjects are requested to invent arguments contrary to their own beliefs, Janis and Gilmore would suggest that an incentive such as money can motivate the subject to do two things: generate convincing counterattitudinal arguments, and at the same time suppress thoughts about arguments supporting his original belief. What are the effects of these two processes? Janis and Gilmore propose that acceptance of the counterattitudinal position will increase as incentives for counterattitudinal "role playing" increase. This argument holds together so far, but what about the existing research? For example, as will be seen in Chapter 5, Festinger and Carlsmith (1959) found more attitude change when the monetary incentive was a mere $1, compared against an incentive of $20.

To answer this question Janis and Gilmore raise the possibility of *negative incentives.* One kind of negative incentive would be a sleazy experimenter who asks the subject to role play for apparent illegitimate reasons. Another kind of negative incentive occurs, ironically, if the subject is offered too much monetary or other material inducement for his role playing. Specifically, Janis and Gilmore raise the possibility that subjects offered $20 for a mere counterattitudinal performance might become suspicious about the experimenter's motives. Such negative incentives are supposed to work as interference factors, inhibiting the subject's acceptance of his counterattitudinal performance. Their argument adds up to a rationale for the Festinger and Carlsmith result, completely independent of dissonance-theory thinking.

In order to test the foregoing ideas against the implications of dissonance theory Janis and Gilmore created a rather elaborate three-factor experiment. About half of the subjects (overt role playing) were requested to write a 10-min counterattitudinal essay, advocating additional mandatory physics and mathematics courses for college students. It was presumed that subjects would disagree sharply with such a position. The remaining subjects (no overt role playing) simply filled out the questionnaire without any counterattitudinal performance, but expected to write an essay later. A second variable was the degree of monetary inducement. Patterned exactly after Festinger and Carlsmith, subjects were offered either $20 or $1. Finally, a "sponsorship" variable was introduced. Some subjects (public welfare sponsorship) found that their essays were needed by a national research organization, while others (commercial sponsorship) were led to think that their essays would be instrumental in an advertising campaign for science textbooks.

As viewed by Janis and Gilmore the latter two variables provide a test of dissonance theory versus incentive theory. They suggest that more dissonance should be aroused when subjects are paid just $1, and dissonance should also be greater under conditions of commercial sponsorship, since there is less justification for essay writing given that the essay is to be used for questionable purposes. They see incentive theory as predicting just the opposite. Twenty dollars may well arouse suspicion or distrust, and operate as a negative incentive. Analogously, commercial sponsorship should also operate as a negative incentive and reduce attitude change.

The results were mixed, but if anything supportive of the Janis and Gilmore incentive reasoning. The monetary variable had no impact on attitudes toward mandatory mathematics and physics courses, but there was a significant interaction between the other two variables, indicating that public welfare sponsorship produced more favorable attitudes than commercial sponsorship, but only among subjects who were overt role players. Just the opposite result was obtained among no overt role playing subjects, who expected to write their essays at a later point. This result seems consistent with their reasoning: the greater the incentive for role playing, the greater is the motivation to think up positive arguments and suppress negative arguments.

A very important feature of this experiment is revealed by looking at the quality of essays written. Quality was higher under public welfare than commercial sponsorship, and was also higher given a high-monetary inducement. The first of these findings coincides with the basis for an incentive theory approach: positive incentives are supposed to motivate the person to "think up all the good positive arguments he can . . ." and in turn lead to attitude change.

The quality-of-argument results are all perfectly appropriate in order to produce incentive theory effects, but are quality differences desirable in order to establish conditions for testing dissonance principles? The theoretical thinking relative to the forced-compliance procedure should be reviewed quickly. When a person engages in a dissonance-inducing action, the amount of dissonance is proportional to the absence of external justification for performance. Ideally the act itself retains a constant quality across all subjects, while justification is varied. Given the same dissonance-arousing action, dissonance reduction will result when justifications are minimal or inadequate. But what happens when the quality of counterattitudinal performance is correlated with amount of justification? The most obvious result that comes to mind is that two dissonance-enhancing factors then come to work in opposition. The higher the quality of the subject's arguments, the more dissonance there should be, assuming an initial disagreement with the advocated position. At the same time, there should be less dissonance among subjects who write high-quality essays, for they are the same ones who receive justification in the form of public welfare sponsorship. In short, the experiment becomes ambiguous when viewed from dissonance theory, and given the result of differential essay quality the study serves as a demonstration of incentive processes and nothing more.

A highly similar study was conducted by Elms and Janis (1965), also for the purpose of evaluating the incentive hypothesis against what might be expected from dissonance theory. The attitude issue was different from that of Janis and Gilmore, but in most other respects the two studies were conceptually similar. The results, however, departed from those of the first experiment. The major attitude change result in this second study consisted of a second-order interaction whereby the combination of high monetary incentive and favorable sponsorship produced a substantial positive attitude change, but only under overt role playing. Given the nonovert treatment the monetary and sponsorship variables operated differently, such that unfavorable sponsorship tended to produce more positive attitude change than did favorable sponsorship. In general these results are not strong evidence for either of the theoretical positions in question here, but perhaps the important point is that dissonance theory might have led us to expect the greatest attitude change in the overt role playing, unfavorable sponsorship, low monetary incentive condition. In fact, the greatest change took place in another condition, where dissonance should not have been terribly high.

The quality-of-essay results were also a departure from the Janis and Gilmore experiment. In the present study there was no systematic relationship between attitude change and essay quality, and in fact, the only consequential difference among essays came from an analysis of number of words, which showed that the quantity was greater as monetary payment was increased. This finding, of course, could partially explain the "incentive effect" obtained within the overt role playing favorable sponsorship condition. In order to implement dissonance theory correctly it would have been necessary to hold constant the quantity of persuasive material written.

The research just reported has been predicated on the assumption that the offering of monetary payment to subjects can operate as a "negative incentive." The idea is that Festinger and Carlsmith, or possibly other researchers, have offered subjects so much money that other motives enter the situation—motives that lead to results which appear as dissonance reduction, but which in fact develop out of the extraordinary and suspect offer of $20. If fact, Festinger and Carlsmith arranged their procedure so that the $20 condition would indeed be one of low dissonance and of low suspicion or distrust. Brehm (1965) notes that the $20 offer was entirely reasonable because subjects expected to be "on call" for work in further research, and further, that Festinger and Carlsmith reported virtually no suspicion relative to the $20 payment.

Brehm also remarks that it is not difficult to create conditions of suspicion by offering too much money, and this may well be what was accomplished by the preceding two studies. Unlike the Festinger and Carlsmith experiment, there was no effort in the above-reported experiments to make the high payment seem reasonable. In fact, Janis and Gilmore report that subjects who were offered $20 expressed "a great deal of puzzlement . . ." Therefore, it should not be surprising that the result departed from other dissonance-theory experiments involving payment.

There is one other questionable feature of the Elms and Janis study, this facet implying a possible cognitive dissonance interpretation. Brehm (1965) has noted that the attitudes held by the Elms and Janis subjects may have been extremely resistant to change, particularly in the unfavorable sponsorship condition. This observation was based on the nature of the attitude and on comments of subjects reported by Elms and Janis. If the noxious position to be taken in the essay causes the subject's original attitude to be resistant, and if extremely unfavorable sponsorship creates even more resistance, it is then unlikely that dissonance reduction would take place through positive attitude change. Instead, as Brehm notes, subjects might exaggerate the pressure placed on them to comply, or perhaps tell themselves that their dissonance-arousing arguments would not be believed by the students who were to be misled by the arguments. Further, subjects might even bolster their earlier positions, and in the data Brehm finds some suggestion that this is indeed what happened.

In summary, Brehm's criticism of the Elms and Janis study implies that conditions were not optimal for finding positive attitude change as a function of dissonance arousal. Instead, the experiment seems better suited for observing boomerang change effects or whatever other effects might result from subjects' suspicion. Independent of Brehm's criticism the Elms and Janis study shares with the Janis and Gilmore experiment a problem of confounding: Unless subjects can be made to compose essays of equal length and quality, dissonance theory does not receive an adequate test.

Explaining "incentive" effects in terms of perceived choice.   Independent of effects such as puzzlement or suspiciousness, the overpayment used in the forementioned research might also have created a feeling of high volition, with consequent greater dissonance. It may sound paradoxical that too much justification, or pressure, could enhance feelings of choice, but the following analysis and experiment illustrate the operation of this notion.

In a typically low-choice condition the subject feels less responsible for his actions than his high-choice counterpart. Because he has not initiated the action himself, he should feel little sense of being the determiner of the act. Instead, his behaviors will reflect the fact that the act has been largely determined by environmental constraints. However, Cohen and Brehm (1962) imply that a feeling of internal determination might result when force reaches a point of illegitimacy. When constraints are too imposing, arbitrary, or illegitimate, the person might feel motivated to become the internal director of his behavior once again. Ironically, the *feeling* of being the personal origin of the discrepant act might increase as force reaches an objectionable level. With these ideas in mind, the Cohen and Brehm study can be spelled out.

In line with the above reasoning, an illegitimate coercive force was employed to make college students agree to participate in an unpleasant task. A questionnaire measured the participants' perceptions of the coercive force, volition, and task valuation. The effect of the illegitimate coercion was made clear by having conditions of low and high threat as well as a control condition that involved no threat.

The subjects consisted of 30 Yale undergraduates. Arrangements had been made with pledgemasters of the various fraternities to send pledges to the experimental room "to help out in some research for a short period of time."

A general condition of illegitimacy was established in the following way. First, the pledges were told by their pledgemasters that they were to report for a short project of 15–20 min duration, whereas the experimenter then demanded that they sign up for a boring and profitless task that would take 3–4 hr. Above all, however, the experimenter was a professor who had no connection whatsoever with any of the fraternities involved. To make the coercion completely illegitimate, the experimenter threatened to have the pledge's fraternity penalize him if he failed to participate in the unexpectedly long task. Since such an influence by a professor on a fraternity's business would be very unusual, it was expected that the attempted coercion would be seen by the pledge as illegitimate. The exact procedure follows.

When the subject arrived, he was told that he was expected to participate in three to four continuous hours of copying random numbers. It was emphasized that participation would be extremely dull and that there was nothing the subject would learn from it, but that his help was needed in order to "establish norms for other research." After being shown an example of the task, the subject was given one of the following coercion manipulations:

High Coercion: Now we need your cooperation, and if you don't cooperate, I'm afraid we'll have to report you as uncooperative to your pledgemaster and the other fellows and really push for some severe penalities. This can have very bad effects; we'll try to see that it has very strong consequences for extending your pledge period considerably and even for keeping you out of the house permanently.

Low Coercion: Now we need your cooperation, and if you don't cooperate, I'm afraid we'll have to report you as uncooperative to your pledgemaster and the other fellows and see that you get some hours of extra duty as a pledge.

In the control condition the subjects were told, "Now we need your cooperation." Nothing was said to them about any possible penalties for noncooperation.

After the manipulation, the subject was given a schedule sheet on which to indicate his free hours. All subjects with the exception of one in the low-coercion condition agreed to participate and filled out a schedule sheet. Perception of the coercive force, perceived choice about whether or not to participate (volition), and evaluation of the number-copying task were measured on a questionnaire given immediately after commitment to participation.

The test of whether dissonance depends on the coercive force itself or on volition arising from the coercion assumes that the experimental conditions have resulted in a direct relationship between coercion and volition: the greater the coercion, the greater the volition. Subjects' responses to the question on felt volition show a statistically reliable difference between the high coercion and control conditions (beyond the 1% level), and a strong but nonsignificant trend for high-coercion subjects to report feeling more volition than low-coercion subjects. This latter trend is crucial for testing the idea basic to this study, since in other research in this chapter it would generally be expected that high coercion (or other justification) would lower felt volition.

If coercion (or in general justification) is the controlling determinant of the magnitude of dissonance, revaluation of the task should vary inversely with coercion (and volition) as has been demonstrated in other research. But if volition is the controlling determinant of dissonance, then revaluation should vary *directly* with coercion (and volition). The measure of revaluation—subjects' satisfaction with being assigned to the experiment—shows that subjects in the high-coercion condition were more satisfied than subjects in either the low coercion ($p < .05$) or control conditions ($p < .01$). These results therefore support the contention that volition is an important determinant of the magnitude of dissonance.

The results of this experiment seem somewhat startling in the context of the earlier studies of choice, and for this reason it is important to keep in mind the theoretical reasoning. When coercive forces become too strong, or "illegitimate," it is possible to impart an *increased* feeling of freedom by way of increments in those same forces. This notion is not an integral part of dissonance theory, but is a worthwhile consideration when dissonance arousal is analyzed in the context of varying pressures to comply. Reactance theory (Brehm, 1966) might be seen as a suitable interpretation of this relationship between force and felt choice, for that theory deals explicitly with negative reactions to coercive attempts. In fact, Brehm (1966) has suggested that a threat to freedom of choice may be accompanied by feelings of increased internal determination. By implementing the variables of reactance theory it should be possible to specify better the preconditions of the effect obtained in this experiment, although at this point reactance theory will not be given a detailed coverage.

Perhaps the lesson to be learned from this experiment concerns the theoretical variables being dealt with by dissonance theory: felt choice or felt sense of being the origin of one's behavior is the crucial variable mediating the effects found in this chapter. In light of the experiment it would be misleading to say that increased force always reduces dissonance, even though virtually every experiment shows this. For an understanding of dissonance processes it is necessary to comprehend better the psychological consequences of that force, for effects similar to those of Cohen and Brehm could arise whenever the forces used to bring out discrepant behaviors are too restrictive.

Returning to the Janis research, which stimulated this discussion, it can be seen that illegitimate or overly coercive forces of any kind can potentially increase dissonance. The idea in implementing money, social pressure, or other justifications in setting up low-dissonance conditions is to provide an amount that would normally be expected, or equitable, given the situation. When the justification exceeds that level, the situation becomes ripe for the sort of reaction witnessed by Cohen and Brehm (1962). Unfortunately there is no method within the Janis and Gilmore and Elms and Janis research to evaluate this possibility, but we should keep it in mind as a general possibility for accounting for "incentive" effects.

Negative evidence of Rosenberg. A study by Rosenberg (1965) parallels the Janis and Gilmore paper in three major respects: There is an extratheoretical interpretation of certain previous dissonance theory findings, a model is proposed to explain why there should be a positive relationship between incentive and attitude change, and finally, the results appear to run contrary to dissonance theory expectations.

First the criticism of earlier studies: Rosenberg contends that a substantial monetary incentive, $20 for example, can bring forth an "evaluation apprehension." This is a state in which a person will think that his "autonomy, his honesty, his resoluteness in resisting a special kind of bribe, are being tested." These considerations will, according to Rosenberg, cause the subject to resist changing his attitude. To demonstrate attitude change would give the experimenter evidence of the subject's less-than-scrupulous ethical standards.

If evaluation apprehension is ruled out, what effect will incentive have? Here Rosenberg (1956, 1960) draws upon his own consistency theory to suggest that a reward will effect "development and stabilization of . . . new cognitions." This means that attitude change following a counterattitudinal performance will be a positive function of amount of payment. Parenthetically, it has been noted elsewhere (Collins & Hoyt, 1972; Nuttin, 1975) that this objection to dissonance paradigms was handled earlier in the Festinger and Carlsmith (1959) experiment, where the induction of dissonance and measurement phases were separated in such a way that "evaluation apprehension" should have been circumvented.

Rosenberg's study centered around his effort to reduce evaluation apprehension. He argued that if the person who offers the incentive is unconnected with the person who measures the attitude, evaluation apprehension should not be reflected on the dependent measure. Supposedly, the subject's evaluation apprehension assumes that one person is "testing" the subject, by both offering money and measuring the attitude. The subject should not have to worry about displaying his loose ethical principles if the two events are separated.

It was fairly assumed by Rosenberg that his subjects (Ohio State University undergraduates) would favor their football team's going to the Rose Bowl.

Accordingly, they were induced to compose an essay supporting an antibowl position. The incentive promised for this performance was either $.50, $1, or $5. In line with the evaluation apprehension reasoning, Rosenberg created a distinct separation between the induction-of-essay-writing phase and the attitude-measurement phase.

The results coincided quite well with Rosenberg's balance-theory prediction: The $5 group showed more essay-consistent attitude change than did the combined $.50 and $1 groups. But there is an additional interesting result. When the essays were scored for persuasiveness, it turned out that the most persuasive comments were made by $5 subjects. This result offers a perfect parallel to the findings of Janis and Gilmore, thus with respect to testing dissonance theory the same ambiguity exists as before. More dissonance should be created by a persuasive essay, yet at the same time those subjects who wrote the most persuasive essays were offered the high-monetary justification, which should have *reduced* dissonance. If anything the result seems to be good support for the Janis–Gilmore incentive model, which allows that attitude change accruing from large incentive will come by way of higher quality essays. But the important point is that dissonance theory is not adequately evaluated by a procedure that allows differential essay quality.

Another important commentary on the Rosenberg procedure comes from some extensive research reported by Nuttin (Chapter 1, 1975). Belgian students were asked to compose counterattitudinal essays, much in the manner as Rosenberg's subjects. The incentive was varied over four levels, between 5 and 500 Belgian Francs. (At the time of the experiment 50 BF equaled approximately $1 U.S.) The dissonance-arousing phase and measurement phase were separated, just as in Rosenberg's study, but the attitude change results were exactly contrary: There was an *inverse* monotonic relationship between amount of payment and attitude change in the direction of the essay. Although Nuttin reports no data on essay quality or quantity, it may well be that such confoundings were responsible for the negative results reported by Rosenberg. To make the point more convincing, Nuttin also reports an experiment in which the two phases were not separated, and in which there was also an inverse relationship between payment and attitude change. Evidently the evaluation apprehension process does not adequately account for the earlier finding of Cohen (1962; discussed in Chapter 5 of this volume) where there was no separation of experimental phases.

Rosenberg and Finkelstein (see Rosenberg, 1970) conducted a study which underlies the preceding reasoning regarding essay quality. The procedure was vaguely similar to the Festinger and Carlsmith basis for all of this research. Subjects were paid either $.50 or $2.50 for lying to a prospective subject, and as an innovation, the amount of time given subjects to profess their lies was varied—between 6 and 1.5 min. The results indicated an interaction between the two variables, with an incentive effect in the 6-min condition and a tendency toward a dissonance effect within the 1.5-min condition.

There was an important difference in quality of counterattitudinal presentation within the 6-min condition, such that 6-min subjects paid $2.50 were more positive in their descriptions of the task than were $.50 subjects. It should be obvious by now that the incentive effect of Rosenberg and Finkelstein can be easily interpreted in light of this content difference. It is also notable that in the 1.5-min condition, where there were no measurable differences in essay quality, the results leaned toward an *inverse* relationship between monetary payment and attitude change.

Rosenberg (1970) concludes his discussion of this experiment by suggesting that the conditions for obtaining incentive versus dissonance results seem to be delineated. He proposes that "counterattitudinal performance involving only an assertion of position, but not elaborated with any advocacy or argumentation, will tend to follow the dissonance dynamic, and probably for the reasons that the dissonancers have advanced" (Rosenberg, 1970, p. 198). He further implies that somewhat more elaborate counterattitudinal performance is necessary in order that an incentive effect be obtained.

Rosenberg's distinction may be valid in the context of negative evidence viewed thus far. Certainly incentive effects have resulted where there has been ample opportunity for subjects to vary, depending on amount of payment, in the convincingness of their counterattitudinal statements. Surely if subjects were given just 1 sec to compose essays or lie to another subject it would be difficult for differential payment to produce variations in performance quality. But this is only to look at the incentive effect question. What of Rosenberg's thesis that dissonance effects occur in this paradigm only as long as counterattitudinal performance involves just an assertion? Certainly there is no basis in fact for this statement, in light of the numerous essay-writing or speech-making experiments reported throughout this volume. Many of the studies already examined or to be discussed below incorporate lengthy verbal performances that constitute far more than a simple "assertion." And finally, a more general point should be made: For a test of dissonance theory the length or quality of the advocacy is not a prime consideration as long as the incentive, reward, or justification variable does not produce differences in the quality or length. If there are such differences, the circumstances are too ambiguous to call the endeavor a test of the theory.

Summary

In light of the foregoing evidence it seems clear that incentives of various kinds can increase acceptance of an acted role, a written essay, or of other attitude-discrepant actions. The "incentive effect" is simply a derivation from a more general principle of secondary reinforcement, and there is probably reason to think that it extends to attitudes, liking, or development of affect. Certainly there is adequate precedent for theoretical thinking along these lines (Byrne & Clore, 1970; Doob, 1947; Lott & Lott, 1972; Staats, 1968). Therefore, even if the quality of counterattitudinal performance had not varied with incentive (justification) in any of the present "negative evidence" experiments, a simple extension of the secondary reinforcement principle would hold that attitude change should increase with amount of monetary, scientific, or other incentive for performance.

We are dealing here with a case of two counterposed factors: secondary reinforcement and dissonance reduction. Why is one sometimes stronger than the other? Probably because the factors in the situation leading to secondary reinforcement effects are sometimes dominant, and sometimes factors creating dissonance carry the most weight. On a conceptual level this seems simple, but what are the factors that control dissonance and reinforcement processes, particularly in the forced compliance paradigms examined here that seem to comprise the major indictment of dissonance theory? We shall deal with two general answers to the question. Probably the best answer, in terms of the investigator's having maximal control over the outcome, is to vary other factors basic to dissonance (such as choice or other bases of responsibility) in addition to justification. The other answer, which we will discuss first, assumes that increases in justification upward from 0 first have a dissonance-reducing impact, then, once dissonance is at a sufficiently low level, incentive effects begin to appear. The trick and potential tripping-up point in this approach is implied in its parametric nature, which will become more obvious as we explore the relevant research.

PARTIALING OUT INCENTIVE EFFECTS: A QUESTION OF DEGREE OF JUSTIFICATION

Gerard, Conolley, and Wilhelmy (1974) have proposed a model of justification effects that views the incentive versus dissonance controversy as one along a continuum of reward, whereby undersufficient justification produces dissonance reduction, but oversufficient justification generates incentive effects. The model assumes the same dissonance prerequisites assumed in general throughout this volume: Choice and foreseeability are central antecedents of dissonance arousal.

A key concept in this analysis is "resultant justification," meaning the degree to which reasons for performing a certain action outweigh the reasons against performing it. Such reasons, of course, may be located within the person or in external sources. If a person is in a position to choose to perform a potentially dissonance-arousing act, a certain level of resultant justification (the "action" threshold) is required simply to cause him to choose that behavior. Obviously the actual amount would be determined empirically. Beyond that critical value further increases in resultant justification will serve to reduce dissonance created by the choice, and if attitude change toward an advocated position is the index of dissonance reduction, such change will decline as resultant justification increases.

With further increases there will be reached a point called a "comfort threshold," defined as a point where whatever dissonance exists can be tolerated with no efforts toward dissonance reduction. Further increases in justification will have no bearing on dissonance effects. However, shortly beyond the comfort threshold a "sweetness threshold" is found, and to increase resultant justification beyond this level is to generate incentive effects. This means that the relationship between justification and attitude change will be curvilinear. Somewhere in a midrange, between the thresholds of comfort and sweetness, attitude change will be minimal.

Is there any evidence for this notion? One of the more convincing studies is by Gerard, del Valle, Olivos, Rodriguez, Sanchez-Sosa, Thatcher, and Zadny (1971), which varied resultant justification over three levels. All subjects were offered $1.50 to perform the onerous experimental task, but certain bogus information was given about the amounts paid to other subjects in order to create feelings of insufficient, sufficient, or oversufficient justification. There were also three levels of choice, but we will deal here with just the "before choice" condition, in which subjects knew the level of justification at the time of deciding.

The onerous task consisted of tasting bitter solutions, thus dissonance could be reduced by an increasingly favorable rating of the solutions. The data were exactly in line with the previous reasoning, and suggest that the authors were successful in locating the in-between stage at which neither dissonance nor incentive processes play a role. There was a slight, but negligible decrease in rated pleasantness of the solutions in the sufficient justification condition, while the other two conditions showed strong positive changes.

A further illustration of the curvilinear hypothesis comes from Hochgürtel, Frey, and Götz (1973), whose procedure resembled that of Gerard et al. (1971) in some respects. Subjects were asked to perform a tedious task, after the manner of Freedman (1963), and were offered either the amount that was announced beforehand, a lesser amount, or a greater amount. Hochgürtel et al. (1973) also ran variations in whether or not the payment was foreseen prior to commitment, but we will comment just on the "before" conditions. The results, which were based on rated attractiveness of the task, were remarkably similar to those of Gerard et al. (1971). The "relative deprivation" and "relative gratification" conditions both showed a fairly high level of liking relative to the "congruent reward" condition.

How general a solution is the Gerard et al. (1974) model of our question of dissonance versus reinforcement effects? First, it should be emphasized that the model is intended to apply only to those instances where behavior is freely chosen and consequences are foreseen prior to commitment. It is clear from the "unforeseen" conditions, run in both the Gerard et al. (1971) and Hochgürtel et al. (1973) studies, that fait accompli justification is monotonically and positively related to subsequent liking-for-task. Certainly this necessity of choice and foreseeability is no limitation of the model, although the implication is that a researcher requires a certain sensitivity to the choice and foreseeability questions. If a pattern of results failed to show the curvilinear function, it would always be possible that responsibility had not been sufficient.

Second, a genuine limitation of the idea lies in the necessity of being able to specify just where the crucial midrange of resultant justification lies. The two research projects just summarized evidently located the critical point, but this is not to say that paying a person the same as everyone else, or simply abiding by a preannounced level of payment, would inevitably place subjects in the zone of sufficient justification.

Third, there is an empirical sense in which the model falls short. Overjustification does not inevitably make the task more attractive, but most certainly has been shown in other contexts to have just the opposite effect (cf. Lepper, Greene, & Nisbett, 1973). It remains to be seen whether or not there are critical differences between the paradigms just discussed and the overjustification approach exemplified by Lepper *et al.* (1973), but for the present the question remains open.

PARTIALING OUT INCENTIVE EFFECTS: RESPONSIBILITY

A second solution to this central dilemma is to appeal to other factors basic to cognitive dissonance, particularly the variable of responsibility, and to vary those factors rather than simply attempt to bring them to a high level. This section offers good evidence that personal responsibility for commitments is a powerful mediator of the insufficient justification phenomenon.

There would be a direct way to deal with incentive effects if more were known about the variables controlling such effects. By analogy, it is easy to deal with curiosity effects that run counter to dissonance-reducing selective exposure once it is understood that subjects are curious (Chapter 12). Their curiosity must be abated, then the selective exposure implications of dissonance theory become manifest. But it is by no means obvious how to effect the minimization of incentive processes other than by eliminating incentives. This, of course, is impossible within the ares of insufficient justification implied by dissonance theory, since incentives must be varied in order to test the theory. At least it is impossible within the scope of the research of this chapter.

Looking beyond the scope of this chapter, the elimination of incentives is easy, and certainly has already been accomplished. The greater proportion of research to be reviewed, and already reviewed, contains no variable that bears any relation to the incentives of this chapter. It is also notable that the "nonincentive" research contains relatively few instances of negative evidence. For example, in the "free-decision" paradigm there are to our knowledge no negative results, except insofar as postdecisional regret (Chapter 8) may be viewed as an exception.

Just because a factor can, under some circumstances, bolster dissonance arousal should not mean that the factor will inevitably have this effect across all possible circumstances. The case in point is the issue of incentives for performing discrepant behaviors. There seems to be good evidence that incentives can create so-called secondary reinforcement effects, whether the measure be liking, attitude change, or similar constructs. But no matter what overall impact an incentive has, the introduction of choice should make the incentive operate more in line with dissonance principles, as will be illustrated in this section.

Imagine an experiment involving children, where each subject is induced to deliver a counterattitudinal speech, proposing a 10-hr school day. Half of the subjects are promised an ice-cream cone for their behavior while others expect nothing. The other variable is a choice manipulation along the lines of that performed by Cohen and Latané. Following delivery of the speech subjects' attitudes toward a lengthened school day are assessed.

Hypothetical Result 1 assumes an overriding incentive effect, generally stronger than the dissonance effect. There would be a positive relationship between incentive and attitude change no matter what choice condition is considered. However, the introduction of choice should weaken the positive relationship.

Hypothetical Result 2 assumes that the incentive effect does not override dissonance effects when there is sufficient choice. Incentive effects might be expected when dissonance is minimized (no choice), but when conditions are ideal for dissonance arousal (choice), the negative relationship between incentive magnitude and amount of attitude change appears.

To avoid any possible confusion it should be noted that these two hypothetical results both support dissonance theory. It makes no difference whether the choice variable makes itself known within a context of an overall incentive effect or in the context depicted by Hypothetical Result 2. In either case *dissonance arousal* is shown to be lowered by an incentive under conditions of choice.

Hypothetical Result 3 would also be conceivable, where there is no evidence of incentive effects, but that is not necessary to the discussion. At this stage a number of experiments will be examined, the results of which all resemble the second hypothetical result. Each of these studies varies an incentive factor in addition to choice.

The best-known of these studies is a pair by Linder, Cooper, and Jones (1967). The first experiment was patterned approximately after Cohen's (1962a) well-publicized attitude change study performed at Yale University, to be discussed in detail in Chapter 5. Two levels of monetary inducement were used by Linder *et al.* (1967) in inducing subjects to write counterattitudinal essays praising a speaker ban at their college: $.50 and $2.50. For no-choice subjects the experimenter merely acted as though he expected everyone to write the counterattitudinal essay, but his treatment of free-decision subjects was more elaborate. At the outset he indicated that he would explain the study to them, and then they could decide for themselves whether or not to write the essay. Similar comments were also made again, after the payment was mentioned. Following the essay writing the relevant attitude measure was taken, and the results were similar to the Hypothetical Result 2: a positive relationship between incentive and attitude change among no-choice subjects, but a negative relationship for the free-decision condition.

Experiment 2 by Linder et al. (1967) was addressed specifically to Rosenberg's experimental "evaluation-apprehension" critique of dissonance theory, summarized above. In one set of conditions their study was as similar to his as they could make it. The subject was greeted by the first experimenter, who indicated that he was running late. He then suggested that the subject might help someone who was running an independent experiment. In the prior-commitment condition the subject was given no explicit license to refuse to assist the second experimenter, but in the free-decision condition the first experimenter indicated:

> All I told this fellow was that I would send him some subjects if it was convenient, but that I couldn't obligate my subjects in any way. So, when you get up there, listen to what he has to say and feel free to decide from there.

The remainder of the procedure followed the Rosenberg study. Subjects were offered either $.50 or $2.50 for writing a discrepant essay, and consistent with the first experiment by Linder et al. (1967), the results took the form similar to those of the first study.

The effects obtained by Linder et al. (1967) are by no means isolated events. Sherman (1970a) undertook a near replication of their second experiment. Free-decision subjects were offered payment before deciding to write, while no-choice subjects learned about the money only after they were committed by the experimenter to carry out the discrepant act. Sherman obtained the same crossover interaction observed by Linder et al. (1967).

A similar effect was observed by Holmes and Strickland (1970), with a singularly weak and yet surprisingly effective manipulation. Subjects were gathered in groups, and were asked to compose a counterattitudinal essay under either free choice or no-choice conditions. Choice was induced among free-choice subjects with the comment, " . . . we'd like your discussion group to write . . . ." No-choice subjects were told, " . . . we're going to have your group write . . . ." Incentive was varied through an offer of either one or two experimental credit points for composing an essay. Once again the effect paralleled that of the previous studies, even though the strength of the choice manipulation was seemingly negligible.

A further study, by Frey and Irle (1972), lends itself to the same conclusion as these other experiments. The authors varied the amount of incentive (translated from West German marks, the variation was approximately $.25 versus $2 U.S.), choice versus no choice, and anonymous versus public conditions. The investigation was designed in large part to examine the joint effects of choice and publicity, and as might be expected, certain combinations of these two variables produced the most extreme attitude effects. The monetary variable produced a substantial dissonance effect within the choice–public condition, while a strong incentive effect occurred within the no choice–anonymous condition. The other two conditions (choice–anonymous, no choice–public) also produced incentive effects, although these effects were short of significance. The important feature of this study as far as this chapter is concerned is that a combination of features that should make for dissonance arousal (choice and publicity) do indeed cause the monetary justification variable to operate as predicted by dissonance theory.

Length and Quality of Essay as Mediators

It will be recalled that the negative evidence compiled by Elms and Janis (1965), Janis and Gilmore (1965), Rosenberg (1965), and Rosenberg and Finkelstein (in Rosenberg, 1970) was apparently dependent on variations in the length and/or quality of the essays composed. A large incentive in those studies effected longer or qualitatively superior essays, and it appeared that subjects' agreement with their essays was determined in part by the length–quality factor. From the standpoint of cognitive dissonance considerations such differential essay quality and quantity serves as an experimental confound. Dissonance theory makes a clear prediction as long as the counterattitudinal performance is held constant, but the theoretical reasoning becomes ambiguous when increased incentive produces either longer or shorter essays. For one, it might be argued that a shorter essay shows that the subject is especially averse to taking the discrepant position, and therefore should experience a relatively high degree of dissonance. An opposite argument can also be made, one which coincides quite well with the negative evidence. The subject who writes the longest and most persuasive argument is engaging in the most discrepant act, meaning that he has the most dissonance reduction to accomplish. With the latter line of reasoning the "negative" results reported above can easily be interpreted by way of dissonance principles, although to do so is a spurious exercise in that an opposite pattern of results could have been explained as well.

If those previous negative findings were mediated by differential character of essays, the findings of this section may have been consistent with the theory because essay length and quality were constants. It is an easy matter to check on this possibility. Linder et al. (1967) analyzed the essays of both experiments for length, organization, and persuasiveness, finding no differences among any of the conditions. Sherman also analyzed his subjects' essays, finding no difference between conditions for length, but an interesting effect on persuasiveness. Within his high-choice condition persuasiveness of essay did not vary as a function of payment, but there was an effect among low choice subjects: the higher the pay, the more persuasive the essays. This result is particularly interesting for it parallels that found in the negative evidence of the preceding section. This suggests, perhaps, that those experiments were low in choice.

The important point here is this: When essay quality and quantity are held constant, as they should be for an unambiguous test of the theory, choice interacts with incentive in the predictable manner. Further, under conditions of high choice, there was an inverse relationship between incentive and attitude change in all four of the present experiments. This result is quite dramatic, and not totally necessary as evidence for the theory. As illustrated in Hypothetical Result 1 (above), the theory receives support if an overall incentive effect is weakened by the introduction of choice; an actual inverse relationship is not crucial as evidence provided that choice is varied. In summary, much of the negative evidence of the previous section seems reasonably well accounted for in light of the evidence for quality and length of discrepant performance.

MORE EVIDENCE: CHOICE AS A MEDIATOR OF OTHER DISSONANCE-AROUSING FACTORS

The previous section dealt only with evidence directly relevant to the negative evidence based in incentive effects. Since those negative effects primarily involved an incentive variable, the previous several studies were grouped together to demonstrate how the choice factor can ferret out dissonance effects from reinforcement effects. The present section is more broadly conceived, and summarizes briefly a number of studies in which dissonance-arousing variables other than monetary incentive have a differential impact as a function of choice.

Greenbaum, Cohn, and Krauss (1965) examined the relationship between negative feedback on a task and choice. Subjects either chose a task to perform or were assigned a task, then after working on the task for a short time they received feedback about their performance. Some subjects received negative feedback while others were told nothing. A clear means of dissonance reduction in the situation was an increase in liking for the performed task relative to a nonperformed one, and consistent with the theory, negative feedback produced more task enhancement than no feedback, but only among subjects who chose freely. There was no effect for feedback among no choice subjects.

A conceptually similar study was performed by Jones and Brehm (1967), in which agreement with a communicator was the mode of dissonance reduction. College students were either made to think that a communicator was negative (he showed disdain for undergraduates) or positive. Second, they either chose freely to listen to a counterattitudinal communication given by him, or were accidentally exposed, without choice, to the same communication. Subjects given choice showed agreement with the communication to the degree the communicator was negative, but just the opposite relationship held among no choice subjects. It is interesting to note that the outcome of this study parallels exactly the experiments of the previous section, by Linder *et al.* (1967) and others, although the earlier "high payment–low payment" variable is replaced here by a "positive communicator–negative communicator" variable. In case the reader is interested in further evidence for the Jones and Brehm hypothesis, a virtually identical effect is reported by Himmelfarb and Arazi (1975).

A further study involving degree of negative consequences and choice is reported by Hoyt, Henly, and Collins (1972). Subjects were given high or low choice to write an essay debunking toothbrushing. Prior to commitment subjects found that their essays would either be effectual, or not, in influencing innocent junior high school students toward abandoning tooth brushing. It was argued that more dissonance would be aroused in the influential case, since the essay would be causal in bringing about tooth decay. After subjects wrote their essays they responded to a "toothbrushing is healthy" attitude measure, and the predicted interaction between variables was apparent. In fact, choice subjects who thought their essays would have dire consequences showed the most attitude change, while the other three conditions were nearly identical.

A pair of experiments on dissonance as aroused by aggressive behaviors is also relevant here. The first one is by Davis and Jones (1960). Subjects were induced, under either high- or low-choice conditions, to make derogatory remarks to a person who was presumably a student being evaluated on several personality dimensions. Further, some of the subjects were told that they would be unable to inform the target person of the false nature of their negative evaluation, while other subjects were led to believe that they would confront the target person and could dispel any belief he might have in their negative evaluation. The latter group of subjects was, therefore, relatively uncommitted to the negative evaluation and should have experienced less dissonance. Dissonance reduction was ascertained by the subject's attitude toward the target person. Presumably dissonance could be reduced by derogating that person, and consistent with their expectations there was a change toward more negative evaluation only among subjects given choice and given no opportunity to rescind the derogation.

A study in the same vein was conducted by Glass (1964). Subjects were asked to shock a target person under choice or no-choice conditions, and the second variable was self-esteem. The author proposed that injuring an innocent person is especially inconsistent for a person who thinks highly of himself, meaning that high self-esteem subjects should experience the greatest dissonance. The results indicated that derogation of the target person was greater among high self-esteem subjects than among low, but only within the choice condition. Self-esteem had no impact on derogation in the no choice case. It appears, therefore, that the argument relating self-esteem and derogation is well supported among subjects who were given ample choice.

The last of several experiments reported by Pallak, Brock, and Kiesler (1967) investigated the impact of making dissonance salient. Subjects were given either high or low choice to perform a dull paired-associates task, and second, the dissonant cognitions were made salient or not by reminding some subjects of the tedious nature of the tasks. The measure, number of paired-associates remembered, was construed as an index of dissonance *avoidance* rather than *reduction*. The authors argued that subjects could throw themselves into their work, memorizing the associates, and thereby avoid concentrating on the dissonance-provoking features of the situation. It was further argued that dissonance should be especially strong when the relevant cognitions are salient, but less so when the subject is distracted from concentrating on those cognitions. The results generally supported their reasoning: Among subjects who were distracted there was a tendency toward better retention under low choice than high, while for subjects who were reminded of the dissonance-arousing aspects of the situation there was better retention under high choice than low. In short, it appears as though the choice variable affects dissonance avoidance in the predicted manner as long as the relevant cognitions are to some degree salient.

SUMMARY

The variable of choice has shown to be a consistently potent means of varying dissonance, at the same time allowing the investigator to tease dissonance effects out from other phenomena that result from dissonance-relevant variables. The variable of incentive for counterattitudinal advocacy is the most notable instance of a cause of multiple effects. One of these, the so-called "incentive effect," simply means that there often tends to be a positive relationship between amount of payment for an attitude-discrepant act and subsequent attitude change in the direction of that act. Since dissonance theory predicts that dissonance arousal varies inversely with amount of payment, there is immediately a question about which process will win out, and in fact there is a body of literature in which either one or the other result has been shown.

The present chapter discusses two general solutions to the ambiguity raised by incentive manipulations. One solution suggests a curvilinear relationship between incentive magnitude and attitude change. Despite potential problems of implementation, there is good evidence for this notion. The second solution simply involves the introduction of choice as a mediating variable, and has consistently resulted in a successful discrimination between incentive and dissonance phenomena.

Independent of incentive as a dissonance arousing variable, choice has also been shown to mediate the dissonance-arousing potential of such diverse variables as liking for a communicator, persuasiveness of one's own counterattitudinal comments, equivocality of the commitment, self-esteem in an aggression-delivering context, and salience of dissonant elements.

4

Foreseeability and Responsibility

There are two crucial respects in which dissonance theory can be distinguished from its balance theory counterparts. First, the variable of commitment is all important, and plays a role in virtually every dissonance analysis. The second critical ingredient of the theory is responsibility for the commitment, a two-component concept consisting of the dimensions of choice and foreseeability. The previous chapter spelled out the experimental determinants of choice and its effects, and in all of that research foreseeability was held at a constant high level. In fact, every piece of research reported thus far has held the foreseeability aspect of responsibility at a high level, simply by insuring that subjects understand the consequence of the discrepant actions before committing themselves.

Why must consequences be foreseen at the time of commitment? Wouldn't more dissonance be aroused if a person were taken by surprise? Certainly there should be a sense in which a person would be made to feel uncomfortable by the onset of unexpected and disagreeable consequences; however, as will be shown in several pieces of research, the state of discomfort does not always seem to be one of cognitive dissonance. When a person commits himself to a discrepant action and later discovers that his actions will lead to the irreparable harm of a fellow student, such knowledge will certainly have some psychological impact. This impact could easily be labeled frustration, anger, surprise, or a variety of other terms. There may be many physiological consequences due to surprise, and a great many motivational processes may get underway. However, dissonance reduction does not appear to be one such consequence, for as long as the individual did not anticipate the consequence at the time of his commitment, there is a real sense in which he is not a personal causal agent. In fact, there is a close tie between the surprised person and the person who undertakes an action under heavy constraint. The latter individual may understand the consequences when he unwillingly undertakes the action, but neither he nor the person who is surprised can reasonably be considered the personal cause of the undesired consequence.

The first part of this chapter will focus on the theoretical point that foresee-ability is normally a prerequisite for dissonance arousal, since foreseeability leads to responsibility. Later in the chapter some exceptions to this rule will be cited; and in particular, there is some research indicating that a sense of personal responsibility can be created even when the consequences are unforeseen at the time of commitment. This latter research implies that there are methods for generating responsibility that bypass foreseeability. This point will be taken up in some detail later, but first, several studies will be reviewed that make the general point about foreseeability.

FORESEEABILITY AS A PREREQUISITE

Unexpected Negative Consequences

In the last of three experiments reported, Freedman (1963) asked subjects to write a long sequence of random numbers, a decidedly unpleasant task. Approximately half of the subjects (high justification) were told that the data from their performance would be extremely useful, and the remainder found that their efforts would be to no avail (low justification), since the data to be analyzed had already been collected. According to dissonance theory the high justification should have reduced dissonance arousal and consequent liking for the task. Freedman's other variable is the one of special interest here: each of the justification conditions was subdivided such that half of the subjects received justification (high or low) prior to task performance, while justification was not mentioned to the other subjects until their performance had been completed. The justification, or lack of justification, given after performance may be characterized as a *fait accompli*—an unforeseen consequence not controlled or expected by the subject.

The results were clear cut: Dissonance reduction in the form of rated task enjoyment was inversely related to amount of justification only if the justification had been introduced early. But as a *fait accompli*, the justification proved ineffective. In fact, when the justification was given following performance there was a tendency toward higher task ratings with high justification.

The Freedman experiment serves as a model for a number of later experiments, all of which found a parallel result: When a variable that would potentially affect dissonance is introduced following the behavioral commitment, that variable no longer has an impact on dissonance arousal—or at least, on dissonance reduction.

In 1968 Helmreich conducted a study in which some subjects expected to receive painful electrical shocks (high fear), while others expected a milder stimulation (low fear). Aside from that variable the procedure was a near replication of Freedman's study. Under high fear there was no evidence of effects for either of the variables, but among subjects who received the low-fear induction there was a clear replication of Freedman's results.

Linder, Cooper, and Wicklund (1968) aroused dissonance in subjects by requesting that they listen to a counterattitudinal speech. To raise dissonance, some of the subjects were asked to commit themselves to an effortful task (random number copying) prior to hearing the speech. In addition, half of the effort condition subjects were told about the effort as a *fait accompli.* That is, they were informed of the effort only after they had committed themselves to a discrepant act of listening to the tape. The results, attitude change toward the advocated position, were as might be expected: The effort increased dissonance reduction only when introduced previous to commitment.

Cooper and Brehm (1971) report two experiments bearing a conceptual similarity to the Freedman study. In the second of those experiments subjects were asked to commit themselves to a dull task (threading needles) and discovered that they would receive no money for their needle-threading performance. Dissonance arousal was varied by telling subjects that others were receiving either $2 for the session, or just $.50.

It was presumed that dissonance would be greater among subjects who were relatively deprived the most. The other variable was whether knowledge of the relative deprivation came before, or after commitment to the task. Predictably, subjects indicated satisfaction with their participation in the research project to the degree they were relatively deprived, but this variable operated in that way only when it was introduced before commitment. When the relative deprivation came as a *fait accompli,* satisfaction varied inversely with it.

Given all of these consistent results, one might wonder whether or not the *fait accompli* versus forewarned dimension might be treated as a continuous variable. In the research above subjects either knew about a dissonance-arousing variable before commitment or did not. In other words, experiments tried to vary expectancy to an extreme degree—between a 100 and 0% expectancy concerning the dissonance-relevant event. Watts (1966) undertook to vary expectancy along a dimension of intermediate probabilities, in the following way.

Subjects were led to think there was a chance of their receiving a painful electrical stimulation. Some subjects thought there was a 95% chance of receiving the stimulation, while others thought there was just a 50% chance. All subjects were asked to take a bitter anesthetic, some under conditions of choice and others under no choice. As far as the subjects were concerned this anesthetic was designed to minimize the impact of possibly imminent electrical shock. About half of the subjects then found they would not receive the shock after all. This knowledge certainly should have been dissonant with the fact of having taken a bitter anesthetic, particularly among subjects who had a choice about taking the anesthetic. But the bigger question here is this: Will the choice variable operate less strongly among the subjects who thought there was a 95% chance of being shocked? For them, the failure to receive shock was almost unexpected, and almost a *fait accompli* as the notion has been used in the above experiments.

On a combined measure of dissonance reduction, including exaggeration of sensitivity to pain, choice subjects showed a stronger effect than no choice subjects with the 50% condition. However, within the 95% condition, which approximated a *fait accompli* treatment, there was no such effect for choice. There is some suggestion here that the expectancy dimension does operate as a continuous variable, such that dissonance arousal is positively related to the strength of a person's anticipation that the dissonance-arousing event will transpire.

Cooper (1971) has also investigated the relationship between the choice variable and unexpected consequences. Subjects were introduced to a partner with whom they were to work on a task with the purpose of winning a prize. From the subject's standpoint it was desirable that the partner be neither too braggartly or timid, for either extreme would interfere with winning. The experimenter assigned the subject a partner, who was described to half the subjects as a braggert and as timid to the other half. The experimenter thus created an expectancy about a partner characteristic that might reduce their outcomes. Choice was emphasized for some subjects by giving them an option of changing partners, whereas no-choice subjects were under constraint to keep the original partner. Then, once the task progressed it became clear that the partner did in fact possess the expected undesirable trait, or else the partner turned out to be exactly the opposite, and equally undesirable. Thus all subjects were stuck with an undesirable partner, although at the time of original commitment only half of the subjects expected the particular kind of undesirability that was manifested during the task.

The results were as follows: Under no-choice conditions liking for the partner (dissonance reduction) did not depend on whether or not the trait was unexpected. However, among choice subjects the data closely resembled the experiments discussed thus far. The more extreme the partner was with respect to the *expected* undesirable trait, the more liking was engendered. Just the opposite result appeared when the trait was unexpected.

Unexpected Positive Consequences

All of the above experiments have dealt with the effect of expectancy on dissonance created through negative consequences. But it should be perfectly obvious that a similar process should operate for positive consequences. For example, if someone commits himself to a discrepant act, dissonance will be minimized to the degree that some benefit accrues from the commitment. However, if the preceding results can be generalized to the case of positive consequences, such consequences will have an impact on dissonance only when expected at the time of commitment. Brehm and Jones (1970) carried out an experiment that was explicitly designed to test this idea.

Subjects were given a choice between two long playing records, and some of them were told that by choosing the right record they could obtain two movie tickets. Receipt of the movie tickets would quite clearly be consonant with the choice of the record. Other subjects were not forewarned about the possibility of winning movie tickets. Then, about half of the subjects actually received free tickets and half did not. If dissonance can be reduced by the occurence of an unexpected positive consequence, postdecisional spreading in rated attractiveness of the choice alternative records should be less when the subject wins a free movie ticket. The results show this exactly, but only among forewarned subjects. Subjects for whom the tickets were a *fait accompli* were not differentially affected by receiving tickets. In conceptual terms, the addition of a positive consequence does not seem to reduce dissonance unless it is anticipated prior to commitment.

A study by Lepper, Zanna, and Abelson (1970) makes a similar point in the context of the "forbidden toy" paradigm established by Aronson and Carlsmith (1963). Kindergarten children were taken into a room with six toys, asked to rank-order the toys, then were given some time alone to play with the toys. Before leaving the room the experimenter requested that the subject not play with a particular toy, and this suggestion was backed up with either a strong or mild threat of punishment should the child transgress. It was argued, as did Aronson and Carlsmith, that dissonance would be aroused more in the case of the mild threat, since a mild threat does not furnish much support for the child's commitment not to play with Toy *X*.

A second variable was also manipulated, this one being crucial for our purposes here. Some subjects were given social support for not playing with the toy in the form of knowledge that peers had abstained from it. Some subjects were given this justification before subjects had to undergo the tempting play period and resist the toy, while other subjects were given the justification after the play period (*fait accompli*), just before the final ranking of toys. Dissonance reduction in this experiment can be defined as subjects' derogation of the critical and nonplayed with toy. The results indicated that dissonance reduction was greater in the mild-threat than severe-threat conditions. The social support variable made no difference in the severe-threat condition, where dissonance was already low. However, within the mild-threat condition the social support did effect lower dissonance reduction, but only when the social support was received prior to commitment. As a *fait accompli* the social support was ineffective. In short, this study and the Brehm and Jones experiment make a similar point.

A study by Cooper and Goethals (1974) also addresses itself to unforeseen sources of dissonance reduction. All subjects were asked to taperecord a counterattitudinal speech, and at the time half of them were informed that their recording would definitely be played later to a group interested in the taped issue. It was argued by the authors that dissonance would be increased by the inclusion of the latter element. The other half of the subjects were told that the speech "might" be played to the group, thus they should have been able to foresee either outcome (i.e., play to group or not play to group).

Subsequent to taping the speech, half of the subjects found that the tape would indeed be played to the group, and half discovered that it would not be played. Within the "foreseen consequences" ("might" be played) condition, dissonance reduction (attitude change) was decreased when subjects learned that the tape would not be played. However, the exclusion of the group's listening did not lower dissonance arousal among subjects who were surprised by the exclusion.

WHY FORESEEABILITY?

The line of thought initiated in this chapter concerns responsibility. We have proposed that there must be a psychological connection between the person and his discrepant act before dissonance will result. He must feel as if he is the author of the consequences that bring about discrepant cognitions, and one clear way of imparting such a feeling to a person is to insure his foreknowledge of the consequences of his decisions. But before pursuing this line of thought it is important to consider some other reasons for the necessity of foreseeability. It may be that the notion of responsibility is only one of several possible interpretations.

Frustration

When an unexpected negative outcome is encountered, there is a real sense in which a person is frustrated. This state of irritation could easily generalize to the entire experimental situation, and thereby interfere with the dissonance-reduction process of coming to like some aspect of the setting. Although this kind of interpretation might be viable for the studies with negative outcomes, it would be difficult to invoke the frustration interpretation universally: Certainly the dissonance-reducing *fait accompli* in the experiments by Cooper and Goethals, Jones and Brehm, and Lepper *et al.* (1970) should not have caused frustration.

Prior Dissonance Arousal as a Prerequisite

Brehm and Jones (1970), Cooper and Brehm (1971), and Sherman (1970b) have all raised the possibility that an unexpected consequence will affect dissonance only if the original commitment created dissonance. As with the frustration explanation, this kind of reasoning might be applied to the experiments with negative unexpected outcomes. However, the studies with surprise positive outcomes demonstrated that dissonance was aroused by the initial commitment, yet the *fait accompli* events in those studies failed to affect dissonance. Apparently the preexistence of dissonance arousal is not an adequate precondition to force dissonance processes to result from *fait accompli* consequences. Accordingly, this kind of reasoning does not apply effectively to the body of research taken in entirety.

Cognitive Irreversibility

Lepper *et al.* (1970) have summarized several theoretical statements bearing on problem solving, all of which lead to the conclusion that certain psychological processes, once initiated, are not reversible. For example, problem solvers are said to fall into a blind pattern of problem solution which they transfer to new problems even though fairly obvious and more efficient alternative approaches to the new problem are available. In addition to problem solving applied to the usual tasks of the psychological laboratory it is reasonable that defensive processes, emotions, balance restoration, and other phenomena operate similarly. Once the mode of drive reduction, defense, or balance restoration is set into action, that mode will follow a course until the "problem" is solved, after which time additional information relevant to the "problem" will be powerless to unfreeze the person from his original solution.

When a person engages in a dissonance-arousing action, the theory predicts that he will examine the cognitions relevant at the time of commitment and proceed to reduce dissonance. If additional and unexpected discrepant cognitions should arise after the initial dissonance reduction, the increment in dissonance should create further dissonance reduction according to the original theory. Further dissonance reduction will not result according to the irreversibility argument, for the "dissonance-reducing" problem has already been solved and additional cognitions will not break the person's fixation on his original act of dissonance reduction. Applied to the *fait accompli* experiments above, this reasoning appears at face value to fit perfectly. One need only assume that dissonance reduction ("problem solving") ensues shortly after commitment, and that the dissonance reduction process is irreversible, or "closed." Then, when the *fait accompli* is encountered no further cognitive adjustments are made, for the preexisting dissonance reduction processes are not subject to modification.

Perhaps the major difficulty with this interpretation concerns the forementioned experiments with negative consequences. In order to apply the irreversibility interpretation there must have already been dissonance arousal and reduction, but this precondition was largely absent in the studies with negative consequences. The interpretation of Lepper *et al.* (1970) might still be invoked, but only by imputing an unmeasured dissonance reduction into those experimental situations.

There is another difficulty with the interpretation, even if unmeasured dissonance reduction due to the original commitment can be assumed. It has never been suggested by Festinger (1957, 1964) or any other dissonance theorist that dissonance reduction is instantaneous, but instantaneous dissonance reduction is probably an important assumption for the irreversibility account of the preceding *fait accompli* studies. Those who have written about the temporal aspects of dissonance reduction (e.g., Brehm & Wicklund, 1970; Jecker, 1968; Miller, 1968; Walster & Berscheid, 1968; Wicklund, 1970) have favored the idea that dissonance reduction can proceed over a considerable interval, and can even be preceded by regret (the opposite of dissonance reduction). If an experiment on unexpected consequences is arranged with a very short time interval between commitment and introduction of the *fait accompli,* it seems likely that the subject's dissonance reduction would be in progress at the time the surprise event is encountered. And if so, the stage of irreversibility should not yet have been attained, thus the *fait accompli* should at that point contribute to the dissonance reduction process. Because the time interval between commitment and surprise event was extremely short in at least one of the preceding experiments (Linder *et al.,* 1968) the irreversibility account runs into trouble.

In summary, the irreversibility explanation is appealing, but has two shortcomings due to assumptions that must be made for its application: (a) it must be assumed that dissonance reduction processes are sometimes unmeasured, and (b) it is necessary, at least in the case of one experiment, to suppose that dissonance reduction is nearly instantaneous. Finally, a more general problem associated with the irreversibility thesis is an experiment that is directly relevant, discussed in Chapter 9: Götz–Marchand, Götz, and Irle (1974) have found definite evidence that subjects do show reversibility when given an opportunity to employ a more comfortable mode of dissonance reduction.

Regret and Other Sequential Effects

Festinger (1964) has postulated that a commitment is often followed by "regret," an effect involving the individual's realization of the unfortunate aspects of his decision. The regret phenomenon will receive detailed treatment later, and for now it is necessary only to deal with the postulated effects of regret, which are opposite to dissonance reduction. For example, the theory generally predicts that a person will come to like that which he has chosen. However, shortly after the decision (during the regret phase) he may temporarily *increase* his liking for the unchosen alternative, and *lower* his attraction to the chosen alternative. Subsequently, according to Festinger, dissonance reduction will supercede the regret phase.

It is instructive to note that all of the preceding experiments involved a time discrepancy between the "forewarned" conditions and *fait accompli* conditions. In every case the interval between time of knowledge of the crucial cognition and time of measurement differed for forewarned and *fait accompli* subjects.

Accordingly, it may be that *fait accompli* subjects, who never had as much dissonance reduction time as "forewarned" subjects, were still in the regret phase at the time of measurement. This being the case, these subjects would be relatively unattracted to the chosen alternative at that point, manifesting less dissonance reduction than their forewarned counterparts. Such an interpretation might be applied readily to those experiments with negative surprise outcomes, for dissonance reduction in those studies was always *less* when the knowledge was in the form of a *fait accompli* rather than being introduced prior to commitment.

How does this interpretation fit the Brehm and Jones (1970), Cooper and Goethals (1974), and Lepper *et al.* (1970) experiments on surprise positive outcomes? In regard to the time interval between commitment and knowledge of the positive outcome, these experiments parallel the rest of the research. That is, the interval was longer when subjects knew of or suspected the positive outcome prior to commitment than when the positive outcome came as a surprise. Therefore, it may be argued that "forewarned" subjects were further along in their dissonance reduction process than *fait accompli* subjects, and should therefore have shown more dissonance reduction. The problem with this analysis is that the results were exactly contrary to this prediction; thus, the regret explanation of the previous studies seems somewhat implausible.

There is an interpretation coined by Gailon and Watts (1967) that resembles the regret interpretation. They propose that the sudden introduction of a *fait accompli* consequence generates negative affect, necessitating a lapse of time before the subject overcomes his surprise reaction and begins dissonance reduction. They report an experiment (Experiment II in their paper) in which a negative event was introduced either with foreknowledge or as a *fait accompli*. Time of measurement was also varied: some subjects received the measure immediately, and others after 20 min. Their thesis was quite well supported. At the time of immediate measurement subjects showed dissonance reduction only if they knew of the consequence prior to commitment. In contrast, subjects in the *fait accompli* condition showed dissonance reduction after 20 min.

Although their interpretation fits the negative consequence experiments reasonably well, their interpretation runs into trouble when applied to surprise positive consequences, and for approximately the same reasons. If anything, their notion would predict *less* dissonance reduction in the surprise case—not more—and further, it is hard to understand why a positive surprise should inhibit dissonance reduction via creation of negative affect.

Summary and a Note on Responsibility

The foregoing interpretations all seem to have some merit with respect to interpreting the failure of negative surprises to instigate dissonance-reduction processes. But as has been shown, they all suffer in generality: They simply fail to account in any convincing way for the repeated finding that surprise positive consequences have no impact on dissonance arousal.

A more general interpretation appears to be the one with which we began. The individual apparently must have a feeling of being personally responsible with respect to dissonance-increasing and lowering elements. Without that sense of responsibility dissonance is either not aroused or not manifested.

Responsibility is a multifaceted concept as far as we are concerned. One aspect of it is choice, covered in the previous chapter, and another aspect is foreseeability, which is the focus of the present discussion. The research already summarized seems to make the point quite evident: Unless a positive or negative consequence is foreseen at the time of commitment, it will fail to have an impact on dissonance reduction efforts.

Before the reader is led to think that responsibility is completely pinned down by the stipulation of both choice and foreseeability, it is crucial to proceed to the next section, in which serious questions are raised about the twofold characterization of responsibility. Until this point we have assumed, and concluded from research, that the combination of choice and foreseeability is a prerequisite for the onset of dissonance, but this conclusion is seriously challenged in the next section. In fact, there now appears to be evidence suggesting that a person can be made to feel responsible even though he in no way could have objectively brought about the dissonance-provoking consequence.

IS FORESEEABILITY NECESSARY?
ANOTHER LOOK AT THE RESPONSIBILITY CONCEPT

The purpose of this section is to examine research that has found foreseeability unnecessary for the arousal of dissonance. In the process of considering the evidence we will attempt to demonstrate how a subject can come to feel responsible with respect to consequences for which he is not at all objectively responsible.

The first investigation of *fait accompli* consequences was by Brehm (1959). Unlike the research reported above, all of which followed Brehm's experiment, this study indicates that unanticipated consequences can have an impact on dissonance arousal.

Brehm's (1959) study was directed toward providing evidence for the notion that a postchoice event can create dissonance. In this experiment, junior high school students were induced to eat a small dish of a disliked vegetable in order to obtain a prize. Eating the vegetable follows from the opposite of disliking it, and thus we would expect all subjects to experience some dissonance. Then, to see whether a further inconsistent cognition would increase the magnitude of dissonance, the experimenter told some of the subjects, after they had nearly finished eating, that he would be writing a letter to their parents to indicate what vegetable they had eaten. The implication of such a letter was that the subjects would be expected to increase their eating of that vegetable at home. Prechoice knowledge of the letter would have militated against the decision to eat. But as the procedure was set up, the subject could escape neither from having agreed to eat nor from having the letter sent. In short, the letter constituted an event inconsistent with the commitment to eat and was outside the control of the subject.

The magnitude of dissonance was measured in terms of increased liking for the vegetable. Dissonance from having to eat the vegetable could easily be reduced by increased liking. If exposure to this event creates dissonance, then subjects exposed to it should show greater increase in liking for the vegetable than those not told about the letter. This expectation was clearly supported by the results.

This experiment was conceptually similar to the one by Freedman, and all of those to follow. Why, then, should Brehm's experiment have been the only one to obtain an effect for the unexpected consequence? Was there an element in his situation that led subjects to feel responsible for the undesired consequence? Before trying to embark on a theoretical understanding of this experiment it should be noted that there is an important methodological difference between this experiment and the others. There was no condition in which the consequence occurred with foreknowledge, leaving open the possibility that dissonance reduction in the *fait accompli* case would have been less than in a parallel "foreknowledge" condition. Still, the fact of the *fait accompli* having an impact above that of the "no *fait accompli*" has to be explained, and there are a couple of reasonable possibilities. For one, when subjects learned about the letter a new decision may well have entered the realm of possibilities. At that point they had to decide whether or not to eat undesirable vegetables at home, and assuming that many of the subjects chose favorably, dissonance reduction and consequent vegetable liking would have been the result. The second possibility assumes that social influence was created by the knowledge of the latter. Presumably informing the subject of the letter reminded him of his parents' desires for him to eat more vegetables, and with the source of influence (parents) reinstated, there was a consequent positive shift toward vegetables. A third possibility is, of course, that a *fait accompli* can under some circumstances be presented so that a person will view it as a product of himself—as a product of his own responsibility. The cogency of this suggestion can best be evaluated by turning to several recent experiments.

Convincing the Subject of a Feeling of Responsibility

Kruglanski, Alon, and Lewis (1972) induced elementary school students to play a competitive group game. Subjects were given the explicit opportunity to decline participation; thus, choice was clearly present. At the time of commitment there was no mention of any reward for playing the game, but upon completion of the competition subjects in the "Prize" condition were told this:

> As we said before, members of the winning team will be awarded special prizes as tokens of their victory.

This statement obviously was a lie, from the standpoint of an observer, yet the experimenters had good reason to think subjects would accept it. To the extent that this happened, subjects would have seen a causal connection between their commitment and the reward. For the "no-prize" condition there was no mention of any reward.

The results showed a genuine *fait accompli* effect: subjects in the no-prize condition enjoyed the games more than did prize subjects. It may be well to keep in mind that the unexpected outcome here was unexpected only from the standpoint of the observer. Certainly subjects had reason to think that they had anticipated the reward.

Worchel and Brand (1972) conducted an experiment very similar to that of Cooper (1971), the major difference being a variation in how responsible subjects should have felt for the negative consequences of their choices. The subject learned that he would perform a task with a partner, and he was required to choose a partner from one of two potential partners. The decision was to be based on personality descriptions of the partner, derived from a bogus personality inventory. Just as in Cooper's experiment one of the descriptions indicated that the person was timid, while the other came across as a braggart. It was indicated that either of these traits taken to extreme would interfere with task performance and ultimately could cost the subject money.

In order to manipulate what they described as responsibility, Worchel and Brand characterized the inventory, on which the personality descriptions were based, in one of two different ways. In one case (test-responsible condition) there was an effort to insure that responsibility for the actual traits of the partner could be attributed to the inventory. It was said that the inventory is extremely effective, and the subject was also assured that his partner would be much as described in the inventory. In the subject-responsible condition the inventory was played down and depicted as inaccurate. There was also an effort to convince the subject of his responsibility for his choice of partner;

> . . . it has been found that people [who] are socially sensitive, and those who work to try and integrate the information provided in the inventory can make amazingly accurate predictions about the personality of the test taker. Thus, with the information provided in the test and with work on your part, you should be able to form an accurate description of the other two subjects [Worchel & Brand, 1972, p. 89].

After the subject had chosen a partner from the descriptions, the two proceeded with the task and generally failed. The failure was easily ascribable to the partner's being too extreme in the expected trait (whether timid or braggartly), or else too extreme in the opposite and unexpected trait.

It might be recalled that dissonance reduction was found in Cooper's experiment only when the extreme behavior was consistent with what was expected, and only under high choice. Since Worchel and Brand (1972) ran all subjects under conditions of choice, they would definitely expect some dissonance reduction when the trait was as expected. However, they propose some additional reasoning for the case of the violated expectancy. Following the lead of Aronson (1968) they argue that disconfirmed expectancies will generate dissonance, but with the stipulation that only disconfirmed expectancies for which the person feels responsible will arouse dissonance. They further imply that a given negative consequence will increase its potential for creating dissonance to the degree that it is unexpected, or disconfirms an expectancy, but only when the person feels responsible for the event. This means that the *fait accompli* in their study should generate more dissonance than the expected consequence, but only in the subject-responsible condition.

Dissonance reduction was measured by subsequent attraction to the partner, and the pattern of data was as expected. The difference within the subject-responsible condition, which was significant, demonstrated that the *fait accompli* negative outcome actually produced more liking than the corresponding *expected* negative outcome. But when the test was responsible, the *fait accompli* resulted in *less* liking, just as in Cooper's (1971) study.

What is the theoretical meaning of these results? Have Worchel and Brand demonstrated that dissonance reduction can occur through a *fait accompli*, and if so, does their experiment require a broadening of our concept of responsibility? It seems that two approaches might be taken toward integrating their results into this discussion:

1. One might argue that subjects in the subject-responsible condition did in fact foresee the possibility of winding up with the opposite of what was chosen. Since subjects were initiates in the procedure of making a decision from personality inventories, they may well have conceived of almost anything happening as a result of their particular choices. There is nothing in the data bearing on this interpretation, and it must remain as a possibility.[1]

2. Assuming that subjects in no way foresaw the eventuality of the supposed timid person turning into a braggart or vice versa, there may still be a sense in which the subject felt responsible. The responsibility induction emphasized the subject's abilities, noting that people who are socially sensitive and who try to integrate the information can make accurate predictions.

---

[1] Cooper (personal communication) proposed that a degree of foreseeability is indeed necessary for dissonance arousal, and interprets studies such as the present one from the standpoint that the consequences were (at least in retrospect) foreseeable by subjects. More specifically, he would argue that consequences of an act can arouse dissonance as long as a "reasonable person" might, albeit in retrospect, have some basis for expecting the consequences.

Given these instructions, the subject who encountered the *fait accompli* could easily conclude that he didn't try or that he didn't possess the requisite abilities. In other words, there would be a direct connection between the subject and the *fait accompli,* a connection consisting of not trying hard enough and/or being inept at the task. This kind of connection has nothing to do with foresight. According to this interpretation foresight would be just one of several routes whereby responsibility might be engendered. The other sources of responsibility could be insufficient efforts or skills, either of which might operate independently of foresight.

Granting this conclusion tentatively, we would do well to examine the second experiment reported by Pallak, Sogin, and Van Zante (1974), in which subjects were induced to take responsibility for surprise consequences. Pallak *et al.* (1974) varied choice and justification, running all subjects under *fait accompli* conditions. The procedure, which required subjects to write random numbers, was reminiscent of Freedman's (1963) experiments. The dissonance reduction measure was task enjoyment. In what was called the "no-consequences" condition, which might also be labeled the "unspecified-justification" condition, subjects were told nothing about whether or not their random numbers would be used. In the context it was reasonable for them to assume their numbers could be of use to the experimenter. "Negative-consequences" subjects found that their numbers could not be used, and blame for this was laid on the subject. The experimenter implied to the subject that something about the way she had constructed the random numbers made it impossible for them to be used.

The results of this experiment are shown in Table 2. Looking just at the high-choice condition, it is evident that task enjoyment was higher in the low-justification condition than in the unspecified justification condition, and this effect was significant. Among low-choice subjects there was no effect for justification, and the interaction was significant. In short, it seems evident that a *fait accompli* effect has again been found, this time consisting of increased liking for a task as a result of an unanticipated negative consequence.

In a second experiment, Sogin and Pallak (1974) explicitly examined locus of causality for negative consequences as a determinant of responsibility and dissonance reduction effects. Using the general method of Pallak, Sogin, and Van Zante (1974), they gave subjects high or low choice about producing random numbers. Half of the subjects were told that their numbers should be useable, while the other half were told that whether or not their numbers would be useable was largely a matter of chance. This information was intended to vary the extent to which subjects thought the usefulness of their production was their own responsibility. It was given to some subjects prior to their producing numbers while it was given to others subsequent to their producing numbers. Thus, the latter group of subjects was led to believe that they were or were not responsible for the usefulness of their work only after they had finished their assignment.

TABLE 2
Task Enjoyment

Choice	No consequences	Negative consequences
High	35.1	46.7
Low	30.8	24.0

Postexperimental ratings of the number task revealed that it was seen as more enjoyable in the high than in the low-choice conditions, but only where subjects were led to feel responsible. Furthermore, the responsibility induction had the same effect whether it was given before or after the production of the numbers. Thus, these results demonstrate not only that responsibility for consequences affects dissonance reduction, but also that responsibility can be induced for unforeseen effects that have already occurred.

The final study in this section was conducted by Aronson, Chase, Helmreich, and Ruhnke (1970). Subjects were asked to engage in a counterattitudinal act, which sometimes had potentially disastrous consequences, and these consequences were either foreseen or not. The subjects were female undergraduates from the University of Texas, all of whom were strongly opposed to governmental regulation of family size. They were asked by the experimenter to make a videotaped speech, which would later be played to an audience of students. Their speeches were to be based on an outline given them, proposing severe limits on family size including governmental regulations and forced contraception. Subjects in the before condition were either told that their speeches would have no impact (low persuasibility) or that the students should be easy to persuade (high persuasibility), and this knowledge was conveyed before the speech was made. The after condition was similar, except that the persuasibility information came as a *fait accompli*. There were two additional conditions, but they are not crucial for our purposes here. Mean attitude change in the direction of the speech indicated that dissonance-reducing attitude change was positively linked with persuasibility within the after condition ($p < .05$) as well as in the before condition ($p < .005$).

This experiment again demonstrates a *fait accompli* effect, although under somewhat different conditions than those of the previously described studies. Subjects in this study had no reason to think that the experimenter had forewarned them (as in the experiment by Kruglanski, Alon, & Lewis, 1972), nor had they reason to think that the negative consequences resulted from their own inadequate abilities. The *fait accompli* here was simply a strong negative consequence of the subjects' taking an attitude-discrepant public stand. Under these conditions, then, is there any reason to think that the subjects may have felt responsible for their negative consequences when they were not forewarned about them? At least three considerations would suggest an affirmative answer:

1. Aronson *et al.* (1970) suggest that when consequences of an act become sufficiently severe it is difficult for a person to excuse himself on the basis of inadequate foreknowledge. According to this line of reasoning, the more severe a consequence is, the more likely the individual who caused it is to feel responsible for it.

2. Unlike negative consequences in other experiments in this problem area, the negative consequences for the subject accrued from causing negative consequences for other people (being persuaded to limit family size). Thus it may be that unforeseen consequences are likely to evoke self-attributed responsibility when others are affected adversely.

3. It may be that the act of attempting to persuade others always implies responsibility for opinion change in the target of persuasion. Unless one learns that the target person was not persuaded, or that the persuasion was due to some other factor, one could hardly avoid feeling responsible for any attitude change produced.

There are, then, at least three plausible reasons why subjects in the Aronson *et al.* (1970) experiment may have felt responsible for the outcome even when they were not forewarned. We may tentatively conclude that this *fait accompli* effect, like previous ones that have been described, can be understood in terms of responsibility for the discrepant cognitive relationships that occur.

Summary of Evidence on Responsibility

These several experiments evidently contradict the conclusion stemming from the research of Freedman and others, who found no dissonance reduction in response to *fait accompli* consequences. We indicated that those earlier findings are interpretable through the concept of responsibility. If a person feels no psychological connection between himself and the consequence, dissonance will not be arroused. The present experiments imply that responsibility in the context of dissonance theory may have a broader meaning than "choice plus foreseeability." Based on the procedures of these studies the defining limits of responsibility have been expanded, and to illustrate this, the studies will be reconsidered from the perspective of defining responsibility. We will take them up in reverse order.

Though the experiment by Aronson *et al.* (1970) may have involved foreknowledge on the part of subjects, it is also plausible that their *fait accompli* dissonance reduction effect resulted either from the magnitude of the negative consequence or from the fact that the negative consequence involved other people than the self. Both of the latter possibilities suggest that responsibility for consequences occurs for reasons other than "choice plus foreseeability."

The experiments by Pallak, Sogin, and Van Zante (1974), Sogin and Pallak, and the one by Worchel and Brand make an interesting point regarding the definition of personal responsibility. Even when the consequences of a person's act are not foreseen, there is still a direct psychological connection between his *abilities* and the consequences. The experiments demonstrate that if a person tries to make a wise decision, or tries to effect an adequate performance in an experimental situation, dissonance is aroused by the consequences of his actions even though the effects are completely unforeseen, and even though the psychological connection of responsibility for the consequences is made only after the fact.

How do the experiments by Pallak *et al.* (1974), Sogin and Pallak, and Worchel and Brand differ from the earlier studies that found no *fait accompli* effect? The earlier studies involved an unforeseen consequence that had little relation to the subject's abilities. For example, Freedman's subjects found that they had been wasting their time on a task, for the experimenter already had enough previous task performance to analyze. In the Cooper and Brehm (1971) study the experimenter simply withheld relevant information. In Cooper's (1971) experiment the subject chose his partner on the basis of personality inventory information, and there was no intimation (as in Worchel and Brand) that the personality inventory was inaccurate. In contrast with these studies, Pallak *et al.* (1974), Sogin and Pallak (1974) and Worchel and Brand (1972) gave subjects definite indications of the connection between their abilities and/or efforts and the end result.

The first experiment discussed was by Kruglanski *et al.* (1972), and it is of a slightly different nature. Rather than implying a modified approach to defining responsibility, the study indicates quite clearly that people can be induced to think that they were forewarned. This is an especially important point, for it is not foreseeability per se that is basic to responsibility—it is the subject's feeling that he did know, or at least should have known.

In the interest of clarifying a potential confusion, we should note that self-rated "responsibility" is not necessarily an adequate precondition for dissonance reduction effects. For example, Wortman (1975) asked subjects to draw a marble in order to win a prize, entirely within the context of a game of chance. Some of the subjects knew, before drawing, which color marble stood for which prize. Other subjects did not have this information. In still another condition the experimenter did the drawing. Following a blind drawing (by the subject in the first two conditions, by the experiment in the third), the subject received whatever prize was indicated by the marble drawn. Then measures of responsibility and prize attractiveness were taken. The subjects who drew the marble themselves and who had foreknowledge of which marble stood for which prize showed greater rated responsibility than subjects in either of the other conditions. Evidently the fact of the subject's choosing himself, plus the knowledge of the marble–color–prize contingency, was sufficient for the subject to assign himself a relatively high-responsibility rating. However, rated responsibility bore no apparent relation to changes in attractiveness of the prize. The prize was rated equally attractive on the postmeasure in all three conditions.

This experiment illustrates an important point: An individual may well admit to being responsible even when conditions are not right for bringing about dissonance. "Responsibility" may have numerous meanings in the English language, and a person's acceptance of "responsibility" cannot be taken as a substitute for knowledge of the conditions under which a potentially dissonance-arousing act is performed. From Wortman's results it is evident that an outcome received through a chance process is not subject to evaluative changes because of dissonance arousal.

BROADENING THE NOTION OF RESPONSIBILITY

This chapter is not meant to be a philosophical treatise on the nature of responsibility. Our intent is to spell out some determinants of responsibility, the sense of personal causation, in order to comprehend better the workings of cognitive dissonance.

Why is responsibility important for dissonance arousal? The concept of responsibility can be viewed as a direct outgrowth of Festinger's (1957) comments on the relations between cognitions. Cognitions can be either consonant, dissonant, or not related psychologically at all. This latter class Festinger (1957, p. 11) calls "irrelevant relations." When dissonance theory was first postulated, the examples of irrelevant relations were fairly extreme and obvious. For example, Festinger (1957) indicates that the length of time for a letter to travel from New York to Paris is probably irrelevant to the bases of Iowa's corn crop.

Then, in *Explorations in Cognitive Dissonance,* Brehm and Cohen (1962) proposed that all consequences of a volitional act are relevant whether they are foreseen or not. However, the evidence on which this proposal was based was ambiguous, and the proposition was not adequately tested until later.

Now it appears that Brehm and Cohen's proposition was quite wrong in that choice (or volition) is not a sufficient condition to make all consequences bear on dissonance processes. Subsequent research has demonstrated that many consequences of choice are irrelevant to dissonance reduction effects. We might return to the Freedman (1963) experiment in order to illustrate the point.

Subjects invested considerable effort into a dull task, only to discover (*fait accompli*) that the experimenter did not intend to use the products of their efforts. What does the dissonant relationship involve here? On the one hand, there is the subject's knowledge of having worked hard, but on the other, he now discovers that he has toiled in vain. These two cognitions seem conspicuously dissonant. Certainly the individual's commitment to work should be consonant with any rewards or useful outcomes stemming from his efforts, just as his commitment should be dissonant with punishments and disappointments resulting from work. But this analysis may be incorrect, as would be suggested by the lack of dissonance reduction in the Freedman study. It is just possible that the cognitions are, for the person, psychologically irrelevant unless there is a perceived causal connection between his effort and the cognition of no reward for working. Irrelevance, according to this conception, would not be defined by the rules of symbolic logic, but instead by the rules of personal responsibility. Although we do not pretend to comprehend fully these latter rules, it is appropriate at this time to review the present conception of responsibility—which apparently serves to make cognitions relevant (dissonant or consonant).

First, the person must have some degree of choice upon entering into his commitment. If environmental forces are totally responsible for his behavior he can easily point to them as the cause of whatever accrues. As a result he will not perceive the relevance of his behavior to the consequences—but instead, only the relevance of environmental forces to the outcome.

Second, foreseeability most certainly contributes to responsibility, as evidenced in the first set of experiments of this chapter. There is an important distinction to be drawn while on the subject of foreseeability. Apparently a consequence need not be *intended* in order to create dissonance. It suffices that the consequence is foreseen. This point is well illustrated by Goethals and Cooper (1972). Subjects delivered a counterattitudinal speech that either had aversive consequences or not. Subjects were apprised of the possibility that the aversive consequence might result, and even though they intended not to bring about that consequence, it created dissonance reduction when it did occur. The important element, presumably, was foreseeability.

We have encountered at least three potential determinants of responsibility in addition to choice and foresight. Two of these came from possible ways to understand the results of Aronson et al. (1970). It was speculated that a sense of personal responsibility ensues whenever the consequence of one's behavior is "sufficiently" aversive, and/or whenever one causes aversive consequences for other people (for whom aversive consequences are not intended). The third determinant, found useful for understanding the research by Pallak et al. (1974) and the experiment by Worchel and Brand, is the adequacy of one's own performance. When a person attributes the cause for negative consequences to his own inadequate performance, dissonance processes occur. This interpretation was strongly supported by Sogin and Pallak's experiment, in which the causal attribution for negative consequences was explicitly manipulated to be due to the person or the task. It will be interesting to see in future research whether causal attributions to a person's own ability, as opposed to attributions to effort, are equally efficacious in producing the feelings of responsibility that give rise to dissonance reduction processes.

Considering how easy it seems to be to convince a person of his responsibility, in light of Kruglanski et al. (1972), Pallak et al. (1974), Sogin and Pallak (1974), and Worchel and Brand (1972), there may be an even more direct route to imparting a sense of personal responsibility. Why not merely tell the person he is responsible? Collins and Hoyt (1972) attempted this very manipulation, and even though their experiment does not deal with *fait accompli* consequences, their study is instructive in the present context. Subjects were asked to write a counterattitudinal essay, and as in earlier experiments, amount of monetary inducement and severity of consequences were both varied. At the time the subject was asked to commit himself, one of the following statements was made:

> (Low responsibility) . . . you are, of course, in no way responsible for the effects your essay might have [Collins & Hoyt, 1972, p. 573].
> (High responsibility) . . . you are, of course, responsible for the effects your essay may have [p. 573].

The manipulation was very effective. The monetary inducement variable and consequences variables made a difference only among high-responsibility subjects, suggesting that subjects given the low-responsibility instructions became convinced of an absence of causal connection between their behaviors and the end result.

In conclusion, there now seems to be good evidence that dissonance arousal requires the perceptions of a strong causal link between oneself and the potentially dissonance-arousing event. Unless such a connection is perceived, the behavior and consequence are two irrelevant cognitions as far as the person is concerned, and the terms *consonance* and *dissonance* are not applicable.

At the same time, many questions remain about the concept of responsibility, not the least of which concerns the role of personal causation. The Sogin and Pallak (1974) experiment made clear that responsibility is a function of locus of causality for the consequence—the locus must be internal for the individual to feel responsible. But Wortman's (1975) experiment showed that feelings of responsibility engendered by knowledge of playing a causal role in the determination of a chance outcome did not produce dissonance reduction effects. Somewhere between these two experiments lies a conceptual distinction that could help to clarify the role of responsibility in the determination of dissonance processes.

Finally, it should be noted that there is a paradoxical aspect about the notion of responsibility for the occurrence of that event can mean that one is blameworthy and has done a stupid thing. To protect or bolster self-esteem it would be better to deny responsibility. But if responsibility is denied, then dissonance reduction cannot occur, and if dissonance reduction does not occur, one means of ameliorating the negativity of the event is lost. Perhaps, then, where a negative consequence is enduring and difficult to avoid or ignore (e.g., a broken leg) there would be a tendency to assume responsibility so that dissonance reduction processes could further psychological adaptation to the situation. But where a person could easily avoid thinking about a negative consequence so that adaptation to it is not paramount, denial of responsibility could be a suitable response.

SUMMARY

The purpose of this chapter has been to illustrate the development of the concept of responsibility within the context of cognitive dissonance theory. To the extent that dissonance theory has evolved since 1957, the evolution has been primarily due to the discovery that responsibility is a prerequisite for effects that we call dissonance reduction. While the precise parameters of personal responsibility will only be uncovered by additional research, the present chapter has reviewed a number of research projects that offer telling conclusions. Two of these seem particularly important:

1. Responsibility, hence dissonance reduction, evidently come about readily when a person engages in a discrepant act under conditions of high choice and when he is able to foresee the potentially dissonance-arousing consequences of that act.

2. Relatively recent research shows that unforeseen consequences can arouse dissonance under special conditions, one of these being when the individual's abilities are connected to the consequence. The possibility that responsibility can accrue even when the aftereffects of actions are not foreseen is one of the most researchable questions relevant to the theory at this point, for a more complete statement of the theory will eventually require a precise understanding of whatever factors are basic to dissonance-producing responsibility.

5
Evidence on Fundamental Propositions

The paradigms discussed by Festinger (1957) were for the most part simple variations in the proportion of dissonant cognitive elements. The well known free-decision and forced-compliance models are the prime examples. The present chapter focuses specifically on these research models, and deals with research that varies, in a straightforward manner, the proportion of cognitive elements dissonant with a specified behavioral commitment. The chapter is divided into a fourfold classification, made possible because the research herein has varied the proportion of dissonant elements in one of the following ways: (a) number of positive attributes of the chosen alternative, (b) number of negative attributes of the chosen alternative, (c) number of positive attributes of the rejected alternative, and (d) number of negative attributes of the rejected alternative. The reader will find that many classical dissonance experiments are included here, and further, that the research reported in the present chapter does not bear directly upon the special issues for which other chapters have been written.

POSITIVE ATTRIBUTES OF THE CHOSEN ALTERNATIVE

Monetary Inducement

From the formula for dissonance arousal given in Chapter 1, it should be evident that monetary inducement associated with the chosen course of action will reduce the total magnitude of dissonance. This is because monetary inducement, being consonant with the chosen behavior, operates to lower the proportion of dissonant cognitions relative to the consonant elements.

The paradigm implied by the above reasoning was begun by Festinger and Carlsmith (1959). They asked college students to perform a boring and tedious task and then asked each to tell the "next subject" that the task was interesting and enjoyable. The positive attribute attached to making this false statement was varied in magnitude by offering to pay some subjects $1.00 and others $20.00. Subsequent to making the discrepant statements, all subjects were interviewed in order to measure their evaluation of the boring and tedious task about which they had made the false statements. To ascertain that the task really was unpleasant, a third group was interviewed after it had performed the task and without having been asked to make a discrepant statement. It was assumed that dissonance aroused by making the statement discrepant with one's private evaluation of the task would tend to result in a more positive evaluation of the task. The results for the three groups confirmed that: (a) the task was unpleasant; (b) making a statement discrepant with one's true evaluation tends to produce change in evaluation toward the position of the statement; and (c) the amount of change in evaluation decreases as the amount of money offered for the discrepant statement increases. These results thus confirm the theoretical expectations.

This paradigm has provided the groundwork for some of dissonance theory's more classical and publicized research efforts. The next one, a conceptually similar study by Cohen (1962a), is reviewed in some detail as it has never been printed in journal form.

In Cohen's (1962a) study there was monetary variation over a wide range of values. College students were offered either $.50, $1, $5, or $10 to write an essay against their private view on a current issue on campus. Under the guise of a "general survey," 30 Yale students were asked to write an essay "in favor of the actions of the New Haven police." The attitude issue was chosen because in the spring of 1959, just prior to the study, there had been a student's "riot" at Yale with resulting accusations of police brutality toward the students. There was thus an assurance that: (1) motivation and interest on the part of the students were maximal; (2) every student was on one side of the issue, that is, extremely negative toward the police and their actions and sympathetic toward the students; and, therefore, (3) any subject asked to write an essay in favor of the actions of the New Haven police would be taking a position clearly inconsistent with his own attitudes.

The students were approached in their dormitory rooms on a random basis; only one subject to a room was selected. The experimenter introduced himself as a fellow student who was a member of a research team from The Institute of Human Relations. He said that the researchers were "interested in and concerned with the recent riots" and that the subject knew that the "university administration and the public are very concerned with the issue." Thus the research group felt that the study had some "relevance and importance, especially in the light of recent events." The experimenter went on to say that, "It has been shown that one of the best ways to get relevant arguments on both sides of an issue is to ask people to write essays favoring only one side. We think we know pretty much how you feel about the students' rights in this matter." Here the experimenter paused for the subject's reaction, and after a usual indication of felt infringement on the part of the subject, the experimenter continued by saying, "What we really need now are some essays favoring the police side. I understand that you have very different views on the matter, but as you can see, it's very interesting to know what kinds of arguments people bring up in their essays if they have very different opinions about it."

The experimenter then went on to say that he would like them to write the "strongest, most forceful, most creative and thoughtful essay you can, unequivocally against your own position and in favor of the police side of the riots." The reward manipulation was then introduced. The experimenter said, "Now as part of our study, we have some funds available, and we are prepared to pay you $_____ for writing the essay against your own position." All reward groups were told exactly the same thing, except that some were offered $10.00 ($N = 6$), some were offered $5.00 ($N = 10$), some were offered $1.00 ($N = 6$), and some offered $.50 ($N = 8$). All groups were told that the decision to write the essay was entirely their own choice. However, in order to prevent their refusing to participate, they were also told that the experimenter did need their help in the study since he was a student and this was part of his research paper. Thus, while the latter "constraints" might reduce the absolute amount of dissonance occasioned by compliance, it prevented any considerable differential loss of subjects and therefore any self-selection bias. After the reward manipulation, the subjects were again reminded that they were to take as strong and unequivocal a stand as possible against their own position and in favor of the police.

After each subject wrote his essay on a blank sheet entitled, "Why the New Haven Police Actions Were Justified," the postmeasures were given. The subjects were told, "Now that you have looked at some of the reasons for the actions of the New Haven police, we'd like to get some of your reactions to the issue; you may possibly want to look at the situation in the light of this. So, would you please fill out this questionnaire." Subjects first filled out an opinion scale asking, "Considering the circumstances, how justified do you think the New Haven police actions were in the recent riot?" This constituted the major dependent measure of the experiment. Checks were then made of the experimental inductions to clarify the possible effect of differential reward on attitude change. In particular, subjects' recall of the amount of money offered was tapped, and they were also asked for an estimate of the strength of their essays.

It should also be noted that the design included a control group, which received no manipulations, to be used as a baseline for attitude change. This was important as no premeasure of attitude was given in the other conditions.

The check on the reward manipulations indicates that the subjects perceived accurately the rewards they were to receive for writing the essay. It was also found that the subjects, in writing their essays, perceived that they were to take a strong and unequivocal stand against their own attitude position and that this perception was constant and high no matter what rewards they anticipated. On the scale where maximum strength of discrepant essay was seven, the mean for the $10 group was 5.72, for the $5 group it was 5.80, for the $1 group it was 5.58, and for the $.50 group it was 5.82. All of these means indicate strongly discrepant essays, and they do not differ reliably from one another. We may thus assume that the basic conditions for examining the effects of differential incentives in producing dissonance and attitude change have been fulfilled here: The subjects accurately perceived that they would be getting differential rewards, and any differences in attitude change as a function of reward would not be a function of the strength with which the subjects perceived that they had taken the discrepant stand.

The data on attitude change are entirely consistent with the notion that dissonance and consequent attitude change vary inversely with the amount of incentive for taking a stand discrepant with one's cognitions. The results in Table 3 show that as reward decreases, attitudes toward the police become more positive. Among experimental groups, the rank order of attitude effects is exactly what was expected, and the linear trend is significant beyond the .01 level. When the range of scores, including the control group, is tested for differences by the Duncan Multiple-Range Test (Edwards, 1960, pp. 136–140), the specific differences between experimental groups emerge. The $10 and $5 conditions are not significantly different from each other or from the control condition, but the $1 condition is different from the control ($p < .10$) as is the $.50 condition ($p<.01$). Furthermore, the $1 condition and the $.50 conditions are both different from the $10 condition ($p < .05$ and $< .01$ respectively). Finally, the $.50 condition is itself different from the $1 condition ($p < .05$) as well as from the $5 condition ($p < .01$). These results are clearly in line with the derivation from dissonance theory regarding the effects of consonant information.

A third study, an often-cited improvement on the Festinger and Carlsmith study, was conducted by Carlsmith, Collins, and Helmreich (1966). Just as in the Festinger and Carlsmith (1959) design, subjects were asked to lie to a subsequent subject in an effort to convince her of the interesting nature of the task. They were offered one of three amounts of money for performing this deed ($.50,

TABLE 3
Mean Attitudes toward Police Actions

Control	2.7[a]
$10.00	2.3
5.00	3.1
1.00	3.5
.50	4.5

[a]The higher the mean, the more positive the attitudes toward the police.

$1.50, or $5), obviously a variation in the number of elements consonant with the chosen behavior. In addition to a face-to-face lying condition, which should have led to considerable dissonance due to the general difficulties and norms associated with lying, there was also an "anonymous essay" condition. In this latter condition subjects should have experienced considerably less dissonance. For one, there was no face-to-face contact with the next "subject," and second, it was made clear that the subject's essay would be used only as a source of ideas upon which the experimenter would draw when writing a standard essay. In short, the subject's actual efforts would not have a direct influence on other subjects.

The results within the face-to-face condition paralleled those of Festinger and Carlsmith, such that subjects found the experimental test interesting and fun in inverse proportion to the payment provided. In direct contrast, essay-writing subjects found the study most interesting (and fun) when they were paid higher amounts. The important point here is that under conditions where dissonance should have been maximal (face-to-face lying), monetary payment served to reduce dissonance.

A conceptually similar experiment is reported by Cooper and Duncan (1971), in which subjects were asked to deliver a speech taking a conservative position on abortion, while being videotaped. It was first established that subjects were not sympathetic with such a position. An amount of either $.50 or $2.50 was offered for this behavior, and consistent with the above-reported results, attitude change in the conservative direction was inversely related to amount of payment. In the same experiment there was also an examination of the impact of self-esteem, but since that variable was ineffective, we may treat this study simply as a demonstration of the effect of positive aspects of the chosen alternative.

Scientific Value and Related Inducements

Another positive attribute of the chosen alternative is the "prestige" or "scientific merit" associated with carrying out the task. For example, in a study by Cohen, Brehm, and Fleming (1958) subjects were requested to write a counterattitudinal essay, and as an external justification some subjects discovered via the experimenter that their performance was ultimately helping the experimenter, the school administration, and science. Other subjects were given only minimal reasons for their performance. Just as in the research on monetary incentives, attitude change following commitment was greater given fewer consonant cognitions. Highly similar effects have been obtained subsequently by Greenbaum and Zemach (1972), and Rabbie, Brehm, and Cohen (1959).

The Greenbaum and Zemach study is of special interest because it amounts to a crosscultural replication, albeit a conceptual replication, of the Cohen experiment described above. Shortly before the study Konrad Adenauer, Chancellor of the Federal Republic of Germany, made a visit to the Hebrew University in Israel. A number of students had assembled to protest his visit, and the police reportedly dispersed them in somewhat brutal style, beating several students. Accordingly, the stage was set for a replication of the Cohen (1962a) study, with a strong antipolice sentiment among the student body. The remainder of the procedure was similar to that of Cohen, except that justification was provided by telling subjects that their counterattitudinal essays would be instrumental in determining future university policy. The results were exactly as would be predicted: attitudes against the police became less intense to the degree that the discrepant act was not adequately justified.

A study by Weick (1964) manipulated whether or not subjects received experimental credit for their work on a concept attainment task. Presumably those receiving no credit would experience more dissonance, and Weick reports the predicted effect on a number of innovative dissonance reduction measures. For example, the no-credit group persisted longer with an insoluble problem, attained completion on more trials, forgot less relevant information, and held a more performance-based level of aspiration. This experiment serves to illustrate the effectiveness of dissonance manipulations on behavioral measures.

NEGATIVE ATTRIBUTES OF THE CHOSEN ALTERNATIVE

It is possibly this category that contains some of the most ingenious research conducted within the theory. The sizable number of studies included here attests to the simplicity of the paradigms that have varied negative aspects of the chosen course of action. We also find the quantitative impressiveness of this research to reflect investigators' intrigue with the phenomenon of the human coming to justify having chosen an undesirable state of affairs. The first, and lengthiest, subcategory of research we will examine deals with physical or mental effort as an accompaniment of various behavioral commitments.

Physical and Mental Effort

A series of four papers has reported a relationship between effort expenditure prior to exposure to a communication and subsequent belief in that communication. The dissonance analysis of this effect is straightforward. When a person commits himself to be exposed to a point of view, particularly one with which he disagrees, dissonance is aroused to the degree that he must also suffer or strain in order to gain exposure. One clear means of dissonance reduction is subsequent agreement with the communication. Conceptually, this is no different from the end result of the underrewarded individual's committing himself to write a counterattitudinal essay. In both cases the proportion of dissonant elements is high and can be reduced by moving toward agreement with the communication, which conceptually amounts to deleting dissonant elements.

The first in this series was by Cohen (1959a), who asked subjects to read a communication that was disparate from their own views. Effort was manipulated simply by suggestion: Some subjects were told that understanding would be problematic, while others expected it to be easy. There was also an individual difference variable. Subjects were divided according to whether their initial opinions were moderate or extreme, on the assumption that dissonance would be greater among those initially extreme. The attitude change results were in accord with expectations: The effort variable increased agreement with the counterattitudinal communication, but only for subjects who strongly disagreed with it at the outset.

Also using a measure of attitude change, Zimbardo (1965) reported two experiments in which subjects either improvised or read a counterattitudinal communication while being subjected to different levels of delayed auditory feedback (DAF). The results indicated that a long and irritating DAF did operate as a dissonance-arousing factor. The longer the feedback delay, the greater acceptance of the communication.

A pair of experiments by Wicklund, Cooper, and Linder (1967) entailed subjects' anticipated exposure to an attitude-discrepant communication. In the first experiment subjects expected to wait either a short (or long) time before having access to the communication, and in the second experiment they expected to sit quietly (or run in place) for several minutes prior to hearing the message. Even though subjects were not actually exposed to the discrepant communication and were told only its general position, the effort manipulations in both studies operated in accord with the theory. Attitudes favored the position of the expected communication more in the high-effort conditions.

These two "anticipation" experiments raise a point that is often discussed in the context of dissonance theory and which has a simple answer. From the theory it is sufficient that the person commit himself to the discrepant behavior. Dissonance arousal does not await actual performance. There is already ample evidence for this point in studies by Brehm and Cohen (1959a), Brock and Blackwood (1962), Rabbie, Brehm, and Cohen (1959a), and in two more recent studies to be described below (Arrowood & Ross, 1966; Shaffer & Hendrick, 1971).

A final experiment on effort and attitude change was reported by Linder and Worchel (1970). The study resembled that of Cohen (1959a), except that difficulty in comprehending the communication was manipulated by actual difficulty instead of by suggestion. The communication argued that cigarette smoking causes lung cancer, and was potentially dissonant for smokers. The results showed the predicted interaction, whereby the effort manipulation made a difference only for smokers.

Yaryan and Festinger (1961) developed what might be called the "preparation for test" paradigm. They considered the situation of a person who has expended considerable effort preparing for some future event and who also knows many things that indicate that the event will not actually occur. Thus, the information that he did expend effort in preparation is dissonant with the information he has that the event will not occur. At least one way the person can reduce dissonance in such a situation is to persuade himself that the possible future event is indeed likely.

In this experiment all subjects were given a standard set of instructions concerning the exact probability of their having to take an examination in the future. Subjects in the high-preparatory effort condition had to commit to memory a list of difficult symbolic definitions in preparation for the aptitude test they might have to take. Subjects in the low-preparatory effort condition merely had to look them over in order to get some idea of what they were all about. After the subjects finished with the list of symbols (either memorizing it or familiarizing herself with it), they were asked on a six-point scale whether they believed that they were one of the people selected to take the test. The results showed that subjects in the high-preparatory effort condition clearly had a stronger belief that they would have to take the test.

A subsequent study by Arrowood and Ross (1966) was in many respects similar to the Yaryan and Festinger design, except that the effort was anticipated rather than actual. The purpose of the anticipated nature of the effort was to eliminate a class of alternative explanations possibly applicable to the original study. For example, from subjects' viewpoints the high-preparatory effort might have been a signal that the prepared-for test was indeed impending. As might be expected, Arrowood and Ross demonstrated that the paradigm operates perfectly well even though effort has not been exerted.

Another original effort justification paradigm was begun by Aronson (1961), consisting of an "effortful fishing" experience. Aronson was interested in demonstrating that the degree of effort a person expends in attempting to obtain a reward has an effect on the relative attractiveness of stimuli associated with rewarded versus unrewarded trials. The hypothesis was that as effort increases, dissonance will increase and that there will be a corresponding increase in the relative attractiveness of stimuli associated with unrewarded trials.

To test the hypothesis subjects performed a task that involved fishing for containers in order to obtain money that was inside some of them. For some subjects, the task was made easy; for others, the task was made difficult. The rewarded containers were of a different color from those of the unrewarded containers. Subjects were asked to rate the relative attractiveness of the two colors before and after performing the task. The results were in accord with the prediction. In the easy condition there was an increase in the relative attractiveness of the rewarded color. In the effortful condition, however, there was no change in the relative attractiveness of the two colors. Thus the direct effect of reward (possibly through secondary reinforcement) tends to be reversed to the extent that effort, and presumably dissonance, is involved.

Fromkin (1968) has conducted a highly similar experiment, with nearly identical results. In his factorial study (high–low effort versus rewarded–nonrewarded) the rewarded stimuli were perceived as higher in attractiveness than nonrewarded stimuli under low-effort conditions, but this was not so under high-effort conditions. Just as in Aronson's experiment it appears as though secondary reinforcement processes operate in the absence of dissonance, but that under high effort, dissonance processes counter such secondary reinforcement effects. This pattern of phenomena has already been treated in some detail in Chapter 3.

In a research effort involving task evaluation, Shaffer and Hendrick (1971) requested subjects to circle random numbers. High-effort subjects were given fairly elaborate rules for working on the numbers, whereas the task was easy and straightforward for low-effort subjects. In the first experiment subjects actually engaged in the task, whereas actual engagement versus anticipation was a second variable in the second experiment. The results of both experiments were similar and were independent of the actual versus anticipated variable: The greater the effort, the more highly the relevant task was evaluated.

Two further experiments on physical effort both involved turning a crank, although neither of the studies is an exemplar from the standpoint of strength of results. Lewis (1964a) asked children to turn a crank in order to obtain chips that were evidently valued by the subjects. On a behavioral measure of preference for chips, high-effort subjects indicated a stronger effort justification effect than low-effort subjects. However, this result was limited to the younger of two age groups used. Also with a cranking device, Ostrom (1966) arranged an apparatus whereby subjects had to turn a crank either rapidly (high effort) or slowly (low effort) in order to keep a communication illuminated. As would be expected, there was a positive relationship between effort and persuasion, although the effect was of questionable significance ($p < .09$).

Finally, in examining a behavioral measure of "rigidity" Knight (1963) demonstrated that mental effort could lead to fixation on a particular mode of problem solution. Subjects were required to develop certain types of problem solutions in difficult cognitive tasks, and it was found that the more effort required to develop a method of solution, the more the subject fixated on that solution when it was no longer appropriate.

In summary, it appears as if the effort justification paradigm has given consistent support to the theory, even though the experiments are remarkably simple. Provided that an important attitude-discrepant behavior is involved, and given that subjects have some degree of volition, there is reason to think that increased effort will generally lead to an increased attraction toward or agreement with the event requiring effortful responses. In fact the phenomenon apparently can operate even without these precautions, as witnessed by Lawrence and Festinger's research with rats (Chapter 11).

Embarrassment

One of the most often cited dissonance studies is the "initiation" experiment of Aronson and Mills (1959). They tested the proposition that when a person decides to engage in an activity, the dissonance consequent to that decision increases as the number or importance of the reasons against engaging in the activity increases. In their experiment, dissonance was induced by requiring female college students to take an "embarrassment" test in order to join a sex discussion group for which they had volunteered. Each subject in the low-dissonance condition was required to read a list of sex-related words to the male experimenter. Each subject in the high-dissonance condition was required to read a list of *obscene* sex-related words to the same experimenter. Subsequent to the test the subject was allowed to audit a purported group discussion, which was actually tape-recorded, and designed to be dull and uninteresting. Finally, subjects were asked to indicate how good they thought the discussion was and how much they liked the group members.

Having a favorable attitude toward the discussion and the group constitutes a cognition consistent with joining the group: Hence, dissonance created by engaging in the embarrassment test in order to get into the group can be reduced by an increased favorable attitude toward the discussion and group members. The more embarrassing or painful the test to get in the group, the more dissonance is created, and the more favorable should be the attitude.

The results showed that attitudes of subjects in the mild embarrassment conditions did not differ from those of control subjects who took no test, while attitudes of subjects in the severe-embarrassment condition were more favorable than those of either the control or mild-test groups.

The Aronson and Mills study has also been one of the most heavily criticized, on the basis of there being several conceivable alternative explanations (see Chapanis & Chapanis, 1964; Gerard & Mathewson, 1966; Schopler & Bateson, 1962). For example, it might be argued that the banal sex discussion offered a certain relief from having read the anxiety-provoking material, resulting in an increased attraction to the group. In a similar vein, a simple contrast hypothesis would argue that the group would appear as relatively pleasant by virtue of its contrast with the noxious initiation rite. One Chapanis and Chapanis suggestion is the "afterglow" hypothesis. According to this account the subjects in the severe-initiation treatment may have had a feeling of accomplishment for having struggled successfully through the initiation, and as a consequence, this "glow" rubbed off onto the evaluation of the group discussion.

A simple way to eliminate these explanations is to create an experimental condition in which the effort and group discussion bear no contingent relationship. From the standpoint of these explanations it makes no difference whether the sex discussion is dependent on the initiation or just an event following it in time. But from dissonance theory a contingency is necessary in order that the cognitions about the initiation be relevant to cognitions about the discussion. Gerard and Mathewson accomplished this exactly. They also substituted an electric shock variable for the obscene reading variable, and their results validated the outcome of the original Aronson and Mills (1959) experiment. Liking for the group was positively related to severity of shock, but only when group membership was contingent upon the shock experience.

A Less-Than-Likable Inducing Agent

In 1961 Smith reported a study in which Army reservists were induced to eat grasshoppers, either by an ostensibly likable or unlikable experimenter. It was found that subsequent liking for grasshoppers was in proportion to the nastiness of the inducing agent (experimenter). From the theory this finding seems predictable, for a negative inducing agent is simply one more negative facet of eating grasshoppers.

A number of difficulties with the Smith experiment were raised by Jordan (1964), the major problem being that a "no-influence" control condition showed as much grasshopper liking as did the "negative inducing agent" condition. The various inadequacies were corrected in a much stronger experiment by Zimbardo, Weisenberg, Firestone, and Levy (1965). It was found that subjects who chose to eat grasshoppers under the direction of a hostile and otherwise dislikable communicator came to like the grasshoppers better than did subjects in a set of control groups in which there was no grasshopper eating.

Risk of Losing a Prize

A study by Rahman (1962) involved giving subjects an initial choice between taking the allotted experimental credit and trying to win a prize instead of the credit. If subjects chose to work for the prize (as most of them did), they were put to work on a ten-trial game that could eventually result in an attractive gift. After six trials subjects were given information about their chances of winning the prize once the next four trials were complete, and at this point they again were allowed to choose the experimental credit as a conservative and safe way out of the game. Some of the subjects had highly favorable odds of winning, thus for them, choosing to remain through the end of the game and to forego the experimental credit did not strongly imply the possibility of going home empty handed. Other subjects were given less favorable odds.

There were a number of variations in chances of success, but the strongest effect involved the difference between the "high-expectation" and "very high-expectation" conditions. Subjects in the "very high" condition had every reason to expect to win the prize, thus the decision to proceed should have led to no dissonance. This was not true to the same degree among "high" subjects. On a dissonance reduction measure of attractiveness of the prize, the "high-expectation" subjects showed a significantly greater effect than subjects in the "very high-expectation" condition.

POSITIVE ATTRIBUTES OF REJECTED ALTERNATIVES

The first study in this category was by Brehm (1956), who reports an experiment demonstrating that postchoice dissonance increases as the attractiveness of the rejected alternative increases. College students were asked to rate the desirability of eight different consumer articles, to choose between a specified two of them, and then to rate them all again. One of the two articles involved in the choice was always highly attractive while the other was made to vary from nearly equally attractive to relatively less attractive. It was expected that the highly attractive rejected alternative would create more postchoice dissonance than would the slightly attractive rejected alternative, and that whatever dissonance was created would manifest itself in pre- to postchoice changes in the desirability of the alternatives. The dissonance could be reduced by increases in desirability of the chosen alternative, and by decreases in desirability of the unchosen alternative. The actual changes in the pre- and postchoice desirability ratings confirmed these theoretical expectations: Enhancement of the chosen alternative and devaluation of the rejected alternative were directly proportional to the manipulated attractiveness of the rejected alternative.

Change in the number or importance of positive attributes in the rejected alternative can be effected not only through change in the attractiveness of the rejected alternative, but also through variation in the amount of "cognitive overlap" of the chosen and rejected alternatives. What is meant by "cognitive overlap" is simply the extent to which the alternatives have attributes in common. It is obvious that as the proportion of common attributes increases, the proportion that can be dissonant with the choice decreases, hence the amount of dissonance created by the choice will tend to decrease. That is, the number of positive attributes lost or negative attributes avoided by rejection of one alternative decreases as the chosen alternative includes more and more of the same attributes, other things being equal. When the two alternatives have the same attributes—that is, they are identical—nothing is given up or avoided by choosing one over the other. And, conversely, as the number of common attributes decreases, and with attractiveness of the alternatives held constant, the magnitude of postchoice dissonance increases.

Two studies have been designed and conducted specifically to test the effect of overlapping cognitions on postchoice dissonance. As with the above studies on the attractiveness of the rejected alternative, they were not concerned with the rejected alternatives' positive attributes per se but rather with the degree of attribute similarity, regardless of whether the attributes involved were positive or negative. Since the alternatives were highly attractive, we again assume that variations in similarity are essentially variations in similarity of the positive attributes.

In the first "free-choice" experiment (Brehm & Cohen, 1959b), grade-school children were individually asked to indicate on a scale how much they liked each of 16 toys both before and after being allowed to choose one. Some were given a choice between qualitatively similar toys (e.g., between metal crafts sets, or between sets of table games) and others were given a choice between quite dissimilar toys (e.g., between swimming fins and a ship model). It was expected that the magnitude of dissonance would be reflected in pre- to postchoice enhancement of liking for the chosen alternative and decrease in liking for the rejected alternative. The obtained liking changes confirmed not only the expected direction of change, but also the theoretical derivation of particular interest here, namely, that dissonance reduction (and presumably dissonance) is greater with dissimilar than with similar choice alternatives.

An experiment by Brock (1963) also bears on the derivation regarding the similarity of alternatives. As part of a larger experiment, children aged 3–12 years were given a choice between similar objects (two bags of crackers or two toys) or dissimilar objects (a bag of crackers and a toy). Dissonance and consequent revaluation of the chosen objects from before to after choice were greater for those children choosing between dissimilar objects: They increased their liking for the chosen alternatives and decreased their liking for the rejected alternatives more than in the case of the children who chose between similar objects.

The Brehm and Cohen (1959b) choice experiment also provides evidence concerning the effect of number of choice alternatives on postdecision dissonance. Theoretically, the more alternatives a person has, the more he is giving up by ultimately coming to a decision. This means that total number of alternatives will generally function as a variation in attractiveness of rejected alternatives.

A final study in this category is a unique variation on the familiar forced compliance paradigm. Darley and Cooper (1972) offered subjects either $.50 or $1.50 as an incentive to write a counterattitudinal essay on the topic of school dress codes, but unlike other dissonance experiments, the authors expected subjects to decline to write the essay. In order to facilitate subjects' refusal, the essay-writing task was couched in a highly objectionable format. Indeed, subjects did decline to write the essay, and as would be expected from other research in this section, those offered the higher incentive showed the greatest subsequent dissonance reduction. Dissonance reduction in this case consisted of attitude change in the direction of the subject's original position.

NEGATIVE ATTRIBUTES OF REJECTED ALTERNATIVES

The classic study in this category is the "forbidden toy" paradigm of Aronson and Carlsmith (1963). In their experiment they were concerned with the degree to which coercion used to force the rejection of a desirable alternative would produce attitude change regarding that alternative. Their subjects were nursery school children who were shown five toys and asked which toy in a given pair they would like to play with. By presenting the children with all ten pairs, a ranking was derived for the most preferred toy to the least preferred toy.

The experimenter then placed the second-ranked toy on a table and introduced the experimental manipulations. Half of the children, those in the mild-threat condition, were given a mild admonishment not to play with the toy on the table; in the severe-threat condition, the children were strongly admonished not to play with the toy on the table under threat of the experimenter's anger, annoyance, and rejection of the child. The experimenter then left the room. After the children were allowed to play with the other four toys, the experimenter returned and the children reranked the toys in the same manner as eariler. The dependent variable in this study was the change in the child's relative ranking of the crucial toy from before to after the threat was administered.

Aronson and Carlsmith expected that a mild threat of punishment for playing with a desired toy would lead to greater dissonance than a severe threat. That is, having committed themselves to the discrepant behavior of not playing with something they found desirable, the children would experience greater dissonance the fewer the cognitions supporting the discrepant commitment. Severe threat is a cognition more consistent with giving up a desirable object than is a mild threat. Thus the subjects in the mild threat condition would experience greater dissonance and could reduce it by devaluing the crucial toy more than those in the severe threat condition.

The results strongly support the hypothesis: The toy decreased in attractiveness more in the mild threat condition than in the severe threat condition. Thus, the children who refrained from playing with the toy in the absence of a severe threat reduced the dissonance between not playing with the toy and the cognition that it was attractive.

Subsequently the effect was replicated by Freedman (1965c), Pepitone, McCauley, and Hammond (1967), and Turner and Wright (1965). In the Freedman (1965c) and Pepitone *et al.* (1967) studies there was additional evidence that the dissonance arousal led to an internalization of the value regarding the specific toy. Pepitone *et al.* (1967) assessed latency of playing with the forbidden toy once the ban was lifted, and these results paralleled exactly the attractiveness ratings. Freedman found evidence that the attractiveness effects persisted over several weeks.

SUMMARY

In this fourfold classification of research we have reviewed a number of classical and less-than-classical experiments that have varied the proportion of dissonant cognitions. In each case is a clear example of how investigators set out to raise dissonance and measure the effects said to result from dissonance arousal. While procedures as simple as these do not inevitably meet with success (witness Chapter 3), it is possible at this point to come to some understanding of factors that might cause such designs to go astray. These factors, most notably personal responsibility, have already been elaborated upon in the previous two chapters.

6

Energizing Effects of
Cognitive Dissonance[1]

In their review of theory and research on motivation, Cofer and Appley (1964) remarked, "Dissonance theory (and its research) needs more anchoring in the concepts of prior work than it has had to date [1964, p. 798]." Cofer and Appley were concerned about a one-sided emphasis they saw in dissonance research at the time they wrote. Most psychologists agree that to designate a variable as "motivational" ascribes to it properties of energizing, directing, and reinforcing behavior. Berlyne (1964) has expressed this well: "To attack motivational problems means to seek factors that govern the organism's degree of alertness and activation, that bias the organism toward certain forms of behavior, and that determine what events will provide reinforcement for learning processes and how effectively [p. 488]."

Until 1964 nearly all research on cognitive dissonance had followed a simple and sovereign strategy. In experiments to validate dissonance theory, investigators aroused cognitive dissonance and then examined the subsequent dissonance-reducing effects. As we have already seen, numerous such effects have been accumulated in the experimental literature. While reliable experimental findings are welcomed by any theory, this body of evidence does not, by itself, make a conclusive case for the assertion that cognitive dissonance is a motivational variable. Consider the reliable patellar reflex (knee jerk) phenomenon. Typically individuals extend the leg in response to a tap on the patella. But few psychologists would wish to say that this response is performed in order to reduce a motivational tension state. We should also be reluctant to conclude that cognitive dissonance is a motivational variable simply on the basis of studies showing that dissonance arousal produces "dissonance-reducing" reactions.

It has been noted above that Berlyne lists three criteria by which we may judge a variable as motivational. One of these has to do with the impact of the variable

[1] We are indebted to the late Nickolas B. Cottrell for writing substantial parts of this chapter.

on biasing the organism toward certain forms of behavior. Most of the research of this chapter falls into this category, and it is this research that makes the strongest case for dissonance as a motivational process. Another criterion is whether the variable in question activates the individual. We will see a certain amount of evidence for the impact of dissonance on physiological change, but that is clearly not a central part of this chapter. Finally, a third criterion is whether cognitive dissonance determines what events are reinforcing. This question has been virtually untouched in dissonance research, and we will have no further discussion of it. In short, the case for dissonance as a motivational process rests primarily on its energizing impact on behavior, and to a small degree on physiological manifestations.

In examining relevant research it is useful to draw upon the theory and methods of modern, eclectic stimulus—response theory (e.g., Miller, 1959; Weiss & Miller, 1971). Although these analytical tools are not customarily used by social psychologists, they are germane because of their extensive use in research on motivation. Furthermore, Festinger has indicated that the motivational status of cognitive dissonance should be evaluated by the same criteria used in evaluating more traditional motivational variables. He defines dissonance as a motivational tension state with behavioral consequences identical to those of the homeostatic drives. More specifically, he has noted that terms such as "hunger," "frustration," or "disequilibrium" could each be substituted for "dissonance" without significantly altering the character of the theory.

INTRODUCTION TO THE DRIVE X HABIT NOTION

The most extensive work on motivational variables as energizers of performance is attributable to scholars examining proposals from Hull—Spence theory (see Brown, 1961; K.W. Spence, 1956). These efforts have resulted in a theory that predicts clearly in simple performance situations such as classical avoidance eyelid conditioning. The theory can also be used to analyze more complicated situations. However, dialogues such as that between J.T. Spence (1963) and Battig (Battig, Wright, & Gescheider, 1963) indicate that there are several complex situations where the theory's predictions are a matter of controversy. Independent of the more complex situations, it will be useful at this point to summarize the more important features of the D X H notion and its associated research. This will place us in a favorable position for examining the numerous dissonance studies that purport to raise general drive by means of dissonance arousal. The reader who is interested in a more comprehensive overview of the D X H conception might refer to Brown (1961) or Cottrell (1972).

Hull—Spence theory distinguishes between variables that direct behavior and those that energize behavior. Hebb (1955) used the analogy of the difference in function of the steering gear and the engine of an automobile. Some variables primarily alter the direction behavior takes. For example, the number of trials on which a response has been reinforced and the number of extinction trials are both important influences of the strength of the directional component of behavior. The conceptual term for the directional aspects is termed "habit" (H). Other variables primarily alter the vigor and intensity of behavior but do not determine the particular behavior that is performed. These latter phenomena (vigor and intensity) are said to result from the general drive state (D) of the organism.

The theory states that the H and D factors combine multiplicatively (D X H) to determine overt performance. The theory was primarily designed to explicate simple learning situations. Thus, the interactive relationship of the D and H factors can be illustrated well by the results of research on the classical conditioning of the eyeblink response. These studies involved presentation of a neutral stimulus, such as a tone, that pilot work had indicated did not elicit eyeblinks. Shortly after each presentation of the tome an airpuff was delivered to the individual's cornea. The airpuff served as an unconditioned stimulus, for it reliably elicited an eyeblink from individuals. With repeated presentations of the tone-puff sequence, the tone gains in strength as an elicitor of the eyeblink as a conditioned response.

The multiplying effect of D on behavior in this situation was shown by Spence (1956, p. 68–70). Drive was defined in terms of the intensity of the air puff, and based on the D X H reasoning, it would be expected that the conditioning process would be manifested more strongly among the high drive subjects. This is precisely what happened. The high-drive group increased its margin of superiority over the low-drive group as the course of acquisition continued.

Another property of D and the D X H mechanism is the irrelevant drive hypothesis, and the related notion of drive summation. These hypotheses assume that any motivation-increasing factor can (within as yet unspecified limits) be substituted for another, since the D produced by each is identical. Thus, if a response has high probability of being elicited by a stimulus when a subject is hungry, it should also be elicited when the subject is thirsty or in pain.

Experiments to verify this hypothesis involve training a response with one sort of drive relevant to the conditions of reinforcement and then testing comparable trained groups under different levels of an irrelevant drive. For instance, Webb and Goodman (1958) trained hungry rats to press a lever to secure food. After 60 trials of training they were satiated for food and returned to the test box for two successive 5-min extinction test sessions. During the first session the animals pressed the bar an average of 1.8 times. In the second period the investigators increased the irrelevant drive of fear by flooding the box with water. This produced a dramatic increase in the incidence of bar pressing. The still satiated animals made more than four times as many presses (the mean was 8.4) as they had during the preceding 5 min. Similarly Miller (1948) showed that the irrelevant drive of shock can increase the occurrence of a response learned originally to secure food.

With this preamble on drive theory as a background, the reasoning and methodologies of the following cognitive dissonance studies will now make sense. Many of the paradigms to be discussed below are direct outcomes of the earlier research we have just mentioned—such as experimentation on the impact of drive on responses of different strengths. Our discussion is categorized according to the type of paradigm used, and includes the following topics: (a) A reinterpretation of certain equity research, (b) the impact of dissonance on hierarchy of competing responses, (c) dissonance and the individual's response to material that is internally competitive or not, (d) dissonance and incidental retention, and (e) the energizing of dissonance arousal through irrelevant drive states.

A REINTERPRETATION OF FINDINGS
ON EQUITY AND TASK ENHANCEMENT

The results of certain research on the effects of cognitive dissonance on task performance are consistent with the assumption that dissonance arousal increases the individual's general drive (D) level. For example, Weick (1964) found that subjects who were induced to perform a task with inadequate justification performed the experimental task more proficiently than controls and also rated the experiment as significantly more interesting than controls. It is entirely possible that the enhancement of task attitudes and improved task performance resulted from different processes. The improvement in performance might have resulted from increased generalized drive increasing the probability of emitting appropriate task responses for individuals experiencing dissonance. In this view, increased favorability of attitudes regarding the task and the experiment are not necessary for dissonance arousal to produce changes in performance. Subsequent work by Ferdinand (1965) supports this view. He manipulated dissonance in the same way as Weick and also found that high-dissonance subjects performed the dependent variable task more proficiently than did controls. However, the dissonance subjects did not show greater liking for the task or the experiment than controls. Apparently the dissonance was reduced by other means. Nevertheless dissonance arousal produced reliable changes in performance.

Experiments to test Adams' (1963) dissonance analysis of the effects of inequity upon task performance are also pertinent. Adams proposed that individuals adjust their performance levels to redress dissonance resulting from inequity between own inputs and/or outcomes and those of a comparison other person (see Chapter 13 for a more complete discussion of dissonance and inequity).

A study by Weick and Prestholdt (1968) is consistent with the notion that inequity-produced dissonance increases general drive (D) level. In this study individuals were either paid equitably (control condition) or inequitably (dissonance conditions) for their work on a marble-dropping task. There were two dissonance conditions: overpayment and underpayment. Adams' inequity formulation predicts that overpaid subjects should increase their performance in order to reduce dissonance, while underpaid subjects should reduce their task performance. Surprisingly, the results showed that both dissonance groups worked at a faster rate than the controls. The drive theorist would propose that dissonance-produced drive energized the sequence of responses involved in dropping marbles, one by one, through a round hole. The fact that the underpaid subjects acted in a way so as to increase their dissonance (they increased, rather than reduced their work rate) is evidence that subjects did not cope with dissonance through changes in work rate. These findings did not seem to result from a task-enhancement process either. The three conditions did not differ on measures of interest in the task.

These intriguing findings are not conclusive proof that dissonance augments D. More precise information is needed on the habits involved in the dependent variable task in order to make a compelling interpretation. For certain arrangements of task-relevant habits increased drive improves performance, but for other arrangements drive impairs performance. Definitive tests of the hypothesis that dissonance augments generalized drive (D) require that the investigator have a priori knowledge of whether increased D will improve or degrade performance. Also helpful is knowledge of the impact on performance of known and reliable sources of drive. The view that dissonance augments drive gains credibility if dissonance-induced performance changes are similar to those produced by manipulations already known to augment D. Many of the studies discussed below were designed with these considerations in mind.

EFFECT OF DISSONANCE ON A HIERARCHY OF COMPETING RESPONSES

Cottrell and Wack (1967) and Cottrell, Rajecki, and Smith (1974) examined the effects of cognitive dissonance on the hierarchy of competing responses. Each subject first practiced saying aloud two novel foreign words at each of the following frequencies: 1, 2, 5, 10, 25. This training served to establish a hierarchy of verbal habits of varying strengths. The dependent variable task was ostensibly a tachistoscope-recognition task for the alleged study of subliminal perception of the foreign words they had practiced reading aloud. On about 80% of these trials the subject saw a brief flash. Pretests indicated that subjects saw something wordlike, but were not biased to any of the 10 verbal responses. These were the so-called subliminal perception trials. Instructions required subjects to call out one of the foreign words on each trial and to guess when unsure, thus placing the verbal habits established earlier in competition with each other.

Drive theory is explicit about the effect of increasing drive upon a hierarchy of competing responses: An increment in drive increases the frequency of emission of responses governed by strong habits at the expense of responses governed by weak habits (see Cottrell, 1972, for a summary of relevant research). These effects on responses should be produced by dissonance arousal if cognitive dissonance augments generalized drive.

Cottrell and Wack (1967) manipulated dissonance with the same procedures used by Weick (1964)—inadequate justification for task performance. The results confirmed the drive hypothesis. Dissonance subjects emitted more highly practiced verbal responses and fewer less practiced responses relative to controls.

Cottrell et al. (1974) used the irrelevant drive paradigm to determine whether or not making a decision increases generalized drive. The rather complicated procedure involved two experimenters and two laboratory rooms. The coed subjects studied 12 consumer articles (e.g. scrap book, pair of bookends) and rank-ordered them for desirability. Then the subject received training in saying the foreign words at different frequencies. Following this training they were given either their fourth ranked article (gift-control condition) or allowed to choose between their fourth and fifth ranked articles (decision condition). Then followed the subliminal perception task, and a second rank ordering of the 12 articles. Results confirmed the hypothesis. Relative to controls, individuals who made a decision emitted more highly practiced verbal responses at the expense of the less practiced responses.

EFFECT OF DISSONANCE ON REACTIONS TO COMPETITIONAL AND NONCOMPETITIONAL MATERIAL

Spence, Farber, and McFann (1956) devised two paired-associates lists for testing drive theory predictions. The *noncompetitional* list consisted of word pairs with strong within-pair associations and weak associations between terms from different pairs (e.g., *adept–skillful, barren–fruitless*). In the *competitional* list there were some strong within-pair associations, but many more strong associations between terms of different pairs (e.g., *barren–fruitless, arid–grouchy, desert–leading*). Since drive is presumed to increase the effectiveness of strong associations, the theory predicts that drive would improve performance on the noncompetitional list. On the competitional list, drive is presumed to increase the effective strength of the numerous strong, task-inappropriate associations and thereby impair performance. These predictions have been verified by experiments using drugs, electric shock, and social facilitational treatments as sources of drive (see Cottrell, Rittle, & Wack, 1967, for a summary of these studies).

Waterman (1969) aroused dissonance by asking individuals to agree to write an attitude-discrepant essay. Control subjects agreed to write a consonant essay. Half of the subjects in each group subsequently learned a noncompetitional paired associates list to a criterion of two successive repetitions, while the other half learned a competitional list to the same criterion. A significant dissonance X list interaction on the dependent variable of number of errors confirmed the drive hypothesis. Dissonance subjects tended to be inferior to controls on the competitional list, but superior (made fewer errors) on the noncompetitional list.

Lombardo, Libkuman, and Weiss (1972) used these lists to determine if dissonance resulting from disagreement was a source of drive. Dissonance arousal involved hearing a confederate posing as another subject state five opinions that were in disagreement with the individual's position on issues that were relatively important for the individual. The confederate stated an agreeing opinion on five relatively unimportant issues. In the low-dissonance condition the confederate stated agreeing opinions on the five important issues and disagreeing positions on the five relatively unimportant issues. Next, each subject learned one of the lists to a criterion of two perfect trials. The significant dissonance X list interaction supported the hypothesis. Relative to low-dissonance controls, high-dissonance subjects took more trials to reach criterion and made more errors on the competitional list, but required fewer trials and made fewer errors on the noncompetitional list.

Our major reservation concerning the Lombardo et al. (1972) experiment has to do with the nature of the dissonance induction. Contrary to the other research we shall report here, it is debatable whether their subjects felt responsible for exposure to contrary opinions, thus it remains a possibility that the increased drive experienced by "high-dissonance" subjects was instead simply a response to an unexpected and unpleasant experience. Instead of "dissonance," that unpleasant experience may well have been labeled "frustration" or "surprise."

A final study in this section of competitional and noncompetitional situations is by Pallak and Pittman (1972), who explored the effects of dissonance resulting from choice to perform a boring task. They used two versions of the Stroop (1935) color word interference task. The high-response competition task was the traditional Stroop task. The individual viewed a series of color labels printed in different colors (that is, "red" in green type, "blue" in green type). The words were presented at the rate of 1 per sec. and subjects were to name the color of the type. This task presumably produces more competition between criterial (naming the color of the letters) and noncriterial responses (reading the color label) than the low-response competition task. The stimuli for this task were color neutral words, such as "safe" and "lot," printed in either red, green, or blue. From drive theory one may predict that increased drive impairs performance most on the high competition task via the D X H mechanism. The results confirmed the hypothesis. Dissonance from choosing to perform the boring task impaired performance on the high-competition task and improved performance on the low-competition task. In an extended replication they found that choice-induced dissonance could be blocked by giving high justification for performing the task after the choice, but before doing the Stroop Color Word Interference Task.

EFFECT OF DISSONANCE ON INCIDENTAL RETENTION

Pallak and his associates (Pallak, 1970; Pallak & Andrews, 1970; Pallak, Brock, & Kiesler, 1967) have conducted an extensive program of research on the effects of dissonance on the retention of incidentally learned material. In these studies subjects copied a list of nonsense syllable pairs. The rationale for this activity was that the subjects were in the control condition of an experiment on verbal behavior that involved copying the list a number of times. After copying the list the prescribed number of times, subjects received a second booklet that contained the first syllable from each pair, and were asked to write down the second syllable for each pair. Since subjects had not been instructed to learn the pairs and had copied them for a different reason, retention in this sort of situation has typically been termed "incidental" retention.

Studies have shown that traditional sources of drive increase incidental retention. For example, Pallak (1970) examined the incidental retention performance of subjects who were instructed that the second part of the experiment (after copying task) involved receiving intense electric shock. Instructions to the no-shock control subjects stated that the second part was a study of the effects of visual stimulation on motor performance. The results showed that subjects threatened with shock retained more pairs than the controls. Pallak and Andrews (1970) replicated this study and obtained identical results. These authors also examined the effects of magnitude of reward on incidental retention. Instructions to subjects stated that the second part of the experiment involved the effects of visual stimuli on motor performance. High-payment subjects were told that they would receive $4.50 for the second part, while low-payment subjects expected $1. The results showed that the anticipation of a relatively large monetary reward produced the greatest incidental retention. These studies indicate that both anxiety (from threat of electric shock) and incentive motivation (K. W. Spence, 1956) from the anticipation of a large reward improve subsequent incidental retention. Thus, under the drive hypothesis, there is reason to believe that the induction of cognitive dissonance prior to the copying task will increase subsequent incidental retention of the nonsense syllable pairs.

Six experiments (Pallak, 1970; Pallak, Brock, & Kiesler, 1967) have shown that cognitive dissonance increases incidental retention. Using the task procedures described above, high-dissonance subjects were offered high choice of whether or not to perform the copying task, which was described as dull and boring. In the low-choice condition instructions stated that subjects were required to do the copying task.

Pallak (1970) studied this effect in what may be called an irrelevant drive paradigm. In the irrelevant drive conditions all subjects were given low choice regarding performance of the copying task. Subjects were, however, given either high or low choice with regard to writing an attitude discrepant essay; this choice was offered before the copying task, and the writing was to be done after copying. The results showed that dissonance from this irrelevant source significantly increased incidental retention.

WHEN DISSONANCE REDUCTION IS ENERGIZED BY OTHER DRIVE STATES

If cognitive dissonance can be shown to have generalized drive properties, thus enhancing various kinds of overlearned or dominant responses, it should also be true that a measure of dissonance reduction will show an enhanced dissonance effect when the individual is experiencing increased drive from another source.

Brock (1963) examined the summation of relevant and irrelevant drive in the postdecision situation. Children made a decision either between dissimilar or similar alternatives. The more dissimilar the alternatives, the greater the postdecision dissonance, and the greater the relevant drive. Prior to the decision all of the children were tempted in another "game" to be dishonest in order to assure winning a prize. Some children cheated and some did not, creating two further conditions. Brock reasoned that the irrelevant drive of guilt would serve to accentuate the difference between similar and dissimilar alternatives on the dissonance reduction measure, which consisted of spreading of the alternatives in attractiveness. His results for these four conditions are in keeping with the idea that dissonance arousal can be bolstered by an irrelevant drive such as guilt: The smallest dissonance-reducing change was witnessed in the nonguilty–similar alternatives condition, while the strongest effect occurred in the guilty–dissimilar alternatives condition. The other two conditions fell midway between the first two.

These findings are consistent with several detailed aspects of Hull–Spence theory. After a decision, the dominant response tendencies elicited by the evaluation-of-alternatives task are those involved in making ratings that reduce dissonance. Increasing the dissimilarity of decision alternatives increases the relevant drive and increases the effective strength of the dominant response tendencies. As reported above, the dissonance reduction index was greatest among guilty subjects for those who chose from dissimilar alternatives. Irrelevant drive from guilt also increases the effective strength of dominant response tendencies via the $D \times H$ mechanism. As noted above, individuals choosing from similar alternatives and who had reason to be guilty showed greater efforts at dissonance reduction than those who should not have been guilty. When combined, these two sources of drive have a nearly perfect summative effect upon the magnitude of postdecision efforts at dissonance reduction.

In a much later piece of research (Worchel & Arnold, 1974) it was hypothesized that the drive states created by task interruption and by dissonance would summate. Dissonance was varied through differential degrees of choice in hearing a counterattitudinal communication. For some of the subjects this communication was interrupted immediately before completion, while others heard the message in its entirety. According to reasoning of Lewin (1951), Zeigarnik (1927) proposed that task interruption would arouse a tension that had to do with task completion. Presumably such tension would be absent in the individual who completes his task. In fact she obtained evidence for this hypothesis, as did Worchel and Arnold (1974). But more important for our present concerns, it was also found that dissonance reduction (agreement with the communication) was greater in the interrupted-choice condition than in the noninterrupted-choice condition. This result means, quite simply, that a tension state seemingly irrelevant to cognitive dissonance can feed into the tension that produces dissonance effects.

The effect noted by Brock (1963) and by Worchel and Arnold (1974) would not hold for all irrelevant sources of arousal. For example, in a study by Drachman and Worchel (in press) subjects were exposed to arousing (or nonarousing) visual stimuli while composing a counterattitudinal essay, and the impact of these stimuli was to *reduce* the dissonance effect. They argued that the subject relabeled his dissonance-based arousal in terms of the exciting visual stimuli. The major question then is this: When dissonance arousal and an alternative source of arousal occur together, what determines whether the arousal is processed as dissonance, after the manner of summative drives, or as tension belonging to the alternative stimulus? The fact that either possibility can occur does not have a direct bearing on the original dissonance theory, but remains as an interesting and researchable question.

DISSONANCE AS A SOURCE OF PHYSIOLOGICAL AROUSAL

Some scholars (e.g. Duffy, 1962; Malmo, 1959) interested in the alerting and activating aspects of motivation have emphasized neurophysiology and the study of measures of autonomic activity. Unlike the Hullians discussed above, arousal theorists focus on nervous and cranial activity; their efforts at behavioral analysis are pallid compared to those of the Hullians. The Hullians, on the other hand, almost completely ignore the neurophysiological level of analysis. However, a complete theory of motivation should ultimately combine the complementary strengths of these two approaches.

Many experimental manipulations widely presumed to be sources of Hullian drive produce reliable effects upon indices of autonomic activity. For instance, Cofer and Appley discuss evidence showing that heart rate increases both as a function of intensity of electric shock and also as a function of length of deprivation for water. Accordingly, the question addressed in the present section is whether the arousal of cognitive dissonance creates changes in autonomic activity in the same way as do traditional sources of motivation.

Gerard (1967) manipulated magnitude of dissonance by varying the closeness of value of decision alternatives. Arousal was measured by a finger plethysmograph that measured the volume of blood in the subject's finger tip. This apparatus gave a continuous measurement of vasoconstriction–dilation. Ten of 12 subjects in the high-dissonance condition showed vasoconstriction from the pre- to postdecision period, but only 4 of 11 low-dissonance subjects showed constriction over the same period. Gerard cites prior work that indicates that manipulations increasing stress and Hullian drive produce vasoconstriction, thereby illustrating the parallel between cognitive dissonance and traditional bases of motivation.

Within a different context it has also been shown (Drachman & Worchel, in press; Pittman, 1975; Zanna & Cooper, 1974) that this arousal state can be relabeled when there are other plausible cues present to serve as explanations for the individual's excited state. This research is covered in detail in Chapter 16. Thus there exists some evidence that dissonance arousal does have properties of physiological excitation.

SUMMARY

The studies discussed above give strong and diverse support to the conclusion that cognitive dissonance is a source of generalized drive (D). The arousal of cognitive dissonance increases the emission of dominant responses in a hierarchy of competing responses in a bogus subliminal perception task, in the learning of competitional and noncompetitional paired-associates lists, and in color word interference tasks. In addition, cognitive dissonance improves the incidental retention of paired associates. The conclusion that dissonance arousal augments D is especially warranted since dissonance had the same effects upon performance as predicted by Hull–Spence theory and as shown by prior studies of the effects of acknowledged sources of drive. Moreover, a variety of dissonance arousing operations produced these effects: commitment to perform a task with inadequate justification, peer disagreement on important issues (this one is debatable), commitment to write an attitude-discrepant essay, choosing to perform a boring task, and making a decision. It has been shown here that dissonance is a source of D when dissonance is the relevant drive as well as when it is an irrelevant drive. Further, Brock (1963) has shown that increased drive from varying the magnitude of dissonance combines summatively with the irrelevant drive of guilt in affecting postdecision reevaluation of decision alternatives. We have also seen that dissonance reduction can be increased by the existence of seemingly irrelevant drives (guilt, tension from incompleted tasks), and finally, there is some evidence for dissonance arousal as a state that carries physiological arousal.

7
Awareness of Inconsistent Cognitions

As set forth by Festinger (1957) dissonance theory sounded much like a model of consciously mediated cognitive activity. The person becomes aware of a contradiction between sets of cognitions, then proceeds to reconcile the contradiction. At least it is easy to infer such conclusions from the original statement of the theory. Although Festinger (1957) was not totally explicit on the issue of whether consciousness is necessary, he took a more definite position in 1964 in the context of discussing postdecision regret. At this writing he indicated that a person would be likely to focus attention on dissonance immediately after behavioral commitment. More important, Festinger suggested that the purpose of such focused attention would be that of reducing dissonance. He questioned that there could be any route to dissonance reduction other than focusing on and directly dealing with dissonant relations.

There is an implicit model of human being in the above suggestion. In order for dissonance to be experienced, and hence to be reduced, conscious attention must be directed toward the cognitive elements involved. In this respect dissonance resembles any other theory of cognitive activity, for it is generally assumed that cognitive work is at a conscious level and that the cognitive contradictions antecedent to dissonance reduction must be experienced directly, or consciously. But such assumptions are not necessarily warranted. The a priori imputing of conscoius mediation to dissonance reduction processes assumes certain psychological processes, the occurrence of which is not shown directly in the numerous experiments on dissonance reduction. This imputed process involves the conscious realization of conflicting cognitions, followed by an active phase of coping directly with such cognitions. But dissonance reduction could proceed by an alternative process.

For one, responses to the dissonance-provoking situation may take place through an unconscious psychodynamic process. Certainly psychoanalytically oriented personality theories assume that unconscious patterns of response inconsistency can be motivating, for such unconscious conflicts are said to lead to a great variety of defensive and adaptive behaviors. Second, even if one is hesitant to postulate an active unconscious (cf. Hilgard, 1969), it is possible to place dissonance reduction into the realm of overlearned responses that require little, if any, direct focus of attention.

From the observer's point of view it may be difficult to imagine how dissonance reduction could be effected without the assistance of attention directed toward the dissonance. The observer, who is sometimes also an experimenter, is perfectly aware of the contradictory cognitions, and for this reason it may be awkward for him to conceive of that cognition going "underground" or not receiving focused attention. But this is only a problem for the observer whose model of man leads him to impute a specific attention-mediated psychological process. In fact, the observer typically knows nothing of the dissonance-reducing process except for the end result.

A unique position on consciousness has been taken by Brock (1968), who suggests that dissonance reducion may actually be reduced by conscious attention. His argument assumes that a commitment becomes stronger, or less changeable, when the person has no conscious access to knowledge of his commitment. As partial evidence for this position it is possible to point to Brock and Grant (1963), who conducted a study specifically designed to minimize subjects' focal awareness of dissonant elements. The experiment is reported more fully in Chapter 10. Brock may be right, but in the larger mass of applications of dissonance theory there is no particular problem with respect to strength of commitment. Normally a recent behavioral commitment is taken to be the basis of the cognition most resistant to change, and to make the person unaware of that cognition in order to reduce its changeability would only be superfluous. It is not about to change anyway. Other than Brock's suggestion there is nothing explicit in the theory that would imply reduced dissonance reduction as a result of awareness. And implicitly, dissonance theory as a cognitive theory would almost have to assume an enhancement of dissonance arousal when attention is increasingly turned to the dissonance.

There are a number of ways in which attention can focus toward relevant cognitive elements, and we might spell out the logical possibilities. First, attention can be focused increasingly on one or the other of the dissonant elements. Presumably such an increase in attention would increase the probability of that cognition being realized as part of the dissonant relationship. Of course, if total attention were given to just one element, awareness of the contradictory element, hence awareness of dissonance, would be precluded. This latter possibility does not loom as a serious possibility, and more important, the research to follow indicates that reminding a person of just one cognition increases the realization that the element is part of a dissonant relationship. Second, the person can be made aware of the dissonant relationship per se, including the relevant cognitions. Operationally these first two possibilities are easy to distinguish, but for all practical purposes they are identical. This is because it is quite likely that attention that is turned to one of the dissonant cognitions will also come to focus on the dissonance per se, thus the two methods should be approximately equivalent as far as psychological impact is concerned. Finally, a person can be made aware of himself in general. This latter technique assumes that a person in whom dissonance is aroused will be more likely to realize that dissonance when he is brought to consider himself as an object even though the method of creating such self-focused attention does not directly point to the dissonant relationship.

RESEARCH ON THE IMPACT OF ATTENTION

In discussing the research pertinent to the question of attention on dissonance we will try to make explicit the ways in which attention is brought toward the dissonance, and whenever possible we will refer back to the above categories. There is a reasonable quantity of research relevant to this problem, and for the most part it supports our reasoning that self-focused attention advances the dissonance-reduction process.

Attention Focused toward Dissonant Cognitions

The first study designed to confront subjects with dissonant cognitions was by Brock (1962). In the context of the familiar essay-writing paradigm nonCatholic subjects were asked to write an essay on "Why I would like to become a Catholic." The amount of choice to undertake this task was varied, and to vary what Brock termed "confrontation," subjects were asked to rewrite their essays under one of the following sets:

1. In the high-confrontation condition the subject was requested to write out his essay again and rank the sentences according to persuasibility. It was assumed that these instructions would call the subject's attention to the counterattitudinal nature of his work.

2. Low-confrontation subjects were given a similar request, except they were to focus on grammar instead of content.

Presumably the attention given to grammar would only interfere with the salience of the dissonance. As evidence for the effectiveness of this manipulation Brock asked his subjects how much they "deliberated upon the implications and consequences" of their "reasons and arguments," and as expected, high-confrontation subjects reported the most deliberation. The effect of the choice variable was consistent with the research of Chapter 3, and the confrontation variable operated as we might expect: Under high confrontation the choice variable made a significantly greater difference than under low confrontation.

Although this study suggests that dissonance-reduction processes can be prompted or bolstered by forcing attention to the dissonance, Brock's experiment does have a reasonable alternative explanation. When subjects rewrote their essays and were requested to give attention to persuasiveness, they may have generated additional dissonant cognitions, thus the actual discrepant commitment may have been more substantial in the high-confrontation condition.

Looking back at the classification of the various ways to force attention onto the dissonance, Brock's technique falls within the first. He explicitly instructed subjects to think about their discrepant commitment, meaning that attention given one of the dissonant clusters of cognitions was increased. As implied in the results, this increased attention to the commitment evidently caused an increased attention to the entire dissonant relationship, thus the bolstered dissonance reduction effect.

An experiment by Brehm and Wicklund (1970) also entailed a forcing of attention onto the discrepant behavior, although in such a way that attention was not confounded with strength of commitment. Subjects were asked to choose between two approximately equal alternatives, each with one conspicuous negative characteristic. The alternatives were people, and the negative characteristic was manifested in the pictures of the two individuals. After the decision half of the subjects were forced to continue to examine a picture of the chosen man while making ratings of the two men, while the other subjects were given no salience induction. Using postdecisional spreading in attractiveness as the index of dissonance reduction, the salience was found to bolster the dissonance reduction effect, although just at a marginal level of significance ($p <$ .07).

Two additional experiments were conducted in a similar vein by Carlsmith, Ebbesen, Lepper, Zanna, Joncas, and Abelson (1969). The experimental paradigm was taken from Aronson and Carlsmith (1963). It will be recalled that the original study involved a situation where a child was tempted to play with an attractive toy, and then leading the child to commit himself not to play with the toy. In the Aronson and Carlsmith study dissonance was varied by threatening the child with either a severe or weak punishment should he play with it. Of course it was found that subsequent dissonance-reducing derogation of the toy was greatest when there was only a weak reason for abstaining from playing with it. The results of Carlsmith *et al.* (1969) were similar although they added a salience-of-dissonance variable. This variable was introduced during a play period, during which time the subject was making a continuing commitment not to play with the toy. In the first experiment salience was increased when a janitor entered the room, ostensibly to borrow a chair, then pointed to the forbidden toy, asking the child why he was not playing with it. In the second study salience came about when a light directly above the toy flashed repeatedly, calling the subject's attention to it. The results were identical to those of Brehm and Wicklund, in that salience magnified the dissonance reduction effects. Further, the results of the first study were replicated in a somewhat more elaborate procedure by Zanna, Lepper, and Abelson (1973). This latter study showed an interaction between level of threat and forced attention to dissonance, such that the focusing stimulus tended to increase dissonance effects under mild threat (i.e., under the high-dissonance condition), but tended to weaken dissonance effects under severe threat.

Pallak, Brock, and Kiesler (1967) conducted a series of studies on avoidance of dissonance. They argue that a subject who commits himself to a tedious task can avoid the subsequent dissonance arousal by throwing himself into his work. Their argument is that hard work on the task will reduce subjects' mulling over the fact of their having chosen a tedious activity. They found evidence of this postulated increased effort in posttask incidental recall of the paired-associate words of the task. For example, in their first several experiments they found that retention was greater under high choice than under low. Their fifth experiment was designed more directly as a test of the dissonance–avoidance notion. Presumably the desire to avoid dissonance would increase as the commitment becomes more salient, thus they introduced a salience manipulation similar to those of the previous experiments. During a feigned break in the task some of the subjects received a communication. In the relevant-communication condition subjects were informed that experiments are frequently boring or tedious, while irrelevant-communication subjects were exposed to some material unrelated to their commitment. Using the retention measure as an index of dissonance avoidance, there was the predicted choice–no choice difference for subjects who received no communication, as evidenced in Table 4. The choice effect was very similar for subjects in the relevant-communication condition, indicating that this communication did not call any additional attention to the dissonance. The interesting effect is in the irrelevant-communication case, where the choice effect is reversed. Apparently the amount of attention turned toward the dissonance was already at a high level before the communication. Then, when attention was drained away from the dissonance by means of the irrelevant communication, dissonance avoidance was no longer a prominent need, and consequently the choice variable no longer made a difference. This study seems especially informative because it demonstrates that the need for dissonance avoidance can be reduced by distracting the subject from the dissonant cognitions—a process similar to experiments already discussed.

A study by Allen (1965) was also specifically directed to the question of the relationship between distraction and dissonance reduction. Subjects chose between two art prints, then either 2 or 8 min. elapsed before subjects rated the choice alternatives. Within each of the temporal variations half of the subjects were provided with an absorbing technical task throughout the time interval. The results showed that dissonance reduction increased with time elapsed following the decision, but more important, the distracting task totally eliminated dissonance reduction effects.

TABLE 4
Effects of Choice and Communication on Paired-Associate Retention

	No communication	Relevant communication	Irrelevant communication
High choice	6.0	5.3	3.8
Low choice	3.8	3.4	4.3

Zanna (1975) employed a similar procedure, although with a forced-compliance essay-writing procedure. Dissonance was varied through high- versus low-choice instructions, and half of the subjects were distracted for 10 min following their essay writing by an interesting puzzle. The results showed more dissonance reduction among high-choice–low-distraction subjects than among the other three conditions combined.

Self-Focused Attention

The previous section illustrated the impact of forcing attention onto dissonant cognitions, and this section accomplishes the same, although by a less obvious route. When attention is drawn to any aspect of a person there follows a general orientation toward self-examination (Duval & Wicklund, 1972). If, for example, a person examines himself in a mirror, he then has a heightened tendency to become aware of himself on other salient self-related characteristics. If the person has just recently committed a serious hypocrisy, the hypocrisy will be a salient part of the self. Then, if he is forced to become self-aware—whether through his mirror image, the sound of his taperecorded voice, or by the stares of an attentive audience—there will be a resultant self-focused attention with regard to that salient aspect of himself.

It should be evident that this line of thought can be extended to dissonance arousal. If a person has just engaged in a dissonance-arousing behavior, the dissonance will be relatively salient. However, the person will not necessarily focus complete attention on that dissonance unless given special prompting, as shown in the preceding research. If this person is then made self-aware in any respect, that is, through his mirror image or by being the target of a camera, increased attention should then be given to the salient dissonance arousal.

The first experiment to test this idea directly was by Wicklund and Duval (1971). Subjects were placed in an essay-writing procedure and were asked to compose counterattitudinal essays on each of five issues. Half of these subjects were told they were being videotaped while they composed their essays. A television camera was aimed directly into the subject's face, this being the device used to stimulate self-focused attention. For other subjects there was no camera.

On measures of attitude change toward the positions taken in the essays there was significantly more change among subjects in the camera condition.

A study similar to this was conducted by Insko, Worchel, Songer, and Arnold (1973). All subjects were asked to defend a counterattitudinal position (legalization of LSD), under conditions of high- or low-anticipated effort. In addition, subjects were induced into the high- or low-effort conditions under conditions of high or low choice. Finally, to manipulate self-focused attention, half the subjects were run through the procedure with a television camera aimed at them, and were told that they were being videotaped. The results were in terms of the amount of attitude change in the direction of favoring legalization of LSD, and the results can be summarized best by noting that the camera increased dissonance reduction among subjects who should have experienced the greatest dissonance arousal. In other words the camera created an increment in attitude change for subjects in the choice–high-effort condition. It might be added that the choice and effort variables themselves were ineffective without the benefit of the camera.

It also should be added that the experimental variables had an impact only for females, and whatever the reason for this, such a result might suggest interpreting the results with caution. Finally, and more important, there was one condition in this study with an anomolous result. The low effort–no choice–no camera condition produced just as much attitude change as its opposite counterpart (the high effort–choice–camera condition), suggesting that a complete interpretation of this study is problematic.

While on the subject of self-focused attention, it is worth noting that the distraction research discussed above (Allen, 1965; Pallak *et al.*, 1967; Zanna, 1975) is not necessarily research on *distraction from dissonant elements* per se. It is distraction away from self-focus in general, and the implication is that an even more general form of distraction might mitigate dissonance effects. Deindividuation is one such possibility. Frey (1971) has remarked that dissonance effects might often be decreased when the individuals concerned are closely associated with groups, that is, when the person is a member of a diad or triad. He suggests that responsibility might be diffused through numbers, which is another way of saying that any given member's focus upon himself is mollified by the presence of other group members. It is noteworthy that virtually all dissonance experiments have avoided group paradigms, or "group" dissonance reduction, and perhaps this avoidance has been serendipitous.

SUMMARY

In light of these experiments on forced attention to dissonance we might well conclude that awareness of dissonance can sometimes be crucial if the theory is to predict accurately. In most of the experiments we have considered dissonance effects were weak and sometimes nonexistent when attention was focused neither on the person nor his discrepant cognitions. Analogous to this, the relatively strong dissonance avoidance effects found by Pallak *et al.* (1967) were eliminated by distracting the subject from attending to the relevant dissonant elements. Since the evidence is consistent, and has been arrived at both through direct focusing of attention on dissonant cognitions and through the indirect method of focusing attention on irrelevant features of the self, it is safe to say that dissonance effects can be reliably strengthened to the degree the person is attuned to his dissonance.

8
Regret and Other
Sequential Processes

As originally posited, dissonance theory contained no specification of the temporal aspects of dissonance reduction. Dissonance-theory researchers have acted on this lack of specificity in that the possibility of sequential effects has been universally disregarded, save for a handful of exceptions to be discussed here. Throughout the history of research on cognitive dissonance there has been an implicit assumption that dissonance reduction ensues immediately after dissonance arousal, and is measurable at virtually any interval following that arousal, whether that interval be a few seconds or a couple of months. In fact the range of measurement times is approximately that—a few seconds in many experiments to approximately two months in a study by Freedman (1965c).

Since dissonance reduction has been obtained at widely varying arousal-measurement intervals it is appealing to conclude that time makes no difference whatsoever. But does such a conclusion make any sense theoretically? What basis is there for thinking that time intervals would make any difference? We might begin by imagining dissonance theory to be a nonmotivational theory. That is, suppose dissonance theory were a notion about judgmental processes, requiring only that the subject perceive certain stimuli and draw a logical conclusion based on his scrutiny of the stimuli (see Chapter 16). If this were the case, "dissonance reduction," which would be the logical outcome of the person's calculations, would proceed approximately as fast as the mental calculations could be performed. If the person were dull, sleeping, or inept at logical thinking, the time for dissonance reduction would be increased. But granting a moderately intelligent and alert group of subjects, and not too difficult a cognitive "problem," dissonance reduction should take place rapidly and the outcome should not change once the person has arrived at his "solution." This chain of events assumes that dissonance theory is simply a judgmental theory and has no motivational components. But in contrast, what conclusion do we find if we consider the theory as it has been stated by Festinger?

Cognitive dissonance is said to be a motivational state, and it follows that we should be able to isolate two distinct phases of the dissonance process. One of these phases is the dissonance arousal itself. Independent of the person's efforts to bring his cognitions into consonant relation there should be manifestations of the drive state of dissonance. And it seems necessary that these manifestations precede dissonance reduction. Thus implicit in the original theory is the possibility of measuring two distinct events. But now the question of measurement arises: How are we to recognize the presence of dissonance independent of attempts to reduce that motivational state?

At this point Festinger's (1964) modification of the theory enters. Perhaps surprisingly, he has suggested that an effect opposite to dissonance reduction can result when the individual focuses on dissonant cognitions, provided dissonance reduction has not taken effect. For example, if a man has purchased a 400-horsepower Cadillac after the onset of a fuel crisis there no doubt would be dissonance arousal. Festinger is suggesting that the presence of dissonance can be detected in the man's *derogation* (however temporarily) of his recent purchase, and in enhancement of various Volkswagens, motorcycles, and other economical but rejected alternatives. These counterdissonance reflections of dissonance arousal are said to result simply from the person's focusing on dissonant cognitions, and these effects are labeled "regret" by Festinger.

Already we can see that the motivational state of dissonance implies effects more complex than would a simple judgmental theory. If dissonance reduction were simply a matter of noting relevant cognitions and proceeding to a reasoned conclusion, there would never be any reason to suspect the appearance of regret. Festinger's notion of regret carries additional complexities as will be shown below, but the important point is this: Regret, defined operationally as effects opposite from those of dissonance reduction, can be taken as one manifestation of dissonance arousal.

THE ONSET OF DISSONANCE
AND THE ONSET OF DISSONANCE REDUCTION

Since the original theory postulated a tension state (dissonance) as basic to dissonance reduction, it seems evident that the tension state would precede efforts at dissonance reduction. Festinger's (1964) discussion assumes this very sequential process, but his discussion also raises another issue of some complexity. He implies that the conditions necessary for dissonance arousal (thus regret) are not necessarily adequate to instigate dissonance reduction. From our earlier discussions it may be recalled that the concept of behavioral commitment is so important to the theory because it allows a specification of the directions to be taken in dissonance reduction. Surely there can be dissonance aroused between two private, nonovert events, but we would find it difficult to predict how dissonance reduction will proceed unless one of those events is clearly more resistant to change than the other. That is, as observers of the person who holds a set of contrary attitudes, we might reasonably infer the presence of dissonance, but very little can be said about the direction or mode of consequent dissonance reduction.

To return to Festinger (1964), he notes that a person can experience dissonance without proceeding to reduce that dissonance, and that this can happen when the consequences of the person's decision are not entirely clear. If the consequences of action are ambiguous, the action does not serve as a point of orientation around which dissonance reduction is organized. Still, a decision with ambiguous consequences can arouse dissonance—the only difficulty for analysis being that the observer and/or the person experiencing dissonance do not know precisely how dissonance reduction will proceed.

An example may help to illustrate this point. Festinger and Walster (1964) recruited coeds for an apparent market research study. First each subject was asked to *rate* 12 hairstyles according to attractiveness, then each style was *ranked*. Finally the subject chose to have her hair done free of charge in one of the styles. The only variable in this experiment was the point at which the subject learned the identity of the choice alternatives. In a no prior-decision condition the subject was informed of which two styles were decision alternatives only after her ranking had taken place, while in the prior-decision condition this information was disclosed before the ranking. Festinger's argument is that the prior-decision subject implicitly chose by virtue of rank-ordering the alternatives, since she performed an overt discrimination among the alternatives. For no prior-decision subjects this kind of implicit decision was impossible, since they were totally unaware of decision alternatives at the time of ranking.

Should the implicit decision have aroused dissonance? Festinger assumed so, presumably because the implied choice of an alternative and rejection of another should have had at least some of the same effects as an actual, less reversible choice. To recapitulate the reasoning in our early chapters, the implicit choice of one hair style would be dissonant with perceived virtues of the other hair style and with deficits of the preferred style. However, there is very little basis in this experiment for predicting the direction to be taken in dissonance reduction. Since the decision was not binding it would not necessarily create a cognition highly resistant to change, for the ranking is obviously malleable. This being the case, Festinger and Walster seem to have created a situation in which dissonance exists in a suspended state. Dissonance reduction as we know it could not very well take place until a style has actually been chosen, or until some other relevant cognitions are highly resistant to change.

What evidence is there for our conclusion? If the ranking of prior-decision subjects created dissonance there should have been a resulting regret, as a manifestation of the tension state. Regret in this context was measured by the subject's reversal of preference between the time of the original rating and the actual decision. A reversal of preference would demonstrate regret. It turned out that 62% of the prior-decision subjects showed such a reversal, while only 28% of the no prior-decision subjects reversed. In short, among subjects who could have experienced dissonance there was good evidence for dissonance arousal in terms of preference reversal (regret). At the same time this was a situation in which dissonance reduction was not likely, for the decision was not a binding behavioral commitment. Indeed, if prior-decision subjects had not been attempting to reduce dissonance following the ranking they should have shown more consistency than no prior-decision subjects, but instead, they demonstrated more of what can be called the opposite of dissonance reduction.

There is another example of the suspension of dissonance reduction in the second of two studies by Jecker (1964). Subjects were asked to choose among two records, the chosen one to be kept by them as a gift. Subjects were told prior to the decision that there was some possibility of their receiving both records, since there were extra records available. It was further explained that a random device would be used to determine whether or not the subject would receive both. Then the experimenter asked the subject to decide which record she wanted in case it turned out that she would receive only one. The subject proceeded to make this decision, having no idea whether or not she would receive only the chosen record. Some subjects thought there was a 1/20 chance of receiving both records and others were led to think that the odds were 19/20. In a control condition subjects chose under more "usual" circumstances: There was no chance of receiving anything except the chosen alternative. The results showed that dissonance reduction, in the form of postdecisional spreading of attractiveness of alternatives, occurred only in the control condition. If there was a chance, however slight, of receiving both alternatives, dissonance reduction was not apparent.

This experiment illustrates an important point: Evidently dissonance reduction does not ensue until the implications of the behavioral commitment are highly resistant to change. In one of Jecker's conditions a decision was made to reject an alternative after having been given a 5% chance of actually receiving that alternative later. This meant that the rejection was not entirely resistant to change, due to the eventuality of receipt of both records at some time following the decision. Since the cognitive elements corresponding to the decision were susceptible to change, subjects had no clear method of reducing dissonance, and as was noted, actual dissonance reduction took place only when the implications of the decision were clear.

The similarity between the Jecker (1964) and the Festinger and Walster (1964) experiments has to do with the ambiguity of some kinds of behavioral commitments. Both studies indicate that dissonance reduction is unlikely when the behavioral commitment is less than definite, and the Festinger and Walster study also informs us that regret, a manifestation of dissonance, can result even when conditions are not entirely conducive to dissonance reduction.

These two experiments have been cited to demonstrate that dissonance reduction does not proceed when a decision or statement of preference has indefinite implications. In addition to this general finding, there was also evidence in the Festinger and Walster (1964) experiment, which they interpreted as dissonance arousal (manifested in regret) occurring in the absence of a dissonance reduction. But a study by Wicklund (1970) sheds considerable doubt on their interpretation of that effect as dissonance arousal.

Wicklund's study was in some ways similar to that of Festinger and Walster, in that half of the subjects gave precommitment ratings while aware of which alternatives were to be decision alternatives, and the other half were unaware of the specific alternatives. In addition, there was a variable of amount of justification for choosing the initially more attractive of the two alternatives. According to the analysis of Festinger and Walster, precommitment dissonance arousal should be less given justification for eventually choosing the highest-rated alternative, and it would follow that regret, or preference reversal, would be less. Wicklund's results demonstrated just the opposite. Relative to the unaware control condition, aware subjects who had been given justification for choosing the highest rated choice alternative manifested a significantly greater tendency toward convergence of ratings of decision alternatives than did subjects given no justification. This means that subjects who should have experienced the *least* dissonance showed the greatest precommitment preference reversal, implying that there is as yet no evidence that dissonance arousal occurs in the absence of a definite commitment.

Summary

One extremely important kind of sequential effect has been uncovered by the combination of the Jecker and Festinger–Walster experiments. We now know that decisions do not inevitably lead to dissonance reduction, and that they do so only when the consequences of the decision are clear—that is, highly resistant to change. There is another implication. If we are interested in changes in dissonance reduction over time, it is important to establish first that there is a firm behavioral commitment, or at least that some cluster of cognitive elements is highly resistant to change. In the absence of this prerequisite the investigator does not know how to ascertain and predict dissonance reduction, and it would appear that the person experiencing dissonance has equal difficulty in marking out a direction for the reduction of dissonance.

SEQUENTIAL EFFECTS OF DISSONANCE AROUSAL AND REDUCTION

An Experiment on Recall of Discrepant Information

A study by Brehm (1962a) is one of a very small number of experiments that directly show the presence of dissonance arousal independent of dissonance reduction. Rather than regret, or "contradissonance reduction" as the measure of dissonance, Brehm assessed subjects' recall for dissonant information. The study suggests a sequential process in line with what has been suggested above: Dissonance arousal, or at least manifestiations of it, are maximal early, and at a later measurement the arousal dissipates or possibly is supplanted by dissonance reduction.

College students recruited from introductory psychology classes were asked to bring a friend to their experimental session, and both served as subjects. When the pair of friends arrived at the experiment room, they were informed by the experimenter that they were to take part in a survey for a nationally circulated magazine devoted to television. The survey's purpose was stated to be a study of the relationship between the personality of types of television stars and of the individuals who watch them. The friends were then placed in separate rooms for the remainder of the session.

Each subject was given a list of 40 personality traits, some desirable (e.g., intelligent, kind) and some undesirable (e.g., sly, lazy). Each trait was accompanied by the following scale responses: "not at all," "moderately," "very," and "extremely." Issues of high and low importance were created by having all subjects rate both themselves (high-importance issue) and their favorite television star (low-importance issue).

The introduction of discrepant information was accomplished by having each subject rate his friend or his friend's favorite star, as well as himself, and then showing some subjects fictitious ratings of themselves (high-importance condition) and other subjects fictitious ratings of their favorite star (low-importance condition), purportedly made by the friend. The ratings on 30 of the 40 traits were made identical with those of the subject, while the remaining 10 ratings were made to differ from those of the subject by two points on the four-point scale. The same traits were made discrepant for all subjects, whether referring to the subject himself or to his favorite star.

In showing the subject the ratings made by the friend, the experimenter said;

> "Now we are interested in your ability to remember the items as they are checked on your friend's inventory. I will give you your inventory, your friend's inventory, and a blank inventory. I will give you 10 min. to look over the two inventories that have been filled in, and then I will collect them. You may take as much time as you like to fill the blank inventory, but it should not take you more than 5 min."

The purpose in these instructions was to insure that the subject would look closely at the friend's rating in the low-importance condition as well as the high-importance condition, so that exposure to the discrepant information would be about equal between conditions.

When the blank inventory had been completed, the subjects were asked to return exactly one week later in order to fill out some additional questionnaires. They were asked not to talk about the study to each other during this interval. On returning, they were again instructed to indicate their friend's ratings on a blank inventory. When finished, they were apprised of the true purpose of the study and the reasons for the deceptions.

It was expected that discrepancies on the high-importance (self) issue would create more dissonance than those on the low-importance (television star) issue. The index of dissonance in this study was salience or relatively good recall immediately after testing, and *forgetting,* or relatively poor recall, one week after testing, of the discrepant information compared to the nondiscrepant.

The results of the immediate recall test, seen in the upper half of Table 5, yielded clear support for the theoretical expectations. While subjects in the low-importance condition recalled a smaller proportion of discrepant than non-discrepant ratings, subjects in the high-importance condition recalled a larger proportion of discrepant than of nondiscrepant ratings, this interaction being significant at the 5% level. However, the expected salience of discrepant information in the high-importance condition is not very strong, probably because of a ceiling for recall, since five of the ten subjects in the high-importance condition recalled all 10 of the discrepant ratings. Because of this ceiling effect, the salience of discrepant information can be seen more clearly by counting the number of subjects who recalled a greater proportion of discrepant than nondis-crepant ratings, six in the high-importance condition and one in the low. This difference is significant by an exact test at the .05 level, *one tail.*

It was also expected that, by one week later, the discrepant information would be less well recalled than the nondiscrepant and that this differential effect would be greater for high-importance subjects than for low. Again referring to Table 5 it may be seen that the proportions of correctly recalled items fall off more sharply for the discrepant than for the nondiscrepant information (significant at better that the 5% level by t tests), but that this effect does not differ between the high- and low-importance conditions. Thus the data indicate that dissonant information does tend to be forgotten more rapidly than does conso-nant, although they fail to show that the rate of forgetting is a function of the importance of the information. We can only speculate that the failure to find greater forgetting of dissonant information in the high-importance condition is due to the salience of the dissonant information, as shown on the immediate recall test. That is, if one finds that a close friend has given one a rating of "unintelligent," that knowledge may be so dissonant, and consequently so salient, that a considerable time is needed to forget it. Indeed, it may even be that the forgetting of highly dissonant information is extremely difficult, and that when one is exposed to such information, the resulting dissonance can be reduced only by methods other than forgetting of the information itself.

The notion that dissonant information may be salient immediately after dissonance is produced—although not having been explicitly derived from the theory—is an entirely plausible phenomenon and quite consistent with the theory. Immediately after dissonance is produced through exposure to discrep-ant information or as a result of a choice, the dissonant information may be

TABLE 5
Recall of Discrepant and Nondiscrepant Information

	Mean percentage of items recalled correctly	
Time of recall	Nondiscrepant	Discrepant
Immediate		
Low importance	82.3	71.0
High importance	89.4	93.0
Delayed		
Low importance	64.1	31.0
High importance	74.8	57.0

most salient for the person as he is confronted with the consequences of his discrepant act. It is only over a period of time, as the person attempts to reduce his dissonance, that he may manage to change the dissonant information from being salient to being forgotten. In effect, the individual must suppress that which is initially salient.

The Temporal Sequence of Postdecision Processes

The preceding experiment by Brehm demonstrated a waning of a direct manifestation of dissonance arousal, and the present experiment by Walster (1964) is a complement to that study. Walster attempted to show how dissonance reduction varies following the point of decision, and in keeping with Festinger's (1964) modification of the theory, it was expected that regret would occur soon after the decision, to be superseded by dissonance reduction.

New draftees were asked to rate the attractiveness of 10 different occupational specialties, any one of which they might hold for their remaining tenure in the army. After the initial rating an experimenter selected out two jobs close in attractiveness, then the subject was directed to choose one as his occupation for the next two years. The next step was an administration of a second attractiveness measure. The time interval between decision and the second measure was varied so that one group of subjects gave their second ratings immediately after the decision, a second group responded to the measure after 4 min, a third group after 15 min, and a fourth group after 90 min. Using as a dependent measure the mean change in scale distance between the two alternatives, Walster found regret (tendency toward crossover) at 4 min, with at least a tendency toward spreading in the other three conditions (see Table 6). The regret was not significantly different from zero, but was reliably different from the spread in the immediate

TABLE 6
Change in Discrepancy
of Two Decision Alternatives

Condition	Change in discrepancy
Immediate	.7
4 min	−1.3
15 min	2.1
90 min	.3

and 15-min conditions. The only statistically significant dissonance reduction was at 15 min.

Does this experiment confirm Festinger's reasoning? He proposes that a person will, immediately after a decision, focus attention on the dissonance "in an attempt to reduce it" (Festinger, 1964, p. 128). Not only will there be such a focusing, but it even appears as though this focused attention will serve as an instrument to dissonance reduction: "After all, how else can we expect dissonance to be reduced other than by focusing on, and trying to do something about, the dissonant relations?" (Festinger, 1964, p. 128) The argument seems to be that focused attention on the dissonance will accompany decisions, such focused attention will result in regret, and finally, that such focusing will facilitate effective dissonance reduction. Walster's results confirm Festinger's postulated sequential effect only in part. It is true that regret was manifested soon (4 min) after the decision, and that dissonance reduction followed, but it is also true that a tendency toward dissonance reduction was the immediate effect of the decision. It is possible that the dissonance reduction found in the immediate condition was insufficient or incomplete for the subjects, necessitating a more careful and regret-generating reexamination of the dissonant elements. It is also possible that factors other than dissonance arousal control the emergence of regret, and it is the next experiment that treats this possibility.

Forced Attention to Dissonance and Regret

If attention given to dissonant elements is the primary mediator of regret, it should be possible to elevate regret through a simple procedure of artificial salience of dissonant cognitions. Brehm and Wicklund (1970) designed such an experiment in order to test this aspect of Festinger's account of the sequential processes involved in dissonance arousal and reduction.

Subjects were led to think that they were taking a personality test and that they would be evaluated on the basis of whether or not they could choose which of two men was better qualified for a certain position. A list of several traits was furnished to aid the subject in her choice, and a picture of each man was also supplied. In each case the picture reflected a negative aspect of the man. The subject was shown the trait list and corresponding pictures of men, then was asked to rate them (premeasure) prior to choosing. Immediately after the decision the salience manipulation occurred. In the no-salience condition all information about the two men, including the picture, was removed. But in the salience condition the picture of the chosen man remained for the subject to examine—in fact, the subject could hardly avoid attending to it. Finally measures of attractiveness of the alternative men were taken at 1-min intervals for a total of 10 min, the first of these being immediately after the decision.

Table 7 shows the mean rating changes at each of the 10 intervals, and also listed are the "mean maximum regret" and "mean maximum dissonance reduction" scores. The most important finding for our purposes are the maximum regret data. Contrary to the extrapolation from the 1964 modification of dissonance theory, regret was greatest when the dissonance-arousing picture was *not* present following the decision. Also of interest were the sequential effects over the 10-min rating period: Dissonance reduction tended to increase over that interval in both conditions, an effect that would be expected on the basis of Festinger's postulated regret-dissonance reduction sequence.

TABLE 7

Mean Changes from Prechoice Ratings[a]

Minutes after choice	High dissonance— no salience[b]	High dissonance— salience[c]
1	−3.8	−1.8
2	−4.0	−1.0
3	−4.9	−0.3
4	−2.7	−1.8
5	−2.5	−1.2
6	−2.2	−1.8
7	−2.9	0.3
8	−2.7	1.2
9	−2.7	1.3
10	−3.1	1.2

[a] Mean changes are based on the rating of the chosen alternative minus the rating of the unchosen alternative.

[b] Maximum regret = −6.91 and maximum dissonance reduction = .36.

[c] Maximum regret = −4.67 and maximum dissonance reduction = 3.50.

Summary

Do the three foregoing studies on sequential effects add up to a consistent conclusion? If we disregard the focused-attention variable of the Brehm and Wicklund (1970) experiment there is a constant theme running through these experiments. The Brehm (1962a) study suggested strongly that regret dissipates with the passage of time from decision, and complementing this finding was evidence in the latter two experiments for an increasing dissonance reduction as time passed. The evidence from Walster's experiment was not altogether convincing, primarily because of a brief period of dissonance reduction preceding the regret found at four minutes, and further, the trend in the Brehm and Wicklund study was not significant. Still, the three experiments taken together imply that regret and dissonance reduction are separable processes, and that as regret fades, dissonance reduction takes hold.

Independent of these general sequential effects, is there any other evidence for Festinger's thesis? Festinger's explanation of regret assumes that the phenomenon results from the salience of dissonant cognitions, implying a good method of creating regret. Shouldn't regret be found if a person's attention can be brought to those aspects of a decision that make him uncomfortable? This was accomplished in the Brehm and Wicklund (1970) experiment, and perhaps surprisingly, subjects appeared to react defensively to the salient negative trait of their chosen alternative. Forced attention brought on dissonance reduction instead of regret.

Does the salience finding of Brehm and Wicklund invalidate the dissonance-theory analysis of regret? More specifically, does the experiment show that regret has nothing to do with dissonance arousal? The experiment attempted to rub subjects' noses in inconsistent cognitions, and this process increased dissonance reduction while decreasing regret. It is conceivable, then, that regret is a phenomenon that occurs for theoretical reasons completely independent of dissonance arousal, and that focused attention given to inconsistent cognitions serves only to magnify dissonance reduction effects. But there are other possibilities as well:

1. The salience manipulation may have increased both regret and dissonance reduction, but the process may have been so accelerated that the regret was manifested even before the first postdecision measure. This eventuality obviously cannot be ruled out. Nevertheless, it does not seem likely. For one thing, Walster's experiment produced a regret 4 min after the decision, and assuming that the information to be processed by her subjects was not more complex than the information of Brehm and Wicklund, we find it difficult to imagine that regret would have been instantaneous in the latter study.

2. Regret may indeed be the natural outcome of focusing on dissonant cognitions during the dissonance-reduction process, as proposed by Festinger. As the dissonance becomes salient in the person's contemplations of the elements of decision, regret is thereby manifested. But when the salience is introduced

artifically, being forced upon the person who has decided, there may be a defensive reaction. Forced salience probably does not fit naturally into the person's ongoing efforts at dissonance reduction. When various cognitive elements are forced into salience by outside influences, those elements may have already been dealt with by the person, hence a defensive reaction could result, or else he may not yet be ready to deal with them—also resulting in a defensive reaction. Unfortunately, if this reasoning is correct a test of Festinger's analysis of regret does not seem likely, since the researcher who must wait for a "naturally occurring" salience of dissonant cognitions is not in a position to manipulate experimentally that salience. At best, Festinger's proposal might then be tested by correlating within individuals the amount of regret with the amount of dissonance reduction, not that this approach would be especially informative.

Given the research discussed thus far, what conclusions might be drawn? The most important finding is the fact of a sequential process. It does seem clear that regret, whether measured through recall of disonant cognitions or tendency toward preference reversal, is a real phenomenon. It also appears as though dissonance reduction is less then instantaneous, and builds as time beyond the decision elapses.

HOW LONG DOES DISSONANCE REDUCTION LAST?

Research discussed thus far has been concerned with events near the decision point. We have seen (in Festinger & Walster, 1964) that preference reversals can occur just prior to the decision, and we have also seen that regret seems to manifest soon after the decision. But how long does the dissonance reduction phase continue, and more important, is that even a meaningful question?

We might begin by looking at three experiments. One of these, the one most often cited for its demonstration of long-term effects, is by Freedman (1965c). Using the "forbidden toy" paradigm of Aronson and Carlsmith (1963), Freedman ran subjects through the manipulations, then measured their attraction to the toys at least 23 days later, and up to 64 days later. The behavioral measure of desire for playing with the forbidden toy provided clear support for the theory, even after that long interval.

Another relevant study is by Walster (1964), cited above. It might be recalled that her strongest dissonance finding was for subjects measured at 15 min after the decision, whereas at 90 min there was only a nonsignificant trace of dissonance reduction. Finally, an experiment by Crano and Messé (1970) shows the same kind of effect as in Walster's (1964) 90-min condition, but more dramatically. Subjects engaged in the now-familiar essay-writing task, and composed counterattitudinal essays advocating the drafting of college students. Some subjects were offered $.50 for their performance, and others were promised $5. Half of the subjects received the attitude measure immediately after their essay-writing performance, but the other half were asked to perform an irrelevant drawing task before finally receiving the measure 15–20 min later. The results indicated that the dissonance theory prediction was supported only at the time of the immediate measurement. A so-called reinforcement effect resulted at the later measurement.

These three studies do not add up to a unitary conclusion. Walster found a diminution of dissonance-reduction effects after 90 min, Crano and Messé found the obliteration of dissonance effects after only 20 min, yet a substantial effect was obtained by Freedman after a month or two. Turning first to Freedman's (1965c) results, how should this dramatically persistent effect be interpreted? It is tempting to say that dissonance arousal lingered on for two months, or alternatively, that dissonance arousal and reduction were reinvoked once the subject was placed back into the situation involving previous choice objects. According to either of these alternatives the effects would be a direct reflection of active efforts at dissonance reduction. But alternatively, it is equally plausible that all of the dissonance reduction took place immediately after the decision, and that the consequent attitude change simply persisted. It is as though subjects' attitudes, once changed in the service of dissonance reduction, persisted in unaltered form in the absence of any other forces toward change. If this is true it would never be surprising to find remnants of dissonance reduction even after years, unless other forces have entered to alter the dissonance-produced attitude change. If this latter alternative is at all viable, no one should be astonished when dissonance reduction appears to sustain itself over a lengthy interval, for such effects certainly do not necessitate the indefinite continuation of the motivational state.

Returning to the contradictory findings, it seems quite evident that dissonance reduction, once demonstrated, does not persist inevitably for great intervals. For one reason or other an immediate measurement tapped into dissonance effects in the Crano and Messé (1970) experiment, while in the case of Walster, the strongest dissonance effect was at 15 min. Perhaps the most striking finding of these two experiments was the reinforcement effect obtained by Crano and Messé at 15–20 min. Ironically that is almost exactly the point at which Walster found the most dissonance reduction.

If it may be assumed that the Crano and Messé subjects in the "delayed-measurement" conditions were attempting dissonance reduction immediately after the decision (even though they weren't measured then), why did the effect dissipate? The same question may be asked of Walster's 90-min condition. It seems obvious from these results that the outcome of a person's dissonance reduction does not easily become a fixed part of his cognitive structure, and the results clearly imply a falling off of the arousal state of dissonance over time. Otherwise Walster's 90-min subjects should have been as motivated to reduce dissonance as her 15-min subjects; and analogously, Crano and Messé's 15–20-min subjects should have demonstrated effects similar to those measured earlier. Apparently the sequence of events in those two experiments was this: Fairly early after the decision subjects proceeded to manifest dissonance reduction, no matter whether a measure was taken or not, and as dissonance arousal dissipated (or declined for other reasons) the dissonance reduction effects also slipped away.

The preceding explanation of the two experiments showing a declining effect makes good sense in terms of a theory about drive, for if the drive state is the sole determinant of the person's responses, there presumably is a point at which the drive is satisfied, and the responses cease. But is this reasoning sensible in the context of dissonance arousal? The "drive" is satisfied by the person's changing his attitude in the three studies we are presently considering, but it does not seem that attitude change would be a very satisfactory solution for the person unless it were permanent. Just as a meal is only a temporary solution for the hungry individual, attitude change that subsequently reverts to the premeasured attitude would leave the person in the same state of dissonance arousal he started with. But would a "regression" in attitude change have this effect? Only if the dissonance-arousing cognitions were still salient, and it seems quite likely that the salience of discrepancies between attitudes and behaviors does not persist indefinitely. Brehm's study of recall suggests directly that a person's recall of dissonant relationships slips quickly.

The conclusion we can draw from this reasoning is the following. Dissonance reduction effects can be either short or long lived, depending on the presence of at least one of two factors:

1. If the attitude change or behavior change entailed in dissonance reduction freezes, just as a new response in the person's repertoire, then we would expect to find dissonance reduction effects no matter when the measure is taken. This kind of persistence no doubt assumes the absence of strong forces toward returning to one's original attitudes, and such forces most certainly existed in the Crano and Messé study, in which subjects were asked to take a highly unpopular position. In contrast, subjects in the Freedman study would probably not have experienced strong forces toward returning to their "original" attitudes toward the toys, for their exposure to the toys prior to dissonance arousal was quite limited.

2. If dissonance reduction effects are viewed solely as the product of contemporaneous dissonance *arousal*, long-term effects would be expected only if the dissonant relations remained salient at future points of measurement. Unless something definite is known about conditions leading to increased salience, the only fair statement about longevity of dissonance reduction effects is that the longevity will depend largely on whether or not the circumstances of dissonance arousal lend themselves to a continued salience.

WHAT MEDIATES POSTDECISIONAL SEQUENTIAL PROCESSES?

The dwindling of apparent dissonance reduction with time can easily be explained in terms of the falling off of salience. At the time of induction of dissonant elements, whether experimentally or otherwise, the various elements should be highly salient, accounting for the typical finding of evidence for the theory when measurements are taken soon after dissonance-arousing decisions. As noted in earlier studies (Brehm & Wicklund, 1970; Carlsmith et al., 1969), salience does make a considerable difference. It seems highly plausible that the person would come to think about other matters as the original dissonance-arousing situation gradually becomes past history.

But what mediates the incremental effect, most notable in Walster's experiment and suggested in Brehm's recall experiment and in the Salience condition of Brehm and Wicklund? Evidently there can be an interval following the decision during which dissonance reduction builds, and thus far we have noted only that elapsed time is the determinant. What happens during those first several postdecisional minutes? An experiment by Davidson (1964) offers a definite hint.

After the manner of Davis and Jones (1960) male subjects were induced to derogate someone who ostensibly was another subject. The format was much the same as the original experiment, although all of Davidson's subjects were run under conditions of high choice and none of them anticipated an opportunity to explain the circumstances of their insults to the target person. Subjects first heard a supposed tape-recorded interview involving the target, then half of the subjects were induced to consider carefully the attributes of the target. This was accomplished by asking them to fill out a 16-item questionnaire, giving their first impression of him. Subjects were then goaded into reading a highly critical and uncomplimentary evaluation to the target person, then a measure of liking for the other was given. A second experimental variable was the timing of the liking measure: Some subjects received it immediately following the discrepant act and others waited for 8 min.

The measure of dissonance reduction was the subject's dislike for his insulted target person. In comparing the four conditions it was found that the least dissonance reduction occurred among subjects not given prior familiarity and whose liking for the target was measured immediately. The other three conditions showed more dislike and were not significantly different from one another. Within the condition of low prior familiarity it was evident that dissonance reduction increased over the 8-min interval, a finding consistent with Brehm and Wicklund, and Walster. But more important are the results for prior familiarity. Davidson found a main effect for the familiarity variable, such that subjects who were induced to become knowledgeable about the target person manifested a greater degree of dissonance reduction. The impact of prior familiarity was especially great among subjects measured immediately, but it had no effect at the 8-min measurement point.

These results suggest that a time interval (8 min) which is important for the dissonance reduction process can be supplanted by an experimentally created familiarity with facets of the dissonance-arousing situation. It would appear, therefore, that one function of the time interval immediately following the dissonance-producing act is to allow the person to gain familiarity with the dissonant cognitions. Festinger (1964) may be correct in his analysis of regret—it is entirely possible that the individual thinks carefully about the dissonant elements in order to deal better with his dissonance, and it would follow that dissonance reduction should then be most apparent after the person has had time to familiarize himself with the elements. Davidson's procedure allowed some subjects to substitute a predecisional familiarity for what may be the more common self-generated postdecisional increase in familiarity of cognitive elements.

Why Familiarity?

If familiarity with the cognitive elements does bolster dissonance reduction, why does it have this effect? Returning to the Davidson procedure, what precisely were the dissonant cognitions? First, the cognition most resistant to change was the behavior of having derogated the other, a cognition that should have been quite clear to the subject. One of the more obvious dissonant cognitions would have been any virtues associated with the other person, thus we might presume that dissonance would be considerable to the degree that the subject realized that his target possessed laudable traits. In a subsequent experiment Davidson obtained independent evidence that the effect of his familiarity induction was that of increasing liking for the target. This effect was on a predecisional measure, which means that subjects given prior familiarity in the original experiment possessed a relatively high number of dissonant cognitions upon committing themselves to a fairly uncivilized act. It is no wonder, then, that they showed more dissonance reduction. Similarly, those measured 8 min later presumably had time to reflect on the characteristics of the target person, and it is reasonable that this reflection would have brought to mind positive characteristics, in a way analogous to the predecisional familiarity induction. Accordingly, dissonance reduction increased over the 8-min interval for subjects who did not already have a substantial familiarity.

As it happens, the small number of experiments on enhanced salience have given the subject a greater familiarity with cognitive elements that were inconsistent with his choice, and in this respect were similar to the Davidson study. Brehm and Wicklund reminded the subject of the negative feature of the chosen alternative, while Carlsmith et al. (1969) and Zanna et al. (1973) made salient an attractive toy that had been rejected. But this is not to say that increased salience, or familiarity, will inevitably bring higher cognizance of dissonant elements. Davidson easily could have arranged things so that increased familiarity would mean familiarity with objectionable features of the target person, and certainly the same could have been accomplished by Brehm and Wicklund (1970), Carlsmith *et al.* (1969), and Zanna *et al.* (1973). This would mean that the passage of time after a decision would not always bring about an increment in dissonance reduction. In some situations the passage of time would bring most people to think about the consonant features of their course of action, and the result would be a lessened predisposition to dissonance reduction.

There is another line of reasoning that could be taken. In the *fait accompli* research (Chapter 4) it became evident that the person who is largely ignorant of the consequences of his actions fails to show dissonance reduction when unanticipated consequences arise. If familiarity with the decision alternatives is slight and a person makes a decision, there is a sense in which he can profess ignorance about the consequences of his actions. For example, even if he understands generally that his actions may be injurious to an innocent victim, he can conceivably excuse himself from responsibility on the grounds of a less than complete understanding of the entire situation. If he is only vaguely familiar with the victim, or is only vaguely familiar with the nature of the injuries he brings about, he can allow himself to feel that he was not completely in control. Responsibility may be attributed to others, especially to whoever brought him to commit the injury. But as he devotes additional thought to the circumstances and nature of his action he would arrive at a much clearer picture of his dissonance-arousing situation. The personality of the victim may become clearer in his mind, there may be more definite comprehension of the possible consequences of his actions, and there might also develop a firmer realization that he could have elected to do otherwise if he had so chosen. As the picture of the entire situation becomes more distinct, so should develop a feeling that the consequences were not anticipated. A sense of responsibility should develop, resulting in increased efforts at dissonance reduction.

If this latter explanation is correct, familiarity would in most cases have the result of enhancing dissonance reduction. But this is not the case for the first interpretation, whereby familiarity might have either of two opposing effects, depending on whether it is primarily dissonant, or consonant cognitions that are uncovered as the person gains increased familiarity.

SUMMARY

The purpose of this chapter has been to review evidence bearing on sequential processes associated with dissonance arousal and reduction, and to hazard some explanations for these sequential effects. It was noted first that an investigator's ability to understand when commitment occurs is central in analyzing sequential processes. This is because dissonance reduction does not seem to be set in motion until the decision is definite, nor until the person knows with certainty what he is accepting and rejecting by making his decision. There is a possibility that dissonance can be created prior to a definite commitment, as evidenced by one experiment that showed considerable predecisional preference reversal. Such preference reversal may, however, be entirely attributable to psychological processes other than dissonance arousal. Thus, the important point about the predecisional period is the following: There is no evidence that the dissonance reduction processes are set in motion until the person has reached a definite decision.

Following the decision there is evidently a transitory period during which the person appears to be increasingly aware of the discrepant nature of his actions. This phase can be reflected in heightened awareness of dissonant elements, and by cognitive changes that move in directions opposite to dissonance reduction. As time progresses these regret phenomena are supplanted by dissonance reduction, and most of the evidence shows that dissonance reduction increases as time after the decision elapses. This increase is easily explainable in terms of the person's heightened familiarity with cognitive elements that are basic to the decision. Dissonance reduction does not necessarily last indefinitely, and may in many instances be extremely short lived. More important, the attitude and behavior change serving dissonance reduction are by no means permanent: There is good evidence that the person reverts to predecisional attitudes and behaviors once the dissonant relations are no longer salient. This is not true in every case, but should be especially likely if there are forces operating on the person toward reverting to his original, predissonance-arousal cognitions.

9
Modes of Response to Dissonance

There are three broad classes of behaviors that can result from the prior arousal of dissonance. The first of these consists of those responses that mirror the presence of cognitive dissonance, such as the recall of discrepant information and regret discussed in Chapter 8. The second is the active attempt to cope with dissonance, consisting of adding consonant cognitions or subtracting dissonant cognitions. Finally, independent of these first two, there are behaviors carried out in the interest of dissonance avoidance. Such behaviors might be directed either at taking the person's conscious attention off the dissonant relations, or alternatively, off the circumstances that prompt him to think of the dissonant relations. This chapter focuses on the last two, and has been written in an effort to capture the variety of circumstances that lead to the many forms of dissonance reduction and avoidance.

While it is true that some research has examined individual differences as sources of differential reactions to dissonance arousal, this chapter will not discuss such investigations. This is because individual differences in the use of any particular mode of dissonance reduction (or avoidance) can reflect processes other than the differential preference for modes. For example, a person who makes little use of the mode of selective avoidance of information may do so because of an ability to tolerate dissonance, or alternatively, because the circumstances did not create much dissonance for him in the first place. Since all of the relevant individual differences contain this kind of ambiguity, they will be reserved for a Chapter 14, which is devoted entirely to individual differences. Within that context the question of preferences for modes will be raised again.

RESISTANCE TO CHANGE

Aside from the magnitude of dissonance, we have seen that the most general factor controlling dissonance reduction is the resistance to change of relevant cognitions. This follows from the fact that once dissonance occurs, it can be reduced or eliminated only by elimination of dissonant cognitions, addition of consonant cognitions, or change in importance of relevant cognitions. The sources of resistance to change are at least two: the physical or psychological difficulty of changing a bit of "knowledge" (e.g., the extent of commitment), and the extent to which a given change would create further dissonance.

In certain cases none of the relevant elements in a dissonant relationship will be easily changeable, and under these conditions one might expect dissonance reduction to take some form other than change in one or another cluster of relevant elements. One such possible form, as we have seen, is the addition of consonant cognitive elements. The addition of consonant elements reduces the proportion of relevant elements that are dissonant with each other.

The resistance of a cognitive element to change is a function of the difficulty of changing whatever reality it represents, on the one hand, and the ambiguity of its significance on the other; that is, resistance derives from the difficulty of changing its physical source and from the difficulty of changing one's perception or judgment of it.

We do not mean to imply that only physical or social objects other than one's self are sources of resistance to change. Indeed, the same factors control the resistance to change of cognitions about the self. For example, cognitions about one's own emotions and motivations can be relatively changeable or not, depending upon the clarity with which such a cognitive element is associated with unambiguous physiological symptoms or overt behaviors, or more generally, with some undeniable reality about the self.

Throughout the history of research on dissonance theory investigators have assumed, usually implicitly, that a specified and explicit behavioral commitment serves as the basis of a cognition highly resistant to change. Very seldom is there any effort to spell out a hierarchy of cognitive elements with respect to relative resistance. The person is required to make a decision, and it is then assumed that cognitions other than the knowledge of having decided will be altered—meaning either subtracted or added. There is seldom any attempt to locate the cognitions least resistant to change in an effort to measure them, but instead, it is typically assumed that any relevant cognitions other than the behavior are subject to be rearranged in the interest of cognitive consistency.

This assumption about resistance to change of the behavior has proven to be quite workable. We have seen in numerous experiments that a great many cognitions are changed by subjects, in an apparent attempt to align such cognitions with whatever behavioral commitment is assumed to be highly resistant to change. Postdecisional change in attraction to chosen and/or unchosen alternatives has been the most common cognitive change measured, but we have also noted behavioral and physiological effects of dissonance reduction. In addition, there has been selective exposure, which entails the person's bringing himself into contact with consonant elements. Not all of the various effects of attitude change, behavior change, physiological change, or exposure need to be listed here, for virtually all of these effects fall into the following simple paradigm: The person makes a decision, which is presumed to be the basis of a cognition highly resistant to change, then change in *some other* cognitive element is measured. This line of research tells us very little about modes of dissonance reduction, except insofar as we might be interested in detailing the particular dimensions of attitude change, or the varieties of attitude-related behaviors that result in dissonance reduction. In fact, the line of research says more about researchers' assumptions concerning what is changeable and what is not than about subjects' preferences for various modes.

There is a possibility, about which we know very little, that the behavioral commitment is not always the basis of the most resistant cognition. Behavior change, or attempted behavior change, is seldom measured. This means that in many of the numerous studies examined thus far the subject may be telling himself that his behavior is other than what it is in fact, or he may have every intention of attempting to rescind that behavior as soon as possible. Even though he probably cannot actually rescind it in the experimental situation, he may find ways to take it back psychologically, by denying it or changing its meaning. This opens the consideration that subjects may often be changing cognitions about behavior, rather than just the attitudes discrepant with behaviors. To the extent that this is true, the tests of the theory are probably conservative; attitude change should be greater if it is the only changeable cognitive element. Further, it is also possible that "failure" experiments fail not because of a lack of dissonance, but because the behavioral element was easily changeable relative to the cognitions being measured.

The point of this discussion is that it would be profitable to develop a means of calculating the relative resistance to change of cognitive elements. And since this is not likely to be done with any great expediency, the alternative is to take safeguards with respect to the behavioral commitment—to see that a person would have difficulty in changing his cognitions about it.

PREFERENCES AMONG LESS RESISTANT MODES

Given that a specifiable behavioral commitment is the resistant element to change, do people exhibit preferences among other avenues of dissonance reduction? They certainly should if the theory is correct, since the use of a particular dissonance-reduction mechanism should be in proportion to its susceptibility to change. A finding of Brock and Buss (1962) is informative in this respect. Male and female subjects were asked to administer electric shock to either a male or female victim, under choice or no-choice instructions. Consistent with the expectations, subjects in the choice condition minimized the pain to the degree that the shock was high. But this happened only when the victim was male. The results were backward given a female victim, suggesting that the cognition of a young woman receiving severe shock was highly resistant to change. If dissonance was indeed aroused in those choice subjects who administered high shock to females, it should be expressed elsewhere.

Perceived Obligation

Brock and Buss report a measure of perceived obligation to administer the shocks. One way to reduce dissonance (add consonant elements) would be to see oneself as constrained in the shock giving, and this was apparently the mode chosen by subjects who shocked females. More obligation was expressed under high than low shock, and there was also more felt obligation when the victim was a female than when a male. Evidently there was a preference among modes in this experiment. Independent of whether or not the behavioral commitment to shock was the most resistant cognition (we may assume it was), subjects expressed clear preferences among the minimized-painfulness and perceived-obligation avenues of dissonance reduction, probably because of the difficulty of convincing oneself that a severe shock does not hurt a female victim.

A study by Cohen (1962b) resulted in much the same phenomenon as that just cited. This design was intended to explore the effect of repeated dissonances in a situation where those individual instances of dissonance arousal were on different dimensions. Of primary interest was the question of whether or not those separate arousals would cumulate.

We have no precise theoretical formulation to predict what the effect of repeated dissonance arousals might be, but we can indicate the logical possibilities and describe relevant evidence. The possibilities are that the occurrence of a given dissonance has no effect on reactions to subsequent unrelated dissonance, that it reduces the reaction to a subsequent unrelated dissonance, or that it increases the reaction to a subsequent unrelated dissonance. Increased reaction might occur if the psychological tension involved has aspects that are not specific to the arousing situation, thus allowing the accumulation of dissonance where there is insufficient opportunity to reduce it from one situation before another is presented. Increased reaction could also occur from increased sensitivity to all dissonances from the occurrence of a given one, or from behavioral dissonance reduction sets or practice effects that could carry over from one dissonance to another. On the other hand, decreased reaction could occur from avoidance tendencies aroused by previous dissonances, from learning to tolerate dissonance, and so forth. In the absence of any further theoretical knowledge about these and other possible mechanisms, we will simply describe a relevant study by Cohen.

A group of 48 Yale College students was used, all of whom were on the same side of each of five different current issues on campus. The issues were: (a) compulsory chapel for all students at Yale; (b) compulsory coats and ties at Yale, at all times, at all places, for all activities; (c) language requirement of compulsory Latin and Greek; (d) elimination of all cuts at Yale, that is, compulsory attendance at all classes; and (e) complete elimination of all intercollegiate athletics at Yale. The subjects indicated their positions on each of these issues, and were all at the negative end of the scale on all five issues.

Three weeks after the initial attitude measure, each student was asked to write an essay supporting one side or the other on each of the issues. This was done under the guise of a survey being carried out by a student for his honors research project under the auspices of "The Institute of Human Relations." It was "aimed at obtaining a clear and objective view of students' opinions for and against these proposals." All subjects were told that essays supporting both sides of each issue were being requested, though certain kinds of essays were then needed more than others. Some subjects were then asked to write an essay *supporting* their own position on each of the first four topics (the preconsonance condition); other subjects were asked to write an essay *opposing* their own position on these four topics (the predissonance condition). Thus some subjects engaged in behavior consonant with their attitudes; others engaged in behavior dissonant with their attitudes.

For the fifth topic, the elimination of all intercollegiate athletics, all subjects were told that essays in opposition to their private attitudes were needed. Thus, for all subjects, the fifth essay was inconsistent with their attitude. In addition, the subjects who had engaged in consonant or dissonant behavior were divided into two further groups: Some were given low justification for writing the discrepant fifth essay while others were given high justification. The justification consisted of various science-related reasons for the essay writing, plus the experimenter's need to complete the research.

The major concern in this study is with the effect of the repeated consonant and dissonant experiences (preconsonant and predissonant conditions) on reactions to the final dissonance–arousal situation. Since the latter involved the writing of an essay discrepant with private attitudes, it would ordinarily be expected that subjects would show some attitude change toward the position supported in the essay. Furthermore, such change would be expected to be inversely proportional to the force inducing the discrepant essay. Hence attitude change should be positive and greater in magnitude in the low-justification condition than in the high. This expectation applies directly to subjects in the preconsonance condition, for they are, theoretically, in a situation that has been shown by previous research to produce dissonance and consequent attitude change. The interest, then, centers on the comparative reactions of subjects in the predissonance condition. These subjects may, as noted before, react either more or less strongly because of having experienced a series of situations that presumably created dissonance.

In Table 8 are presented the attitude change scores for each of the experimental conditions on the intercollegiate athletics issue, the one on which all subjects wrote discrepant essays. An analysis of variance performed on the data indicates that while there was no main effect of the justification manipulation (F

TABLE 8
Attitude Change on the Fifth (Discrepant) Issue

	Justification	
	High	Low
Predissonance	.3[a]	−.1
Preconsonance	.1	.6

[a] A positive mean represents dissonance reduction.

= .08), the main effect of practice and the interaction between practice and justification were both significant (practice, $F = 4.73$, $p < .05$; practice X justification, $F = 8.53$, $p < .01$).

As was expected for the preconsonance condition, there was greater positive attitude change among those subjects receiving low justification than among those receiving high justification. In the predissonance condition, however, there is essentially no effect of the justification manipulation (the only difference being a slight trend in the negative direction), nor is there evidence of any attitude change consistent with attempts to reduce dissonance. As was said, the analysis of variance test of the interaction indicated that the justification manipulation had less of the predicted inverse effect in the predissonance condition that in the preconsonance condition. Thus, at least under the present conditions, repeated but essentially unrelated dissonances minimize the effect of a subsequent dissonance.

It should also be noted that within the low-justification condition (high dissonance) there is a difference in perceived obligation to take the discrepant stand: The predissonance subjects perceived that they were obliged more than the preconsonance subjects (3.41 versus 2.85; $p < .05$). The fact that the predissonance subjects were requested to write four discrepant essays prior to the central attitude issue, while the preconsonance subjects had only to write the last one in a discrepant manner, may have increased their sense of being forced.

On the other hand, change in obligation may be viewed as a potential mode of dissonance reduction, either complementary to or substitutive for attitude change. In the present experiment, given this difference in obligation, it may be assumed that the predissonance subjects reduced their dissonance in this manner more than the preconsonance subjects, and therefore did not use the avenue of attitude change. Thus the differences in attitude change (−.1 for the predissonance subjects, .6 for the preconsonance subjects) may be comprehensible not only in terms of differential prior experience in reducing dissonance, but perhaps even more because of the differential use of the avenue of perceived obligation as a mode of dissonance reduction. Once having reduced dissonance by increasing their perception of obligation, they may have had less need to do so via attitude change.

In any case, it may be well to dwell for a moment on the conditions under which this test occurred, particularly since there are no other data to help clarify the problems. First of all, it should be noted that the dissonance-arousal situations are not entirely dissimilar. They all involved writing an essay discrepant with one's private attitude, the only difference being the issue on which the essay was written. Although this relative similarity of dissonance-arousal conditions may make no difference conceptually, since the theory would not treat them as similar, it may make a difference in terms of the setting in which the study was done. That is, the issues all concerned possible actions about regulation of student activities by the school administration. Thus, if a student experienced dissonance on writing the first essay, he might have tried to reduce it by convincing himself that the administration is probably correct about such issues. Once he had convinced himself of this, he would experience little or no dissonance nor need to change his attitude on subsequent issues. Similarly, a student might have experienced dissonance on the first essay or two, but reduced it by convincing himself that college life should be hard and full of unpleasant regulations. Again, once convinced of this tenet, he would experience little or no dissonance in regard to the final test issue. In short, as far as dissonance theory is concerned the dissonance-arousal situations are similar in that they have some cognitive elements that can overlap, especially in regard to reduction of the dissonances.

A second general characteristic of this test is that the separate dissonance-arousal situations were presented one right after the other. If the obtained phenomenon of reduced reaction to a dissonance–arousal situation depends on a defensive reaction, or even perhaps a tolerance buildup, then it might also depend on this quick succession of events. Where dissonance-arousing situations are more widely spaced, defensive reactions and tolerances might have time to wear off between dissonances.

A third characteristic of this test is that the dissonance aroused by the preliminary essays should have been relatively slight, since there was little or no choice involved in taking the discrepant stand. What might happen with more intense preliminary dissonances is unclear, though the trends in the obtained results would indicate a possible reversal of the ordinary effect of justification.

In conclusion, it remains an open question whether the low-justification subjects in the predissonance condition changed less as a result of less dissonance arousal or whether they reduced dissonance via the mode of obligation increase, thereby obviating the need to change their attitudes. The fact that both obligation change and attitude change are inversely related within the practice conditions suggests that the repeated use of attutude change may not be a means of reducing dissonance for the predissonance subjects but, rather, that they increase their perception of being forced to comply with the discrepant request.

Varying the Reality Base of Relevant Cognitions

One source of resistance to change is whether or not a cognition has some basis in reality, especially when that reality can be perceived by others. If a person chooses among two alternatives, and expects the chosen one to be evaluated objectively by experts in the near future, his cognitions about that object should be resistant to changing away from their predecisional level. Given the prospect of forthcoming "objective" information, there are constraints against exaggerating the virtues of that object, and dissonance reduction efforts should be more seriously directed toward changing the evaluation of the nonchosen item. Walster, Berscheid, and Barclay (1967) designed an experiment to test this thinking.

Boys between approximately four and six years of age were asked to rate a number of toys, then were allowed to choose one to take home. Subsequent to the rerating that followed, resistance to change of evaluation of one of the toys was manipulated. The experimenter claimed that he would return to the subject the next week, on each of the five days, with information about the chosen (or nonchosen) toy. This information was supposedly to be based on reports of other young boys who had played with that same toy (whether the chosen or unchosen). Assuming that a marked change in evaluation of a toy might clash with forthcoming reports of the experimenter's survey information, such a change would only serve to increase or sustain dissonance. Therefore, all of the change should be exhibited with respect to the toy about which no forthcoming information was anticipated. Table 9 supports this reasoning convincingly: note that the dissonance-reducing evaluative changes are considerably bigger when the subject's cognitive work is not constrained by anticipated information about what other boys think of the toy.

TABLE 9
Mean Amount of Dissonance Reduced by Changes in
the Chosen and Rejected Alternatives by
Subjects in Various Conditions

Expectation	Chosen alternative	Rejected alternative
Subjects who expect to hear objective information on chosen alternative	.7[a]	1.0
Subjects who expect to hear objective information on rejected alternative	1.6	.2

[a]Positive values represent dissonance reduction.

The Walster *et al.* (1967) experiment is one of very few that have systematically rendered difficult the use of certain modes of dissonance reduction. The experiment is especially compelling because of the way that one set of cognitions was tied to objective reality. The study implies that derogation of the rejected alternative may often be the preferred method of dissonance reduction, for there are many circumstances in which people are likely to encounter further information about their chosen alternatives, especially information that will force cognitions to be veridical with reality (Brehm, 1972). Surely this is true whenever someone purchases an automobile, or any other material commodity which others also own and upon which others are likely to comment.

The research of this section has implied a negative relationship among avenues of dissonance reduction: If one mode is resistant to change, another will be used in its place. Rather than specifically blocking off individual modes, Steiner and Rogers (1963) took the tack of correlating subjects' use of the various modes, assuming that if one type of dissonance reduction were adopted, another would not. Subjects were placed into a conformity bind in which they would feel pressure to comply with the judgments of an unlikable confederate. Presumably dissonance was created by the mere discrepancy between judgments. Not only was the degree of conformity measured, but Steiner and Rogers also took note of other possible routes of dissonance reduction, including rejection (negative evaluation) of the confederate and underrecall of the number of times disagreement with the confederate was manifested. If a subject deals with dissonance arousal by conforming to the judgments of the other, he should tend away from the use of other routes. The results showed this very effect: The use of rejection was negatively correlated with conformity, and so was underrecall of disagreements negatively correlated with conformity.

CHANGING THE BEHAVIORAL COMMITMENT

Unfortunately the literature on dissonance theory has fostered the idea that behavioral commitment is inevitably the starting point from which we can calculate changes in cognitions. This is patently false. First of all, there are studies in which dissonance has plausibly been created without the subject's overtly committing himself to an observable behavior (e.g., Aronson, Turner, & Carlsmith, 1963; Bochner & Insko, 1966; Bramel, 1962, 1963; Zimbardo, 1960). In some of these studies assumptions (implicit or not) were necessary about the relative resistance to change of a person's opinion when confronted with a persuasive communication. Bramel's research required assumptions about the resistance to change of the person's own opinion of his heterosexuality. These investigations contained no overt behavioral commitment around which subsequent cognitions might be aligned, and even if there were such a commitment, it would not necessarily be absolutely resistant, a point which the following studies illustrate.

When a person engages in a discrepant behavior there is a definite sense in which uncommitting himself (when possible) takes the least psychological toll. Uncommitment allows a circumvention of the cognitive work necessary given commitment, and restores the person to what may have been initially an equilibrium with respect to consistency of cognitions. The Davis and Jones (1960) experiment shows that when subjects could uncommit themselves, they did not change their attutudes. However, those subjects whose discrepant behavior was irrevocable became more negative toward the person they had derogated. Having chosen to commit themselves, and with their discrepant behavior clear and unambiguous, they could only change their attitudes toward alignment with behavior as a way of reducing the dissonance engendered by that behavior.

A gambling experiment by Festinger (1957) makes the rather dramatic point that the original behavioral commitment can change provided dissonance grows to such an extent that the commitment becomes the most readily changeable element. His subjects were provided with a small amount of money for use in a card game, and could choose which side to play. On the basis of information provided before the decision there were definite hints that one side should be superior to the other. After several hands of the game some subjects found that they were winning slightly, and others found that they were losing, anywhere from a slight amount to a substantial loss. The primary measure of dissonance was selective exposure to a complicated graph that was supposed to show the subject his true probability of eventually winning the game. Festinger argued that as losses became increasingly significant, subjects would tend more to avoid examination of the graph, out of an expectation that it would tell them they chose the losing side. The results generally followed this expectation except among subjects experiencing *extreme* losses, who showed more interest in the graph than moderate losers. The latter exposure was interpreted by Festinger as reflecting subjects' intention to switch sides (which they were allowed to do for a slight penalty). Festinger argues that if the dissonance is so large as to almost overcome the resistance to changing behavior, a person might then be expected to increase the dissonance temporarily so as to change behavior. Indeed, over half of the subjects who were suffering extreme losses elected to alter their behavior and switch to the opposite side.

We may conceptualize this experiment, and a replication by Cohen, Brehm, and Latané (1959), as cases of dissonance between behavioral commitment and monetary disadvantage implied by the commitment. These two studies are unusual in the literature on dissonance in that the behavior could be changed— the commitment was revocable. But the monetary loss was irrevocable, difficult to deny, and although it could be minimized psychologically, there was no way to change the monetary outcome. Since the behavior was subject to change, thus less resistant than the fact of monetary loss, it was changed when dissonance grew to considerable proportions.

The Davis and Jones study and the gambling experiments of Festinger (1957) and Cohen *et al.* (1959) underline the point that dissonance theory is not inevitably a theory about attitudes coming to be consistent with behavior. Behavioral commitment should be viewed as the source of cognitions that can be relatively resistant to change. Typically experiments are designed such that the behavior is irreversible and quite undeniable, but it is important to know that the theory can also predict revocation of the original commitment if other cognitions are strongly resistant to change.

SELECTION OF A MODE: TAKING WHATEVER IS AVAILABLE

Our thinking until this point has neglected the possibility that subjects may be less aware of some dissonance-reducing mechanisms than others. In discussing the studies of Brock and Buss (1962), Cohen, (1962b), Steiner and Rogers (1963), and Walster et al. (1967), it was assumed implicitly that the possible avenues of dissonance reduction were equally accessible in the sense of subjects' awareness of them, but not equally accessible with respect to resistance to change. It is conceivable that dissonance reduction might be spread over a number of possible modes provided they are all susceptible to change and provided the person is aware of their potential for restoring consistency within his cognitive framework. But if the person were kept in the dark about certain of these avenues of consonance, those few modes of which he is aware should absorb the brunt of his dissonance reduction efforts. An experiment by Götz–Marchand, Götz, and Irle (1974) is the source of this thinking about differential awareness of modes, and they report an experiment designed to examine the idea.

Sixteen-year-old males initially received an intelligence test. They also gave estimates of their own intelligence in numerical terms coinciding with the scale associated with the test. They were contacted again a week later, expecting to receive their test results and to answer a questionnaire. At the outset of the second session they all received rather negative feedback ostensibly based on the prior IQ test. Each subject received a score 18 points below his own Session 1 self-estimate, certainly a dissonance-arousing source of information. Even though the subject did not knowingly choose to receive a low score, he should have felt responsibility for the outcome of the test since IQ should be seen as related to one's abilities. As noted in Chapter 4, forseeability of a consequence is not necessary as long as the individual believes that the outcome is a product of his own performance.

How is such dissonance dealt with? Two modes selected for study by Götz–Marchand et al. (1974) were acceptance of the low score—hence a revision downward of self-estimate, and rejection of the test as a meaningful instrument for measuring intelligence. Götz–Marchand et al. (1974) conceived of these two modes as differing radically in resistance to change. Since a person's intelligence is a central, presumably stable aspect of himself, there should be strong resistance to lowering it to reduce dissonance. Besides, the obvious fact of desiring to

be intellectually capable serves as a clear source of resistance to change. Derogation of the test, in contrast, seemed to them a ready dissonance-reduction
device, and certainly subjects felt no long-lasting commitment to a positive
evaluation of any particular test.

Following the IQ reports subjects responded to a form that listed five possible
dissonance reduction devices. The first and the fifth of these were the modes just
noted, while the second, third, and fourth were modes that the authors preferred
not to analyze because the resistance to change of those modes was in question.
For half of the subjects the revised IQ estimate measure came first and test-rejection last, while the opposite order was used for the remaining subjects. The
crucial variable was whether subjects were aware of the fifth item while filling
out the first. Half of them proceeded through the questionnaire without reading
ahead; the others read all five items before filling any of them out. Therefore,
some of the subjects could have anticipated use of the dissonance-reduction
mode located at the fifth position in the questionnaire, while others had no idea
what was coming from item to item.

The results are shown in Table 10. The revised IQ-estimate measure was scored
so that a high score means a shift downward, in the direction of feedback. The
data indicate that this mode served as a major source of dissonance reduction (X
= 10.1) only when subjects did not know what other modes might be forthcoming. In all other cases it was used much less, consistent with the thesis that
changes in self-estimate of intelligence are highly resistant to change. The
interaction of these four conditions was highly significant. The test-rejection
mode was scored such that a low score represents a low evaluation of the test, or
dissonance reduction. The interaction was also significant here, but the pattern is
slightly different. The only place that test rejection was conspicuously *not*
employed was in the condition where it appeared fifth in the series of questions

TABLE 10
Means of Revised IQ Estimate and Test Rejection

| | | Order of modes on questionnaire | |
| | | Revised IQ | Test rejection |
Measure	Awareness condition	estimate first	first
Revised IQ estimate measure[a]	Aware of subsequent items	4.7	5.1
	Not aware of subsequent items	10.1	4.5
Test rejection measure[b]	Aware of subsequent items	3.2	3.1
	Not aware of subsequent items	6.8	2.6

[a] A high value represents dissonance reduction.
[b] A low value represents dissonance reduction.

and subjects did not anticipate it ($\overline{X}$ = 6.8). In all other cases it was used equally and to a high degree.

These results are completely consistent with the reasoning of Götz–Marchand *et al.* (1974). The cognition about one's own intelligence, being highly resistant to change, was employed significantly only when subjects saw no other clear alternatives to dealing with their dissonance. Conversely, the only time subjects resisted the use of test rejection was when they were unable to anticipate its placement in the questionnaire.

We find these results to be intriguing. It is evident that people do not have liberal access to the plethora of dissonance-reduction mechanisms designated as such by investigators. The subjects of Götz–Marchand *et al.* (1974) employed a mode of dissonance reduction only to the degree that it was made evident through the questionnaire, suggesting that even the relatively "obvious" modes of dissonance reduction are used systematically only when all subjects are made aware of them. It would appear that devices for coping with dissonance are idiosyncratic, and that universal use of any given mode might be made only to the degree that it is made salient. Of course salience would not always require an experimental induction. If a person is in a familiar dissonance-arousing setting we might suppose that he would take advantage of whatever avenues of reduction he used on previous occasions.

The present results should not be taken to imply that dissonance reduction can result only by filling out a questionnaire, for the Götz–Marchand *et al.* (1974) study does not show this. But the experiment does demonstrate that making the person aware of easily changeable cognitions results in his reduced usage of cognitions that are highly resistant. It is not as though the person in the "known" condition understood that a good mode of dissonance reduction was waiting for him in Item 5, and then saved his dissonance until actually arriving at that item. Instead, it seems highly plausible that he took advantage of that mode as soon as he was made aware of it, with resultant decreased dissonance reduction on the first mode measured.

With these results as a taking-off point, it would be easy to think of previous research that might be explained in ways consistent with the present results. For example, Götz–Marchand *et al.* (1974) note that among the four dissonance-relevant questions asked of subjects by Festinger and Carlsmith (1959), positive results were obtained only on the first. Dissonance reduction may have been reduced sufficiently through that one mode, even before subjects became aware of specific alternative approaches to dissonance reduction. Returning to the chapter on focused attention, it is possible that focused attention on specific decision alternatives or on the person himself served to make salient the specific modes being measured. It was assumed in that chapter that focused attention had the effect of enhancing the person's awareness of the dissonance per se, but the present experiment implies that the experimentally induced focusing may have served to bring modes of dissonance reduction into focus. The results of that chapter would, of course, have been the same no matter whether it was the modes or the dissonance, or both, that were affected by the forced attention techniques.

A varying attention given to alternative modes could also be the basis of almost any variety of sequential effect. For example, if a person showed dissonance reduction on a questionnaire shortly after the decision, such effects might appear to dissipate upon later measurements if he became increasingly aware of other modes as time passed. This suggestion would necessarily assume that dissonance reduction on a specific mode would not become frozen, but instead, that a person might discard early dissonance-reduction efforts as he encountered routes involving cognitions that were more readily changeable. This might have occurred in the Crano and Messé (1970) experiment of Chapter 8, in which the inverse relationship between payment and attitude change vanished, and even reversed, after 15–20 min. There is no way to know what other modes may have usurped attitude change as a way to coping with the dissonance arousal, but it does seem reasonable that a person left to his own devices would come to think of novel methods of attaining cognitive consistency.

An Experiment on the Hydraulic Relationship among Modes

How reasonable is the assumption that an initial dissonance-reducing response will be withdrawn or abandoned when a more workable one enters the picture? ("Workable" refers here to the qualities of not being resistant to change and of not implying further dissonance.) There was no evidence bearing on this question in the first Götz–Marchand et al. (1974) experiment, but they report an Experiment II that seems to answer this question quite well. A simplified version of the first study was run whereby subjects received two modes, in one order or the other, and under conditions where subsequent questionnaire items could not be anticipated. As soon as the questionnaire was completed, they were asked to respond to a second copy of it, with the excuse that "We are interested in your answers after you know all the questions and had time to think about them." The results showed dramatic changes in usage of the two modes in the condition where the most resistant mode appeared first in the questionnaire. In that condition the tendency to lower one's own IQ estimate was reduced substantially on the second form, whereas there was a marked increase in test derogation. These same tendencies were significantly less apparent in the condition where test evaluation appeared first on the questionnaire. This is the first evidence we have seen for such flexibility in the workings of dissonance reduction modes, and the experiment clearly demonstrates that the continued use of an avenue of dissonance reduction is not inevitable. If a more satisfying and less resistant mode occurs to the person, highly resistant modes engaged earlier will be abandoned.

AVOIDANCE OF DISSONANCE

Independent of adding consonant elements, removing dissonant ones, or lowering the importance of either, there is a mode of coping with dissonance that simply involves not thinking about the dissonant relations. We cannot say at this point whether avoidance will generally be preferred to actual dissonance reduction, or vice versa, although certainly one factor contributing to a relative preference would be the availability of easily changeable cognitive elements.

One of the few studies directed specifically at the avoidance issue was Brehm's experiment on recall (Chapter 8). As was emphasized in that chapter, there was an especially good recall of dissonant cognitions immediately after the dissonance was introduced, but after a week the motivation to avoid became apparent: At that point there was better recall for consonant than dissonant elements, showing that avoidance can result if sufficient time is given to allow for the manifestation of memory differences.

The research on selective exposure might also be interpreted as an avoidance phenomenon. When a person shows a preference for exposure to messages consistent with his choices there is no evidence that he is performing cognitive work in form of adding consonant or subtracting dissonant elements. Of course it is possible that selective exposure is carried out for the purpose of aiding the person in finding new, consonant bits of information, but it is also perfectly reasonable that exposure is a tactic to allow a decreased awareness of dissonant relations. When someone immerses himself in an advertisement for a recently purchased automobile, it becomes possible temporarily to forget the negative features, and the more intense the exposure was, the better.

Avoidance of dissonance does not necessarily have to be limited to avoidance of actual dissonance arousal. Conceivably dissonance could be anticipated predecisionally and averted before it is even aroused. For example, Braden and Walster (1964) offered subjects a choice between two records under either of the following conditions. In an "anticipated consonance" condition the subject found that she would have to read recommendations of the record she received to groups of girls, while "anticipated dissonance" subjects discovered that the record *not received* would have to be promoted by them to other girls. Subjects then had a choice of methods of receiving a record: They could either choose it freely or be assigned a record by the flip of a coin. It was thought that anticipated dissonance subjects could readily avert the dissonance that would be aroused through a decision, and this proved correct: 71% of these subjects elected to abide by the coin toss rather than decide, compared against only 19% for the anticipated consonance condition. The only weakness with this study is that it is difficult to conclude with certainty that the avoidance was avoidance of dissonance per se. For example, the anticipated dissonance instructions undoubtedly led to higher conflict in that condition, and the experiment might also be labeled as a study of conflict avoidance.

Returning to avoidance of postdecision dissonance, a number of studies are reported by Pallak *et al.* (1967) and Pallak (1970) which suggest that a person will attempt to take attention off dissonance arousal through activity. An aspect of the Pallak (1970) experiment serves to illustrate the point. In one pair of conditions subjects were asked to write a counterattitudinal essay under either high- or low-choice conditions. After committing themselves, subjects then found that there would be a half-hour delay before writing the essay, and during that time they were told to perform a copying task—seemingly irrelevant to the dissonance-arousing task. Subjects in the choice condition subsequently showed greater retention for details of the copying task than did low-choice subjects, an effect that may reflect choice subjects' efforts to distract themselves from the dissonance.

In summary, a clear alternative to actual manipulation of cognitive elements is the avoidance of focusing on them. This mode of coping with dissonance has only begun to be explored, and it remains to be seen how the alternatives of reduction and avoidance operate when juxtaposed. The original theory makes no definite statements about this interrelationship, and this would seem to be an especially fruitful area for research.

SUMMARY

Our discussion of alternative methods of dissonance reduction can best be summarized by noting four ideas that have been discussed:

1. In the familiar paradigm in which a recent behavioral commitment is viewed as the source of a highly resistant cognition, dissonance reduction can be reflected in behavior change, attitude change, and certain cognitive changes that don't explicitly fit into either category. Almost all of the research discussed in this volume fits this paradigm.

2. There is now ample evidence that the use of a given mode tends to preclude the use of other modes. This has been shown in experiments where resistance to change of certain cognitive elements was heightened, forcing change in others, and the point has also been made through simple correlations among modes.

3. Behavioral commitment is not always the most resistant cognition around which dissonance reduction is organized, as demonstrated in at least two studies.

4. People do not necessarily have access to as many modes as the investigator might think. It has become apparent that the use of any particular route to dissonance reduction is facilitated by the investigator's making that avenue salient.

10
Motivational Effects of Dissonance

There seems no reason why dissonance theory cannot readily be implemented to predict the rise and fall of various biologically based motives. For example, in the familiar forced-compliance paradigm it would be an easy matter to require a person to commit himself to eating a sizable meal. To the extent that he had just eaten there should be a good deal of dissonance, for continued eating would be inconsistent with a feeling of being satiated. Following the model of the forced-compliance paradigm an increment in subjectively reported hunger should result. That is, at the very least this person's cognitions about his hunger should change in a direction specified by the theory. Whether the noncognitive aspects would change concomitantly is a question raised later in this chapter.

The above example might be turned around so that the person decides not to eat even though he is hungry. To make the example more theoretically convincing we might add a variable such as justification. Suppose a person has fasted, then is asked to commit himself to an additional fast without external justification. The resulting dissonance should bring him to minimize his hunger, and more so than would someone who is paid to continue abstaining from food. The first section of this chapter will deal specifically with this example.

HUNGER

The first experimental study of hunger as affected by dissonance was by Brehm and Crocker (1962). All subjects were asked to skip breakfast and lunch, and upon arriving at the experimental room in the afternoon they were shown some food which they expected to eat later in the session. The experimenter proceeded to take a premeasure of hunger. Then the subjects were engaged in an irrelevant task necessitated by the rationale of the experiment. Following that task, the deprivation request was introduced. All subjects were asked to commit themselves to several more hours of fasting—until 8 or 9 p.m. in the evening. High-dissonance subjects learned that no additional credit points could be given for this additional participation, whereas low-dissonance subjects were offered $5 for their assistance. If dissonance is arroused in proportion to the absence of justification existing for the discrepant commitment, it should be reflected in self-ratings of reduced hunger. This is exactly what Brehm and Crocker found. High-dissonance subjects lowered their estimates of hunger when a postmeasure was given, and low-dissonance subjects showed an increase. As additional evidence for the major proposition subjects were asked to indicate how many sandwiches, cookies, and pints of milk they would like to have at the 8 or 9 o'clock evening session. In support of the subjective rating results, high-dissonance subjects did not desire as many food items as their low-dissonance counterparts.

The Brehm and Crocker (1962) experiment may be viewed as a direct extension of the forced compliance research of earlier chapters, with hunger substituted for attitudes. As the theory would predict, an unjustified commitment to a discrepant act (fasting in the face of previous fasting) serves to engage the same dissonance reduction process as observed in the attitude change research. The next two experiments take a similar tack, although instead of commitment to further fasting, the dissonance-arousing act consists of choosing to eat a quantity of noxious food.

In his "forced-compliance" experiment, Smith (1961) varied the characteristics of the communicator (i.e., experimenter or authority figure) at whose behest the person commits himself to the dissonance-producing discrepant act. The subjects were Army reservists undergoing training at an Army Reserve Center who, under the guise of a study of survival in food-emergency situations, were induced to eat grasshoppers. They were told by the experimenter, who was introduced to them as someone doing research for the Army Quartermaster, that in the "New Army," smaller units would have to be more mobile and possibly live off the land more. Therefore the researchers were going to find out "what your attitudes and reactions are toward an unusual food that you might have to eat in an emergency. This food is grasshoppers."

All subjects were then given a prequestionnaire, which included an attitude scale on their liking for grasshoppers as a food. Then, with half the subjects, the experimenter acted in a friendly, warm, permissive manner throughout the experimental period (the positive-communicator condition). He smiled frequently, referred to himself by nickname, sat on the counter, said that the subjects could smoke if they wished, that they should relax and enjoy themselves. The other half of the subjects (the negative-communicator condition) were treated throughout in a formal, cool, official manner. The men were ordered rather than requested; they were told that they could not smoke; the experimenter never smiled; he stood in a stiff pose and replied in a sharp manner to all questions.

After the subjects in both conditions had been induced to eat at least one grasshopper (encouraged by the offer of $.50), they were permitted to go ahead and eat as many as they liked. The subjects in the two conditions ate almost exactly the same mean number of grasshoppers. After eating, the subjects filled out the attitude measure again.

When the change scores in liking for grasshoppers were examined, it was found that the subjects in the negative communicator condition showed more increase in liking for grasshoppers than those in the positive-communicator condition. Although this evidence is not entirely unequivocal because of the different numbers of subjects complying with the request to eat, it does show that for those complying with the discrepant request, the more negative the characteristics of the inducing agent, the fewer are the cognitions supporting commitment and the greater the dissonance. Having once eaten, the subject can reduce dissonance by changing his attitude to be more consistent with the behavior.

A study by Zimbardo, Weisenberg, Firestone, and Levy (1965) was similar to Smith's experiment, but contained some major refinements. First, the communicator did not act in a differentially authoritarian manner toward the subjects in this experiment. Instead, subjects had the opportunity to witness either his favorable or foul disposition as passive onlookers. This is important because Smith's procedure might have led the subjects who were bossed around to think that they were expected to indicate a positive attitude toward grasshoppers—independent of dissonance processes. Once a negative or positive communicator had been established, all subjects received an identical plea to eat grasshoppers. In fact, approximately 50% of the subjects in both conditions (positive and negative communication) abided by his request. (Since the percentages were nearly equal, the subject self-selection problem of Smith's experiment is minimized here.) Finally, ratings of the grasshoppers were taken in a room separate from the main experiment, in the absence of the communicator. Again, this procedure served to minimize an artifact that might have resulted from subjects feeling differential pressure to comply publicly with the communicator's wishes. Presumably most of the dissonance would be experienced among subjects who decided to consume a grasshopper, and among the "eaters" the hypothesis is supported: With the negative communicator 55% of the subjects became more positive toward the grasshoppers, whereas only 5% increased their positivity if the communicator was positive. A test–retest control condition, without the experimental treatment, showed a 10% rate of increased favorability.

The theoretical thinking behind these two studies should be summarized briefly. When someone commits himself to an attitude-discrepant act, such as consuming a grasshopper, dissonance is aroused to the degree that few cognitions are present to support his commitment. If there is justification in the form of scientific worth, monetary compensation, a high degree of force, or even pleasant characteristics of the inducer, dissonance arousal will be minimized.

Ironically then, the more negative the inducer, the greater is the tendency to increase one's liking for a very disliked food.

The Noncognitive Effects of Dissonance:
Change in Level of Free Fatty Acids

Mobilization of plasma-free fatty acids has been shown to reflect energy demands, according to M. L. Brehm, Back, and Bogdonoff (1964). Free fatty acid level is generally related to the length of food deprivation, for under conditions of deprivation there are clearly increased energy demands on a person. In short, the hungrier a person becomes, the more that person should mobilize free fatty acids.

Returning to the reasoning of the Brehm and Crocker (1962) hunger experiment, what should be the effect on fatty acid level of a person's committing himself to food deprivation? To the extent that dissonance is created by such a commitment the individual will try to convince himself that he is not hungry, and if successful, he may also affect his level of fatty acid mobilization. If a low level of free fatty acids normally reflects the nonhungry state, dissonance-arousing commitment to fasting should occasion a lowering of free fatty acid mobilization. This was the reasoning behind two experiments by M. L. Brehm *et al.* (1964).

Subjects were initially asked to fast from 4:30 p.m. until 8:30 a.m., next morning, at which time they reported at the laboratory. In the morning session a baseline of free fatty acid mobilization was taken, then subjects were asked to commit themselves to an additional eight hours of fasting. Dissonance was varied by offering some subjects $25 and others nothing. The postmeasure of free fatty acid level was taken when subjects returned to the laboratory following their additional 8 hr fast.

In analyzing the data M. L. Brehm and her colleagues argued that dissonance should be aroused only among subjects who were hungry at the time of commitment to the additional fast. Based on self-ratings of hunger taken just prior to commitment, the subjects were divided into "hungry" and "not hungry" categories, thus a four-condition experiment was created. Given these two variables, there should be a direct relationship between amount of payment and mobilization of free fatty acids, especially among subjects who were hungry at the time of commitment.

The pattern of data was generally in the form of the predicted interaction. First, note that the relationship between payment and free fatty acid increase was opposite from the dissonance-theory prediction among not-hungry subjects. For some unspecifiable reason subjects not expecting payment showed a substantial increase. In contrast to this, the hungry subjects behaved in line with the original prediction, although the low- versus high-dissonance difference for hungry subjects was not significant. Looking at all four conditions together, the tendency toward an inverse relationship between payment and fatty acid level was greatest among hungry subjects, although the interaction in this study was slightly short of significance ($p < .10$).

The second study by M. L. Brehm et al. (1964) was similar in most respects, except that the dissonance variable was manipulated somewhat differently. Male subjects were recruited from campus organizations such as fraternities, which were paid for their help. For this reason, subjects in the low-dissonance condition were not offered money as an added justification for the prolonged fast. The attempt to manipulate the magnitude of dissonance consisted of giving some subjects high-verbal justification for the additional fast, while other subjects were given minimal verbal justification. Again the subjects were divided into hungry and not-hungry, and the results were similar to those of the first experiment, although the interaction was considerably stronger ($p < .025$).

These two experiments provided an invaluable extension of the Brehm and Crocker results. While the initial experiment by Brehm and Crocker demonstrated that dissonance can alter cognitions about physiological states, it now looks as if the physiological state mimics the cognitive change brought about by dissonance arousal. This thesis recurs below in a study of pain by Zimbardo, Cohen, Weisenberg, Dworkin, and Firestone (1969).

THIRST

A study by Brehm (1962b) on commitment to thirst parallels closely the Brehm and Crocker investigation of hunger. Male and female undergraduates were asked to abstain from all liquids from bedtime until the experimental session the following afternoon. Upon arriving at the laboratory in the afternoon half of the subjects were confronted directly with a salient reminder of their abstinence: In this high-stimulation condition a pitcher of water with paper cups sat on the testing desk throughout the session; these stimuli were absent in the low-stimulation condition. A premeasure of thirst was taken, then subjects were asked to continue their abstention until the following afternoon and were offered either $1 (high dissonance) or $5 (low dissonance) for this ordeal.

Brehm administered a check on the manipulation of justification to insure that subjects in the low-dissonance condition would feel underpaid relative to those in the high-dissonance condition. The male subjects showed the expected pattern, but female subjects did not. For some reason the females generally felt overpaid, and to make matters worse, those in the low-stimulation condition felt overpaid more when they were given less money. Accordingly, the results of the females will not be reported here.

Table 11 shows the mean changes in thirst ratings for males. A negative mean represents a decreased thirst rating, and it should be apparent that the only

TABLE 11
Mean Changes in Self-Ratings of Thirst

		Level of dissonance	
		High	Low
Level of	High	−.6	.2
stimulation	Low	−.2	.1

consequential decrease in self-rated thirst is found in the high-dissonance—high-stimulation condition. The difference between that condition and the low dissonance—high stimulation condition is significant, and so is the overall effect of dissonance significant in the expected direction.

Although the main effect of stimulation was not significant, the tendency toward an interaction ($F = 2.14$) is reminiscent of findings in Chapter 7 on awareness. Presumably one method of forcing the person's attention to the dissonance arousal is by rendering salient a positive characteristic of the foregone alternative. In this instance that characteristic consisted of the possibility of drinking water, and it is instructive that the only dissonance reduction effect of any import was produced by the combination of high dissonance and high salience.

Independent of the salience dimension the study stands as an important contribution to the understanding of motivation in terms of cognitive dissonance. It offers clear evidence that a person will try to convince himself of his lack of thirst when he has insufficient reason for a commitment to deprivation from water.

Another study on dissonance and thirst, by Brock and Grant (1963), will be discussed briefly. The subjects consumed either a very hot, or somewhat less hot sauce, thereby experiencing differential thirst. Following that experience half of the subjects were given a hypnotic suggestion that they would feel water bloated. This latter cognition surely would be dissonant with having previously consumed hot sauce, and subjects were therefore expected to convince themselves that they were not thirsty. This minimization of one's own thirst should have been reflected in decreased water consumption, and, indeed, "thirst" subjects who were given the water-bloated suggestion consumed less water than subjects in other conditions. In fact, they even drank less than their low-thirst counterparts.

These two studies have made the same theoretical point, but in much different ways. Brehm's (1962b) experiment shows that a person who commits himself to doing without water will reduce his felt thirst to the degree that abstinence is not otherwise justified. Brock and Grant (1963) take a different tack: They deal with a person who has contradictory bits of knowledge. When a person has a cognition of satiation, yet at the same time there exists a cognition of having recently consumed a thirst-inducing hot sauce, dissonance can be reduced by minimizing the thirst arising from that hot sauce. Ironically the person with contradictory knowledge will indicate a lower level of thirst than someone who did not eat a hot sauce. This result offers convincing evidence of the motivational relationship between thirst-inducing stimuli and actual thirst.

Broadening the Dissonance-Leads-to-Thirst Hypothesis

Mansson (1969) conducted an experiment in keeping with that of Brehm (above), the major innovation consisting of multiple measures of dissonance-mediated thirst reduction. Different levels of dissonance were created through various combinations of (a) length of anticipated water deprivation and (b) justification for deprivation. Subjects in the high-dissonance condition anticipated 24 hr of deprivation and received only minimal justification. Low-dissonance subjects were at the other extreme—they anticipated only 4 hr of deprivation and received high justification. The Moderate condition was created through combining the elements of the High and Low conditions.

Shortly after subjects had committed themselves to water deprivation five different indices of dissonance reduction were administered.

1. The first of these consisted of thirst ratings, and the effects were completely in line with Brehm's (1962b) results.

2. When given the opportunity to drink water, the high-dissonance group consumed the least, a result that parallels the thirst ratings convincingly.

3. The third measure can be labeled "thirst words perceived and preferred." In a situation where the criteria for selecting a correct word were ambiguous, the high-dissonance subjects were less likely than the other groups to choose thirst-related words. This finding assumes that thirsty people tend to project their thirst desires into an ambiguous situation, and to perceive glasses of water, oases, or thirst-related words. For example, Atkinson and McClelland (1948) showed that the tendency to perceive food-related items in Thematic Apperception Test (TAT) cards was positively related to length of food deprivation. From this reasoning it again appears as though the high-dissonance subjects were convincing themselves of their lack of thirst.

4. The fourth measure relates thirst to rapidity of learning, and requires some explanation. Mansson has taken some earlier research (Epstein & Lewitt, 1962; Spence & Ehrenberg, 1964) to imply that thirst can facilitate learning of paired associates, particularly when the members of those paired associates are related to the thirst drive. Accordingly, he measured the number of trials his subjects took to learn a list of food-related paired associates. High-dissonance subjects, who apparently minimized their thirst, showed the worst performance. Thus the learning measure is consistent with the other reflections of dissonance reduction

in a thirst context, and makes the point that dissonance affects thirst no matter how indirect the measuring device might be.

5. On the fifth measure, frequency of need-for-water themas generated in response to TAT cards, no clear dissonance effects emerged.

Summary

If there was doubt in the Brehm and Crocker (1962) hunger study that dissonance alters hunger level in ways other than subjective reports, the M. L. Brehm et al. (1964) experiments on free fatty acids provided evidence against such doubts. Analogously, if there were uncertainty about the viability of extending Brehm's findings on thirst to actual behavior, Mansson seems to have abated those uncertainties. Not only did Mansson find that dissonance had an impact on amount drunk, but differential thirst was also reflected in a projective measure and in rapidity of learning thirst-related words. These latter findings contribute substantially toward the case that dissonance significantly alters the motive state (thirst), and not simply a verbal representation of thirst. On the basis of this research it now is evident that cognitive dissonance theory can be implemented to interfere with the normal relationship between deprivation and desire. When a person voluntarily commits himself to deprivation, and when abstention is unjustified, dissonance processes give the person a capacity to convince himself that he does not suffer.

At this point we will turn to the final extension of dissonance theory to biological drives—control over the experience of pain.

PAIN

As the sections on hunger and thirst have demonstrated, the person who commits himself to an uncomfortable state of food or water deprivation employs cognitive changes to reduce the severity of his suffering, but only to the extent that deprivation is not externally justified. This section on pain takes a similar approach.

The first study of cognitive dissonance and pain was by Zimbardo, Cohen, Weisenberg, Dworkin, and Firestone (1969). The experiment was rather complex, and just two of the conditions will be described here. After an initial experience with painful shocks subjects were introduced into the familiar forced-compliance paradigm, and were asked to volunteer for additional shocks. Some of the subjects (low-dissonance condition) were provided with numerous justifications for participating, with emphasis on the scientific merit of the study. High-dissonance subjects were given a minimal justification for continuing to participate. Following commitment all subjects attempted to learn a list of words while receiving numerous unavoidable shocks. These shocks were uncorrelated with the subject's performance. In addition to recording the rapitidy of learning, the experimenters also took physiological measures. These two measures are the two modes of dissonance reduction we will examine, and the rationale behind them is as follows.

With respect to learning the list of words, Zimbardo et al. (1969) provide evidence for the assumption that electric shocks should raise drive level, with consequent impairment of learning. The reader may note that this assumption appears inconsistent with one made in Mansson's (1969) thirst study, but there is an important difference. The idea here, which is different from Mansson's study, is that increased drive will interfere with learning when the discriminations to be made among words are difficult. In keeping with this notion, Zimbardo et al. (1969) employed groups of adjectives that were semantically similar. In Mansson's experiment the words to be learned were directly related to the drive, and his reasoning revolved around that fact. The second measure, galvanic skin response (GSR), has been shown previously to reflect directly the administration of electric shock. The predictions and results should now make sense. If commitment to electric shock is dissonance arousing, the subject can come to terms with his discrepant commitment by lowering his felt level of pain. In line with this idea high-dissonance subjects demonstrated a quicker learning rate, suggesting that the pain did not interfere with their performance as much as it did for low-dissonance subjects. In addition, GSR responses were higher for low-dissonance than high-dissonance subjects, showing rather dramatically that the physiological impact of the shock had been diminished by dissonance reduction.

An experiment by Grinker (1969) bears some similarity to the previous study of pain. Again, a certain relationship between pain and extent of learning is established on the basis of prior evidence, then pain is varied through manipulations of dissonance arousal and the impact of dissonance is reflected in learning.

In this experiment the learning was classical eyelid conditioning. It has been found previously by Spence and Goldstein (1961) that threatening the subject with a more intense unconditioned stimulus produces an emotional response, with consequent bolstering of the conditioning effect. How can dissonance theory be introduced here? If a threat of an aversive stimulus facilitates conditioning, it should then be possible to attenuate the threat-conditioning relationship by arousing cognitive dissonance with respect to the threat. Grinker gave some of his subjects a certain degree of choice in whether or not to commit themselves to additional conditioning trials with an aversive unconditioned stimulus. They were told that the intensity of air puffs was to increase, and that an increase was likely to be unpleasant. Among those who were given choice, half received high justification and half received low justification, manipulated in a way similar to the previous electric-shock study. The results confirmed Grinker's reasoning convincingly: Subjects given low justification, who would be expected to minimize the noxiousness of the unconditioned stimulus (US), showed weaker conditioning than did the high-justification group. Therefore, it appears that emotionality, as generated by an aversive US, can be reduced through dissonance processes with consequent decrement in conditioning.

A related investigation is reported by Glass and Mayhew (1969), in which skin conductance was the primary measure. Subjects first watched a short segment of a highly aversive film depicting crude surgical operations, then half of the subjects were requested to sit through a longer segment of the same film. This first condition embodied an element of free choice, whereas in the control condition subjects were simply instructed to sit through the longer segment. Following the reasoning of Zimbardo *et al.* (1969), who also measured skin conductance, a subject who voluntarily commits himself to a stressful experience can reduce dissonance by way of minimizing his stress reaction. This implies that physiological reactivity to the longer film segment should not have been as great among choice subjects as among controls, and this is precisely what Glass and Mayhew found. Control subjects were the highest in skin conductance.

Summary

This concludes our discussion of the impact of cognitive dissonance on biological drives. To return to an example given at the beginning of this chapter, it seems entirely plausible that a person who is hungry, and who commits himself to food deprivation, will come to minimize his hunger. By "minimize his hunger" is meant a change in his own cognitions about hunger level. Dissonance theory is a theory about cognitions and predicts at the very least a cognitive adjustment in admitted amount of hunger. This derivation is not qualitatively different from the research with counterattitudinal essays in which cognitions about the issue are realigned to be more consistent with the behavioral commitment. The qualitative difference enters when the supposed noncognitive facets of the biological drives enter the picture. As it turns out, the cognitive changes specified by dissonance theory are eventually manifested in physiological changes as well, and in other seemingly noncognitive reflections of the motive. The free fatty acid effects and GSR effects testify to this point. Similarly, when a motive state (thirst or pain) is said to affect learning, and dissonance arousal then is shown to mediate that effect, we have increased confidence that the dissonance-produced changes are more that just cognitive.

At this point we will turn to other areas of psychology that have been dealt with historically in theoretical terms other than dissonance theory. The purpose of introducing dissonance theory into these areas will be the same as with the biological drives: Dissonance arousal can often mediate previously-specified relationships between a motive and its satisfaction. Just as the relationship between deprivation and hunger is modifiable through dissonance arousal, it will now be shown that the functioning of nonbiological drives and other psychological processes are similarly modifiable.

AVOIDANCE OF FAILURE

A "forced-compliance" experiment by Cohen and Zimbardo (1962) represents an attempt to deal directly with the effects of cognitive dissonance on the behaviors assumed to stem from social motivation.

One of several important factors affecting the magnitude of dissonance in a situation where a person commits himself to deprivation of an important motive is the amount of deprivation to which he commits himself. According to the present theory, greater deprivation should result in a greater discrepancy between motivation and goal availability; we therefore assume that, holding constant initial motive strength and incentives for commitment, commitment to greater deprivation should result in greater dissonance and consequent reduction of motivation and thus in fewer responses directed toward satisfying the particular motive involved. By actually decreasing his motivation, the person reduces the dissonance created by the discrepancy between his knowledge of his motivation and his knowledge that he has committed himself to further deprivation.

If a person wants very much to achieve some success in an important task, he should, everything else being equal, desire to avoid performing the task in a situation that provides failure. However, if for some reason the person commits himself to a situation promising failure, he can reduce his dissonance by lessening his failure–avoidance motivation. That is, one way of making consonant the relationship between one's motivation to avoid failure (or achieve success) and one's commitment to failure is to reduce the motive to avoid failure (or to succeed). A decrement in failure–avoidance motivation should then be reflected in less behavior guaranteed to promote success. Thus the greater the prospect of failure to which the person commits himself, the more dissonance he should experience and the more he should attempt to reduce that dissonance by a decrement in avoidance motivation, which will be reflected in less concern with changing the conditions so as to ensure a greater probability of success on a subsequent trial.

Subjects were first given instructions designed to instill a motive to succeed. They were told that the study was a test of their ability to memorize and interpret verbal materials under adverse conditions. Then they were asked to memorize a poem and discuss its psychological implications under the disruptive influence of a delayed auditory feedback of .2 sec. Generally subjects did not experience much success from this initial experience, and it might be presumed that they became motivated to avoid the task in the future.

With this negative experience as a background, subjects were then requested to undergo a similar experience again, although for a much longer interval. The dissonance created by this commitment was varied by giving subjects differential expectations about their chances of performing well during the longer session. High-dissonance subjects were told that they would "perform very poorly, among the worst subjects we have ever run," and low-dissonance subjects learned that they would "perform not too badly, about average or a little less than the average subjects we have run."

How might dissonance be reduced in this situation? Given that high-dissonance subjects committed themselves to a situation in which they were bound to fail, one clear mode of dissonance reduction would consist of lowering the motive to avoid failure. One manifestiation of this would be for them not to take advantage of an opportunity to improve conditions for performing. Accordingly, all subjects were given the chance to change the delayed auditory feedback setting.

After agreeing to return, subjects were told that the initial testing was over and they were brought into the "apparatus room" and shown the DAF equipment. They were shown the recorder and the dial indicating the delay interval. They were told that in the initial session the interval was extreme and constant at Point 13 on the 15-point scale. It was stressed that the size of the delay determined the amount of speech disruption and presumably the amount of failure the subject experienced and that a shorter delay would enable one to perform much better. Subjects were then told that, since they knew their own subjective reaction to the situation, we would like them to choose the point on the dial with which they would like to begin the next session (and keep for at least half the session). The subject then adjusted the dial himself in response to the request that he select the interval he wanted to experience in the second session. The subject could see how the tape loop changed speed as a function of the direction and extremity of dial setting.

The major issue in the present experiment concerns the changes in actual behavior that are assumed to reflect dissonance-produced changes in motivation. When we examine the major dependent variable, we see a strong effect of the dissonance manipulation: Nine out of ten subjects in the low-dissonance condition decreased the delayed auditory feedback interval, whereas only two out of ten in the high-dissonance condition decreased it. In fact, those in the high-dissonance condition kept the dial approximately as it was set, while the lows reduced the interval considerably, presumably as a function of their stronger avoidance motivation. The mean change for the high group is +.03; for the low group it is −3.42. The difference between the conditions is significant at less than the .05 level. These results are entirely consistent with the reasoning behind the study. Evidently a commitment to failure can, through dissonance reduction, lower the motive to avoid failure, as illustrated by the seemingly irrational behavior of high-dissonance subjects: When given a chance to improve their chances of success, they generally declined to take advantage of the opportunity.

An experiment by Schlachet (1965) was derivative of the work by Cohen and Zimbardo (1962), and it introduced the additional variables of chronic need for achievement and monetary incentive for commitment to future failure. As in the Cohen and Zimbardo study subjects were asked to commit themselves to a task that did not promise great success. Some subjects were given a definite expectation of failure (10% chance of success), while others were led to expect approximately a 50% chance of good performance. The amount of incentive for this commitment was also varied: some subjects were offered $5 and others $1. Subjects then proceeded with the task, which involved trying to estimate how many dots formed a given nonsense word. All subjects were given identical performance feedback and found that 13 of their 18 judgments were incorrect. Schlachet reasoned as follows: If subjects have committed themselves to a difficult task for minimal justification, dissonance can be reduced by minimizing one's motivation to avoid failure. Dissonance reduction should take place to the degree that the subject definitely expects failure and to the degree that his behavior is unjustified. Therefore, if subjects are asked to recall the components of the task (i.e. the 18 nonsense words), dissonance should increase the number of failure-associated words recalled. On an index of tendency to remember failure words better than success words, subjects given a strong expectation of failure were significantly higher than subjects given a 50% chance of failure. Further, this result was particularly strong among subjects promised a low incentive ($1) for taking part in the dot-guessing task. Although the interaction between probability of failure and incentive was not significant, the pattern of results is at least in keeping with what dissonance theory would lead us to expect. Further, and more important, the results are an exact parallel of the Cohen and Zimbardo (1962) result, but with a different measure of motivation to avoid failure.

As a second measure of failure–avoidance motivation, subjects' reaction times to the 18 nonsense words were measured. It was assumed by Schlachet that negative affect would be reflected by slower reaction times to failure-related stimuli than to nonfailure stimuli. Therefore, as dissonance increases, and the motivation to avoid failure thereby diminishes, reaction times to failure stimuli should become faster. The data generally followed this form, the major statistical evidence consisting of a difference between subjects committed to failure versus the combined subjects from the low-probability-of-failure conditions and a control condition in which there was no choice or monetary justification.

In summary, the experiment reproduced the probability of failure results shown in the previous study, and with more sophisticated measures, but the other two variables (monetary justification and chronic achievement motivation) produced no dissonance effects by themselves.

Summary

This section, based largely on Zimbardo's (1969) review, exemplifies the extension of dissonance theory to a central problem area of psychology. Motivation to avoid failure has long been studied by psychologists, and our attempt here has simply been to show how dissonance processes can alter straightforward effects occurring in this area. In the research on motivation to avoid failure, Cohen and

Zimbardo (1962) and Schlachet (1965) have made an expecially important point: Although common sense might reason that a person who is committed to almost certain failure would try to improve his working conditions in order to reduce the chance of failure, it turns out that the individual with a moderate chance of success is the most likely one to take advantage of an opportunity to improve his working conditions.

There is a potentially important parallel between this last point and a theory of motivational determinants of risk-taking behavior by Atkinson (1957). It is proposed by Atkinson that people who have a relatively strong need for achievement, and comparatively weak fear of failure, will exert maximal efforts when given a task of intermediate difficulty. Although it is not clear that Cohen and Zimbardo (1962) were dealing with subjects who fulfilled these individual difference requirements, it is interesting to speculate on the assumption that their subjects were predominantly achievement oriented. To recapitulate: Cohen and Zimbardo virtually guaranteed failure to some subjects, but led others to think that their performance would be about average. Then all subjects were given a chance to improve their subsequent performance by shortening the delayed auditory feedback level. Granting the previous assumption about the nature of the subjects, Atkinson (1957) would predict that the subjects who saw a moderate hope of success would make the most of the situation—and hence shorten the DAF interval. This is, of course, precisely what happened.

A study reported in Chapter 5 (Rahman, 1962) provides a second parallel to Atkinson's thinking—this parallel occurring toward the high end of the proba-bility-of-success dimension. It will be recalled that subjects engaged in a game that could lead potentially to an attractive gift. Part way through the game some of the subjects were provided a "very high expectation" of success upon their continuation of the game, while subjects in another condition were given a slightly more pessimistic ("high expectation" of success) report. Further, all subjects were allowed at this point in the game to choose between a conservative strategy (gaining an experimental credit and giving up the possibility of winning the prize) and a risky strategy (receiving the attractive prize given success, but no credit and no prize with failure). Focusing just on subjects who chose to pursue the prize, more dissonance should have been aroused in the "high" dissonance condition than in the "very high" condition, and the results, in terms of rated attractiveness of the prize, confirmed this expectation.

Looking at this experiment from an achievement–motivation perspective, success at a task should be attractive to the extent that there is a moderate probability of success, and without elaborating, this is precisely what the results demonstrated.

A dissonance interpretation of Cohen and Zimbardo's (1962) and Rah-man's (1962) results is somewhat more clear than the Atkinson extension, primarily because of an assumption that would have to be made about individual differences in achievement motivation. Nonetheless, this parallel provides an interesting lead into the possibility that dissonance theory may be germane to several of the phenomena associated with Atkinson's notions.

PERFORMANCE EXPECTANCY

If a person has a firm expectancy about his performance level, and then is suddenly surprised by a change in performance, there is a serious question about whether or not dissonance should be aroused. The question exists because of earlier considerations: Unforeseen events typically fail to bring about dissonance arousal, except under the special circumstances cited previously (Chapter 4). The question for this section is the following: Is a person's deviation from his expectancies for his own performance one of those special circumstances? It will be recalled that the experiments of Pallak, Sogin, and Van Zante (1974), Sogin and Pallak (1974), and Worchel and Brand (1972) demonstrated a *fait accompli* effect when the surprise event was due to the person's own abilities. We went on to argue that responsibility may be defined in part by a connection between the person's abilities and the unexpected consequence. Returning to the central question of this section, the answer may well be "yes." When a person's performance suddenly changes, even in an unforeseen way, he should feel responsibility for the change in light of the conclusions drawn from the research of Chapter 4.

Aronson and Carlsmith (1962) instigated the performance expectancy line of research. The basic idea was to give subjects a strong expectancy for their performance level, then to confront them with a sudden perceived switch in their own performance rate. Aronson and Carlsmith proposed that this sudden change would create dissonance, to be reduced by attempting to alter performance rate back toward the original level. Their reasoning makes perfectly good sense as long as we assume that the cognition most resistant to change is the cognition corresponding to previous performance, or expectancy. Surely a situation could be created where the performance change itself would be the most resistant cognition, but that will not be relevant here.

Their subjects were administered a social sensitivity test, divided into five sections so that feedback could be given sequentially five times. Some subjects found their performance to be quite poor on the first four feedbacks, while the remaining subjects were led to think their performance during the first four blocks was excellent. Thus an expectancy was created for all subjects, and was of either high or low performance. These two conditions were subdivided on the basis of fifth-block feedback: Half of the subjects were told their fifth-block performance was good, and half were told it was bad. To summarize the design, there were four conditions of performance at this point of the experiment: high–high, high–low, low–high, and low–low. The authors anticipated dissonance arousal primarily in the two "unexpected change" conditions, and in

TABLE 12
Number of Responses Changed on Repeat Performance

		Score obtained on fifth test	
		Low	High
Score expected	High	11.1	3.9
on fifth test	Low	6.7	10.2

order to measure dissonance reduction subjects were given a chance to perform the fifth block of the test again. In this way it would be possible to note how much subjects changed their performance the second time around. If a subject had built up a negative expectancy and then had performed positively, he could presumably return to his accustomed level by changing his answers when he went through the fifth block of trials a second time. The same would apply for subjects with a positive expectancy who found themselves performing poorly on the fifth block. Taking this changed performance as an index of dissonance arousal, the results were as shown in Table 12. The hypothesis is well supported. Perhaps it is not so surprising that high–low subjects showed a good deal of performance change, but the intriguing effect from the standpoint of dissonance theory is the high number of changes in the low–high condition, significantly greater than in the low–low group.

Although this line of research has never been included under the *fait accompli* or unforeseen consequences headings, it seems evident that it belongs there. Certainly subjects did not, with foreknowledge, commit themselves to a change in performance level. It seems entirely plausible that a firm expectancy had been built, followed by a surprise consequence. The explanation in terms of dissonance theory need only assume that subjects felt responsible for this outcome, and since subjects' abilities were the source of the changed performance, there is good reason to postulate that subjects saw a causal connection between their abilities and the outcome.

The apparent attempt of low–high subjects to restore a familiar performance rate captured the imaginations of several investigators, but many of the subsequent studies have failed to replicate that low–low versus low–high difference (Cottrell, 1965; Lowin & Epstein, 1965; Silverman & Marcantonio, 1965; Ward & Sandvold, 1963). It had been suggested first by Ward and Sandvold that the results of Aronson and Carlsmith might be due to the experimenter-demand qualities of their procedure, and controlling for that, Ward and Sandvold failed to replicate. Even without controlling for demand characteristics the original effect has been hard to replicate. For example, Lowin and Epstein (1965) attempted an exact replication and found no hint of the original low–low versus low–high difference. One effect that does recur reliably in several of these studies is an "achievement–motivation" result. Independent of previous expectancy subjects try to change their performance when the outcome is poor, but become conservative when the result is satisfactory. All of these failures to replicate could simply be the result of achievement needs winning out over the motivation to reduce inconsistency. Presumably dissonance reduction was for some reason the stronger process in the original experiment. Before moving on to a more detailed consideration of achievement versus dissonance reduction, research by Brock, Edelman, Edwards, and Schuck (1965) should be discussed, for they provide some direct evidence that the procedures of Aronson and Carlsmith can lead to a replicable finding.

Brock *et al.* (1965) report seven studies altogether. The first was a near replication of Aronson and Carlsmith (1962), and the results were approximately as strong. Most important was the obtained difference between the low–low and low–high conditions. The second experiment requires a short methodological introduction. Aronson and Carlsmith (1962) gave subjects feedback four times prior to the fifth and deviant trial. Each instance of feedback was based on a block of 20 trials, thus there were 80 trials up through the fourth block (and fourth feedback), followed by 20 additional trials to constitute the fifth trial block. Brock *et al.* (1965) reasoned that the stronger expectancy a person has going into the fifth block, the more dissonance should be aroused by a disconfirmation. Following this reasoning they tried to weaken the expectancy in their second experiment by halving the first segment of the procedure. Subjects received just two feedbacks rather than four. The results were slightly weaker, as expected, but still significant and consistent with the finding of Aronson and Carlsmith.

The strength-of-expectancy idea was carried into the next two experiments of Brock *et al.* (1965). Rather than including a block of 20 trials into one performance report, subjects received feedback on every single trial. Presumably this built a strong expectancy, but to the authors' surprise the only effects obtained were of the "achievement motivation" variety.

What might account for the disparity between these last two studies and the first two? After 80 trials of no improvement whatever, and with feedback occurring on every trial, subjects probably did not feel much responsibility for their performance. With repeated failure over the course of 80 trials they must have concluded that they had very little control over their outcomes, and when performance suddenly increased, it is unlikely that they saw the increase as generated by their abilities. At that point they were probably convinced that anything happening to them with respect to the test was due to chance, or unfathomable characteristics of the testing procedure. Therefore, not feeling responsibility for performance level, they would not have felt responsible for the sudden rise, and dissonance would not have occurred. Although this interpretation is only conjecture in the context of the Brock *et al.* (1965) research, there is direct support for such an idea in a more recent experiment, to which we shall now turn.

Marecek and Mettee (1972) worked toward a resolution of two issues that have come up in the last few pages: the interference of achievement needs with dissonance reduction, and the issue of responsibility for change in performance. With respect to the first issue, they argued that a person should be reluctant to accept a positive change in performance if he is chronically committed to poor outcomes. Accordingly, a person with low self esteem who is certain of his self esteem level should be especially resistant to a sudden increase. Note that this approach to performance-expectancy eliminates the interference of achievement needs, for the person who is certain of his low self-esteem should have few desires for achievement. In contrast, someone with low self-esteem, but who is not certain of that low self-esteem may well have a desire to improve. This person, just like the high self-esteem individual, should be relatively willing to accept a sudden change for the better in performance.

The responsibility issue was approached by telling some subjects that the task involved luck, and others that skill was the determinant of success-failure.

Subjects completed a measure of their self-esteem and their certainty about self-esteem level, and then engaged in a task 20 trials long, on which it was possible to ascertain actual performance rate (in contrast to the Aronson–Carlsmith, 1962, procedure). The task consisted of matching geometric figures. After the first 10 trials all subjects received positive feedback, which should have aroused dissonance only for subjects low in self-esteem and certain of their low self-regard. Then subjects proceeded on the next 10 trials, and by comparing the two performances Marecek and Mettee (1972) determined which subjects tended to try hardest for success on the second block of 10. The results were exactly as predicted: Considering just the performance levels for the second block, corrected for first-block performance by analysis of covariance, subjects certain of their low self-esteem in the skill condition performed much worse than subjects in any other condition. Also striking was the similarity of the remaining conditions.

The Marecek and Mettee (1972) experiment provides a most informative supplement to our above discussion of performance expectancy. First, it should be evident that achievement needs can easily interfere with dissonance reduction in the original paradigm, and that a fair test of the theory controls for such needs. This is exactly what Marecek and Mettee accomplished, and the results are convincing. There was no indication that subjects with a strong chronic expectancy for failure were about to accept a good performance. Second, the study makes explicit the role of responsibility in mediating performance expectancy phenomena. Only when the subject could view himself as the cause of his good performance (skill condition) did dissonance reduction appear. This result parallels the skill-chance distinction we imputed into earlier research. That is, the three successful experiments (Aronson & Carlsmith, 1962; first two experiments of Brock *et al.*, 1965) were run under conditions of skill, while there was some reason to think that the second two studies of Brock and his associates approximated chance conditions. This entire pattern of findings lends confidence to the notion that a sudden change in performance, even though unexpected and unforeseen, can arouse dissonance because of the causal connection between subjects' abilities and performance outcome.

One final study that sheds light on the conditions necessary for motivated decreases in performance is by Mettee (1971). The study was patterned much after the original Aronson and Carlsmith procedure, so that we will not delve into exact procedural details. A number of variations were introduced in order to implement Mettee's ideas about the bases of performance expectancy effects. The experiment was rather complex, and we shall deal just with a portion of it.

One of the crucial aspects of Mettee's (1971) procedure involved telling subjects explicitly that the dimension at hand (psychological sensitivity) could not be learned, implying that it is a relatively permanent trait. This was important, according to Mettee, because subjects might be more than willing to embrace a newfound and unexpected success experience if they believe that they have just "caught on." In terms of the language we have used here, Mettee is suggesting that the subject's conception of himself as low in psychological sensitivity must be highly resistant to change in order for the individual to become motivated to try to transform his unexpected success into a failure experience.

Another feature of Mettee's (1971) experiment was a variation in whether or not subjects expected to gain further feedback about their psychological sensitivity following the test feedback. A number of the subjects anticipated an interview with a clinical psychologist on the day following the test, and these subjects were also led to think that the interview usually produced an assessment in concurrence with the outcome of the personality measure. Other subjects expected no such clinical interview. In order to understand the basis for this variation we need to turn briefly to Mettee's reasoning about the various sources of motivation for performance consistency.

Independent of cognitive inconsistency, it is possible to talk about the "instrumental negative components" of unanticipated success. One such negative component arises in the situation where a person receives a sudden success experience, alters his expectation of performance upward slightly, and then encounters further confirmation of his previous failure expectation. A situation that should bring forth such considerations from subjects is Mettee's "future interview" condition, in which subjects had good reason to think that the clinician would find them to be seriously lacking in psychological sensitivity. In contrast, this same "instrumental negative component" should be considerably less pronounced among subjects in the "no future exposure" condition.

The results of Mettee's (1971) study provide good evidence that he has uncovered some of the central bases of individuals' efforts to regain low-performance levels. There was a strong effect for failure versus success expectancy, whereby positive feedback on the fifth section of the test created more changes in answers among the failure expectancy subjects than among the success expectancy group. This was an overwhelmingly strong result, and suggests that it is crucial to convince subjects that the ability in question cannot be learned over the short course of the experimental session. In other words, the expectancy about self must be a high resistance-to-change cognitive element. We might draw a direct comparison between this reasoning and a finding of the Marecek and Mettee (1972) study, which showed that attempts to be consistent with a failure self-image were pronounced only among subjects who were highly certain of their low self-concepts.

   The other result we should like to mention is that changing of answers among failure expectancy subjects was more evident when future feedback from a clinician was expected. This supports Mettee's notion that changes upward in self-concept can sometimes have negative "instrumental" side effects, one such effect being the necessity of later having to shift one's self concept back to a previous, low baseline level. Such "instrumental" considerations are important, because in the performance expectancy paradigm we have examined they work in direct opposition to the predicted dissonance effects.

SUMMARY

The present chapter has delved into the impact of cognitive dissonance on processes that are ordinarily thought to be governed by somewhat unique and powerful motives. It has been shown that the course of events surrounding hunger, thirst, avoidance of pain, and avoidance of failure is not as simple as might be imagined from the viewpoint of a simplistic approach based on specific drives. When a person takes it upon himself to suffer from hunger, the manifest need for food thereby diminishes in proportion to the amount of dissonance involved in his decision. An analogous process takes place in the case of committing oneself to thirst, pain, and conditions conducive to failure.

   The case of performance expectancy research is a departure from the paradigm involved in the above lines of investigation. The major conclusion deriving from this final segment of the chapter is as follows: A person who is committed to a self-image of failure will reject unexpected success experiences to the degree that he is responsible for those successes. With respect to the dimension of responsibility this area of research offers an interesting supplement to Chapter 4, which was devoted entirely to that concept.

11
Resistance to Extinction and Related Effects

The present chapter continues the extension of dissonance theory to various well-established phenomena in psychology. The subject here is the well-documented finding that irregular, or partial, reinforcement results in stronger resistance to extinction than does regular reinforcement. We will also consider the effort-justification hypothesis in the context of research that shows resistance to extinction to be affected by the amount of physical effort exerted during learning. Rather than focusing specifically on a motive state, as in the previous three chapters, this chapter centers on the dependent variable of resistance to extinction. There is another important uniqueness associated with this chapter: the experimental subjects of these cognitive dissonance studies are rats.

Most of the research reported here can be credited to Lawrence and Festinger (1962). In applying dissonance theory to the partial-reinforcement effect (PRE) and other effort-justification phenomena they have created a diverse array of experimental situations in which the organism's behavior definitely should vary due to dissonance arousal, and at the same time they have tried to create conditions to which other interpretations would not apply. Whether other explanations have direct applicability will be taken up after their research is presented. For the present we will stick with the relationship between their reasoning from dissonance theory and the requisite experimental designs.

The rationale behind these studies is no different from that of the effort-justification paradigm with which the reader is now familiar. In fact, the design of these experiments is conceptually similar to those of Aronson and Mills (1959) and Gerard and Mathewson (1966), in which subjects who underwent an embarrassing experience or electric shock in order to join a group came to develop an increment of attraction to the group. What is required of Lawrence and Festinger's rats is no different from requirements for human subjects. The organism must be induced into performing a discrepant act—discrepant in that the act is rewarded only minimally or entails great effort expenditure. Subsequently dissonance reduction is measured in terms of attraction to that action, the goal attained, or some aspect of the goal setting. Since it is difficult to take verbal measures of attraction in rats, a behavioral measure is obviously necessary, and this leads us directly to the measure of resistance to extinction. A rat that suffers or exerts effort, or that is rewarded only minimally, should come to develop an extra preference for the goal box toward which it continuously runs, and this preference can be assessed by the resistance to extinction of approach to the goal box.

Before proceeding to discuss the research an important point must be made concerning the definition of what is dissonant for rats. When a human subject is asked to commit himself to a dissonance-arousing behavior, the investigator can insure that the behavior is dissonant with a specified attitude held by the subject. It is important for the investigator to know this, since many kinds of behavior would not necessarily be discrepant with attitudes. In the case of the rat required to run a maze, how do we know that running under conditions of partial reinforcement is more dissonance-arousing than running under conditions of 100% reinforcement? The answer is simple. There must be some independent evidence of the animal's reluctance to run under partial reinforcement. In the Lawrence and Festinger (1962) research this evidence is abundant, for it is almost always true that the partially reinforced animal runs more slowly during acquisition of the running habit, even though the same animal builds a strong resistance to extinction. This running speed effect does, however, have some exceptions. For example, Goodrich (1959) has shown that in early segments of the runway, partially rewarded animals will run faster than those continuously rewarded, but only toward the end of the training period.

THE LAWRENCE AND FESTINGER RESEARCH

Absolute Number versus Ratio of Unrewarded Trials

According to Lawrence and Festinger (1962) it has generally been assumed in the literature that the primary variable influencing the partial reinforcement effect (PRE) is the ratio of rewarded to nonrewarded trials. As this ratio decreases, resistance to extinction increases. In contrast, the present derivation from dissonance theory would say that dissonance is created on every nonreinforced trial. This seems eminently reasonable, since every bit of nonreinforcement should operate as a cognition dissonant with the commitment to keep running toward the goal. Lawrence and Festinger's search of the literature yielded no definite test between these two apparently opposing positions, since ratio and absolute number are completely confounded among earlier experiments. Therefore, in an effort to demonstrate that dissonance theory has some predictive power in this area, an experiment was conducted by Lawrence and

Festinger addressed to the question of ratio versus absolute number of nonreinforced trials.

The experiment involved running rats through a runway to a goalbox, and varying the number and percentage of unrewarded trials. This procedure was proceeded by a large number of premanipulation trials during which the subjects learned to run the maze. The total number of unrewarded trials was varied between 0 and 72, and the *percentage* of unrewarded trials was varied within each of those levels of "unreward." The results were quite convincing: Absolute number of unrewarded trials was an excellent predictor of resistance to extinction, while percentage of trials unrewarded made no difference whatsoever. The results are consistent with the idea that dissonance is aroused through each instance of nonreward and cumulates to effect a stronger resistance to extinction. More important, the results cast doubt on the commonly held thesis that the ratio of unrewarded trials provides the underlying force behind the partial reinforcement effect. We shall return to this point later.

When an organism suffers in order to reach some desired state of affairs, dissonance can be reduced by finding something attractive about the situation in which the suffering occurs. That is, in addition to the goal itself becoming more attractive, we would expect the organism to justify its behaviors by developing an increased appreciation for almost any relevant aspects of the uncomfortable or effort-producing setting. The reasoning is not so different from that of Aronson (1961), whose dissertation found that subjects came to increase their liking for the color of an object associated with nonreward, particularly when the object was obtained only after considerable effort.

Attraction to a Location Associated With Nonreward

With the assistance of Uyeno, Lawrence and Festinger employed an apparatus designed originally by Amsel and Roussel (1952) consisting of a runway for rats, a starting box, a "mid-box," and an end box. The animals were run from the starting box, through the midbox, and were rewarded on every trial upon reaching the end box. The only difference between conditions involved an experience in the midbox. One group was rewarded every time it reached the midbox; the other group was delayed there for the length of time it took the first group to eat its midbox food. Since the latter group repeatedly committed itself to running to the midbox for no reward, dissonance theory would allow that an extra preference would be built up for some aspect of the unrewarded situation. In short, the animal should come to like the midbox to the extent that reward is lacking. To test this possibility the subjects were run in extinction trials only from the starting box to the midbox and the index of extinction here was the running time. The results showed that extinction was considerably weaker among the rats never rewarded in the midbox. More specifically, as the extinction trials progressed it became increasingly evident that running time to the midbox was faster for nonrewarded than rewarded rats. Assuming that running time is a fair measure of attraction to the box, the experiment appears to be a good demonstration of the theoretical point.

Attraction to a Location Where Behavior Is Delayed

The next experiment by Lawrence and Festinger also involved a delay in a midbox, but this time delay was the only variable. There was no differential reward. The subjects began in the starting box, proceeded to midbox A, then to midbox B, and finally to the end box, where food was delivered on every trial. Some of the rats were consistently delayed in midbox A, then were allowed to run directly through midbox B and on to the end box. The other rats were allowed to run through midbox A, but were delayed at B. To return to the theoretical argument, dissonance should be created by the delay, and if dissonance can be reduced by developing a preference for the place where dissonance is aroused, there should develop a special preference for the box in which a wait was imposed. We might add that this prediction would only make sense if the animals were not completely forced to wait, and indeed they were not, in that trials subsequent to the first were run by the rat with the knowledge that a delay had occurred previously.

For the extinction trials the subjects were run only from midbox A to midbox B. This meant that half of the animals were running to the box where they were delayed and half were doing the opposite. If a preference was established for the "delay" box, there should be a relative hesitancy to run away from it. Thus, the rats delayed originally in box A should show a fairly slow running time toward B. Just the opposite would be expected for rats delayed in box B. The results were entirely consistent with this reasoning: After the third day of extinction the dissonance effects become rather pronounced, such that the animals running *to* the delay box showed a reliably faster running speed.

We might note a parallel between this study and one by Wicklund *et al.* (1967) with human subjects (see Chapter 5). The subjects were led to expect to hear a tape-recorded speech that countered their own opinions, and some of them were asked to wait several minutes before hearing it. The waiting time was arranged in order to pose some inconvenience to the subject's schedule. Just as in the Lawrence and Festinger experiment, the human subjects evidenced the development of a special preference for an aspect of the situation in which they were delayed: they showed more agreement with the anticipated communication than did subjects not expecting a delay.

Physical Effort

The experiments discussed thus far have dealt with nonreward and delay as sources of cognitive dissonance, and the next two experiments involve the creation of dissonance through physical effort. In the first of these effort was reduced for some animals by the experimenter's placing them directly in the end box; in the second, Lawrence and Festinger's (1962) rats were required to climb a 50° incline.

Animals in the first experiment ran an 8-ft runway which led to a goal box. One group was rewarded 100% of the time upon reaching the goal box, and another group received reward on 50% of the trials. A third group was comparable to the 50% reward group except that dissonance arousal was minimized in the following way. On half of the trials the rats were rewarded each time they reached the goal box, but on the other half of the trials the experimenter lifted the animals directly into the goal box, not giving them the opportunity to run, nor giving them a reward. In these "placed" trials there should have been little dissonance arousal, since the effort exertion was minimal. Also minimizing dissonance in this condition was the fact that a reward was received every time on "nonplaced" trials. If this reasoning is correct, the only condition in this experiment that should have aroused much dissonance is the straight 50% reward condition, and the results bear out this prediction. The 50% group took significantly more trials to extinction than either the "placed" or 100% groups.

In another experiment on effort the rats were run in a special 7-ft runway that could be adjusted so that its angle with the floor varied. Some rats were trained to run to the end with the runway inclined at 25°, and others ran up a slope of 50°. Each of the trials was rewarded. During extinction the slopes were left just as they were during training, and again, the measure of dissonance reduction was number of trials to extinction. The 25° group took 20.6 trials to extinguish, the 50° group took 28.3 trials, and the difference was significant. It seems evident from these two experiments that physical effort affects rats just as it affects humans. To the degree that running is difficult (Experiment I) or to the degree that running is required at all (Experiment II), the organism develops special attractions for the goal box to which he runs or for the activity of running.

Independent of the Lawrence and Festinger research program, Lewis (1964b) conducted three experiments on the relationship between effort expended and attraction to a food. Rats were placed into high- and low-effort groups, such that some of them had to displace a rather heavy weight in the course of their progress toward the reward (Rice Krispies), while other rats were burdened with only a minimal weight. After a number of such trials the subjects were placed into a straight maze, allowed to run freely to the goal area, and were rewarded each time with Rice Krispies. Using running speed as the atractiveness measure, the results of all three experiments taken together indicate that rats pulling the heavier weight developed the stronger attraction toward Rice Krispies.

FURTHER THEORETICAL QUESTIONS

In addition to demonstrating the operation of dissonance principles with rats, the Lawrence and Festinger research makes inroads into a heavily researched area of experimental psychology. Dissonance theory is presented by them as a clear alternative approach to explaining the partial reinforcement effect, and this being the case, we should take a more careful look at the kind of explanation they have set out to refute, and also at other possibly cogent explanations of these phenomena.

The Discrimination Hypothesis

The type of explanation Lawrence and Festinger view as contradicted by the first experiment of this chapter might be called generically the "discrimination" hypothesis (first proposed by Humphreys, 1939). The discrimination notion says that the organism has more difficulty discriminating extinction trials from learning trials when learning has been under conditions of partial reinforcement. There is a great deal of common sense embedded in this idea. If learning takes place under conditions of 10% of the trials rewarded, rather than on every trial, the organism will have more difficulty knowing precisely when the extinction phase has begun. This confusion is then likely to lead to continued responding in the face of nonreinforcement.

It should be evident that the clearest route to resistance to extinction, using the discrimination hypothesis, is to make the learning conditions and the extinction conditions as similar as possible. Taking the idea to an absurd extreme, resistance to extinction would be greatest if the percentage of rewarded trials during learning were 0. Since that poses some practical problems in regard to motivating the organism to run, we might try 5%, 10%, or some fairly low ratio, maximizing the similarity between learning and extinction periods. But Lawrence and Festinger did exactly this, and found no effect for differential ratio when the absolute number of nonreinforced trials was held constant.

The research of Lawrence and Festinger (1962) is not the only PRE investigation to cast doubt on the discrimination hypothesis. In the same year that the Lawrence and Festinger book was published, Jenkins (1962) and Theios (1962) reported experiments inconsistent with the discrimination idea—Jenkins with a Skinner box, and Theios with a runway apparatus. Each of these studies showed that the PRE was manifested even though a block of continuous reward trials was interspersed between learning and extinction. If all subjects have the common experience of reward on every trial for several trials before extinction, the extinction phase should then be easily discriminable and the PRE should disappear. But such was not the case. In a more dramatic demonstration of the same point, Donin, Surridge, and Amsel (1967) showed that the PRE can carry through a period of 90 days of no training, then through a block of trials on which reinforcement is given on each trial.

Given all of this evidence the discrimination hypothesis need not be taken seriously as a competitor of cognitive dissonance theory in explaining the PRE. Moreover, it is difficult to imagine how the discrimination hypothesis would handle the two experiments on liking for midboxes, since both of these studies were designed specifically in accord with the theory and do not lend themselves to an analysis in terms of similarity between learning conditions and extinction conditions. But this is not to conclude that dissonance theory remains as the only viable interpretation of PRE, or even the only plausible explanation of the midbox studies. A recent formulation by Amsel (1972) may well have some bearing on the problems considered by Lawrence and Festinger.

Amsel's Theory of Persistence

Dissonance theory's claims to explaining the PRE, delay, and effort phenomena reported by Lawrence and Festinger have been criticized soundly by Amsel (1962) and Mowrer (1963). Their critiques take a similar form in arguing that behavior theory can easily explain the effects in question through a mechanism called "counterconditioning." In brief, the individual subject is viewed as playing an active role in the extinction process. This active role results through the organism's own response to nonreward—a response that may be called "frustration."

   In Amsel's (1958) statement of his theory, a stimulus situation involving blocking, delay, or other inhibiting factors will create in the organism a "fractional anticipatory frustration." This is symbolized "r_F–s_F." The first of these two components is an implicit response to the runway situation, and is evoked by those cues in the runway that tend to create inhibition, such as absence of reward. This first component (r_F) has stimulus consequences (s_F) for the organism which, through repeated trials, become conditioned to the instrumental approach response. Then, when extinction begins, the organism will continue its running to the goal box due to the prior connection between running and absence of reward. In contrast, an organism that has never met with frustration will not have the same conditioning history, and will extinguish faster. In the latter case there is no conditioned cue to serve as a stimulus to the instrumental running response.

   A more recent notion by Amsel is even more obviously germane to the Lawrence and Festinger paradigms, and we will discuss it in more detail. Amsel's (1972) "more general theory of persistence" is intended as a general explanation of persistent behavior, and as such includes the PRE. We should note that this theory is by no means intended only as an account of PRE phenomena, for it applies to a wide range of learning effects including discrimination learning and even drug effects. Amsel's earlier frustration interpretation of PRE (Amsel, 1958, 1962) can be treated as a special case of this broader notion of persistence.

   We will illustrate the theory of persistence with reference to a rat in a straight runway. If the animal is placed in a starting box and is reinforced for running to an end box, a running response will develop quickly. This much we can take for granted. What happens when stimuli that disrupt this response are introduced? Such stimuli should at first set off competing or disruptive responses, and these will interfere with the goal-oriented response. For example, if the proportion of reinforced trials is reduced there will tend to be a disruption in behavior, or if the animal must surmount an obstacle course there will be a disruption. Amsel (1972) goes on to postulate that in the face of these disruptive consequences, there will be a gradual conditioning of the running response to whatever stimuli cause disruption. That is, in the course of habituating to the disruptive stimuli the organism's running response actually becomes conditioned to those stimuli. This means that in addition to whatever stimuli in the runway were already conditioned to the running response, the response is now also cued by disruptive elements in the situation. The result, according to Amsel, should be greater persistence in the face of extinction conditions.

From Amsel's more general theory we may infer that the strength of conditioning of a running response to disruptive stimuli is a function of the number of pairings. For example, if a rat were shocked while running toward the goal, the conditioning of running to shock stimuli would become stronger as the number of shock trials were increased. Returning to the first experiment of this chapter, it now appears as if the effect of absolute number of nonreinforcements on resistance to extinction would clearly be predicted by Amsel, as well as by Lawrence and Festinger. Nonreinforcement tends to disrupt running behavior, and the more disruptions, the more running will come to be conditioned to interfering cues. The same argument can be applied to the studies of delay. Being delayed in a midbox without receiving reinforcement acts to disrupt the ongoing activity of running to the endpoint for food. Since the running response is disrupted in the specific location of the midbox, that response would become conditioned to the midbox as a stimulus associated with delay (disruption). Accordingly, the sight of that box, even during extinction, should set off the running response. It might also be evident by now that the prospect of a $50°$ incline should be disruptive. As the rat continues to make his way up the $50°$ slope of the runway his running response should come to be conditioned to the steep runway, which serves as a disruptive stimulus.

One of the interesting aspects of Amsel's new formulation lies in its overlap with dissonance theory. Lawrence and Festinger indicate that an unrewarded, effortful, or disrupted response will become more resistant to extinction because the organism will develop extra preferences for parts of the unrewarding or effortful situation. For Amsel, such a situation bolsters resistance to extinction because the response becomes conditioned to the disruptive elements. In essence, both positions argue that the durability of responding will ultimately be enhanced by disruptive intrusions into the conditioning procedure. Moreover, both positions would assent that this durability will increase as the number of instances of disruption increases.

Conceivably the two ideas might be discriminated in some carefully designed research, although not all of the variables of dissonance theory would necessarily set it apart from Amsel's notion. "Lack of justification" is a good case in point. To run a rat under conditions of minimal justification would probably mean reducing its quantity or frequency of reinforcement, but it should be evident by now that Amsel would follow the same procedure in setting up resistance to extinction. More generally, most of the stimuli that could be thought of as "dissonant" with the rat's running behavior would also be "disruptive" within Amsel's scheme. Another variable would be the degree of coercion: The more choice an animal exercises in the conditioning situation, the more dissonance. A paradigm might be created where the rat had to choose between two courses of action. With the subtle coercion of an experimenter the rat always chooses Course *A,* containing numerous disruptive (dissonant) features. Coercion would be varied so that the rat is sometimes gently nudged toward Course *A;* at other times the animal would receive more definite guidance. The prediction from dissonance theory is clear based on numerous earlier studies with humans, but what does Amsel's notion say about this variable? Amsel's (1972) view says that persistence develops when an organism learns to approach in the presence of any stimulus "which arouses a competing-disruptive response [p. 411]." It seems reasonable that competing responses are set up in proportion to the animal's degree of choice, since the tendency to pursue Course *B* would consistently be in competition with the tendency to choose Course *A.* Just as nonreinforcement sets up tendencies that compete with running to goal box *A,* the presence of a viable Course *B* would create in the organism a motivation to go elsewhere, and the effect of this competition-producing stimulus should be to strengthen resistance to extinction with respect to running toward *A.* The everpresent possibility of choosing Course *B* serves to disrupt running Course *A.* In short, whether we examine the variable of number of dissonant cognitions or the choice variable there appears to be considerable overlap between the two theories when applied to the phenomena reported by Lawrence and Festinger.

This being the case, might Amsel's framework be extended to the cognitive dissonance work on humans? To answer this we must look at the important differences between the human and rat cognitive dissonance research, and there appears to be just one striking difference: All of these animal studies have entailed numerous trials with the same behavior and same goal, where the human research involves just "one trial." In fact, "one trial" is a misnomer, since dissonance experiments with humans are not conceived as learning paradigms. Nonetheless, to fit Amsel's theory to the human research we would have to talk about a response becoming conditioned to disruptive stimuli without the benefit of systematic, repeated, multitrial exposure to such stimuli. This would be a cumbersome task, and it is doubtful that Amsel's framework would be done justice by attempting this extrapolation.

SUMMARY

The theory of cognitive dissonance is readily extensible to animals, and specifically to the PRE. This application broadens the domain of the theory and is also consistent with a finding in Chapter 7 on whether or not conscious awareness of a cognitive contradiction is a prerequisite for dissonance arousal. In that chapter it was found consistently that dissonance reduction was increased when attention was forced onto the dissonance, yet at the same time, research with young children and hypnotized subjects indicates that conscious attention to the dissonance is not completely necessary—it only helps. It should therefore not be surprising that rats can also express dissonance reduction.

Our conclusion is not designed to imply that dissonance theory is the sole reasonable account of PRE or related effects with animals, for we have just seen that Amsel's theorizing seems to handle these phenomena equally well. From the standpoint of dissonance theory, the point is not that these phenomena are the domain of just dissonance theory, but that they appear to coincide with numerous related effects we have noted among human subjects.

12
Selective Exposure

Selective exposure to information is a form of dissonance reduction and/or avoidance qualitatively distinct from other measures reported throughout this book. There appear to be unique problems associated with this measure, and historically, dissonance research involving selective exposure has been treated as a distinct entity (Festinger, 1957; Freedman & Sears, 1965; Katz, 1968; Mills, 1968; Sears, 1968). For these reasons this chapter will delve into some problems oriented around the measure of selective exposure, rather than focusing on independent variables as has been the custom in other chapters.

SELECTIVE EXPOSURE CONTRASTED
WITH OTHER FORMS OF DISSONANCE REDUCTION

Experimenters who have investigated selective exposure have for some reason been extremely interested in dissonance created by commitment to smoking. Accordingly, an example to introduce this chapter might best begin with a person's commitment to smoking and his subsequent desire to see or hear antismoking information. This hypothetical study has just two conditions. A sample of smokers is obtained, as well as a sample of nonsmokers who are in all other respects similar to the smokers. These two groups define the two conditions. Just to make the idea of behavioral commitment a salient feature, we might assume that the subjects are teenagers who have recently decided to become smokers or nonsmokers. Further, to be clear about the relative resistance to change of the cognitive elements, we might assume that these youthful smokers have committed themselves knowingly to a lifetime of addiction to tobacco—particularly cigarettes. So far the experiment resembles the simplest possible experiment of Chapter 2. We have only a variation in commitment.

What are the sources of dissonance for these two groups of subjects? For the smoker, dissonance should be created by the price of cigarettes, relevant medical information, and immediate side effects. For the nonsmoker, dissonance might be created through social ostracism for his abstinence, and perhaps by the feeling that he is missing something pleasurable. If this were one of the previous chapters, we would look for dissonance reduction in the form of attitude change: Smokers should come to enhance the virtues of cigarette smoking and play down the deficits; nonsmokers should do the opposite. But now we are interested in selective exposure to information, and the predictions for this means of dissonance reduction are quite simple.

Festinger (1957) discusses selective exposure in terms of approach and avoidance of certain kinds of information. If a source of information is potentially dissonance increasing, it will be avoided, while a source of information promising to lower dissonance will be approached.[1] The smokers should seek out supportive information and avoid information that promises to heighten preexisting dissonance. Nonsmokers will, of course, do the same. If a television commercial effectively associates cigarette smoking with one's sexual prowess and occupational success, smokers will be attentive while nonsmokers will be inattentive. But in contrast, nonsmokers will be attuned to the surgeon general's warnings, while smokers will attempt to avoid exposure to such warnings.

There is an important qualitative difference between selective exposure and evaluative change as methods of dissonance reduction. One superficial description of this difference is in terms of the complexity of the measure. In the case of evaluative change the measure does not require the person to exert additional overt efforts or to engage in a learning experience. But selective exposure does ask for these additional behaviors. In selective exposure the person is called upon to delve into previously unexplored information, to evaluate it, react to it, perhaps even to learn it. If indeed there are these differences, what is their import?

Given that selective exposure requires additional behaviors, a likelihood in many cases, it should be true that factors other than the existence of cognitive dissonance will have an impact on exposure. This is because the behavior to be performed (exposure) is unfamiliar and is subject to whatever influences are normally present when someone is about to move in a previously unexplored direction. Evaluative change as a mode of dissonance reduction may also have multiple determinants, but the problem is not of an imposing quality. This is primarily because evaluative change comes entirely from within the person and is a function of relevant cognitions already in his possession. In the case of selective exposure the individual is forced to react to the imposition of unfamiliar, possibly threatening stimuli, and to make decisions about dealing with these new events. There are many conceivable determinants of exposure to

[1] As an additional hypothesis, not derived from the theory, Festinger (1957, p. 131) argues that these selective tendencies will diminish as the amount of dissonance approaches a maximum. However, the only published experiments dealing with this hypothesis are the 1957 gambling experiment by Festinger and its replication by Cohen et al. (1959). Thus, we will not pursue that hypothesis in this discussion.

information, and of course these determinants can interfere with the clear functioning of dissonance principles in exposure to this information. It is our purpose here to examine a number of these sources of variance in order to gain an understanding of the kind of situation that best allows cognitive dissonance to have a measurable impact on exposure to information.

EXTRATHEORETICAL FACTORS BEARING ON SELECTIVE EXPOSURE

De Facto Selective Exposure

Among the numerous possible ways to measure the selective processes of the young smokers and nonsmokers discussed above, the easiest would be to classify each subject's exposure experiences during his usual existence. For example, subjects' actual exposure to cigarette-related advertisements, articles, and lectures might be tabulated, and if the theory is correct, smokers will have accumulated more procigarette exposures than nonsmokers.

But aren't there other possible reasons for such "selective" exposure? Perhaps the differential exposure came prior to the differential smoking habits, or equally likely, it may be that some other factor generated both smoking versus nonsmoking behaviors *and* differential exposure. De facto selectivity means only that smoking and exposure to prosmoking information are positively correlated. There is no necessary motivation to approach or avoid information selectively—it just "happens" that smokers are exposed more to consonant than dissonant information. Freedman and Sears (1965) have developed the distinction between de facto selectivity versus motivated selectivity and have presented evidence consistent with the de facto variety. We will neglect that kind of evidence, for its relevance to dissonance theory is negligible.

The point to remember about de facto selective exposure is this: People who have committed themselves to a behavior such as smoking or drinking can often be depended upon to be in more contact with supportive than with nonsupportive information. But the reasons for this contact may have nothing to do with cognitive dissonance. Because of these ambiguities our attention will be given to experimental manipulations of dissonance and selective exposure situations, simply to insure that the phenomena we list as evidence are more than de facto selectivity.

Curiosity

The preceding example can be altered slightly to make it comparable to some of the research to be reported. Suppose the smoking and nonsmoking subjects are brought into a laboratory where their exposure is confined to a specific body of information. They would then be given the chance to listen to a persuasive communication. One experimental communication is a speech on the degenerative effects of smoking; the other is a potpourri of enthusiastic cigarette advertisements. The subjects would be asked to rate each communication according to desire to hear it. Although the dissonance-theory prediction is perfectly obvious, the nonobvious could easily result due to subjects' curiosity. It may be that smokers are normally protected from medical information during the course of their daily lives, and given a golden opportunity to hear a speech on degenerative effects, curiosity might be stimulated. Contributing to such an effect would be their overfamiliarity with cigarette advertising. Nonsmokers, on the other hand, might be more curious about cigarette advertisements. Their reasons for abstinence could lie in a familiarity with degenerative effects, and assuming that the prospect of hearing more about a familiar topic would not excite them, their curiosity about a variety of advertisements would be especially likely to engage their curiosity.

In the interest of elucidating the relationship between dissonance arousal and selective exposure, it is obviously necessary to control curiosity. This is accomplished in at least four studies to be reported below.

Intellectual Honesty

Someone confronted with a variety of discrepant and nondiscrepant information may be strongly influenced by a norm of intellectual honesty. This is a value placed on exposing oneself to all viewpoints, something that follows from a self-conception of being openminded to all viewpoints. Just as with curiosity, it seems likely that such a need would be satisfied by a sampling of exposure to discrepant information, after which the selective processes implied by dissonance theory would become more prevalent.

Usefulness

Both smokers and nonsmokers might have more use for one type of information than another, independent of the utility of information in dissonance reduction. For example, perhaps the smokers are considering switching to a brand of cigarettes with lower tar or nicotine. If so, they would be well advised to listen to the speech on degenerative effects, for such a speech is likely to inform them about the separate effects of different toxic elements in tobacco. If this were the case they would be especially interested in the "dissonant" communication, but for reasons of usefulness. It follows that the potential usefulness of the information should be held constant, just as curiosity needs to be controlled. Any experimental situation allowing usefulness to covary with the degree of dissonance is not providing adequate conditions for a good test of the theory.

Attractiveness of Choice Alternatives

The factor considered here applies to a situation slightly different from the one considered above. The example should be changed to the following. Numerous smokers are recruited as subjects and are asked to rank-order the desirability of 20 brands of cigarettes. Then each subject's fifteenth-ranked brand is selected out, and the subject is subtly coerced to smoke that brand for the next month. The question now is, how will he reduce dissonance by means of selective exposure? The answer depends heavily on the specific experimental situation, and a suitable dependent measure would be to ask the subject to rate his desire to read each of 20 advertisements—one for each of the 20 brands. Dissonance theory, of course, implies that ratings of the advertisement for the fifteenth-ranked chosen brand will exceed ratings of other advertisements.

Unfortunately, the theory could receive spurious disconfirmation in this situation. Mills (1965a,b) indicates that interest in reading about a product can be a direct function of that product's desirability. This being the case, the fifteenth-ranked cigarette's advertisement may not be as attractive as the advertisement corresponding to more desirable brands, but for reasons completely independent of dissonance processes. If desirability were controlled, dissonance effects might then appear.

Dissonance Reduction by Exposure
to Nonsupportive Information

Festinger's (1957) analysis of selective exposure indicated that dissonance reduction might best be served by exposure to information consistent with one's commitments. To see discrepant information is to be reminded of the possibility of an error in decision. In 1964 he offered an alternative, in fact opposite possibility, which has since been followed up by Lowin (1967, 1969). This recent development allows that dissonance is sometimes best dealt with by exploring the challenge and refuting it. If a smoker realizes that antismoking arguments are available for his viewing, he might do better to become familiar with them and refute them, rather than to pretend they do not exist.

The difficulty posed by Festinger's (1964) change in thinking is simply this: dissonance reduction can sometimes be served by the variety of selective exposure which we have already described, and sometimes by the ostensibly opposite process of seeking out discrepant information (for the purpose of refutation). With these two processes occurring simultaneously the end result could be no systematic bias toward supportive or nonsupportive information. We will see some successful attempts in subsequent experiments to ferret out one or the other of those two opposing selective exposure tendencies.

Does the Research Stand a Chance of Supporting Dissonance
Theory?

In light of the many factors other than dissonance that could lead to various
exposure effects, a great deal of control seems necessary in order to test the
selective exposure extension adequately. If de facto exposure, curiosity, intellectual honesty, usefulness, and desirability are all controlled, it should then be
easy to commit a subject to a behavior and note his dissonance-reducing selective
exposure. But this is not quite the complete solution. Suppose the subject
decides to seek out discrepant information and attack it. There is still a problem
in prediction, but this too can be handled. The ideal experiment should vary the
circumstances conducive to subjects' tending to counterargue or not, and if this
can be accomplished the two opposite forms of exposure can be predicted with
some certainty.

Needless to say, none of the experiments to be described here has met all of
the conditions for the ideal selective exposure experiment. But there have been
various degrees of control over the many possible influencing factors, and by
examining the research we will be able to gather an idea of which factors are
most important to hold constant.

RESEARCH EVIDENCE: EXAMPLES OF REVERSE EFFECTS

In their lengthy review of selective exposure research Freedman and Sears
(1965) tabulated a number of experiments according to whether subjects generally preferred supportive, or nonsupportive information, or showed no preference. Experiments in which no preference was shown are hard to evaluate, for all
of the issues crop up that are relevant to explaining "no outcome" experiments.
If the reader is interested in some "no results" studies, we suggest reading
Freedman and Sears. The purpose of this brief section is to show how several
studies may have been misconceived, or designed incompletely, in light of the
criteria for an adequate dissonance theory test of selective exposure. All of these
experiments have shown results that are evidently contrary to the original
theory. In each of the experiments subjects who were committed to a given
behavior showed a propensity to expose themselves to nonsupportive information, and these results are by no means surprising when viewed with the previous
stipulations as background.

Rosen (1961) asked subjects to commit themselves to take either an essay
exam or a multiple choice exam. One aspect of his dependent measure involved
asking subjects for their preferences among two articles, one clearly supporting
the commitment, the other obviously nonsupportive. For example, the nonsupportive article for a student who chose the essay test was represented as an

opinion that students who favor essay-type exams are likely to perform better on objective tests. The results were in strong contradiction to the selective exposure notion: most subjects preferred nonsupportive information.

Here is a case where curiosity and usefulness could explain the finding. If a subject generally prefers essay exams, then has an opportunity to read an article telling him that people with such preferences generally do better on objective tests, he would no doubt be curious to find out more about himself. Related to this curiosity would be the potential utility of knowing why he, the essay exam taker, should perform better on objective tests. Mills (1968) offers a similar point in noting that people would prefer to read articles about themselves rather than about other types of people.

Feather (1962) examined the information preferences of smokers and non-smokers and found a selective tendency only among smokers, who preferred information contradicting their smoking behavior. Again, this seemingly backward result is not surprising. Curiosity and usefulness of information could easily have been associated with the smoker–nonsmoker dichotomy. Further, there is always the possibility that the smokers had set out to refute actively the antismoking arguments.

Sears (1965) turned his subjects into simulated jurors. He manipulated their votes by furnishing them with reports either favoring or opposed to conviction. Subsequent to this manipulation he measured the extent of preference for supportive or nonsupportive information and found a strong preference for nonsupportive information. Here we have an extreme example of conditions being created where the selective exposure effects discussed by Festinger (1957) could certainly not appear. The dice are loaded in the opposite direction. There is a strong norm of fairness and of weighing all sides in a courtroom, simulated or otherwise, and this factor alone should stimulate subjects to examine evidence contrary to that which they have already seen. The other factors such as curiosity are also relevant here, but their specific application does not need to be repeated.

Freedman's (1965a) experiment was even more severe than Sears' experiment in its potential for arousing the need to view nonsupportive information. Subjects listened to a taperecorded interview of a college student who had applied for a job carrying great responsibility. The student came across as either "very good" or "very bad" on the tape recording. Each subject was asked to record his judgment of the student job applicant, then was given the opportunity to read evaluations of the job applicant written by other subjects. The subject was given a choice between reading an evaluation agreeing with his own and one that disagreed (i.e., either supportive or nonsupportive).

Before describing the results we might reconsider the procedure. A subject who hears an inept applicant is likely to evaluate the applicant unfavorably, and should do so without much reservation. The decision about whether or not to hire this applicant should seem rather obvious to the subject, and should hardly create much dissonance. Then, he finds that another subject has actually expressed a favorable evaluation of the incompetent applicant. How could the subject possibly keep from being curious about the nature of that favorable evaluation? He would probably even derive a sadistic pleasure from reading the details of another subject's apparent misperceptions. The same reasoning would apply when the applicant appears to be of high caliber and the subject is offered a chance to read a negative judgment. The results, of course, showed an overwhelming preference for the "nonsupportive" material.

RESEARCH EVIDENCE: POSITIVE RESULTS

It should be apparent that the negative evidence just described can be taken as negative only if extratheoretical factors are disregarded. Most of the research contained several elements implying a bias toward exposure to nonsupportive information, meaning that the theory is not adequately tested by those procedures. Obviously none of those experiments was a perfect test in the sense of controlling for curiosity, desirability of alternatives, usefulness of information, and other relevant "nondissonance" factors. But for that matter, neither is any of the experiments in the following review "perfect." It does happen however, that controlling for a small number of those extratheoretical processes allows the theoretically predicted exposure effects to surface. More important, some recent evidence offers suggestions about which of the several factors most needs to be controlled.

Approach versus Avoidance

Festinger (1957) treated selective exposure as two parallel processes—selective approach and selective avoidance. Thus far there has been no need to make the distinction. However, the distinction can be drawn when the information used to assess selective processes is divided into supportive versus nonsupportive, provided that suitable baselines exist from which to infer the separate approach and avoidance components. The *approach* aspect of selectivity is shown when level of dissonance arousal is positively related to approach of supportive information, and in parallel fashion, the *avoidance* aspect becomes apparent when dissonance arousal is positively related to avoidance of nonsupportive material. For the most part the following experimental literature supports the approach derivation, but the avoidance postulate seems more difficult to demonstrate. In fact the phenomenon of avoidance of dissonant information has been demonstrated (Mills, 1965a), but it has yet to be shown that avoidance is a function of the amount of dissonance. This issue will be raised again toward the end of this chapter.

The research will be divided into "early" experiments and "later" experiments. This division is made partly for chronological considerations, and in part because of the differential focus. The early research employed dissonance-related variables without simultaneous efforts to control for the extraneous "muddying" and confounding factors such as curiosity and usefulness, while the later studies have centered more on control of these other processes.

EARLY RESEARCH

The first relevant study involved a "free choice" and was done by Ehrlich, Guttman, Schönbach, and Mills (1957). It was concerned with the consequences of an important decision for selective seeking of and attention to information bearing on the choice alternatives. It revealed that owners of brand new cars read advertisements of their own car more often than of cars they considered but did not buy and of other cars not involved in the choice. These selective tendencies were much less pronounced among old car owners who had made no recent decision. Thus, this finding supports the derivation from dissonance theory that persons seek out supporting or consonant information after an important decision in which they have rejected an alternative having positive attributes.

The study by Ehrlich et al. (1957) also illustrates a secondary determinant of dissonance having to do with the number of choice alternatives. Consistent with the assumption that the positive characteristics of unchosen alternatives are related to dissonance, it might be expected that the more alternatives involved in the choice, the more cognitive elements there are corresponding to desirable features of the rejected alternatives, hence the greater the resulting dissonance. The results showed that there was a tendency for new car purchasers, who named two or more cars as ones they considered but did not buy, to read more "own car" ads than those who considered only one other car or none; the former thus showed greater activity oriented toward reducing dissonance.

The Ehrlich et al. (1957) field study is easily open to criticism, primarily due to its correlational nature, but we do find in it an element of control not evident in other early exposure research. Since the sample of subjects was already familiar with much of the dissonance-relevant literature in question, curiosity and usefulness can probably be ruled out as biasing or interfering factors.

Other evidence, relevant to the effect of a negative choice on dissonance, comes from a "free-choice" study by Mills, Aronson, and Robinson (1959) and a replication by Rosen (1961). In the original study the investigators gave students in a psychology course a choice between taking an essay examination and a multiple-choice examination. An attempt was made to create choices of high or low importance by telling some students that the examination would count 5% (low importance), and others that it would count 70% (high importance), toward their course grade.

Since the subjects in this experiment did not choose whether or not to take the examination, but which of two examinations to take, the choice could have been perceived as having positive consequences, depending on the subject's expectations of how well he would do. However, it seems reasonable to assume that the most salient feature of such a choice situation is the fear of potential failure on an examination the subjects had not sought.

To measure dissonance reduction tendencies, all subjects were given the instruction that the course instructor wanted them to learn something more about types of examinations. Then they were asked to indicate, by a rank-ordering, which one of six research articles they wanted to read. Each student was given a list of titles, three of which were about essay examinations and three of which were on multiple-choice examinations. All the titles of some lists implied that each article, whether about essay or multiple-choice exams, described the beneficial or positive aspects of examination. Titles of other lists implied negative information. It was expected that subjects, to the extent they were experiencing dissonance from choosing one kind of examination rather than the other, would tend to choose positive articles and avoid negative articles about the exam they chose. (It might be noted that the terms "approach" and "avoidance" should not be viewed in any absolute sense, as the experiment had no baseline from which to measure approach versus avoidance tendencies.) Thus, the tendency to choose positive articles and avoid negative articles about the kind of exam chosen should be greater in the high-importance condition than in the low-importance condition.

The average rankings given to the articles showed that the positive articles for the chosen kind of examination were preferred to those for the rejected kind of exam. However, there was no difference in preference between negative articles about the chosen and negative articles about the unchosen, nor was there any effect of the importance manipulation.

Among possible weaknesses in this research is the absence of a method of ruling out curiosity, usefulness, and subjects' value on being intellectually fair about exposing themselves toward all possible positions. We will see an improvement in these respects in the following two "gambling" studies.

In a study by Festinger (1957), discussed briefly in an earlier chapter, college students were given $2.50 with which to play a card game against the experimenter. In describing the rules of the game, it was clearly implied that one side was much more likely to win than the other, and that the subject should easily be able to pick the winning side for himself. After the subject chose which side he would play, 12 hands were played, the subject being able to bet a small amount of his money on each trial. Unknown to the subject, the deck was stacked in such a way that the subject was likely to lose a moderate amount over the 12 trials. The prediction was that after the choice, the greater the loss, the greater the dissonance.

Since the cards were actually shuffled for each hand, some subjects were winning a little by the end of the twelfth trial, while others were losing anywhere from a little to a lot. At the twelfth trial the experimenter announced that before going on, the subject could look at a graph from which the true probability of winning could be computed. The subject was then allowed to look at the graph for as long as he liked. It was assumed that subjects who were, at the 12th trial, either winning or losing only slightly would expect the graph to indicate they had chosen the correct side, while those who were losing moderately to a lot would expect the graph to indicate they had chosen the wrong side. Thus subjects who were winning only slightly or were losing slightly and were therefore experiencing little dissonance would tend to study the graph carefully, with the expectation that the information would reduce their dissonance by informing them that they had chosen the correct side. On the other hand, subjects who were losing moderate to large amounts would be experiencing greater dissonance and would also expect that study of the graph would simply raise that dissonance by disclosing that they had chosen the losing side. In short, those who were winning or losing slightly would be motivated to study the graph carefully, while those who were losing moderately or greatly would tend to avoid study of the graph. This expectation was confirmed by a measure of the amount of time that subjects spent looking at the graph.

This experiment illustrates the proposition that because the magnitude of dissonance is a function of the ratio of dissonant to consonant cognitions, it can be reduced not only by change in the dissonant cognitions per se but also by the addition of consonant cognitions. Conversely, a person who is experiencing dissonance will tend to avoid attending to cognitions that will increase the magnitude of that dissonance.

An interesting further aspect of this study concerns behavioral change as a mode of dissonance reduction. In addition to attending selectively to the graph, most subjects also changed sides when there was extreme dissonance over losing and they were given an opportunity to change.

This study was replicated by Cohen, Brehm, and Latané (1959), with the addition of a questionnaire check on subjects' expectations in regard to what the graph would say about whether or not they had chosen the winning side, and a variation of importance through publicity. The results of this replication confirmed the assumptions and findings of the original study as reported above. It was also shown that when their winnings were to be made public, subjects' attempts at selective exposure were more pronounced than under private conditions.

These two gambling experiments resemble the Ehrlich et al. (1957) experiment in one important respect: Since subjects were allowed actual and sustained exposure to the dissonance-provoking information, any curiosity or value on intellectual honesty leading to exposure should have been satisfied quickly. It is conceivable that this facet of these two studies and of the Ehrlich et al. (1957)

field study was responsible for their success relative to various laboratory experiments attempted by other researchers.

One more comment is necessary in the context of the gambling studies. These are the only existing published experiments in which the behavioral commitment—the cognitive element originally most resistant to change—was reversed by subjects. In his original statement of the theory and analysis of selective exposure Festinger has offered some comments about the conditions under which there might be a sudden exposure to information that is discrepant from a behavior. Specifically, if the dissonant cognitive elements reach such a height that they become in some sense stronger than the behavior, the behavior might then be expected to change. When this happens it is of course true that previously dissonant elements would henceforth be consonant. Festinger (1957) elaborates on the relationship between this change in the most resistant element and exposure to information:

> If the dissonance is so large that it is *almost* sufficient to overcome the resistance to changing the behavior, one may expect that the easiest way to eliminate the dissonance is temporarily to increase it sufficiently so as to change the behavior. Under these circumstances one would expect persons *to expose themselves to dissonance-increasing information.* However, this would occur only in instances of extremely large, near maximum, dissonance. The maximum dissonance that can be produced between any two cognitive elements is, of course, equal to the resistance to change of that element which is less resistant [pp. 163–64].

From Festinger's discussion it should be evident that exposure to consonant information will not always increase monotonically with the amount of dissonance. If circumstances allow the most resistant cognition (usually some behavior) to slip into a status of less resistant, it is true that the analysis must change. Once the behavior is no longer the most resistant cognition the person will not, for reasons of dissonance reduction, attempt to expose himself to information consistent with that behavior.

Festinger's theoretical analysis of the 1957 gambling experiment has sometimes been taken to mean that the relationship between dissonance and exposure to behavior-consistent information will inevitably be nonmonotonic. For example, Rhine (1967a, b) has argued that the theory is adequately tested only when a wide variety of levels of dissonance is introduced, for only then is there some possibility of capturing the curvilinear nature of the dissonance-theory prediction. But this reasoning substitutes the specific analysis of the gambling experiment for the general spirit of the theory. The important factor is understanding what cognitive element is most resistant to change, for only then can the direction of dissonance reduction efforts be predicted. If the behavioral element is totally irrevocable, thus entirely resistant, the theory can predict only a monotonic relationship between dissonance and exposure to behavior-consistent information.

LATER RESEARCH

These studies will be divided into categories, depending on the extraneous factors ruled out by their experimental designs. Incidentally, it might be noted that Freedman and Sears (1965) arrived at their pessimistic conclusion about selective exposure effects before any of these experiments was published. Their pessimism may easily have been premature in light of these findings.

Desirability of Choice Alternatives

The primary purpose of two experiments by Mills (1965a) was to explore the conditions necessary for selective *avoidance* of information. The avoidance postulate was supported in none of the experiments just summarized, nor was it well tested. Mills presumed that the failure of Ehrlich *et al.* (1957) to find avoidance effects stemmed from a tendency of people to be interested in information about desirable products, independent of dissonance arousal. He suggests that the new car owners interviewed by Ehrlich *et al.* (1957) probably found the cars they rejected to be more desirable than cars they never considered. In fact, this would almost have to be true. Therefore, if exposure to advertisements is generally related to product desirability, it is not surprising that ads for rejected cars were read more than ads for cars never considered.

The procedures for Mills' two experiments were almost identical. Female college students rank-ordered the desirability of 10 personal products such as hair spray and deodorant, then the subject was offered a choice among two of the products. Immediately after the choice she rated her interest in reading each of 10 advertisements corresponding to the 10 products. Mills argued that an excessive interest in ads for the chosen product indicates selective approach, while an aversion to ads for the rejected product would show selective avoidance.

The following statistical procedure was employed to control for desirability of the product. A regression equation was derived for each subject on the basis of the eight products not involved in the choice. This regression equation was simply the linear relationship between the product's desirability and the subject's interest in reading an advertisement for it. Based on this regression equation, a prediction could be made for the subject's interest in reading about the chosen product, based on his desirability ranking of it. The same was done for the unchosen product. Given these two equation-derived predictions for interest in chosen and nonchosen products, the approach and avoidance tendencies are easy to calculate. If the subject's *actual* interest information for the chosen product exceeds the predicted value, that constitutes evidence for approach. If her *actual* interest in information for the rejected product is less than the predicted value for the rejected product, then selective avoidance is a reasonable conclusion.

The results of both experiments together show strong evidence for both approach and avoidance effects. At the same time, however, there remains some question concerning what kinds of dissonance-theory factors play a role in initiating these effects. In the first of these two experiments Mills varied the ease of the decision, in the same manner as Brehm (1956). Some subjects chose between products ranked 2 and 9, while others chose between the eighth- and ninth-ranked products. That this manipulation failed to have an impact may possibly be attributed to its relative weakness, a difficulty corrected in the experiment to follow.

Mills (1965b) conducted a near-replication of his previous (Mills, 1965a) research. One of the major changes was the use of 20 products rather than 10, enabling him to manipulate difficulty of decision more decisively. Subjects in this experiment chose either between the second and third-ranked items, or between ranks 2 and 19. Again there was statistical control for desirability, and this time the difficulty-of-decision manipulation had an effect: the more difficult the decision, the more interest subjects showed in reading advertisements for the chosen alternative (selective approach). The difficulty-of-decision variable had no impact on selective avoidance. In fact, the evidence for existence of avoidance was weaker than in the previous experiments, and not statistically significant.

At the very least Mills' research indicates that cognitive dissonance can produce a selectivity in regard to supportive information, given that desirability of alternatives is held constant. Further, his research shows that selective approach of information is mediated by the degree of dissonance, while it still remains to be shown that the *amount* of dissonance affects selective avoidance. But why did the mere controlling for desirability produce positive results, when there are numerous other factors that could have influenced exposure? The best answer seems to be that Mills was able to ascertain which of those several factors would make the most difference in his specific experimental situation. In the context, curiosity and usefulness of information would not have been particularly effective in leading subjects to expose themselves to nonsupportive information. This is because subjects' familiarity with each alternative was approximately equal, thereby handling the curiosity problem. Regarding the usefulness of information, Mills' procedure was designed so that nonsupportive information would be practically useless.

Usefulness

Canon (1964) conducted an experiment that demonstrates the potential confounding or interfering effects of information usefulness in selective exposure studies. The experiment was subsequently replicated by Freedman (1965b), but we will describe only the Canon experiment here. Subjects were first asked to make a series of four decisions regarding business matters, as a test of general ability in decision making and processing of new information. Then, following the fourth decision, they learned that the experimenter wanted them to formulate a written rationale for their fourth decision. In order to "assist" them in composing this short essay, the experimenter described various kinds of relevant information that could be made available to them while they wrote, and under a suitable rationale he asked them the degree to which they wanted to read each item of information. Some of this information was consistent with the subject's fourth decision, and other information was potentially dissonance arousing. Usefulness was varied by giving differential instructions regarding the nature of the essay. Some subjects ("high-useful" condition) expected that their essay would be in the context of a written debate, thus knowledge of the opposition's arguments would be of some utility to them. Subjects in the "low-useful" condition expected only to deliver a simple presentation of their own view concerning the fourth decision; thus, for them, the opposition arguments would not be terribly useful.

The results showed a clear main effect for usefulness of information, such that dissonant information was sought after more when usefulness was higher. Further, among subjects who were rendered confident in their decision-making ability by means of a prior experimental manipulation, there was a definite preference for dissonant over consonant information, given that the information was potentially useful. This latter result suggests that some subjects may have actively sought out dissonant information in the interest of refuting it.

These results make it plain that usefulness of information can be a potent determinant of exposure, and that the specific nature of the usefulness can lead either to supportive or nonsupportive selective exposure. However, the experiment should not be given too much credit for elucidating dissonance processes per se, for the effects could easily have been due to information usefulness independent of dissonance arousal. The important contribution of the experiment is a reminder that usefulness can be a potent factor.

Confidence in Decision and Refutability of Dissonant Information

Canon's (1964) experiment also contained a manipulation of subjects' confidence to make business-related decisions. Some subjects were given low confidence by "demonstrating" to them their ineptitude at choosing the correct solution to a series of case studies; other subjects found that they were able to choose the correct solution quite readily. Then, following the fourth case study in a sequence, all subjects had the opportunity to choose between supporting and nonsupporting information regarding that fourth decision.

The results indicated that low confidence led to a strong desire for supportive information, but the opposite pattern of results appeared among highly-confident subjects, particularly when nonsupportive information was described as useful. The results make perfectly good sense from the standpoint that highly-confident subjects should not have experienced much dissonance upon deciding—they should have felt some security of being correct. The results are also in line with an interpretation that assumes the operation of the alternative form of selective exposure. Assuming that all subjects had some desire to encounter and refute nonsupportive arguments, the highly confident people would have been in the best position to effect such a refutation. Accordingly, their preference for nonsupportive information is understandable. They felt they could beat down the opposing arguments.

Lowin (1967) designed a pair of field experiments to examine explicitly the impact of arguments easy to refute versus arguments difficult to refute. We will describe just the first study here, which Lowin casts as his "main" study. Subjects who favored either Johnson or Goldwater during the 1964 election were mailed the experimental materials. Each subject received in the mail several sample arguments, more of which he could obtain by returning a postcard. Subjects received either weakly consonant, strongly consonant, weakly dissonant, or strongly dissonant arguments. Strength of argument was defined in terms of relative difficulty of refuting it.

We might examine the experiment from the standpoint of a subject. A few sample arguments are received via mail, and the recipient finds that all he need do is return an enclosed postcard in order to receive a brochure loaded with similar arguments. Among subjects who received consonant arguments the tendency to return the postcard should increase with the strength of the sample arguments. Certainly any dissonance aroused by choosing to support Johnson (or Goldwater) could best be reduced through exposure to convincing consonant arguments. The situation is different for a subject receiving dissonant arguments. There should generally be a desire not to see additional information, but presuming that there is an opposing form of selective exposure, in which the subject seeks out dissonant information and refutes it, the tendency to request a dissonant brochure should increase with the weakness of the arguments.

The data follow exactly the form suggested by Lowin (see Table 13). In fact, the data would imply that the refutation-of-contrary-arguments form of selective exposure is as prominent a process as the original type of selective exposure. The percentage of subjects requesting weak dissonant information (24%) is approximately the same as the percentage requesting strong consonant brochures (26%).

Lowin's study could be a crucial stepping point in understanding the antecedents of selective exposure, although there is one weakness in the form of a plausible alternative explanation. Just as in our discussion of Freedmsn's (1965a) experiment on "preference for dissonance information," it could have been that Lowin's subjects found the weak opposition arguments to be amusing and took pleasure out of the opportunity to ridicule the opposing political party or candidate. The joy involved in laughing at one's enemy may have nothing to do with the active refutation supposedly basic to the dissonance reduction process implied by Lowin. A similar criticism could also be applied to a further study by Lowin (1969), which produced evidence in keeping with the initial research

TABLE 13
Subjects Requesting a Brochure

Strength of argument	Consonant or dissonant	Percent
Strong	Consonant	26
Weak	Consonant	12
Strong	Dissonant	10
Weak	Dissonant	24

effort. However, the criticism is weakened substantially by the manipulation of ease of refutation in this experiment (Lowin, 1969): Instead of manipulating the actual content of arguments, ease of refutation was defined in terms of the source being a high school student, versus an expert in the difficult-refutation condition.

Together with Canon's (1964) study, Lowin's (1969) research suggests that subjects will engage in "refutational" exposure when they are sufficiently confident in their ability to refute the arguments. In Canon's experiment this confidence was imparted by way of experience with earlier decisions, and in Lowin's experiment the confidence was determined through the form of the argument. Given these results, some of the weaknesses in earlier research are more comprehensible. It is quite probable that subjects in earlier studies differed in their method of dealing with dissonant information, and unless something definite is known about the ease of refutation, a mixed bag of results is entirely likely.

In the interest of completing the picture about confidence and exposure, we should note that the procedure employed by Canon (1964) does not appear to be easily replicable. Similar efforts to vary confidence by Freedman (1965b), and Lowin (1969) did not produce results in accord with those of Canon, although Rosnow, Gitter, and Holz (1968) did meet with success. This variability in results does not mean that the variable of confidence is suspect, because alternative devices for instilling confidence do appear to operate with more regularity. For example, if ease of refutation of opposition arguments may be construed as one type of confidence, then certainly the ease-of-refutation results of Lowin (1967, 1969) support the notion that confidence allows the individual to expose himself to discrepant cognitive elements.

Effects of Actual Exposure Rather Than Anticipated Exposure

In most of the above research selective processes were measured by asking subjects what kinds of information they would prefer to see or hear. Since they were never actually exposed, but had to anticipate the nature of the arguments, at least two relevant but atheoretical factors may have entered the picture. First, curiosity about dissonant (or consonant) arguments can be an important determinant of exposure to yet-unheard arguments. We have already discussed the ways in which curiosity about the unfamiliar can mask dissonance reduction effects. Second, when subjects are told by an experimenter that there are two kinds of information available, a norm of fairness toward the information, or intellectual honesty, may well be activated. The strength of this norm would have been particularly strong in the Sears "juror" study, but it could easily exist wherever the subject might feel evaluated by an experimenter.

Brock and Balloun (1967) examined selectivity in such a way that subjects did not have to anticipate the information. Instead, selective exposure was measured during the course of actual exposure. Since subjects in such a situation do become quite familiar with the line of thought in the arguments, curiosity and the norm of fairness to each side are fairly well eliminated.

Before discussing the Brock and Balloun (1967) research we might note that the two gambling experiments (Festinger, 1957; Cohen, Brehm, & Latané, 1959) gave all subjects ample opportunity to become familiar with the dissonance-arousing or consonance-creating information, and the measure of exposure was reading time rather than deciding whether or not to expose oneself to the information. With this procedure curiosity should have been largely eliminated as a determinant of differential exposure. This is because a brief initial examination should have handled curiosity, while a more detailed inspection would begin to relate clearly to dissonance arousal.

In four separate experiments. Brock and Balloun (1967) exposed smokers and nonsmokers to dissonant or consonant information. The information consisted of taperecorded messages, which either favored or opposed smoking. The messages were accompanied by a good deal of static, and if the subject desired a clear rendition of the arguments it was necessary to push a button repeatedly in order to hear a continuous static-free message. The measure of exposure was simply the number of static-removing button pushes.

The results of all four experiments were similar, and consistent with Festinger's 1957 ideas. Smokers initiated more attempts than nonsmokers to remove static from a message which disputed the connection between smoking and lung cancer, while nonsmokers tried harder than smokers to clarify a message arguing for a causal link between smoking and lung cancer.

There were some additional issues included in the experiments, but there is no point here of going into more detail. The smoking issue and messages make the point clear: Given actual exposure rather than anticipated exposure, dissonance theory's original prediction is quite accurate.

We might ask why "refutational" selective exposure did not dominate the picture here. The best answer is that subjects who were exposed to dissonant information may have listened to arguments as long as they were able to refute them, or until they had refuted all of them. However, such refutation might not imply the same kind of careful listening as would be manifested by the subject who is attempting to surround himself with comfortable thoughts. Refutation requires only an understanding of the essential points of the argument, and certainly the redundancies and details would not be crucial. But the individual motivated to create an atmosphere of consonant information is likely to enjoy all of the details.

The Brock and Balloun procedure is directly analogous to a television advertisement. Static would be welcomed in the case of a disagreeable appeal, but the recent purchaser of a new car should be interested in clarifying the details of a consonant message.

There is a more general point coming out of the Brock and Balloun experiments. Many of the extradissonance processes we have discussed require only minimal exposure for their completion. Curiosity is satisfied by a sampling of the nature of the arguments, usefulness of the information is exhausted once the essence of the arguments has been absorbed, and the need to be fair-minded or intellectually honest is probably served by a "token" exposure to disagreeable information. The Brock and Balloun procedure allows these various motives to be satisfied quickly, and once they are diminished, dissonance reduction can appear in relatively pure form.

SELECTIVE AVOIDANCE AND UNFORESEEN CONSEQUENCES

Earlier in this chapter we noted that selective exposure, as a dissonance-reducing process, is markedly different from the cognitive changes that are typically assessed in dissonance research. When attitude change or some similar process is measured we have no reason to think that the measuring instrument calls upon the subject to absorb new, unfamiliar cognitive elements. But the case of selective exposure is markedly different. In most of the research we have discussed (Brock, 1965; Canon, 1964; Feather, 1962; Freedman, 1965a, b; Mills, 1965a, b; Mills, Aronson, & Robinson, 1959), the subject knew little about the information at the time his selective exposure was ascertained by the researcher. In all of these above-mentioned cases subjects had virtually no concrete expectations about the information prior to their decisions, and when asked for preferences among pieces of information they usually knew only the title of the selection of information. There have of course been exceptions, most notably Brock and Balloun (1967), Festinger (1957), Cohen, Brehm, and Latané (1959), and Lowin (1967). In these latter investigations the subjects were given a substantial sample (or all) of the information prior to or simultaneously with the experimenter's ascertaining the degree of selective exposure. We have already noted that such procedures can abate curiosity, intellectual fair mindedness, and usefulness, but these same procedures may also be relevant to a more central process within dissonance theory.

It will be helpful at this point to view selective exposure as involving two separate, dissonance-arousing decisions. First there is the decision we have discussed heretofore—for example, the decision to smoke, the decision among consumer items, or the decision about business matters. Presumably it is possible to vary the degree of dissonance created by that decision, as we have seen in experiments by Mills (1965a, b) and others. Further, we must assume for this analysis that a high degree of dissonance due to the first decision will motivate the person to avoid further, related dissonance-arousing decisions.

The second decision concerns whether or not to expose oneself to a particular type of information. Theoretically a person should experience dissonance to the degree that he elects to expose himself to information contrary to a behavioral commitment, just as he would experience dissonance by electing not to receive payment for his efforts in a tedious or dangerous task. However, this decision about exposure will arouse dissonance only to the extent that the person can accept responsibility for his exposure. It will be recalled from Chapter 4 that surprise consequences typically create no dissonance, thus it may well be that dissonance is not created by exposure to information about which the person is ignorant. When a person knows nothing about an essay, or article, except for the title, it is possible for him to deny responsibility for his exposure to its contents. More specifically, he cannot easily anticipate the specific arguments or other persuasive features, thus the various discrepant elements within the communication would not be relevant to dissonance arousal.

This line of reasoning may explain, in part, why it is difficult to obtain evidence for selective avoidance of "dissonance-arousing" information (see Freedman, 1965a; Rosen, 1961; Sears, 1965). It is entirely possible that subjects feel no responsibility for their exposure to such information, thus the motivation to keep dissonance at a low ebb plays no role in their decision to avoid or not.

It follows from this reasoning that selective exposure, as a dissonance-minimizing tactic, will be more prevalent once the individual is apprised of the exact nature of the information. Only then can he make an informed—hence responsible decision, and only then will the decision to expose oneself to discrepant information have implications for dissonance arousal and reduction. Perhaps this is one of several reasons for the marked success of the studies by Brock and Balloun (1967), Cohen, Brehm, and Latané (1959), Festinger (1957), and Lowin (1967; 1969).

SUMMARY

Festinger's original argument assumed the operation of a selective exposure process whereby information that increased consonant elements or decreased dissonant elements would be sought out. It was also assumed that dissonance-increasing information would be shunned. He divided the selective processes into approach and avoidance elements, and the accumulated evidence makes a strong case primarily for the approach segment of selectivity. Even the approach-of-consonant-information hypothesis was on tenuous ground for many years, as documented by Freedman and Sears (1965), but beginning with the Mills research (1965a, b) there have been clarifications of the conditions conducive to selective approach. To name a few, the variables of confidence, curiosity, and values of intellectual honesty or fairness can play a significant role in altering the course of exposure to decision-relevant information. Unless such processes are controlled or otherwise taken into account, the implications of dissonance theory for selective exposure can often go astray, or even appear correct for the wrong reasons.

Still more important are two factors more closely related to the theory. The first of these is the refutational selective exposure suggested by Festinger (1964) and elucidated by Lowin (1967, 1969), which is an everpresent possibility. Unless the investigator is equipped to locate factors that discriminate the two kinds of selective exposure, any dissonance-theory hypothesis about selective process will suffer from ambiguity. Second is the issue of responsibility. If the individual confronted with potentially discrepant information may be cast in the role of decision maker, it is not surprising that he chooses discrepant information when he is ignorant of the contents of such information. Only if he anticipates the nature of the communication can he be described as responsible for choosing among types of information, and unless there is responsibility we doubt that the decision would have much impact on dissonance. The implication is that people will be most selective in exposing themselves to information with which they are completely familiar.

13

Interpersonal Processes

Earlier chapters have illustrated the role of dissonance theory in reactions to others, but within the context of making particular theoretical points. For example, Aronson and Mills (1959) demonstrated that subjects who must come to justify an embarrassing initiation rite will subsequently increase their liking for a group. Brehm and Wicklund (1970) showed that attraction to two people is a function of choosing between them. Just as in any other dissonance-arousing decision, the person choosing comes to see the chosen as increasingly attractive and the unchosen as less attractive. The present chapter also deals with dissonance-mediated reactions to others, but the purpose here is not specifically to demonstrate theoretical issues surrounding the theory. Instead the theory is applied to areas of psychology that have traditionally been studied from theoretical perspectives other than dissonance theory. Just as in the preceding several chapters, our purpose is to show how dissonance theory might provide an alternative approach to phenomena normally dealt with in other conceptual language. Five problem areas have been selected for this discussion of reactions to others: (a) the individual's attraction to a group, (b) motivational effects of social deprivation, (c) aggression, (d) defensive projection, and (e) reactions to inequity.

THE INDIVIDUAL'S ATTRACTION TO A GROUP

Conformity as a Source of Dissonance and Subsequent Liking for Group

Imagine a person who is asked to perform a somewhat difficult discrimination task, consisting of estimating which of two stars has the greater number of points. This person is led to believe either that he has high or low ability at this task. Then he is asked to make a series of discriminations between pairs of stars, but in the meantime he stands a chance of being influenced by a small group:

Just before he gives his own judgment there arises an opportunity to view the judgments of two other people. Obviously this is a potential conformity situation, and the dissonance analysis here treats the conformity response as the cognition most resistant to change.

This situation may be familiar by now. It is an experiment by Gerard (1965) discussed in Chapter 2. It may also be recalled that Gerard was not particularly interested in measuring actual conformity. Instead, he *determined* the degree of conformity by giving subjects "feedback," based on some electronic equipment, regarding whether their "first impulse" in making judgments was to conform or not conform. This is a novel experiment, since the behavioral commitment consisted of the subject's belief that he had a first impulse, independent of his actual behavior.

Returning to the ability dimension, what combinations of high and low ability and high and low conformity should produce dissonance? In the low-ability condition subjects were probably not surprised by either their conformity or deviance. Neither behavior would have aroused much dissonance, for their ability level would not necessarily have led them to expect to be different from or similar to the group. But high-ability subjects who found themselves to be conformers should have experienced dissonance arousal. Their ability level should have led them to expect some independence, assuming that they felt their ability was generally above that of other subjects. How should this dissonance be reduced? The most direct route would be to find the group to be especially attractive, thus liking for the other members should have been greater for high-ability subjects who conformed than those who did not conform. This is exactly what happened (see Chapter 2). Moreover, the low-ability subjects showed just the opposite pattern of results. This latter result is probably orthogonal to dissonance processes and may reflect low-ability subjects' felt dependence on the judgments of others.

How does this experiment qualify earlier findings or theory in conformity? From any theoretical standpoint conformity has always been treated as a dependent variable. And in relation to liking, it would be difficult to find a conformity theorist who would disagree with the statement that conformity to a group increases to the degree that the group is attractive, except, perhaps, with the notable reactance-theory exception of Brehm and Mann (1975). Gerard's (1965) innovation consists of turning this liking-conformity sequence around. With the theoretical impetus of dissonance theory he has shown that conformity can lead to liking, but only to the degree that conformity is dissonant with cognitions the individual holds about his own abilities.

Liking for an Unaccepting Group

The fact that humans generally like others who like and accept them should come as no surprise. This point is well documented in the literature on interpersonal attraction. People who are similar, pleasant or agreeable, and who indicate liking for us come to be liked in return (Aronson, 1969a). With dissonance theory as a theoretical guide, Kiesler and his colleagues have documented some important exceptions to these extensions of common-sense reinforcement theory. This research has been discussed in some detail in the commitment chapter and will be reviewed quite briefly here.

In the first experiment (Kiesler & Corbin, 1965) subjects met in small groups and evaluated paintings. Partway through the experimental session subjects received feedback about their degree of acceptance by other group members, and it will be recalled that acceptance was varied across three levels—high, moderate, and low. Given this much information, we might expect from earlier work in interpersonal attraction that subjects would be attracted to the other members in direct proportion to the amount of acceptance. But now dissonance arousal enters the picture. About half of the subjects were asked to continue in the same group for an additional three hours. For subjects who were given low acceptance, there would have been a discrepancy between a commitment to further interaction and lack of acceptance.

The results showed a direct relationship between acceptance and liking for the group if just the high and moderate-acceptance conditions are considered, and commitment made no difference at those two levels. But the results show a dramatic switch when the low-acceptance condition enters the picture. In this condition there was a marked divergence between committed and uncommitted subjects, such that commitment brings forth an increment in liking. In fact, among committed subjects there was more liking with low acceptance than with moderate acceptance. It should also be noted that these results were virtually identical when conformity to the group was measured (Chapter 2). Interestingly, there is some evidence that these liking effects are mediated by opinion conformity (Kiesler & Corbin, 1965).

Results parallel to these were found by Kiesler and De Salvo (1967) and by Kiesler, Zanna, and De Salvo (1966). Since these were discussed in the commitment chapter we will not go into them again here. The important contribution of this research is that of specifying conditions under which an "unattractive" group becomes impactful, in the sense of producing conformity, and subsequently increasing in attractiveness. The seemingly perverted response of becoming attracted to a group in the face of rejection is not so startling when considered as a dissonance phenomenon. Just as in the Lawrence and Festinger research (Chapter 11), the organism appears to find good reasons for its presence in a situation to which it is committed, and such reasons are invented in proportion to the pain, effort, or rejection entailed by being committed to that situation.

MOTIVATIONAL EFFECTS OF SOCIAL DEPRIVATION

The preceding research on groups provided a serious qualification of the operation of reinforcement principles. Given dissonance arousal with respect to an uncomfortable social situation Kiesler and his associates find that the group becomes increasingly attractive as it increases in its rejecting qualities. Two experiments reported in this section also demonstrate how dissonance arousal can interfere with processes generally presumed to be controlled by reinforcement. More particularly, the research of this section illustrates a breakdown of the "normal" relationship between deprivation from a reinforcer and the reinforcer's effectiveness.

Cohen, Greenbaum, and Mansson (1963) note that social deprivation can improve the effectiveness of a socially based reinforcer. For example, if words of a certain class, such as personal pronouns, are reinforced by means of social approval, the effectiveness of social approval is enhanced by first depriving the subject from such social approval. But suppose a subject whose verbal responses are being shaped is deprived of social approval under conditions of choice, and suppose further that his commitment to deprivation is not adequately justified. The dissonance incurred by this procedure should lead the person to devalue social approval. And if he manages to view approval as insignificant, the deprivation should not be especially effective in raising the power of the reinforcer.

Cohen et al. (1963) began by establishing an operant level for emission of I and we. This baseline was established by asking subjects to respond verbally to a set of stimulus cards. Second, a 15-min interview was conducted with the subject. During the first 5 min of the interview the subject received frequent verbal reinforcement ("good") from the interviewer, and deprivation was manipulated in the following way during the remaining 10 min: In the low-deprivation condition the interviewer continued to reinforce with "good," but in the high-deprivation condition the interviewer remained silent for 10 min. Based on earlier research we would expect the amount of deprivation to affect subjects' responsiveness to later reinforcement. This later reinforcement will be discussed below.

Third, a number of the high-deprivation subjects were randomly assigned to one of two dissonance conditions. In both dissonance conditions subjects were asked to take part voluntarily in an additional interview. The interview was described as something the subject would not enjoy, and the interviewer was said to be highly disapproving, critical, and skeptical. In the low-dissonance condition subjects were offered $5 to volunteer for this further deprivation from social reinforcement, while high-dissonance subjects were offered $1.

Before proceeding we should review the reasoning behind this procedure. If a subject commits himself to social deprivation, voluntarily and for just a minimal monetary justification, dissonance should result. One clear route to reduction of this dissonance is derogation of that which has been foregone, that is, devaluation of social reinforcement.

Subsequently all subjects were administered the same verbal task used to establish an operant level of first-person pronouns. But this time every sentence beginning with I or we was reinforced with a "good" from the experimenter.

The number of *I*s and *we*s over the operant level was the dependent measure of interest. First, considering just the two nondissonance (control) conditions, in which there was no commitment to a further interview, the results showed clearly that deprivation does increase the power of a social reinforcer in the absence of dissonance. But when the dissonance groups are examined, both of which were subject to deprivation, it appears that commitment to deprivation with a justification of only $1 resulted in a minimization of the value of social reinforcement. The high-dissonance condition shows less responsiveness to "good" than either the low dissonance or high-deprivation Control conditions.

Epstein (1968) conducted a study in keeping with the design of Cohen *et al.* (1963). His subjects were grade school children, whereas those of Cohen *et al.* (1963) were college students, and the response reinforced was that of imitating the experimenter's judgments of the loudness of paired tones. In addition, dissonance was varied through different degrees of choice. Otherwise the two experiments were fairly similar. The study began with an operant period to assess a baseline imitation rate for each subject. Then the subject was left alone for 15 min. When the experimenter returned he informed the subject that there would be an additional delay, meaning he would again leave the subject alone. In the no-choice condition the subject was prevented from partaking in any social interaction during the experimenter's absence by the experimenter's order to "Please remain here until I come back. Don't return to your class." High-choice subjects were also asked to wait alone, although the experimenter raised the possibility of their returning to their class, saying ". . . the choice is up to you."

For both groups the experimenter returned from his second absence after 2 min and proceeded with the imitation task. But this time the subject's imitative responses were reinforced with social approval, such as "fine" and "good." The measure was the effectiveness of the reinforcement in producing imitation, and consistent with the dissonance-theory reasoning, there was a tendency for high-choice subjects to imitate less than low-choice subjects ($p < .10$).

Taking the two experiments together, the theoretical idea is supported consistently. When a subject commits himself to social deprivation for low justification (Cohen *et al.* 1963) or under high choice (Epstein, 1968) he comes to devalue social reinforcement, with resultant lowered conditionability. This result might be seen as similar to Mansson's (1969) study of commitment to water deprivation and subsequent learning performance (Chapter 10). It will be recalled that subjects who committed themselves to additional hours of water deprivation under dissonance-arousing conditions showed relatively poor performance in learning a list of thirst-related words. Presumably that decreased learning was the result of subjects' attempts to convince themselves they were not thirsty, thereby interfering with the normal tendency for thirsty individuals to increase their retention of thirst-related stimuli. In light of these experiments, and Mansson's (1969) study of thirst, a more general conclusion can be drawn. Whenever a reinforcer has an impact on learning, the effectiveness of that reinforcer can be curtailed if the individual commits himself, under dissonance-arousing circumstances, to doing without that reinforcer. Cognitive dissonance has the effect of bringing forth derogation of that reinforcer, and it appears that the behavior of a person who convinces himself he has no need for reinforcement is then less subject to being "shaped up" by such reinforcement.

This is not to say that dissonance always operates to lower the effectiveness of reinforcers. The direction and nature of behavioral commitment must first be specified. For example, the previous experiments might have been done in reverse, whereby subjects would first be satiated with social reinforcement. Several experimenters would virtually "good" the subject to death, then he would voluntarily commit himself to additional social approval. Under such circumstances this behavioral commitment would no doubt arouse dissonance, since additional social approval on top of a recent over-abundance would be less than desirable. The less justification provided for consuming additional social approval, the more the person would have to find his own reasons for his commitment. Certainly he should come to value approval more highly, with the result that social approval would gain in effectiveness as a reinforcer.

At this point we will move on to the third topic, aggression. The aggression section doesn't address itself to the interference of dissonance with reinforcement processes, but deals specifically with aggression as a dissonance-arousing behavior and the different routes by which overt aggression is justified.

AGGRESSION

Dissonance and Derogation of One's Victim

A study by Davis and Jones (1960) was the first investigation of the relationship between aggression and derogation of the victim as mediated by dissonance arousal. The theoretical argument behind this study is similar to the reasoning of most research discussed thus far: If a person elects to aggress against someone under highly dissonance-arousing conditions, he will come to find justifications for his actions. One such justification consists of reevaluating the target of aggression, thus rather than feeling sympathy for whoever is the brunt of aggression, the perpetrator will come to dislike him.

Davis and Jones induced dissonance by having college students make derogatory remarks to a person who was presumably a student being evaluated on several personality dimensions. All subjects were informed that this "student" was to hear either a positive or negative evaluation. But some were told that they were assigned to give one of the two kinds of evaluation according to whether they were odd- or even-numbered subjects, while others were told they could give either the positive or negative evaluation, but what was really needed was the negative evaluation. It was expected that dissonance engendered by the choice to rate a person negatively would be reduced by negative shifts in real evaluations of the person. Postexperimental ratings by the subjects of the person they had falsely rated were, in fact, more negative in the high-choice condition than in the low, thus supporting the specific experimental hypothesis and the more general formulation that dissonance increases with choice.

The Davis and Jones study also shows the role of commitment in the choice paradigm which we have been discussing. While some of their subjects in each of the high- and low-choice conditions were told that they would be unable to inform the target person of the false nature of their negative evaluation, others were led to believe that they would confront the target person and could dispel any belief he might have in their negative evaluation. The latter group of subjects, relative to the former, were not committed to the negative evaluation. And, as one would expect, the relatively noncommitted subjects showed no evidence of evaluating the target person more negatively in the high than in the low-choice condition. Of course, it is not clear whether the effect of the revokable commitment is to eliminate the arousal of dissonance in the first place or to change the way by which dissonance is reduced.

Glass (1964) elaborated on the paradigm of Davis and Jones by adding a dimension of self-esteem. At the outset of the experiment subjects were given false feedback on their maturity, intelligence, concern for others' feelings, and egocentricity. Some subjects found that they were highly mature and intelligent, in addition to being of high standing on other dimensions, while the other subjects received quite negative feedback. Subsequently the subjects were asked to administer electric shock to a confederate, and were given either high or low choice in whether or not to deliver the shocks. Glass proposed that the type of aggression in his experiment was inconsistent with a high self-esteem subject's conception of himself. Presumably a person with high self-esteem does not view himself as motivated to inflict physical harm onto others. But a low self-esteem person should not find his unjustified aggressive behavior to be so inconsistent with his self-conception. From this reasoning, subjects with high self-esteem who gave shocks under high choice should have experienced the most dissonance, and the results were consistent with Glass' expectations. Subsequent to the shock administration, liking ratings for the confederate were lower in the choice—high self-esteem condition than in the corresponding no choice condition. The choice variable made no difference in the low self-esteem conditions, suggesting that the aggressive behavior was consistent with a negative opinion about the self.

In summary, these two studies extend the reasoning behind the choice variable to effects of aggression on interpersonal liking. The experiments also contribute two other interesting derivations from the theory.

1. In the Davis and Jones study there is some suggestion that dissonance is aroused only when the dissonance-arousing behavioral commitment is irrevocable. To the extent that the insult can be mollified by a forthcoming discussion with the object of the insults, dissonance reduction is weakened.

2. Glass has demonstrated that some kinds of actions which might ordinarily be construed as dissonance-arousing are not necessarily so, and this is because certain "negative" actions are implied by a negative overall self concept.

Other Methods of Reducing Aggression-Related Dissonance

In a forced compliance paradigm Brock and Buss (1962) showed that attitude change, as determined by changes in evaluation of a subjective experience, is affected by dissonance. Their study dealt with the evaluation of aggression by examining the effects on individuals who chose to deliver noxious stimulation when they were on record as opposing such punishment. After such a choice, the greater the intensity of the aggression, the greater should be the dissonance and consequent tendency to reduce dissonance. The aggressor may reduce dissonance by evaluating the stimulus as less noxious, saying, in effect, "The pain I administered was really rather mild." Thus a main hypothesis of the study was this: When dissonance is high (under the high-choice condition), the greater the intensity of the aggression delivered, the more subsequent minimization of its painfulness.

Subjects who were opposed to the use of electric shock on humans in scientific research were induced to administer mild or extreme electric shock to a "subject" (victim). They were given either high choice or no choice about whether to administer the shock. Before and after these manipulations they received mild shocks, and they rated the painfulness of those shocks. Change in evaluation of painfulness from before to after the experimental delivery of the shock to the victim was the principal dependent variable.

In the high-shock condition subjects were instructed to use only shocks at levels 6–10; in the low-shock condition they were instructed to use only the shock values 1–5. Subjects in the no-choice condition then proceeded with the experiment. In the choice condition, before proceeding with the administration of the shock, the experimenter gave subjects the option to leave and stressed the subjects' choice in whether or not they wanted to continue with the research.

Thus subjects presumably experienced dissonance as a function of behaving in a manner contrary to their values: They shocked others when they were against the use of shock. The more they experienced a choice in this and the more shock they had to deliver, the more dissonance and consequent revaluation of shock as less painful were expected.

The results for subjects within the high-choice condition were much as expected: their subjective minimization of shock painfulness was a positive function of the amount of aggression delivered.

An interesting sidelight in this experiment is that the greater revaluation of shock so as to minimize its painfulness occurred only when the "victim" was a male. When the victim was a female, the effect was reversed. When the victim was a female, rather than changes in evaluation of the painfulness of shock, the preferred avenue of dissonance reduction for the aggressor was evidently an increase in feeling of obligation, the subject saying, in effect, "I gave pain but I was obliged to do so."

It is clear that when the victim is a female, the barriers against reducing dissonance via attitude change (minimization of shock) are greater than when the victim is a male. It is more difficult to feel that a female is not being hurt by the shock than it is to believe that a male is not being hurt. Since there was a great deal of resistance to attitude change where there were female victims, the subjects chose another available avenue that had not been blocked off experimentally: They increased their felt obligation to comply with the request to deliver shock. This result suggests that where resistance to change via one mode of potential dissonance reduction is relatively high, dissonance reduction may then transfer to an alternative mode. In this case, having committed themselves to delivering shock, subjects could reduce their dissonance by attitude change, except when that mode was infeasible due to the fact of a female victim. The question of preference for alternative modes is discussed in more detail in Chapter 9.

Inhibition of Retaliation Following Dissonance Arousal

The present experiment by Firestone (1969) focuses on the inhibition of aggression as an effect of commitment to interaction with a hostile partner. If a person knows that a second individual has been hostile toward him, and then voluntarily enters into a dyad with that second person, dissonance should lead to an increment in liking. This much has been illustrated in the above research by Kiesler and his colleagues. Firestone's experiment goes beyond this already-established point and considers the impact of provocation from the partner once the interaction has begun. His reasoning is as follows: If a person enters into a dyad, by choice, with someone who has already been openly hostile, dissonance processes will set in motion a tendency to like the other. This dissonance-reduction effect may then continue when further hostility is met during the interaction. When the person is provoked additional dissonance will result, and if he has the opportunity to retaliate, the ongoing dissonance reduction process should inhibit the desire to retaliate.

The experiment began with the subject and a simulated partner exchanging self-descriptions. This was done without face-to-face contact, allowing the experimenter to use a taperecorded "partner." At the end of this initial session the subject and partner exchanged evaluations, allowing a manipulation of the partner's hostility. In the no-insult condition subjects received a complimentary evaluation, while subjects in the insult condition found that the partner thought them to be shallow, inconsistent, and egotistical. After the insult manipulation all subjects were asked to participate in an "optional" procedure. The experimenter indicated that this would consist of a 20-min interaction with the same partner, and subjects were induced to engage in this interaction under either choice or no-choice conditions.

During the interaction the subject worked on a task while his partner distracted him. The distraction consisted of blasts of white noise, and the number of blasts to be given was left up to the partner. Accordingly, the partner had the opportunity to be as obnoxious as he desired with respect to delivering the distracting noise. In the low-provocation treatment he gave the subject nine blasts, while 29 blasts of noise were administered in the high-provocation condition. Subsequently the subject had an opportunity to retaliate by shocking the partner, and the dependent measure we will examine is the number of shocks delivered.

Before presenting the shock results Firestone's experimental design and reasoning should be reviewed. First the subject committed himself to interacting with a partner under one of three conditions: no insult—choice, insult—no choice, and insult—choice. Of these three conditions dissonance should have been created primarily in the insult—choice condition. As a check on this assumption an evaluation-of-partner measure was taken just after commitment to interaction, but before the actual interaction, and the results are entirely consistent with the theory: Liking was greater in the insult—choice condition than in either of the other conditions, compared against a baseline liking rating taken earlier. Since there was apparently just one condition in which dissonance was aroused by the anticipated interaction, Firestone expected that the subsequent provocation (white noise) would generate dissonance reduction primarily for subjects in that condition. If we reconsider some of the conclusions of the earlier chapter on responsibility, Firestone's reasoning makes perfectly good sense. Only the subjects in the insult—choice conditions and insult—no choice anticipated hostility from the partner. Subjects in the no insult—choice condition did not enter the interaction with any idea that they would be greeted with hostility, thus the high provocation would have come as a fait accompli, and should have been an ineffective stimulus to dissonance arousal. Finally, and needless to say, subjects in the insult—no choice condition would not experience much dissonance.

The means for the measure of retaliation against the partner (shock frequency) are shown in Table 14. Note that the pattern of results in the first two columns is similar: the higher the provocation, the greater the retaliation. However, this relationship between provocation and retaliation is changed considerably by the onset of dissonance in the insult—choice condition. As shown in the third column there is only a slight, and insignificant tendency for increased provocation to be met with greater shock frequency. It appears that Firestone's reasoning is supported. It might also be noted that the pattern of results was identical for shock duration.

TABLE 14
Retaliation against Partner: Shock Frequency

	No insult— Choice	Insult— No choice	Insult— Choice
Low provocation	9.5	16.2	16.7
High provocation	19.7	24.7	19.1

Note: There is a significant effect for provocation within the first two columns.

DEFENSIVE PROJECTION

In a paper aimed at clinical psychologists, Festinger and Bramel (1962) discuss in detail the use of defensive projection as a means of dissonance reduction. It will have been noted by now that there is a similarity between certain "defense mechanisms" discussed by psychoanalytic theory and certain avenues of dissonance reduction. Certain dissonance-reduction mechanisms appear very much like "rationalization" or "defensive denial," for example.

One reason for this similarity is that once ego-defenses become established as reactions to characteristic conflict-arousing situations as a means of handling inner impulses, they may become behavioral modes themselves and therefore may be used in a wide variety of situations (see Cohen, 1959b). Thus an ego-defensive behavior, as a characteristic individual reaction to tension or conflict in discrepant situations, might reflect itself in a given mode of dissonance reduction. As Festinger and Bramel say, the concept of dissonance and the psychoanalytic concept of "inner conflict" may have overlapping meanings. They go on in some detail to distinguish between the two notions.

Their argument, paraphrased, runs as follows: Psychoanalytic theory is mostly concerned with situations in which the person's perception of some aspect of himself is discrepant from his internalized values (his superego). A person who considers homosexuality an extremely invidious trait and is suddenly made aware of the fact that he has homosexual tendencies may have a fear of disturbing and painful guilt feelings and punishment aroused in him. In order to avoid further anxiety and guilt, according to psychoanalytic theory, the ego will initiate defensive measures, of which the most pervasive appear to be various forms of denial of the threatening information about himself.

Dissonance theory, on the other hand, would first ask whether dissonant relations would be expected to exist among the cognitions involved. Is the cognition that one has homosexual tendencies necessarily dissonant with the belief that such tendencies are bad and that one should not have them? The answer, according to Festinger and Bramel, is no, except for those persons who believe that they consistently live up to their internal standards. For some people, the knowledge that a trait is undesirable may not necessarily imply in itself that one does not possess it. Thus some people who are threatened in the psychoanalytic sense may also experience considerable dissonance, whereas others will not. In other words, according to psychoanalytic theory, the conflict sufficient to produce defensive behavior does not necessarily include what would be defined as dissonance.

Festinger and Bramel do not say that dissonance would be completely absent from the cognition of the person who does not expect himself always to live up to his own standards. For example, when he discovers he has homosexual tendencies, this knowledge may be dissonant with his belief that he is really quite masculine, even though it may not be dissonant with his conviction that homosexuality is a bad thing. In any concrete case to which the psychoanalytic theory is applied, it is quite unlikely that dissonance will be completely absent. However, any contribution which dissonance might make to defensive behavior would be in addition to the factors emphasized by psychoanalytic theory. They say that perhaps the key differences between the approaches are highlighted by the lack of concern for the self-concept in classical psychoanalytic theory. Dissonance theory would place more emphasis on the individual's concept of what he is rather than his concept of what he should be (superego).

Festinger and Bramel ask whether the Freudian defense mechanisms against anxiety could also be used to reduce dissonance in the type of situation we have been discussing. They consider as an example the defense mechanism of projection, which is especially interesting to social psychologists because of its interpersonal implications. A person who has high self-esteem (i.e., he has many cognitions favorable to himself) considers homosexuality a very bad thing and a matter of considerable importance. When such a person is suddenly confronted with information that he is sexually attracted to members of his own sex, this cognition will be inconsistent with his cognitions concerning what a good person he is and also inconsistent with his belief that he is actually quite a masculine person.

Can this dissonance be reduced by attributing homosexuality to other people? One possible way to do this, according to Festinger and Bramel, would be to attribute homosexuality to people who are liked and respected in order to be able to revaluate homosexuality as such. If liked and respected persons possess the trait, perhaps the trait is not so bad after all. Then possession of the trait would no longer be discrepant with high self-esteem and therefore dissonance would have been reduced. A further possibility is that the person, by attributing homosexuality to members of his reference or comparison group, may be able to convince himself that he does not deviate from the persons most important to him. If he is only average in his possession of the trait, then subjectively it does not so strongly disconfirm his favorable self-esteem.

In their paper Festinger and Bramel cite at length an experiment by Bramel (1962) designed to study the use of projection as a mode of dissonance reduction. In this experiment each subject was told that the first part of the experiment was designed to discover what kinds of people had insight into themselves. He was asked to take a number of personality tests that, he was told, would be carefully analyzed by members of the clinical psychology staff. After the tests were scored, he was to learn the "results" in an interview, during which time his self-insight would be measured.

At the beginning of the second session (about a week later), the subject was told that the second part of the experiment was concerned with forming impressions of personality and that he would be asked, in addition to other things, to make some judgments about another subject. The two subjects appeared simultaneously, and, prior to the reporting of the results of the tests, they were introduced to one another. The experimenter asked each in turn (in the presence of the other) a set of questions about himself and his attitudes toward certain current events in order to enable the two strangers to gain some impression of each other in preparation for a later measurement of their attitudes toward each other. The subjects were then separated, and the appropriate test report was communicated to each of them privately.

Unknown to the subject, the "results" that he received had been prepared with no reference to his actual performance. There were only two test reports, one very favorable (the favorable condition) and the other very unfavorable (the unfavorable condition). The tone was objective and the general favorability (or unfavorability) quite consistent throughout the report. One subject of each pair was assigned randomly to the favorable condition and the other to the unfavorable condition. Thus, experimentally, the self-esteem of one subject was enhanced, while the self-esteem of the other was reduced somewhat.

After receiving the "results" of their personality tests, the two subjects were brought together into a room and seated at a long table; in front of each subject was a box containing a dial that faced the subject. Two wires with electrodes on the ends issued from each box; each subject perceived his apparatus immediately in front of him and could not see the other subject's apparatus.

The subjects were first asked to make some judgments of each other, using 11 adjective scales that could be scored for general favorability. A self-concept measure followed, consisting of 16 polar adjective pairs similar to those included in the prior rating of the other person. This scale provided a check on the effectiveness of the experimental manipulation that had attempted to influence their level of self-esteem.

Next, the experimenter read a set of instructions to set the stage for introducing the undesirable cognition that, presumably, should create considerable dissonance for subjects in the "favorable self-esteem" condition but should not produce much dissonance for subjects in the "unfavorable self-esteem" condition. It was explained that psychologists were especially interested in whether or not people could estimate "deeper and more personal aspects of the personality" on the basis of a first impression, and that this part of the experiment would be concerned with the perception of sexual arousal. An elaborate explanation of the physiology of sexual arousal and the sensitive techniques for their measurement followed. Considerable emphasis was placed on the unconscious nature of sexual arousal and the impossibility of exerting conscious control over its expression in the "psychogalvanic skin response." The subject's task was to observe his own sexual-arousal response on his galvanometer for each of a series of photographs of men that would be projected onto a screen. He was to record this figure on a page of a small, anonymous booklet. After recording his own arousal level for the particular picture on the screen, he was to make an estimate of the dial indication of the other subject's apparatus for the same photograph. The subjects were explicitly told that movements of the dial indicated homosexual arousal to the photographs. As a precaution against excessive threat, the subjects were told that persons with very strong homosexual tendencies would consistently "go off the scale." Furthermore, the anonymity and privacy of the situation were carefully spelled out, with the intention of convincing the subject that no one but he would know what his own responses had been.

Unknown to the subject, the experimenter exerted complete control over the movements of the needles, which were identical for the two subjects. Each photograph had been assigned an "appropriate" scale value in advance, so that those depicting handsome men in states of undress received more current than did those depicting unattractive and fully clothed persons. Both subjects were thus led to believe that they were sexually aroused by certain pictures and not by others, according to a consistent pattern. In effect, they were made to believe that they had "behaved" in a manner contrary to their self-images by somehow producing homosexual responses, just as Gerard's (1965) subjects were made to believe that their first impulse was to "conform" or remain "deviate." According to the hypothesis, subjects in the favorable condition should experience considerable dissonance when observing their needle jump in response to photographs of unclothed males. "Behaving" in a strongly undesirable manner is quite dissonant with believing one is an extremely fine person. Subjects in the unfavorable condition, on the other hand, would have more cognitions consonant with having produced homosexual responses and not so many dissonant cognitions. Discovering one has a very undesirable trait is less discrepant from believing one is an undesirable person. Thus, if projection of an undesirable trait is a positive function of the magnitude of dissonance, then subjects in the favorable condition should attribute more homosexual arousal to others than those in the unfavorable condition. The results showed clearly that subjects in the favorable condition evaluated their partners as having significantly higher arousal than did subjects in the unfavorable condition. The average subject in the favorable condition evaluated his partner as having had the same arousal level as he himself had; those in the unfavorable condition generally evaluated the other person as having had less arousal than they themselves had. This difference between the groups in change in evaluation was specific to the trait of homosexuality. There was no difference between conditions in the general favorability with which subjects rated their partners. In short, it would appear that projection occurred in order to reduce dissonance, for there was more projection where dissonance was high than where it was low, even though "threat to superego" was the same for both conditions.

Some of the results derived from internal analyses were especially interesting. It was found, for example, that an identifiable projection effect tended to occur mainly when self-esteem was exceptionally high—in other words, when the discrepancy between the self-esteem and the homosexual "behavior" and resulting dissonance was great. Even within the favorable condition, projection occurred relatively consistently only when measured self-esteem was above the average for that group.

It seemed plausible to Bramel that the major dissonance-reducing effects of projection would occur only if the person onto whom the trait was projected was liked or favorably evaluated. By projecting onto respected persons, an individual might succeed in making homosexuality appear a less undesirable trait, and by projecting onto his reference or comparison group he may conclude that he is no worse than average in the degree to which he possesses an undesirable trait. The data show that subjects in the unfavorable condition attributed more homosexual arousal to people they did not respect. Subjects in the favorable condition also attributed more arousal when their partner happened to be evaluated poorly or moderately. However, this simple halo effect disappeared when these subjects happened to be with a partner whom they respected. Considering only those subjects who rated their partner very favorably, there is a significant difference between the favorable and unfavorable conditions in the expected direction. Thus, subjects in the two conditions differed in their evaluation of their partner as homosexual only when their partner was rated favorably. This suggests that defensive projection occurred only when the available social object was favorably evaluated.

As Festinger and Bramel note, the finding that defensive projection occurred only when the available social object was favorably evaluated differs considerably from usages of the projection concept by writers in the psychoanalytic tradition. Such writers (e.g., Ackerman & Jahoda, 1950) say that projection is generally aimed at persons and groups who are disliked and considered noncomparable and inferior to the projector. It would seem, for example, that the projection concept may have indeed been used too freely in explaining hostility toward out-groups, without any clear specification of the conditions under which it represents defensive attribution or rationalizations of displaced hostility.

As a more direct answer to the question of whether projection is toward outgroups or ingroups, Bramel (1963) conducted a second study of projection of homosexuality. Half of the subjects were given feedback indicating that they had homosexual tendencies, and half received more favorable feedback. The "psychogalvanic skin response" apparatus used in the previous study was again employed to manipulate homosexual feedback. Each of these conditions was subdivided according to the nature of the target person. Sometimes the target was described as a student, and for other subjects he was described as a criminal. The results, again in terms of amount of homosexuality attributed to the target person, demonstrated that projection is a positive function of dissonance only when the target is a student, and this finding is consistent with Bramel's expectations.

Why should dissonance reduction best be served by projection onto a liked or similar other? Bramel (1963) offers one good possibility. If a similar other person is seen as possessing the trait, the meaning of the trait could change such that a homosexual tendency would no longer be seen as a grossly unflattering characteristic.

The result of this second experiment supports dissonance theory, but it would be presumptuous to say that the psychoanalytic notion is thereby incorrect. The issue of denial is relevant here. The psychoanalytic position assumes that projection onto an outgroup will occur provided the person can at the same time deny that the characteristic applied to himself. In Bramel's (1963) study the subject could not make an outright denial of the meaning of the needle movements, so that the dissonance-producing information regarding his homosexuality "response" was unambiguous and consciously available to him. Under such circumstances the commitment to his "own homosexuality response" was very strong and therefore resistant to change. Thus one good way to reduce the remaining dissonance in the absence of refutation of the discrepant information was to try to see others as similar. At this point we might turn to a more recent study, in which the issue of denial versus projection is addressed directly.

In an experiment with fewer explicit Freudian overtones, Edlow and Kiesler (1966) supplied their subjects with feedback concerning decisiveness. In the low dissonance case subjects found that their decisiveness was at a reasonably high level, while dissonance was created for other subjects by informing them that the test feedback revealed exceedingly low decisiveness (fifteenth percentile). The high-dissonance group was subdivided such that the information was easy for some subjects to deny. They were simply told that the validity of the decisiveness test was in question. It was argued that such subjects could reduce whatever dissonance was aroused by refusing to characterize themselves in line with the feedback, while this was presumably made difficult in the "hard deniability" case, where the experimenter attested to the test's validity.

The other variable resembled that of the last study by Bramel, and consisted of varying the projection target between a student and a criminal. The results were consistent with the authors' reasoning: projection of indecisiveness toward the student occurred only to the degree that the feedback could not be denied, while projection to the criminal was virtually unaffected by the ease-of-denial variation.

Festinger and Bramel's use of the dissonance formulation to explain the occurrence of projection raises the interesting issue of the place of dissonance theory vis-à-vis psychoanalytic theory with regard to such phenomena. Do they mean to put dissonance theory forth as an alternative explanation for understanding ego defenses, or, instead, do they visualize dissonance theory as a formulation existing side by side with psychoanalytic theory insofar as both attempt to deal with defensive phenomena? It seems to us that theirs is the latter intention. What then would be the advantage of specifying a dissonance formulation of processes with which psychoanalytic theory has long dealt? The answer would seem to be predictive accuracy. If one assumes that the sorts of variables suggested by the dissonance application to these personality phenomena are more amenable to measurement and conceptualization than the sorts of variables classically identified by psychoanalytic theory, then dissonance theory can certainly be assumed to add precision to the understanding of defense mechanisms. In addition, these concepts are more clearly specified, more easily subject to empirical test, and more easily linked to other empirical operations. Such variables as the self-esteem of the individual or his patterns of liking and respect are different from the variables generally used by psychoanalytic theory to account for ego-defensive behavior. Because of this they may make for more accurate and controlled research into the determination of this kind of behavior.

It is true, however, that Festinger and Bramel make no attempt to join dissonance theory and psychoanalytic theory. The theories remain standing alongside one another, both assumed to have a great deal to say about the phenomena under scrutiny. But we may well ask if there would be any advantage in applying these theoretical models to ego defenses in a more integrated fashion. In order to discuss this point we must first raise the question of whether the person has to be consciously aware of the cognitive conflict he experiences in order for dissonance to be produced.

It should be clear that the dissonance formulation as it stands makes no assumptions about the need for a person to be conscious about commitment to discrepant behavior or about the resultant dissonance. However, all of the aforementioned experiments that we have considered to be rather unequivocal in their arousal of dissonance appear to make at least the implicit assumption that the processes under observation are concerned with some awareness of own responsibility for discrepant commitment on the part of the subject. In Gerard's (1965) experiment, for example, had the subject not felt some uncertainty and decisional conflict and even some twinges toward conformity when he saw the others making responses radically different from his, the manipulation of conformity through the identification of his "first impulse" might not at all have been successful. Thus, when he saw the needle indicating that he had "conformed," he may be said to have had some subjective awareness of having chosen to "commit" himself to the discrepant response.

The same point applies to Bramel's experiment. Even though the subjects were told that the sexual arousal was unconscious, similar processes of choice in commitment may be said to have been operative. Young men just having come into manhood are conscious of their identity and masculinity. When they look at pictures of men in various states of undress, we may assume that they possess a great deal of cultural foreknowledge about the impropriety of sexual arousal under such conditions. They are all eager to behave and feel in the right manner and may therefore feel a good deal of uncertainty and anxiety when viewing the pictures. Thus, when the experimenter feeds back the information that they have experienced some homosexual arousal, it must be seen against this baseline of uncertainty and conflict and the subject's knowledge that he could give either an acceptable "response" or an invidious one. Here also, then, the dissonance experienced is a function of the fact that he has "behaved" to produce an invidious response discrepant from his self-image, that is, his behavior "follows from the opposite of" his motivation to maintain a positive self-picture. In effect, he has "committed" himself in a manner that has created some conflict within himself between an important motive and its satisfaction.

The Festinger and Bramel model is not explicit on the role of the processes of choice and commitment that we have highlighted, and, as a result, it is difficult to see that they are generally speaking about a situation that probably demands some "conscious awareness" of a discrepant commitment. It is precisely this factor of choice in commitment, which may be unique to dissonance theory, that makes it difficult to see how the theory can interact with psychoanalytic theory in explaining, for example, defensive projection. It would seem that a much broader attack might be more valuable than one that permits the two theories to function side by side in dealing with ego-defensive processes.

Festinger (1957, pp. 235–243) has suggested that such a state of affairs as strong emotion without a conscious explanation of it produces dissonance and motivates the individual to invent reasons for his feelings. (The similarity of this notion to the reasoning of Schachter & Singer, 1962, is striking.) According to Festinger (1957), Freud had recognized this phenomenon. From this lead, it would appear that, using the Festinger and Bramel argument as a starting point, a more detailed analysis of at least the processes of projection, homosexuality, and paranoia may be possible. Such an analysis would deal with the interplay between conscious and unconscious forces and may not necessarily assume the person's awareness of a discrepancy.

Berkowitz (1960), in a stimulating paper on the judgmental process in personality functioning, offers an explanation for the dynamics of paranoia and projection that illustrates the potential benefits to be gained by dealing more explicitly with the interplay between the more conscious forces central to dissonance theory and the unconscious forces postulated by psychoanalytic theory. His ideas, although somewhat different from the conventional psychoanalytic formulation, are based on it. Also, while they are not identical to the assumptions of dissonance theory, they are entirely consistent with it, at least as it has been discussed in the present book. As Berkowitz points out, the psychoanalytic concept of projection involves, among other things, lack of insight into (or the repression of knowledge of) the possession of undesirable traits that produce conflict. If this lack of awareness is motivated, it may be due to a perceived inconsistency between the given trait and the individual's self-concept. Also, according to the psychoanalytic formulation, reaction formation must be considered here. In projecting his own characteristics onto others, the person may not only repress awareness that he has those characteristics, but he may also lean over backward in denying them and insist to himself and others that he is just the opposite. This is shown by the paranoid: According to psychoanalytic theory, the paranoid's basic problem involves latent homosexualty, and, since this is threatening to him, he represses the drive and projects it onto important others. However, even the attribution of homosexual desires onto others provokes anxiety, so the idea is transformed from "he loves me" into "he hates me."

Berkowitz's (1960) explanation, on the other hand, runs as follows: Paraphrasing his argument, we may say that, as in psychoanalytic theory, the process commences when the person judges himself (his "real self," i.e., his "behavior") as being toward the homosexuality end of the continuum, whereas his "ideals" are anchored toward the extreme heterosexual end. This discrepancy produced dissonance, and, in defense, the person "represses real knowledge of his self-evaluation," and may believe that he is really the way he would like to be. Such a process could, of course, occur entirely below the level of conscious awareness, though the notion of "judgment" in fact denotes conscious experience of this by the individual at some level. In any case, the individual represses his homosexual attributes but also exhibits reaction formation in characterizing himself as nonhomosexual. Seeing himself as extremely heterosexual, the person may see important others as more homosexual than they actually are. But even this is dissonance producing, since liked others cannot be characterized as having a trait of which one disapproves. The person may reduce such dissonance by increasing his dislike for the person possessing the evil trait. However, since the basis for the hatred is kept from awareness, some tension may still remain. The discrepancy between the tension and no conscious explanation for it motivates the individual to find reasons for his feelings. Thus, Berkowitz proposes that to a considerable extent the paranoid's feelings of being persecuted are the reasons he invents to give conscious meaning to his hatred for others. And extrapolating from Festinger's observations, Berkowitz feels that the magnitude of dissonance and consequent projection and paranoia can be a function of the size of the discrepancy between the way a person behaves and feels and what he thinks of himself.

The major point we wish to make here is that although the mechanism of projection may have been established early in life as a mode of resolution of inner conflict, it can also be seen as serving to reduce the dissonance arising from discrepancies between aspects of the individual's self-concept (both conscious and unconscious) and his behavior. Thus, projection might well be viewed as a consequence of the motivation to reduce discrepancies within the self produced by some choice to commit oneself to a stand that is incompatible with the satisfaction of some important motive, in some cases, the motive for a favorable self-evaluation.

If one followed this line of reasoning, numerous implications for processes characteristically viewed as within the province of personality theory might be uncovered and made amenable to a dissonance formulation. For example, aggression directed against the self and its concomitant of depression could be explored as a function of the exercise of aggression toward others. If a person for some reason hurts or is openly hostile toward some innocuous other person whom he does not necessarily want to hurt, he may be expected to experience dissonance. The higher his self-evaluation, the more would aggression be dissonance arousing since his behavior is more discrepant from his self-concept, the more self-esteem he has. The person can reduce dissonance in this situation by increasing his dislike of the other person, thereby making his perception of the other person consistent with his behavior. If, on the other hand, the other person is a good friend, and barriers to derogation exist, the person can reduce dissonance by increasing his feelings of dislike or hostility toward himself. A bad act is thus made consistent with the kind of person one is. The greater the dissonance, the more the dislike directed toward the self in order to reduce that dissonance. We thus arrive at a rather paradoxical prediction: The higher the person's self-esteem or the more favorable his self-evaluation, the more he will show aggression against the self when he commits a discrepant act of aggression. Such an analysis could conceivably be applied to other personality processes like regression or dependency, reaction formation, and repression or denial. When the motivations, either conscious or unconscious, can be specified, a dissonance-arousing discrepant commitment can be identified and often shown to have effects on perception, cognition, and behavior that might not be expected from other theoretical approaches.

The point here, as well as Berkowitz's argument, represents an attempt to deal explicitly with the interplay between the unconscious forces posed by psycho-analytic theory and the more conscious ones specified by dissonance theory. Such a scheme may permit a better specification of the interaction between the environmental stimulus events impinging upon the person and the inner constraints as they both serve to determine his daily behavior in the social world. In effect, a formulation of this sort might aid in elaborating a more subtle and differentiated view of the relationships between personality and social behavior than we have at present.

Summary

A dissonance theory analysis of social interaction stresses that there are many possible reasons that one person may choose to interact with one or more others. To the extent that there are reasons for not choosing to interact, dissonance will be aroused by the choice to do so. This dissonance can be reduced by magnifying any of the possible reasons in favor of interaction. Thus, given the choice to interact, low personal attraction to the other person, for example, would arouse dissonance that could be reduced by enhancement of the importance of the interaction product, by enhancement of the prestige of the group, by perceiving the interaction activity itself as highly attractive, and related effects. Any factor that affects the tendency to choose to interact with another can affect the magnitude of dissonance from that choice, and all factors that can be seen as reasons for interacting can serve in the dissonance reduction process.

REACTIONS TO INEQUITY

This section is devoted to a special theoretical treatment of social processes not touched upon in the preceding sections. It is based on Adams' (1963, 1965) formulation of inequity theory, which is derived in part from dissonance theory as we know it. Adams analyzes the effects of a person finding himself to be in an inequitable relationship with another. His initial statement of inequity theory appeared in 1961 (Adams, 1961), and was published in 1963, but since his later statement includes and extends the earlier treatment, our discussion here comes entirely from Adams (1965).

The concept of inequity becomes useful whenever two people are in a direct social relationship, or when each of two individuals is in a direct exchange relationship with some third person and the two individuals compare themselves with one another with respect to that relationship. In either of these circumstances the two people will each contribute certain imputs to the relationship, and each will derive certain outcomes. For example, a man and wife each contribute inputs to their marriage, and each expects outcomes. Alternatively, when two individuals are employed by some third party, each one invests inputs (work) while at the same time receiving outcomes—particulary payment for that work. Inequity comes into being when a person perceives his ratio of outcomes/inputs to be different from that of the person with whom he compares. *Different* is to be taken literally. An inequitable outcome–input ratio can be either below or above that of the comparison person.

When a person discovers himself to be in an inequitable situation, a tension is created which is proportional to the magnitude of inequity. Adams postulates that this tension will motivate the person to eliminate or reduce that same tension. We might note the similarity to a central postulate of dissonance theory. Certainly dissonance theory also assumes a tension state which the person becomes motivated to reduce. The similarity is more than coincidental, for Adams (1965) has postulated that "the experience of inequity is equivalent to the experience of dissonance [p. 290]." Not only is the tension state of inequity the same as cognitive dissonance, but Adams also notes that he has borrowed from dissonance theory to derive a number of statements about the ways in which inequity is reduced. We shall turn to these now, for the modes of inequity reduction are the core of Adams' theory.

Altering Inputs

No matter what form inequity takes, it can be reduced by the person's altering his inputs. If a person's outcome–input ratio is greater than that of a co-worker or other comparison person, inequity is reduced by increasing inputs. Stated in other words, if the person thinks he is receiving too great a reward for his investment of work, he can accelerate his work rate or quality. Conversely, if the same person's outcome/input ratio is small relative to someone with whom he compares, he can render his ratio more comparable to the other's ratio by decreasing inputs.

One derivation from the altering-inputs idea has to do with inequitable piece rate payment versus inequitable hourly rate payment. If a person feels he is overpaid according to an hourly rate, he can increase his inputs (work). However, the definition of overpayment on a piece rate schedule is that the person is simply receiving too much money. Therefore, to lower the overall payment he can lower his rate of work. A study was designed by Adams and Rosenbaum (1962) to test this idea. Nine subjects were assigned to each of four conditions: (a) where an hourly rate of $3.50 was paid and the subjects were made to feel overcompensated by stating that they were not qualified to earn the hourly rate of $3.50; (b) where the hourly rate of $3.50 was paid, but the subjects were made to feel that they were fairly paid by telling them that they were very well qualified to earn the rate; (c) where a piece rate of $.30 was paid but the subjects were made to feel overcompensated as in the first condition; and (d) where a piece rate of $.30 was paid but the subjects were made to feel they had been fairly paid as above. The task was to obtain interviews with the general public for 2 hr, and subjects were under the impression that they were hired for an extended time period.

The data support Adams' hypothesis. They show a significant interaction such that subjects overcompensated by the hour show a higher productivity than comparable individuals earning the same pay but feeling equitably compensated, whereas overcompensated persons paid by the piece show lower productivity than comparable persons paid at the same piece rate but feeling equitably compensated. This is assumed by Adams to indicate an increase in performance among the hourly workers who are overcompensated in order to establish equity, whereas the piece workers who are also overcompensated reduce the amount they can earn when they are overcompensated in order to establish equity.

In another experiment Adams and Jacobsen (1964) asked subjects to perform a proofreading task. Some of the subjects (high-inequity condition) were led to believe that they were unqualified to earn the standard $.30 per page, yet they were also told that they would receive that rate. Subjects in a reduced-inequity condition were given similar instructions except that they found their rate reduced to $.20 because of their lack of qualifications. Finally, subjects in the low-inequity condition were made to think that they deserved their $.30 payment. Adams and Jacobsen found the highest quality of work among high-inequity subjects, who performed significantly better than subjects in either of the other conditions. Apparently the postulate about altering inputs is supported: When subjects find their outcome–input ratio to be excessive, they adjust their inputs accordingly.

How does it happen that Adams' principles, ostensibly derived from dissonance theory, seem to be supported while the original theory is at least superficially contradicted? For example, the finding of increased work with excessive payment is not in keeping with insufficient justification phenomena reported earlier. The answer lies in the degree to which his principles are in fact derived from dissoance theory. It turns out that Adams' ideas are somewhat independent of the theory, particularly in two respects: He does not emphasize the role of cognitions most resistant or least resistant to change, and at least as important, he does not incorporate choice or responsibility into his model. These differences will become increasingly apparent as we proceed to describe further modes of reaction to inequity, and below we will make more explicit the contrasts between the two theories.

Altering Outputs

Adams' derivation for changes in outcomes is simply the converse of his comments on changes in inputs. If a person's outcomes are inequitibly high relative to those of someone else, outcome level can be reduced; the opposite holds when outcomes are too low. For evidence, Adams cites studies by Thibaut (1950) and Homans (1953), both of which show that subjects who receive relatively low outcomes express an interest in increasing their outcomes. This should hardly come as a surprise. The other type of inequity, receipt of outcomes too great for one's input, should theoretically result in attempts to decrease outcomes. There is some evidence for this in Adams and Jacobsen (1964), in that overpaid pieceworkers decreased total outcomes while raising quality, relative to control subjects. Further, Aronson and Carlsmith (1962) found that subjects who were accustomed to poor outcomes attempted to return to that low level upon unexpectedly receiving a high outcome. This latter result also occurred in later research, all of which is summarized in Chapter 10.

Cognitive Distortion of Inputs and Outcomes

Adams allows that a person may distort his evaluation or perception of inputs and outcomes in a manner analogous to actually changing those inputs and outcomes. If inequity consists of relative overpayment, the individual can distort downward his payment, or he can enhance his estimate of his efforts. If relative underpayment is the source of inequity, an underestimate of one's efforts can result, or alternatively, there can be an enhancement in the perceived rewards in the situation. This latter alternative has received a great deal of support in research already examined. In addition to a study by Weick (1964), which is cited by Adams as supporting the idea that the underpaid person will find something positive about his task, there is a considerable literature on "insufficient justification" and "effort justification," much of which has been discussed in earlier chapters.

The "cognitive distortion" postulate has also received support in the realm of overpayment. Lepper, Greene, and Nisbett (1973) first established that an activity was intrinsically interesting to children, then some of the children were offered a reward for engaging in that activity. Subsequently it was found that intrinsic interest in the activity dropped off among children offered the reward, suggesting that the overpayment (reward) created an inequity that could be restored by viewing the activity itself as somewhat onerous. Analogous phenomena, using monetary reward, have been found by Deci (1971, 1972), and Kruglanski et al. (1972).

Leaving the Field

This postulate bears some resemblance to an aspect of Festinger's (1954) social comparison theory. According to that theory, a person will cease comparison with others to the degree that a successful comparison is impossible. In the present context, comparison will cease when inequity cannot be reduced. It is as though the person would prefer not to tolerate the inequity if it cannot be eliminated, and perhaps one way not to think about it is to be removed from the comparison person. Adams cites studies by Thibaut (1950) and Patchen (1959) as supporting this notion. In Thibaut's experiment team members who were designated as low status and who suffered relative to others were the most likely to withdraw from the experimental games. Patchen's study found that dissatisfied workers who wanted higher pay had more absences than others. In a similar vein, it was found by Dansereau, Cashman, and Graen (1973) that high performers who were not differentially rewarded for their efforts were especially likely to leave the institution of employment. Finally, in a further study of salary inequity, Finn and Lee (1972) observed that inequitably treated employees were increasingly likely to leave their jobs.

Acting on the Comparison Other

The person does not necessarily have to change himself when inequity arises. He can also strive to alter the others' inputs, outcomes, or even push the other out of the field. The evidence for these ideas is somewhat scanty, and we will not report it here. The important point theoretically is that most of the modes of inequity reduction that apply to oneself can also be applied to the other person in the situation.

Changing Object of Comparison

Adams' (1965) model predicts that another will be chosen for comparison whose outcome–input ratio is identical to one's own. This notion also bears a strong resemblance to an aspect of social comparison theory. Festinger has noted that comparison will cease when a successful comparison is impossible, and by a successful comparison he means a comparison with someone who is similar in opinions or abilities. Festinger also notes that people will seek out similar others, thus Adams' postulate appears to be a specific instance of Festinger's more general comments on opinions and abilities. Adams reports no direct evidence for this derivation.

Preference for Mode of Equity Restoration

In examining the considerable repertoire of responses to inequity that Adams has allowed, it becomes evident that not all could be used simultaneously. In an effort to give his model a testable specificity Adams (1965) has enumerated some bases for thinking that some modes would be preferred over others:

1. There is a reward–cost theme: Changes in outcomes and inputs will be favored to the degree that increases in rewards and/or decreased cost and effort result.
2. Real and cognitive changes that imply a change in the person's self-concept or self-esteem will be resisted. Evidently the person is conceived to be relatively inflexible, or committed, when it comes to his self-image.

3. (Similar to the preceding point) the individual is more likely to change cognitions about others' inputs and outcomes than he is to alter his own inputs and outcomes.

4. The person is assumed to be reluctant to change the object of his comparisons, and implied in this is that leaving the field will be low in priority among reactions to inequity.

Although these distinctions do not allow a totally unequivocal set of predictions, as Adams admits, they do render the theory a good deal more testable. What we find interesting about these distinctions is a certain parallel to the concept of commitment within dissonance theory. The person's self-concept and his usual choice of comparison person are both viewed by Adams as sources of resistance to change, and from this assumption it can at least be predicted that other cognitive or behavioral elements will change in the interest of equity. This parallel to dissonance theory should not, however, be taken to mean that both notions predict the same resolution of inequity. There is an essential noncomparability that was raised earlier and which should be explored now in more detail.

The Difference between Dissonance and Equity Theories

There is a built-in notion of "cognitions resistant to change" in Adams' (1965) treatment of preferences among modes of equity restoration. Certainly this implicit inclusion of a resistance-to-change concept improves the theory's predictive power. However, there is another kind of resistance to change that Adams does not discuss explicitly, but which is the core of the difference between equity and dissonance theories. When dissonance is created through inequity there is one cognition that is stipulated by Adams to be totally resistant to change, although he does not use the language "resistant to change." This is simply the cognition that one's own output—input ratio should be identical to that of a relevant comparison person. All other cognitions, whether one's inputs, outputs, or comparison persons, are susceptible to change. It is these changeable cognitions that Adams has addressed in specifying preferred modes of equity restoration (above). If a person makes a behavioral commitment to a given level of outcome, amount of input, or to a particular comparison person, that commitment is *not* the basis of the cognition most resistant to change in Adams' system. This explains why the underpaid employee is said to be likely to lower his productivity. The worker holds the cognition that his rewards should bear a certain relation to his inputs, and if his situation is inequitable he can lower inequity by decreasing inputs.

It would be interesting to speculate about the relative resistance to change of this norm of justice between cultures. According to Walster, Berscheid, and Walster (1973) the norm of equity only develops through the realization of groups that they can maximize their collective outcomes through the establishment of certain rules about fair distribution. Without such group needs, equity norms would fail to develop. The implication is that cultures characterized by group functioning as a central feature would be more thoroughly imbued with norms of justice and fair distribution, whereas a hypothetical group-free society would be free of these justice norms. Such a society might be found among young, pregroup-interaction children, where the norm of justice would not be salient, well learned, or resistant to change. Instead, the individual "profit" motive would dominate.

At face value dissonance theory would not treat an equity norm as the cognition most resistant to change. Instead, it is likely that the worker's decision to gain employment at an unreasonable rate would be taken as the most resistant cognitive element, and this is also the cognition around which dissonance reduction would be oriented. The worker would be expected to find something positive in his situation, and rather than decreasing his productivity, he may even show increased efforts (see Lawrence & Festinger, 1962).

We are confronted with a dilemma. Which of these two approaches more accurately specifies the cognitive elements most resistant to change—the inequity model, or dissonance theory as construed in this volume? There are at least two potential means of answering this question.

1. The dissonance literature contains a pervasive element of experimentally varied responsibility, usually in terms of the degree of choice given the person. It is often found that "reinforcement" effects appear when choice or other kinds of responsibility are minimal. An example of a reinforcement effect is increased productivity when payment is increased, or taking absence when pay is inadequate. These are exactly some of the effects reported by Adams, suggesting that at least some of his evidence was produced by processes independent of dissonance reduction. Since choice is not varied in the research on equity we have no way of knowing how much responsibility was present in Adams' unequitable situations, and this paves the way for a possible reinforcement interpretation of certain equity effects.

2. The other answer consists of systematically varying the extent to which the equity norm, or alternatively, certain behavioral commitments, serve as the source of cognitions highly resistant to change. This approach would assume that neither theory is correct to the exclusion of the other, but only that either theory could come into play given adequate knowledge about resistance of relevant cognitive elements. Such a test has never been conducted with the equity norm per se, but a study by Kiesler and Corbin (1965), reported in Chapter 2, is instructive regarding the method by which equity restoration and other kinds of dissonance reduction might be separated through the notion of commitment.

It will be recalled that subjects took part in small groups and received differential acceptance from the group members, consisting of high, moderate, or low acceptance. Subsequently there was a measure of how much subjects conformed to a group standard. When subjects were committed to no further group interaction, conformity was positively related to the degree of acceptance. Or in Adams' language, the more positive the outcomes, the greater the individual member's inputs. It is especially important to note that this effect was under conditions of no further commitment to the group, meaning that the person's knowledge of his membership was not a frozen fact, but was free to change. Conceivably then, an equity norm came to prevail under these conditions, and the observed effect fits an equity explanation perfectly well. But there was more to the experiment. Half of the subjects were committed to further group membership, which means that the cognition corresponding to being a group member should have been highly resistant to change. If so, and if that cognition was more resistant to change than the equity norm, a different pattern of results would be expected. Specifically, dissonance should have been aroused especially when acceptance was low, and since the cognition of group membership was highly resistant to change, other cognitions would have to change. One such cognition would be the person's conformity to the group, and the results indicated that there was a relatively high-conformity rate among nonaccepted members who were committed to further interaction.

The Kiesler and Corbin (1965) experiment illustrates one approach that could be taken in disentangling the dissonance-theory and equity applications to unequitable situations. Of course, we have to guess that the equity norm was the determinant of subjects' behavior in the noncommitted conditions, and it remains likely that other processes could have brought about that result. The complete experiment for this purpose would consist of varying the degree of commitment to the group, as Kiesler and Corbin have done, together with an independent manipulation of resistance to change of the equity norm.

As the equity notion stands now, it is evident that Adams has accumulated a substantial amount of support for the most basic premises. (See the reviews of equity research by Adams & Freedman, 1976, and by Walster et al., 1973.) Two major issues remain:

1. Are the "equity" effects due to dissonance reduction in the form specified by Adams, or to reinforcement or other processes?

2. Since the equity model assumes implicitly a highly resistant-to-change norm of equity, the idea is evidently contrary to some central assumptions of the more general dissonance theory.

It is this latter conflict that seems particularly interesting, for Adams' notion is the only one existing that takes issue with the implicit premise of dissonance researchers that a recent behavior is the basis of the most resistant cognition.

SUMMARY

The purpose of this chapter has been to extend dissonance theory to problems lying at the core of social psychology—the individual's reactions to others. The chapter has dealt with five topic areas, and in most of these it was found that the theory implies important exceptions to principles that have long been assumed in psychology.

1. For example, given a commitment to a group, a person will come to conform to the group and increase liking for it in proportion to its rejection of him.

2. Under the topic of social deprivation it has been shown that one common effect of social deprivation can be eliminated through dissonance processes. When the person voluntarily commits himself, for minimal justification, to deprivation from social reinforcers, those reinforcers are subsequently weakened.

3. The research on aggression has also led to interesting findings. Some of the research shows that aggression comes to be justified by disliking the victim, contrary to what a guilt hypothesis might lead us to believe.

4. Bramel's (1963) second experiment on projection of homosexuality contradicts a long-standing psychoanalytic assumption. This assumption is that projection of a denied impulse or trait is toward an outgroup, and this notion has now been directly contradicted by both Bramel (1963) and a further study by Edlow and Kiesler (1966).

5. Finally, the extension of dissonance theory to reactions to inequity poses a curious theoretical problem having to do with resistance to change of cognitions, and implies that a central, highly resistant cognition can sometimes lie in a social motive such as the equity norm.

14
Individual Differences

Until this point our comments on cognitive dissonance research have been based almost entirely on experimental investigations, but it should be obvious that the nature of the theory in no way implies only experimental tests. Preexperimental, more or less permanent differences between individuals provide an entire arena of research possibilities, and the purpose of this chapter is to explicate the role of individual differences in dissonance arousal and reduction processes. The material of this chapter could easily have been interspersed among discussions at various other points in this book, but we have found a number of special considerations in the area of individual differences that warrant a separate treatment. Some of these considerations will be mentioned now, at the outset, and they will become more manifest as the details of the relevant research are explored.

WHAT CAN BE EXPECTED FROM AN INDIVIDUAL DIFFERENCE APPROACH?

Why study individual differences within the present theoretical context? Most apparent is that certain variables having something to do with dissonance arousal are by nature individual differences. It may be more dissonance arousing for a man to walk into the ladies' restroom than for a woman to enter the same restroom. The dissonance created by a choice between toys may be greater for children than for adults, and it is also easy to imagine cultural differences as a source of differential dissonance. The use of individual difference variables is not a necessity for testing the rigor of the theory, but if an investigator happens to be interested in some specific variable such as sex or age and its relationship to dissonance arousal, there is no completely experimental approach to be taken. Perhaps the reason that such variables have not yet surfaced in this volume is that interest in the theory has been focused primarily on theoretical tests. For such tests the investigator can typically deal with experimental variables exclusively, if he wishes to do so, and the necessity of reliance upon individual differences is uncommon. It will become apparent in the applications chapter that many extensions necessarily call up individual differences.

Individual differences are also a potential source of increased predictive power. At the simplest level, an individual difference could be used as a supplement in an experimental study to account for some of the error variance. Used in this way, as a covariate, the individual difference would in no way have to be coordinated to the theory. For example, if hair color, age, or any other chronic factor were found to be correlated with the dependent variable of interest, an analysis of covariance would strengthen the experimental finding. Such an approach could have been taken in any of the research we have discussed thus far. (For example, see Brehm and Wicklund, 1970.)

To employ individual differences in the above way is of some value in increasing the power of experimental tests of the theory, but that is not our primary interest here. Instead, this chapter asks whether or not there are theoretical gains to be accomplished through implementing individual differences. In order to discuss just what might be learned it will be useful to divide the dissonance process into its components, and to consider briefly the present state of knowledge about those components.

THREE FACETS OF THE DISSONANCE PROCESS

A variable that plays a causal role in a dissonance context can be relevant to any of the following: The initial perception of inconsistent cognitions, awareness of and tolerance for dissonance, and the selection of a route by which dissonance is reduced.

The Initial Perception of Dissonant Cognitions

Almost every piece of research we have examined thus far has varied only the ratio of dissonant to consonant cognitions, and as such, has dealt with what may be called the "initial perception" of dissonant cognitions. A person commits himself to a discrepant act, and dissonance arousal is then said to be a function of the proportion of cognitions inconsistent with that behavior. Certainly there is no reason why we should restrict our analysis to experimentally induced cognitions, as has been done thus far. A behavior that creates dissonance for one person may bring about consonance for another, and it is here that individual differences become relevant.

Awareness of Dissonance and Tolerance for Dissonance

Once the stage has been set for dissonance arousal ("Initial Perception," above), there are now questions about the individual's awareness of the inconsistency, the longevity of his awareness, and his extent of tolerance for dissonance once it is experienced. These are questions that we have touched on only lightly in the experimental research reported thus far, for it has generally been assumed by researchers that their experimental variations are relevant only to the initial perception of dissonant elements rather than to the processes of awareness and tolerance. In fact, the original theory said nothing specific about these latter processes, which may account for the scant attention given them.

In the experimental literature there has been some attention given to the question of awareness (Chapter 7), and the findings have been entirely homogeneous: If a person is led to focus more diligently and continuously on discrepant cognitive elements, dissonance reduction proceeds at a greater rate (Brehm & Wicklund, 1970; Insko et al., 1973; Pallak et al., 1967; Wicklund & Duval, 1971; Zanna et al., 1973). The "focusing" manipulations of these several studies were independent of the ratio of dissonant to consonant cognitions, thus it may be said that the individual's awareness of dissonance (and consequent dissonance reduction) is heightened by external events that direct attention toward the dissonance elements. There is no reason why an individual difference counterpart to forced attention could not be found.

Dissonance *tolerance* is a phenomenon related to awareness of dissonance, and presupposes awareness. The idea is simply that certain individuals might be better able than others to live with inconsistency given that they are cognizant of it. Much of the individual difference work in cognitive consistency theory has dealt with various types of individuals who are said to vary in tolerance for ambiguity, need for a black-and-white world, or related states that would imply a propensity toward inner consistency. Thus far no one has dealt with the tolerance concept via experimental means, possibly because the term "tolerance" has definite individual difference (chronic) connotations.

Obviously the time is ripe for a more thorough analysis of the psychological events following the initial incidence of dissonant cognitions. Although the original theory did not deal explicitly with these events, it is apparent that awareness and intolerance of dissonance are prerequisites for eventual dissonance reduction, and ideally, the following individual difference research would shed light on the operation of these processes.

The Mode of Dissonance Reduction

The original theory makes a highly general and useful statement about the routes by which dissonance will be reduced: Festinger (1957) argued that the direction of dissonance reduction could be predicted by the relative resistance to change of the various cognitions, such that cognitions amenable to change would be the first to undergo transformations in the interest of eliminating dissonance. In the experimental literature there has been a small amount of work relevant to alternative routes to dissonance reduction (Chapter 9), and perhaps the most informative is by Götz—Marchand et al. (1974). They made a direct comparison between two possible modes, one of which was specified a priori to be more resistant, and consistent with Festinger's idea, that mode was employed considerably less than the other. They also found that one of the modes was employed only to the extent that the subject was made aware of the possibility of changing the cognitions associated with that mode. This latter finding suggests that a cognition might be resistant to change simply because the person does not realize its potential for change.

In parallel manner to the experimental research on preferential use of modes, it should be possible to study preferential use of modes through individual differences. The clearest theoretical approach, in light of our remarks about resistance to change, is to locate individuals who vary in the extent to which certain cognitions are fixed entities. Should this prove feasible the predictive power of the theory might be greatly enhanced, for there are no doubt substantial variations among individuals with respect to ease of altering specific dissonance-relevant cognitions.

Summary

Given this tripartite division we have reason to expect a great deal from an individual difference approach. Only minimal *experimentation* has been devoted to the latter two categories, but there is encouraging reason to think that tolerance of dissonance and differential preference among modes are concepts especially amenable to an individual difference treatment.

AMBIGUITIES

Although a more exact knowledge of dissonance processes *should* be expected from individual difference investigations, there is a potential stumbling block, residing inherently in the concept of individual difference. This stumbling block is nothing more than the conceptual ambiguity of individual differences. If a test score is taken as an independent variable, it is given a label, such as "authoritarianism." But it is always possible to attach alternative conceptual (or nonconceptual) labels to the same test score, which is approximately the same as saying that authoritarianism, or any other individual difference, is inevitably correlated with numerous other preexisting differences. Why is this a problem here?

Suppose that the Brehm and Crocker (1962) experiment on food deprivation were repeated with separate samples of men and women, with a theoretical eye toward the individual difference of gender. The investigator learns that most of the local women are on a diet and argues that extended deprivation would not create substantial dissonance. He proceeds with the experiment, crosscutting the man–woman variation with a variation in monetary payment. True to the investigator's expectations, Brehm and Crocker's results are replicated only for the men. The women show no changes in rated hunger as a function of payment.

Although the investigator had good basis for thinking that food deprivation would arouse less dissonance for a person on a diet, there remain other sources of dissonance arousal that might be correlated with the male–female differences. For example, perhaps the women in this sample were more wealthy than the men, which would imply that $5 would have less impact on their lives. This could explain the absence of an effect for monetary payment among them. Or it is also possible that the women, for some reason, viewed the research as particularly valuable from a scientific standpoint, meaning that their participation and deprivation would have been well justified. If so, this would also explain the failure of the monetary variable.

These alternative explanations all fall within the first category discussed above, which we have called the "initial perception" of dissonant cognitions. These explanations refer only to the various different routes by which the male–female difference could constitute a variation in the ratio of dissonant–consonant cognitions. But this is not the totality of alternative explanations. Unknown to the investigator, or to anyone else, is whether or not the individual difference might also represent a variation in the second or third categories. Perhaps one sex is more prone toward attending to intraself contradictions, is less tolerant of dissonance, or has a special propensity to use the dissonance reduction mechanism that was made available.

The problem now becomes difficult, not only because of interpretive ambiguities, but because contradictory predictions might be possible if enough were known about the nature of the individual difference. For instance, it may well be that females suffer less than males when placed under food deprivation, but it might also be that females are less tolerant of dissonance. If this were so, what do we predict? Which variable (initial incidence or tolerance) would have the stronger impact, or would the two processes cancel one another? This is only the beginning, for there are numerous ways in which the sexes could differ in factors central to the dissonance process, and rather than spell these out, we will leave the obvious unsaid.

Given these considerations it now seems that individual difference variables may be difficult to coordinate to the theory. Surprising and contradictory results may emerge because of the many dissonance-related factors that can be correlated with an individual difference, and even if results emerge as predicted, the interpretation can lie in any of the three domains outlined above. Keeping in mind these problems we will proceed below to discuss a number of attempts to bring individual differences to cognitive dissonance theory in order to see how these difficulties have been met.

WHAT RESEARCH IS INCLUDED?

A number of discussions exist that relate individual differences to cognitive balance theories in general (e.g. Glass, 1968a, b; Miller & Rokeach, 1968; Steiner, 1968), but the approach to be taken here is considerably more focused.

As noted by Steiner (1968, p. 642), dissonance theorists have dealt primarily with a paradigm distinct from that of other balance theorists, and our purpose here is to attempt to explore that paradigm more thoroughly by means of individual differences. Just because an individual difference mediates certain balance processes is no sign that it will operate in like manner in the situations of interest here. This is primarily because the hallmark of dissonance research is the resistance to change concept, especially where resistance originates in recent behavior. To elaborate, we are not simply asking whether some individuals experience or tolerate more imbalance than others; we are also asking questions about individual differences related directly to the behavioral commitment, thus it is important to limit our discussion to the paradigm familiar to this book in order to gain any definite information about individual differences in that paradigm.

There is one further limitation. In order to examine the impact of individual differences on the dissonance process it is important to vary dissonance arousal independently of the individual difference variable. This will normally imply a factorial design, as it is not sufficient simply to show that a personality or trait variable affects a supposed measure of dissonance reduction, that is, produces a main effect. That trait variable might create differences for any number of reasons, some of which would have nothing to do with cognitive dissonance. Thus it is important to show that the individual difference has a greater impact as dissonance arousal is varied from low to high levels.

RESEARCH: THE INITIAL PERCEPTION OF DISSONANCE

Self-Esteem

A point derivable from the original theory and elaborated upon by Aronson (1968) and Deutsch, Krauss, and Rosenau (1962) is that self-esteem can often play a role in dissonance arousal. We have already seen evidence of this in experiments by Glass (1964), and Gerard, Blevans, and Malcolm (1964). In both of those experiments self esteem was manipulated experimentally, and both of them found that dissonance reduction was greater among high self-esteem individuals. In the Glass experiment subjects were asked to aggress against another, and it was argued that such an act would be dissonance arousing only for someone who had a positive conception of himself. The Gerard et al. (1964) paradigm was substantially different. Subjects were simply offered a choice among related alternatives, and it was argued that high self-esteem subjects would experience more dissonance since the possibility of making an incorrect decision would be especially inconsistent with their high self-concepts. A study of Malewski (1962) is parallel to that of Gerard et al. (1964), with the exception that self-esteem was identified by an individual difference.

Malewski approached the measurement of self-esteem by combining self-reports and sociometric data. It was assumed that a subject who is frequently chosen by peers may be legitimately described as having high self-esteem. His female subjects were given a choice among various consumer articles, and rankings of the items were taken both before and after the decision. Contrary to what might be expected on the basis of the Gerard *et al.* (1964) experiment, self-ratings of self-esteem had no appreciable impact on rating changes. But with the sociometric data the results were substantially as expected: Subjects with a large number of sociometric choices evidenced all of the dissonance reduction, whereas there were only minimal ranking changes among subjects with a low number of sociometric choices. The dissonance reduction effect among frequently chosen subjects was highly significant; however, there was not a reliable difference between the two groups. The results are suggestive evidence that similar processes may be occurring here and in the Gerard *et al.* (1964) study, although we should suspend drawing a strong conclusion in light of some weaknesses. First, there was not a significant difference between groups in amount of dissonance reduction; second, dissonance arousal was not varied independently; and third, the self-report measure of self-esteem failed completely to have an impact. Perhaps this latter difficulty means only that self-reports of self-esteem are not valid as measures of self-conceptions, but we should suspend judgment on this point until reviewing one additional work.

Greenbaum (1966) conducted a study of forced compliance which involved a measure of self-reported self-esteem. He did not predict an interaction between self-esteem and the experimental variation of dissonance arousal, but since he found such an interaction, the study should be mentioned here. The measure was taken from the Janis and Field (1959) self-esteem questionnaire, which is possibly not comparable to the self-report form employed in the Malewski experiment. Subjects were requested to tape-record a counterattitudinal communication, either under choice or no choice conditions, and a relevant attitude measure was given before and after the counterattitudinal performance. The results were perhaps surprising in light of the experiments by Gerard *et al.* (1964), Glass (1964), and Malewski (1962). The choice variable operated according to dissonance theory only for low self-esteem subjects, while there was a slight reversal of this effect within the high self-esteem group.

Before concluding that this result invalidates the previous findings, or is theoretically inconsistent, we might review the reasoning of the earlier studies. Glass' hypothesis assumed simply that unprovoked aggression was a behavior strongly inconsistent with the self-concepts of his high self-esteem subjects, a line of thought that is completely derivable from the theory. The two "free decision" experiments (Gerard *et al.*, 1964; Malewski, 1962) depended upon the assumption that high self-esteem subjects desire to protect a self-image of wisdom, or correct decision-making. But the theoretical reasoning behind Greenbaum's result was not spelled out, though it is entirely possible his findings are explicable within the theory. For example, it may have been that Greenbaum's low self-esteem subjects were more ego-involved in the relevant opinion, that is, for them it was a highly important cognition. If so, the results make perfectly good sense. On the other hand, shouldn't the arguments of Gerard *et al.* (1964) and Malewski (1962) apply here? If their argument is a reasonable general assumption, then high self-esteem individuals should in all decisions be more concerned about the wisdom of their choices—hence more defensive and more subject to the processes of dissonance reduction.

With measures of chronic self-esteem, as opposed to self-esteem manipulations, we now begin to see ambiguities surfacing. Even though perfectly reasonable predictions can be made, based perhaps on an assumption about the propensity of high self-esteem individuals to be defensive when making decisions, it is also easy to conceive of other, equally sound predictions. There is also a question about the validity of self-reports of self-esteem, since these self-reports failed to have an impact in Malewski's study. For these reasons the apparent contradictory finding of Greenbaum need not be viewed as contrary to the theory, but simply as a reminder that self-esteem does not necessarily provide a simple and straightforward variation in dissonance arousal.

Introversion—Extraversion

The use of individual differences, including self-esteem, to define the initial incidence of cognitive dissonance does not seem at face value to be a complex endeavor. But the preceding experiments illustrate how ambiguities can easily result. A more convincing approach has been taken by Cooper and Scalise (1974), who have created both consonant and dissonant conditions for subjects of each of two personality types. Subjects first responded to the Meyers—Briggs Type Indicator, and were thereby divided into introverts and extraverts. Then all subjects were placed in a conformity bind in which there was pressure to adopt a group opinion. The subject was convinced that a piece of apparatus would reveal his first impulse—to conform or remain independent—and, as far as our analysis is concerned, this first impulse may be viewed as the cognitive element most resistant to change. The measure of dissonance reduction was the subject's opinion change on the critical item, and in this case the direction of change is determined by whether the subject is an introvert or extrovert. The Cooper and Scalise (1974) argument is this: The life style of an introvert is one of independent thought. He typically holds to his own opinions and feelings and shows little dependence on others. But the extravert's style is in marked contrast: He is often dependent on others and upon their views of him. Therefore, among subjects whose first impulse is to conform, introverts will experience more dissonance than extraverts. But just the opposite will hold among first-impulse independent subjects. This chain of reasoning may be seen as related to Glass' (1964) self-esteem analysis of propensity to aggress, although the approach taken here is more specific, in that the measure presumably deals with just one facet of self-concept.

Dissonance reduction may be defined as opinion change in a direction consistent with the first-impulse commitment, and the results are shown in Table 15. It is evident that subjects of both types followed the prediction, and further, the interaction is highly significant.

A qualitative difference between this and every other study in the present chapter has to do with dissonance-arousal variations within each personality classification. Cooper and Scalise (1974) could have created conditions that would be dissonance provoking just for extraverts, and then have found no effect among introverts, but this would have opened new ambiguities. Such a design (and results) could then be interpreted in terms of extraverts being more aware of the dissonance, less tolerant of same, or more prone to use the available mode of dissonance reduction. But in fact, both extraverts *and* introverts were found to evidence dissonance reduction, and on the same measure. This suggests rather strongly that the source of difference between the two types was in the initial incidence of dissonance, and not in the second or third categories of the dissonance process.

RESEARCH: AWARENESS AND TOLERANCE

The conceptual difference between awareness and tolerance is quite simple. Awareness of dissonance simply means the degree to which attention is turned toward discrepant elements, while tolerance is the individual's willingness to live with the uncomfortable state of imbalance. Unfortunately the empirical difference between these two has not been as distinct. Most investigators whose research is included in this section claim to deal with tolerance, rather than awareness, although the first study (Wolitzky, 1967) comes closer than any others to the awareness concept.

Cognitive Interference

It is possible to conceive of a dimension of "interference proneness," whereby individuals vary in their ability to keep out cognitions that are irrelevant to or incongruous with an ongoing task, or goal. For example, some people might find it impossible to search for a desired book without also noticing several stimulating alternatives, while other individuals would have no difficulty in keeping their focus on only the desired goal. It is argued by Wolitzky (1967) that people who are highly prone to cognitive interference will readily notice dissonant cognitions, whereas such awareness may be minimal for those who are not so prone. Presumably the person who has committed himself to a potentially dissonance-arousing act could restrict his awareness to just the behavior, or to cognitions consistent with it, as long as he is not subject to cognitive interference. But the other type of individual will notice salient, dissonant cognitive elements.

TABLE 15
Dissonance-Reducing Opinion Change

Condition	Introverts	Extraverts
Conform	5.1[a]	0.7
Independent	0.2	3.7

[a] A positive score represents opinion change in the direction of the first-impulse commitment.

Wolitzky's subjects were first given the Stroop Color–Word Test, which measures the extent to which a person can disregard salient stimuli that interfere with a specified goal. Then the subjects were broken into categories of smokers and nonsmokers. If we may assume that smoking is a goal surrounded by potentially interfering stimuli such as contrasmoking medical evidence, it should be the case that low interference-prone smokers will not admit of a smoking–cancer link. Wolitzky's results showed exactly what he expected: Among smokers there was a greater admission of a connection between smoking and cancer for high interference-prone subjects, while a slight opposite trend existed among nonsmokers.

It is important to keep one crucial conceptualization in mind in interpreting these results. To talk about interference-proneness we must have some firm idea of a goal with which extraneous stimuli might interfere. To make Wolitzky's argument complete we have assumed that the behavioral commitment is one such goal, but this may be a tentative assumption. For example, health is also a goal, and it would be possible to view health as a predominant concern that would receive interference from the knowledge of smoking. As with the other research in this chapter there is, of course, the recurring ambiguity of the precise meaning of the individual difference. This was recognized by Wolitzky, and we will not reiterate that point at present. At least Wolitzky's results are consistent with his reasoning, granting the above assumption about the nature of the ongoing and predominant goal.

The preceding experiment is the only one known to us on individual differences in cognitive interference and dissonance. As there exists no explicit research on individual differences in the tendency simply to be aware of inconsistencies, we will move on to the more substantial part of this section—dissonance tolerance.

Tolerance for Dissonance

It has frequently been supposed that individuals differ in their willingness and/or ability to allow contradictory cognitions to persist in their minds. One of the earlier investigations into tolerance of cognitive dissonance was by Harvey

(1965), who differentiated between "concrete" and "abstract" modes of thought. The concretely thinking person is said to possess a high absolutism of thought, a need for bifurcated evaluations of events, and an intolerance of ambiguity. All of this, needless to say, should imply a strong disposition toward dissonance reduction. In a word, the abstractly thinking individual is just the opposite.

Harvey requested his subjects to take part in the familiar counterattitudinal essay-writing task and assessed attitude change. Some of the subjects were informed that their taperecorded statements would be made public (thereby enhancing dissonance), while others expected no one to hear their readings. Prior to this subjects had been divided into "concretes" and "abstracts" on the basis of a "This I Believe" test, attributable to Harvey. If the results for just concrete individuals are considered, the results of the public–private variations are exactly as would be predicted from dissonance theory, but if anything, the effect was backward for abstract subjects.

The results are in agreement with Harvey's thinking, although there is one special ambiguity here that we might note, particularly since it was raised by Harvey. It is possible that concrete and abstract individuals do not *experience* the same degree of dissonance, and if so, the results of the "This I Believe" measure would be better conceptualized as due to differential awareness, rather than tolerance. Harvey suggested that this problem is minimized by using a procedure with a strong impact, but such a safeguard is certainly not absolute.

An earlier field study by Paul (1956) was not conceived in terms of dissonance theory, but it is conceptually similar to that of Harvey. Paul first divided a number of respondents into high and low authoritarians (Adorno, Frenkel–Brunswick, Levinson, & Sanford, 1950). He then examined subjects' opinions of presidential candidates before and after the 1952 election. In general there was a shift of sentiment toward the victor, Eisenhower, but this shift was significantly greater among authoritarian subjects. This result cannot be taken as strong evidence for authoritarianism mediating the dissonance process, as there was no independent manipulation of dissonance, but we mention it here because of the similiarity of authoritarianism to Harvey's (1965) tolerance measure.

A line of research by Glass and his associates may also be viewed as bearing on the tolerance question. Glass, Canavan, and Schiavo (1968) investigated dissonance reduction as a function of repression–sensitization. As a general personality style, sensitization is the tendency to deal with ego-threats by verbalizing, and then coping with them. The repressing individual is more likely to repress the very existence of the threat–and there ends the cognitive work. Glass *et al.* (1968) placed subjects into a situation where they were committed to a test on which failure was likely (or less likely), then took a verbal measure of the subject's desire to succeed. They also varied the extent of monetary inducement for commitment to work on the task, with the expectation that dissonance arousal would be maximized in the low payment–high probability of failure condition. In such a paradigm dissonance may be reduced if the subject convinces himself that he does not want to succeed (see Cohen & Zimbardo, 1962; Schlachet, 1965). The Glass *et al.* (1968) measure of achievement lowering was a verbal one, in which subjects were asked how much they wanted to perform well and how hard they would try. A second measure was the subject's tendency to derogate the test and the study.

Given this procedural background how might repressors and sensitizers be expected to differ? Glass *et al.* (1968) propose that the sensitizer would allow himself to become cognizant of the threat, and then would attempt to reduce tension through verbalization of the impact of the threat. In the present context, they argue, this implies that the sensitizer would convince himself that he doesn't care about success. However, the repressor is not viewed as open to verbalization of the threat, and instead, he will deny its existence. This implies for Glass and his associates a denial of the forthcoming incompetent performance by devaluing the test and testing situation.

The results on the first measure were exactly contrary to these expectations. *Repressors* in the high probability of failure, low monetary inducement condition showed by far the greatest decrement in reported achievement motivation, while there was no evidence of dissonance reduction among sensitizers. In fact, except for that one repressor cell, there were only minimal differences between conditions. Evidently the minimization of desire to achieve is not a phenomenon limited to sensitizers, but if anything, is more likely to appear among repressors.

Moving to the second measure, derogation of the test and the test situation, the results are in keeping with the original expectations. Repressors evidenced dissonance reduction in the maximally dissonance-arousing conditions, while this was not true of sensitizors.

The results of these two measures can be summed up easily: The independent variables operated according to the theory for subjects classified as repressors, no matter what the measure, but sensitizers showed no evidence of dissonance reduction. At this point it will be useful to discuss some reasons provided by Glass *et al.* (1968) for their surprising results. This list of reasons will be familiar in light of our earlier discussion of ambiguities.

For one, it may be that the two groups experienced equal amounts of dissonance, but that sensitizers used a means of dissonance reduction not assessed in the experiment. One possible route to ascertaining the degree of dissonance, independent of reduction of dissonance, is a measure of "discomfort" included in the Glass *et al.* (1968) procedure. At the end of the experiment it was found that sensitizers indicated somewhat more discomfort than repressors, in the high-dissonance condition. This is taken by Glass and his associates to be suggestive evidence that sensitizers failed to reduce dissonance, although such a measure is of debatable theoretical value. For example, McGuire (1966) has argued that the "felt discomfort" of cognitive dissonance does not necessarily imply a cognitive awareness of such discomfort. In a somewhat different vein, it is also possible that felt discomfort ratings reflect dissonance reduction, thus repressors may have lowered their rated aversion to the situation as a means of coping with dissonance.

Another interpretation offered by Glass et al. (1968) proposes that sensitizers might be better able to tolerate inconsistency. They draw a tentative portrayal of the sensitizer as one who verbalizes feelings of discomfort, while at the same time being able to live with the cognitive inconsistency basic to the discomfort. This interpretation is related to their original reasoning, except that they had anticipated that verbalization of the threat would lead to a specific form of dissonance reduction rather than to mere tolerance.

Still another explanation would allow for more dissonance among repressors. Certainly there could be many differences between repressors and sensitizers in chronic variables related to dissonance arousal, and we need not elaborate on these at present.

Finally, Glass et al. (1968) speculate about a possible difference between groups in self-esteem. Although they had no self-esteem measures on their subjects, they find it likely that the repressors may have had a self-esteem level that would lend itself to greater dissonance arousal, which would be consistent with the chronic self-esteem findings of Malewski (1962).

This investigation of repressors and sensitizers, and the interpretations offered, provide a clear example of the problems we raised earlier. Individual differences are ambiguous in interpretation even when the predictions are borne out, but given the unexpected, the myriad of possible interpretations becomes especially obvious.

We might note that the repressor—sensitizer variable, even if ambiguous, does seem to operate in a consistent manner. Gordon and Glass (1970) provided subjects with a free choice that carried either high or low personal involvement. The postdecisional spreading was greater in the high-involvement case only for repressors, while sensitizers again failed to function according to dissonance theory. This result, unfortunately, does little to clarify the theoretical meaning of repression—sensitization.

RESEARCH ON MODES:
AN ATTEMPT TO DIFFERENTIATE THE THREE PHASES

Thus far we have described attempts to relate individual differences to the initial experience, or onset of dissonance, and to willingness—ability to tolerate the state of dissonance. In the previous research it has been assumed that the individual difference in question was relevant to one specific fact of the disso-nance processes, such as the initial onset or tolerance, but Shaffer and Hendrick (1974) have allowed that a given individual difference might be related to all three facets, and have proceeded in an investigation to ferret the three out separately. Their experiment deals with two related individual differences, but because the results of the two were similar we will deal here with just the first—dogmatism. It should be noted that a similar, but less complex experiment was performed by Shaffer, Hendrick, Regula, and Freconna (1973) using the individual difference of tolerance for ambiguity. Since the results of that study were similar to the present, we will describe just the latter and more intricate experiment.

Subjects were placed in an "effort-justification" setting in which they were asked to perform a boring task under conditions of high or low effort. Subsequently a number of measures were taken in order to assess the three aspects of the dissonance process, and it is these methods of measurement that are of crucial interest here:

1. To measure the onset, or initial experience of dissonance, subjects were asked for their perception of differential mental discomfort. A statistical interaction resulted, whereby the dogmatic subjects rated discomfort as higher in the high-effort than in the low-effort condition. In contrast, the nondogmatic subjects did not strongly differentiate the high- from low-effort manipulation, implying that the dissonance manipulation had an initial impact primarily on dogmatic subjects. There could be numerous bases for this differential initial experience of dissonance, but our immediate purpose here is not to explore these. The important point is that the initial incidence of dissonance can, in theory, be measured by a question asking about felt discomfort.

2. In order to assess possible differential tolerance for inconsistency Shaffer and Hendrick took a repeated measure of mental discomfort. The first one, just reported above, was administered immediately before attempts at dissonance reduction were assessed, and the second discomfort measure came toward the end of the measurements, presumably after subjects had been given opportunity for dissonance reduction. The change scores on this discomfort item indicated a universal lowering in discomfort ratings, suggesting to Shaffer and Hendrick that subjects in all conditions chose to reduce dissonance rather than live with their inconsistent cognitions. Had subjects tolerated their dissonance, we might presume that felt discomfort would not have changed during the course of the measurement phase of the session. There are, however, some questionable assumptions to be made in order to take this change score as a tolerance index, and we will turn to these difficulties shortly.

3. The third phase of the dissonance process is dissonance reduction, and here Shaffer and Hendrick have attempted to examine the use of two different modes as a function of the personality dimension. The first mode was called "interest and enjoyment" of the task, a straightforward measure employed in previous research. On this measure the nondogmatic subjects behaved consistent with the theory, showing greater liking for the task in the high-effort condition. For some unknown reason the dogmatic subjects showed no such effect: They evidenced

no differential liking-enjoyment for the high and low-effort tasks. From this result Shaffer and Hendrick conclude that only the nondogmatic subjects made use of the task-enhancement mode of dissonance reduction, which seems perfectly reasonable. However, their argument becomes difficult to follow when we move to the second mode. Subjects were asked a question having to do with whether or not the experiment was justified, plus two more questions dealing with whether or not the experimenter was competent and justified. These three questions taken together constituted a "derogation index," and it was assumed that low ratings on these three items constituted a type of dissonance reduction. The results showed that only the dogmatic subjects used this "derogation index;" that is, dogmatic subjects derogated more in the high effort than in the low-effort condition.

Shaffer and Hendrick provide a line of reasoning for this latter index, but the problem here is that the two indices (task interest and enjoyment; derogation) should have operated similarly from the standpoint of a simple reading of dissonance theory. Just as dissonance can be reduced by coming to enjoy the task and find it interesting, dissonance might also be reduced by viewing the whole experience as justified and by perceiving the experimenter as competent, or likable, or attractive in any other sense. Since the two indices did not operate in parallel fashion, and in fact led to opposite results, we will not pursue this result. The only clear conclusion to be drawn from these results is that nondogmatic subjects made more use of a straightforward and familiar mode of dissonance reduction.

This experiment is the only one in existence that attempts to consider the three phases of the dissonance process as a function of an individual difference, and at this point we should discuss the relative success of such an approach:

1. First, what of the measure of the initial incidence of dissonance? It will be recalled that the effort manipulation appeared to create differential dissonance arousal, as measured by mental discomfort, primarily for the dogmatic subjects. This being the case, we would expect the dogmatic subjects to proceed to reduce dissonance in a parallel fashion. However, on the interest and enjoyment items it was just the *nondogmatic* subjects who differed as a function of high–low effort. This lack of fit between the mental discomfort measure and dissonance reduction measure raises serious doubts about the validity of "mental discomfort" as a dissonance index. Perhaps more problematic is the assumption that mental discomfort reflects just the existence of dissonance, independent of other processes. For example, subjects might attempt to justify their existence in the situation by reducing felt discomfort, just as subjects in the studies on hunger and thirst (Chapter 10) reduced their subjective discomfort. There is also a serious theoretical question about whether or not the tension state of cognitive dissonance is a psychological event that is reportable as "mental discomfort." This is the point raised by McGuire (1966), reiterated by Glass *et al.* (1968).

Finally, the attempt to measure the existence of dissonance assumes that dissonance has not yet been reduced. This assumption appears to be predicated on the notion that dissonance can be reduced only when the subject is confronted with an appropriate measure, but this has been shown to be erroneous by Götz–Marchand *et al.* (1974). The implication is that dissonance reduction may have been in progress by the time that subjects were asked about their mental discomfort.

2. Similar problems arise in the case of the tolerance measure, because tolerance was defined through change scores on the mental discomfort item. The use of the change score assumes that dissonance reduction, to the extent it occurred, took place between the administration of the two mental discomfort measures, but such an assumption is without theoretical basis. The McGuire objection also applies here, in that we have no way of knowing if the experience of dissonance can be reflected verbally. And finally, in order to make a case for this change score as a tolerance measure it would at least be necessary to show that the most tolerant subjects are the least likely to attempt to justify their commitments, but in the present experiment there is no such evidence.

3. The problem with the two alternative modes has already been discussed, and need not be reviewed here in great detail. There is no point in trying to talk about distinct modes of dissonance reduction that appear to be contrary to one another, and this means that there is no evidence in this experiment for the use of a mode other than enhanced task interest and enjoyment among nondogmatic subjects.

In summary, it is safe to say that the approach taken here has not proved adequate to show how dogmatic versus nondogmatic individuals react differentially to the three phases of the dissonance process. For that matter, even if we disregard the individual difference, this approach has not elucidated any distinct aspects of the three phases of the dissonance process. The reason for this failure, we suggest, lies in the assumption that the stages can be sorted out by asking individuals specific questions about the course of their experiences in dissonance arousal and reduction. As the Shaffer and Hendrick experiment illustrates so well, a question aimed at tolerance of dissonance or the experience of dissonance can as easily become a reflection of dissonance reduction itself.

SUMMARY AND CONCLUSIONS

Predictability and Consistency of Results

This is not our central theme, but it is of interest to note whether or not the results of these several studies have been as predicted. The most notable successes in this respect have been by Cooper and Scalise (1974), Harvey (1965),

Malewski (1962), and Wolitzky (1967). In the other instances there were either unexpected results, theoretically uninterpretable results, or else no conceptual basis for predictions. In addition to these difficulties in successful prediction, there are also inconsistencies among results when experiments are compared. Taking just the self-esteem individual difference, we have found that Malewski (1962) reported most of the dissonance reduction among his high self-esteem subjects, whereas just the opposite result was obtained by Greenbaum (1966). Two different procedures were followed in these studies, as well as different methods of measurement, but that fact does not bring theoretical light to the opposing results.

Another concept leading to inconsistent results is the broad notion of cognitive rigidity—whether called authoritarianism, dogmatism, or concrete thinking. The results of Harvey seem clear and interpretable when taken alone, but juxtaposed with the effects noted by Shaffer and Hendrick (1974) the concept becomes confused. Harvey (1965) labeled his individual difference "concrete versus abstract," and Shaffer and Hendrick (1974) focused on a related notion that was called "dogmatism." It is difficult to find any important theoretical difference between the two concepts, for Harvey and Shaffer and Hendrick have characterized the concrete thinker and dogmatic thinker, respectively, as intolerant of cognitive inconsistency.

Inherent Ambiguities

Early in the chapter we asked what might be expected from an individual differences approach, and we found that chronic differences between individuals might be employed to study the three facets of the dissonance arousal and reduction process. It is particularly the latter two phases, awareness—tolerance and mode of dissonance reduction, that have not been studied in great frequency by experimentalists. What has the research reported here told us about these three facets?

1. *Initial incidence.* The most straightforward application of individual differences is to the initial incidence of cognitive dissonance, and the clearest result we have reviewed is by Cooper and Scalise. It is relatively free from ambiguity because dissonance-provoking conditions were created for subjects who were at both ends of a personality continuum. This feature of their research effectively rules out the possibility that the results might be attributed to differences between groups in tolerance—awareness, or in preference for mode of dissonance reduction. The other research in this category is considerably weaker, either because only one end of the personality continuum was tapped for the high-dissonance condition, or because the individual difference variable was not clearly related to the theory.

2. *Awareness—tolerance.* The study by Wolitzky may be construed conceptually as oriented around awareness of inconsistency, but the case for having established an individual difference in inconsistency—awareness is extremely

weak. As noted by Wolitzky, his measure of interference proneness might easily be an operational definition of other phases of the dissonance process, thus we are left knowing nothing definite. The same problem applies to the seemingly clear study by Harvey, and is made more evident in the case of Harvey's (1965) experiment because of the contrary results of Shaffer and Hendrick.

3. *Mode of dissonance reduction.* The research considered here provides no evidence whatever for the mediation of individual differences in selection of avenues of dissonance reduction. We do not pretend by this that individual differences are not important in determining the mode, for it is entirely likely that individuals differ with respect to what cognitions are more resistant to change, or in their awareness of the malleability of relevant cognitions. It remains to be seen whether or not future research can shed light on this facet of the dissonance process.

A Comparison with the Experimental Approach

If individual differences are of little value in increasing our knowledge about the different facets of dissonance arousal and reduction, the alternative is to depend on the experimental method for these theoretical questions. The immediate issue is whether or not the questions can be answered more clearly in this manner.

On one level it is obvious that the experimental approach is less ambiguous. For example: if the initial incidence of dissonance is varied by altering the number of positive features of a chosen alternative, it then seems highly plausible that there is no difference between experimental groups in chronic tolerance of dissonance or habitual use of modes. The fact of the experimental method completely rules out these differences. There remains, however, another sort of ambiguity that has not heretofore been discussed in the context of dissonance research. Conceivably a variation in the number of dissonant cognitions might at the same time affect a person's ability to tolerate dissonance. For example, the imposition of numerous dissonant elements might bring about a general increased stress, and weakened tolerance for ambiguity, inconsistency, and more specifically, for dissonance. In any given experiment it would be difficult, and perhaps inconceivable, to establish whether or not there exists such a confounding.

But this is as close as we can come to removing ambiguity from the study of cognitive dissonance. Certainly with the experimental approach the investigator knows what he has done to his subjects, as opposed to the individual difference approach which allows no ready means of establishing the exact antecedent condition. The question remaining now is whether the three facets of dissonance can be studied effectively with an experimental approach:

1. First, it is clear that the experimental method is quite adequate for study of the initial incidence of dissonance. Hundreds of experiments have fallen into this category.

2. Second, we have reported earlier several studies of awareness of dissonance, and these results have been surprisingly consistent. If a person's attention is forced to the dissonant elements, dissonance reduction increases, and if he is distracted, there is a resultant decrement in dissonance reduction. Whether or not these variations in focused attention might also constitute variations in preference for a specific mode, or in the ratio of dissonant to consonant cognitions, is a question to be grappled with by the reader and investigator. A priori it seems quite unlikely that the forcing of attention to dissonant elements would increase the *number* of dissonant elements.

Also in the second category is dissonance *tolerance,* a concept that has not yet been brought to experimental investigation. Here there is a question of whether or not the process can be studied experimentally, for tolerance has generally been conceived as an antecedent disposition, on the same level as other traits. Were an investigator to formulate the tolerance concept in such a way that it might be varied, perhaps it could then be studied.

3. Finally, how can the person's selection of a mode of dissonance reduction be altered experimentally? We have seen at least two excellent examples in Chapter 9 on modes of response to dissonance arousal. One of these studies (Walster *et al.*, 1967) simply varied whether or not a potentially changeable cognition had a firm basis in reality. A cognition with a foundation in reality should be resistant to change, and the subject should then have to look elsewhere for methods of dissonance reduction. This is just what happened in the Walster *et al.* (1967) experiment, and is a good example of the implementation of the resistance-to-change concept. The other example assumed that certain avenues of dissonance reduction are not readily available to the person's consciousness, and that such modes will come into use only if they are made salient experimentally (Götz–Marchand *et al.*, 1974).

15
Related Theoretical Developments

Several attempts have been made to improve upon or extend dissonance theory since its inception. These modifications, qualifications, or additions have not been conceived primarily as replacements for the theory, and they were not inspired by a desire to interpret dissonance phenomena in totally different language. Each of them focuses on some particular feature of the theory, such as commitment or the role of the self, and elaborates that feature into a qualification of the theory, or even into a distinct but compatible theoretical formulation. The first of these we will discuss is an elaboration of the idea of "commitment," by Kiesler.

COMMITMENT

Our use of "commitment" thus far has treated the concept as equivalent to behavior. Implicit in our discussion has been an assumption that some behaviors are more resistant to change than others, meaning that the person can be committed to his behaviors in varying degrees, but we have not generally invoked the idea of variations in commitment. This is because the research has not called for the concept of "degrees of commitment." Experimental subjects either decide or they do not, at least in the preponderance of the investigations. Kiesler (1971) has seized on the concept of commitment to turn it into a psychological reality. Although he is hesitant to label his considerations as "theory," we will take the liberty of treating his notion as a theory that is different from dissonance theory, but which builds upon and extends the basic tenets of dissonance theory.

Kiesler does not view commitment as a source of dynamic psychological processes, but instead, as an inert entity with the property of freezing a person to particular acts. To be committed is to be rigid in the face of forces that call for change. Kiesler's treatise (1971) describes a good many forces for change that are ineffective because they call for flexibility on the part of a highly committed person, including forces stemming from dissonance arousal, but it is important to note that these forces are not an integral part of his theory. The theoretical statement simply has to do with determinants of the degree of commitment. The commitment notion becomes useful when forces of change enter the picture, since resistance can then be predicted as a function of the person's extent of being frozen to a given mode of behavior.

What determines commitment? How is it that people develop a high degree of inflexibility in certain behaviors? At least five determinants are discussed by Kiesler, the last of which is most central in his discussion:

1. The explicitness of the act, meaning its degree of public exposure and clarity of meaning for the actor.

2. The importance of the act for the person. We might presume that importance relates to the potential of the act for satisfaction of vital needs.

3. The irrevocability of the act.

4. The number of acts performed. Kiesler views this variable in such a way that the acts basic to a commitment do not have to be identical. We would guess that as long as several acts are quite similar and each implies the other, the performance of any one of those acts should bind the person to related acts.

5. Volition, viewed by Kiesler as "freedom or choice," is the final determinant and the one he treats in most detail in his research. Only if the behavior is instigated by the person's own desires should he defend that behavior in the face of pressures to change. Were a person totally imposed upon to engage in a behavior there is little basis for predicting how he would resist changing that behavior, but the chances are quite good that he would desire to make changes even without the benefit of external pressures.

The important applications of Kiesler's ideas have dealt with pressures toward attitude change, and since we have referred only to "behaviors" thus far in our discussion of Kiesler's ideas, it should be noted that attitudes are just as much a part of commitment as are more explicit and overt behavior:

> However, to the extent that a person is bound to some explicit and attitudinally relevant behavior, he must accept it as integral to himself, to his self-view, and other attitudes and beliefs must be accommodated accordingly [Kiesler, 1971, p. 31].

Although Kiesler has extended his thinking to numerous situations in which there are pressures to change an attitude away from a commitment, we shall focus on just one study by Kiesler, Pallak, and Kanouse (1968) in order to show how his ideas relate to cognitive dissonance processes.

The first part of the experiment was an attempt to create differential levels of commitment to an act consistent with subjects' existing attitudes. The issue dealt with tuition increases at Michigan State (where the subjects attended college), and the subjects were asked to deliver a speech opposing tuition increases. In the high-commitment condition the subject found that his speech would be played to a large audience, that his name would be associated with it, and that the audience would assume his opinion was reflected by the speech. Low-commitment subjects were assured that the audience would not be able to identify them. There was also a no-commitment condition in which subjects delivered a talk on an irrelevant topic.

At this point we should ask what this manipulation accomplishes. All of the essay writing or speech delivering we have seen in the dissonance research has been counterattitudinal, but the subjects in this experiment did not take issue with their personal beliefs. Accordingly, dissonance should have been minimal, but not necessarily absent. After all, the high-commitment subject stands to be embarrassed, attacked, or to suffer other adverse consequences of being publicly identified with a speech. This means there is some possibility of subjects in the high-commitment conditions changing their attitudes to become even more strongly opposed to tuition increases. This eventually is something Kiesler and his associates have tried to avoid methodologically, since they did not want the results to be open to the alternative explanation that the resistance to change stemming from commitment was actually mediated by dissonance, or by other motivational processes. Therefore, the manipulation was intended to accomplish just one result: the greater binding of the person to his beliefs. There is no reason to expect the manipulation to be reflected in attitude change or in any other measureable quantity. The impact of differential commitment becomes manifest only when forces toward change enter the picture.

Following a manipulation of commitment subjects were requested to write a short essay arguing that public universities should become more like private ones. The subjects were told explicitly that one implication of such a change in public universities would be increased tuition rates. Therefore, from the subject's viewpoint, he was composing an essay that ran counter to his previous commitment to low tuition. Dissonance was varied over three levels. There was the familiar high choice–low choice manipulation in addition to a no-dissonance control in which subjects wrote essays irrelevant to the tuition issue.

The dependent measure of primary interest here was attitude change on the tuition-increase issue. The attitude change scores are given in Table 16. Before examining the effect of commitment on dissonance reduction we should point out that commitment in the absence of dissonance (Column 3) does not have a significant effect. This absence of a difference is a necessary baseline from Kiesler's perspective, since that means that the commitment variable cannot be interpreted easily as a variation in dissonance. It should also be noted that the choice manipulation within the no-commitment condition operated just as in other dissonance research: The mean of 16.2 was significantly greater than the mean of 7.2. Turning to the four conditions of high and low commitment and high and low dissonance, it might first be observed that the dissonance variable

TABLE 16
The Effects of Dissonance and Commitment
on the Tuition Increase Issue

Degree of prior commitment	Degree of dissonance		
	High	Low	No
High	11.0[a]	13.5	12.6
Low	19.1	9.2	10.0
No	16.2	7.2	13.4

[a]The higher the number, the more favorable subjects were to increased tuition.

operated as expected within the low-commitment condition. In fact, the effect here was almost identical to that within the no-commitment condition. However, the impact of dissonance arousal was much different when subjects were initially highly committed to not increasing tuition. There was no difference of any consequence between the high-commitment—high-dissonance and high-commitment—low-dissonance conditions, and the direction of difference was even opposite that of the other high—low dissonance differences.

The last difference reported is particularly important for Kiesler's notion of commitment. It is apparent from the data that high-commitment subjects were indeed highly rigid with respect to altering their attitudes. Even when they later committed themselves to an opposite behavior in the high-dissonance condition—defense of tuition increase—the original commitment conferred such resistance to the original attitude that dissonance was not reduced in the manner we have observed so regularly. It is not clear what happened to the dissonance, but that is not the important point here.

Kiesler's model as applied in the context of cognitive dissonance tells us something about the resistance to change of cognitions that have as their basis overt behavior. Virtually all of the research we have reported has been designed with the idea that some salient behavior (behavioral commitment) is the cognition most resistant to change, and it is interesting that this experiment brings into juxtaposition two behavioral commitments. Although the relative resistance of those commitments could not be assessed, the authors did vary the binding quality of one of them, with the result that dissonance reduction then tended not to be organized around the other commitment.

The assumption that salient behaviors are highly resistant may often be correct, but it is useful to understand that cognitions about behaviors can vary widely in their resistance to change. Kiesler has specified several determinants of this kind of resistance, and for this reason his notion offers a most viable supplement to dissonance theory.

CHOICE CERTAINTY

A theory of choice certainty (Mills, 1968; Mills & Ross, 1964) begins with the premise that people desire to be certain, upon making a choice, that their decisions are correct. This motivation to choose wisely is said to apply both before and after the choice point, meaning that unlike dissonance theory, the point of commitment does not serve as the starting point for the motivational effects.

The effects of desire for certainty have been measured primarily in terms of selective exposure to information. As applied to postdecisional information-seeking, Mills' ideas overlap completely with dissonance theory. The less certain a person is about the wisdom of his choice, the more likely he is to be receptive to information which tells him that he has chosen correctly. Conversely, uncertainty will lead to *avoidance* of information that threatens to shake the person's sense of certainty. We have discussed some of Mills' postdecisional research in an earlier chapter, and at that point it was described in the language of cognitive dissonance. Needless to say, those effects could as easily be labeled as subjects' efforts to gain certainty of correctness.

The more unique application of Mills' thinking is to predecisional processes. Unlike his analysis of postdecisional selective exposure, where uncertainty leads to exposure to information favoring chosen alternatives, uncertainty has quite different effects prior to a definite commitment. The more uncertain a person is about which alternative should be chosen, the greater his tendency to expose himself to *any* information. Stated the other way, if a person has some certainty that he will choose an alternative, he will then react "defensively" to relevant information, preferring that which favors his tentative choice. The argument is simply this: If the person is highly uncertain about what to choose, information favoring anything will give him direction, or certainty. Even if he exhibits some slight preferences among the alternatives, those preferences are quite susceptible to change when there is no firm basis for them, thus *any* information input will impart an increase in certainty. However, when the person has some basis for preferring one option, certainty is threatened when information implying the contrary is encountered.

Mills and associates have performed at least three experiments to demonstrate his thesis in the context of selective exposure. In the first of these (Mills & Ross, 1964), college men stated a position on an issue, and some of them also found that their position would be publicized. Others expected no publicity. The subjects were also asked for feelings of certainty about their position on the critical issue, and the results demonstrated that exposure to supportive information was especially pronounced among the less certain subjects, but only when they were committed publicly.

In a subsequent experiment Mills (1965c) offered subjects a choice between an advertised product and another that was highly similar in evaluation. In another condition the choice was between the advertised product and one ranked much higher. Mills then asked subjects to read the advertisement, and found reading time to be greater in the first (uncertain) condition. His explanation follows directly from the above reasoning. If a person is offered a choice between two items rated almost equally, he will have trouble in knowing which way to turn, and information about any one of the products will impart an increased sense of direction. However, if the choice is between two products separated by a considerable distance in evaluation, there already exists some degree of certainty, and an advertisement for the lower-rated product would only serve to shake the person's confidence upon going into the decision.

An experiment making the theoretical point in the context of avoidance was performed by Mills and Jellison (1968). All subjects were offered a choice between two products that were seen as much different in attractiveness. Just as in the Mills (1965c) experiment one of the products had an advertisement associated with it. In one condition (certain—relevant) subjects were offered a choice between the advertised product and a product rated much higher, while in the certain—irrelevant condition the choice was between a product ranked just below the advertised product and a product rated much higher. In other words, the advertisement was not relevant to either product, nor to the decision, in the certain—irrelevant condition. Consistent with Mills' thesis subjects spent more time reading the advertisement in the irrelevant condition, where an endorsement for the product could not have induced uncertainty.

A dissertation experiment making a point similar to that of Mills and Jellison (1968) was reported by Sensenig (1969). Subjects were given a choice between two objects, then, prior to the choice, they had an opportunity to listen to two advertisements. One of the advertisements was relevant to *one* of the choice objects, while the other ad related to an item not involved in the decision. Considering just a condition in which subjects were certain that the critical choice item was not something they would choose, there was a definite propensity not to listen to the advertisement associated with that article. In contrast, the same subjects spent significantly more time listening to an ad for a decision-irrelevant product.

How is the desire for choice—certainty reflected aside from exposure to information? Continuing the parallel to dissonance theory, it should be expected that systematic reevaluation of alternatives might be one outcome of the desire for certainty. Upon making a decision the person who desires certainty may bias his ratings of his options so that he has better "reason" for choosing one over the other. Three experiments on predecisional ratings have been conducted to demonstrate this derivation from Mills' ideas. In these experiments (Mills & O'Neal, 1971; O'Neal, 1971; O'Neal and Mills, 1969) subjects were asked to rate a number of decision alternatives (prior to choosing) on several attributes. Intercorrelations were then computed among the ratings on those attributes, and if Mills is correct, the intercorrelations should be positive, reflecting subjects' motivation to rate some alternatives consistently high and others consistently low. The intercorrelations were indeed positive, and more important, were higher than intercorrelations computed for comparable no-choice alternatives.

These experiments are exceptional in that no other published research has found evidence for predecisional spreading in the attractiveness of alternatives. A study by Mann, Janis, and Chaplin (1969) purports to find a predecisional spreading in attractiveness, but the study contains an important flaw in that numerous subjects who showed decision reversals were deleted. It has never been an easy matter to find research evidence for the predecisional biasing, or spreading, implied by Mills' theory, and without going into the theoretical reasons, there is some evidence that people guard against making overt discriminations between alternatives prior to deciding (Jecker, 1964). Two experiments based on other theoretical considerations, have even shown that spreading of the alternatives *decreases* as the decision point approaches (Linder & Crane, 1970; Linder, Wortman, & Brehm, 1971).

One final issue should be raised in evaluating Mills' demonstrations of predecisional choice certainty. Precautions have been taken in his research in an attempt to insure that the ratings and exposure were predecisional, but these precautions have usually amounted to a request of the subject that he not decide until some later point. Unfortunately this kind of safeguard equates a decision with a public statement of such, but why should this be necessary? For all we know the predecisional exposure and rating measures taken from Mills' subjects were tapping into ongoing dissonance reduction, and the patterns of results of each experiment are consistent with dissonance theory as well as with Mills' analysis. Perhaps the only definite safeguard to keep people from deciding is to withhold from them the ingredients for deciding, such as the knowledge of the consequences of deciding (Jecker, 1964), or information that they believe is critical in making up their minds.

In summary, Mills' theory implies that the desire to be certain of having decided correctly is a process to be found both before and after the decision point, and he has provided demonstrations of his thesis with selective exposure to information and with selective biasing of alternatives. The difficulty in interpreting his results amounts simply to whether or not his findings are truly predecisional, and as of this time that remains an open question. Accordingly, there is as yet no perfectly convincing reason to think that dissonance-like processes are initiated prior to decisions.

EXPECTANCY AND SELF

Aronson (1960, 1968, 1969b) has noted what is no doubt a useful rule of thumb in many applications of dissonance theory. To begin with he proposes that dissonance theory makes its clearest predictions when a clear expectancy is held regarding one of the cognitive elements involved in the dissonant relationship. Whether or not such clear expectancies must also be resistant to change is an open question as we interpret his idea. Second, and more important for his applications of the idea, Aronson proposes that expectancies about one's own self-concept are almost always stronger than expectancies about other events. Accordingly, dissonance theory has its clearest application when a firm expectancy about the self is basic to dissonance arousal.

Numerous experiments already discussed assume, at least implicitly, something about the nature of the self concept. For example, the Festinger and Carlsmith (1959) experiment may be viewed as a question of subjects' discrepancies between their positive self-images and their behavior of lying to an accomplice. Numerous other studies requiring antisocial behaviors have presumed that such behaviors are contrary to the subject's personality makeup. Aronson's rule of thumb regarding strong expectancies, and particularly expectancies about the self, asks the investigator to examine the precise nature of expectancies about the self. Does the person conceive of himself as honest, or as a crook? If a crook, asking for the performance of dishonest or hostile behaviors may be perfectly consistent with the person's self-conception, bringing forth nothing but cognitive consonance. For such a person we should try to arouse dissonance by asking him to carry out the deeds of a Boy Scout. Aronson's rule of thumb would imply that the investigator tailor make his discrepant act for each subject, for there should be many instances in which it would be naive to assume that a person possesses self-concepts of honesty, interpersonal warmth, and other common virtues.

A study and some accompanying reasoning by Deutsch, Krauss, and Rosenau (1962) was rather explicitly related to Aronson's modification, although conceived independently of it. Their experiment was a relatively simple free choice study in which subjects chose among different foods. For some of the subjects this was made an ego-involving decision through explaining to them that people with good "food-taste-judgment" also tend to demonstrate leadership potential, executive potential, and artistic judgment. Other subjects (low self-involvement) received no comparable instructions. The results showed that postdecision reevaluation of the chosen alternative was greater in a dissonance-reducing direction for high self-involvement than low self-involvement subjects.

How do we interpret these findings? If a subject realizes that his choice of a simple food item has implications for his more general self-worth, he stands to lose a great deal by choosing incorrectly. It is this ever-present possibility of having chosen incorrectly that adds a negative element to the chosen alternative among high self-involvement subjects. Subjects had no way of knowing whether or not they chose correctly, thus a major source of dissonance was the threat of having chosen so that a broader incompetence would be reflected. Dissonance can be reduced by inventing some extra attraction for the chosen alternative, and this is exactly the form of the results.

An experiment explicitly derived from Aronson's thinking is reported by Nel, Helmreich, and Aronson (1969). Subjects were asked to make a video recording of a highly counterattitudinal message, and were offered differential sums of money for this performance. The ostensible future audience of these taped remarks was said to be either (a) a group opposed to the position of the speech, (b) a group favorable to the position taken, or (c) an uncommitted group. On the basis of Aronson's self-esteem notion, it was assumed that the greatest self-esteem discrepancy would occur in the latter condition, where the subject stood to do some influential damage. (The position of the speech was that marijuana should be legalized, and subjects were initially strongly opposed to such a plan.) Presumably a subject with a high opinion of himself does not encourage people to assent to an immoral position. In the other two conditions, where the audience does not stand to be greatly influenced, the potential damage is considerably less.

The results indicated a strong dissonance effect for the payment variable, but only within the "uncommitted audience" condition. Within the other two conditions there was virtually no effect, thus the reasoning of Aronson seems well supported.

Perhaps the most influential research stemming out of this theoretical reasoning is the performance expectancy paradigm (Aronson & Carlsmith, 1962). A detailed discussion of this area is included in Chapter 10.

As we have treated "clear expectancy" thus far the term might be replaced by "clear cognition." For example, if a person holds cognitions about his innate dishonesty, dissonance will be aroused when he behaves with honesty. Conversely, the self-described honest man will be subject to dissonance when indulging in unscupulous acts. However, to equate "cognition" with "expectancy" does not do justice to Aronson's term. An expectancy is not mere knowledge. Also involved is a sense of prediction for future behaviors or other forthcoming events. Normally an expectancy is a prediction built out of repeated instances of some past occurrence, and this means that dissonance as conceived by Aronson entails a disconfirmation of a prediction, or set. There is a further implication.

A strong expectancy is one that allows the person to be surprised. If an individual has only a vague expectancy about the longevity of his toothbrush, he will not be terribly surprised when all of the bristles come loose. Nor would he be surprised if it lasted indefinitely. But if there is a firm expectancy for the toothbrush to remain intact and it then rapidly deteriorates, the situation begins to look "dissonant" according to Aronson's analysis. Presumably the strongest, best-established expectancy would allow the clearest application of dissonance theory. This means that dissonance arousal will result to the degree that a person's expectancies are disconfirmed, which is approximately the same as saying that an unexpected event occurs. The expectancy does not necessarily have to be a part of the self; Aronson's model requires only that the expectancy antecedent to the disconfirmation be a strong one.

The difficulty should by now be apparent. From most of the research in Chapter 4 on surprise consequences it was found that an event would bring about dissonance reduction only if it was *expected* at the time of behavioral commitment. Subjects whose commitments did not lead them to expect the potentially dissonance-arousing event, and whose expectancies were then disconfirmed, regularly failed to manifest dissonance reduction. The sole exceptions to this finding occurred where subjects were convinced of their causal role with respect to the unanticipated event—but aside from those exceptions there is good reason to think that dissonance does not necessarily result from strong disconfirmations of expectancies.

Aronson's model can be evaluated from two perspectives. He has performed the insightful service of noting that the self-conceptions of subjects should be understood before dissonance theory is applied in a blanket fashion, and certainly this is sound advice. However, the underlying idea of dissonance as an outcome of contradicted expectancies does not seem to fit the major part of the relevant research of Chapter 4. If anything, dissonance seems best created when the individual is not surprised by the consequences of his actions.

COGNITIVE DISSONANCE AS FEELINGS OF SOCIAL REJECTION

Bramel (1968) has advanced several statements of qualification of the theory, and his comments can best be treated by separating them into two parts. The first part of his discussion deals with distinguishing between two kinds of dissonance; in the second part he postulates a new psychological underpinning of dissonance phenomena.

Two Types of Dissonance

Bramel's (1968) reading of the original theory had led him to conclude that one origin of dissonance arousal is the disconfirmation of expectations. Unfortunately this line of thought leads exactly to the same difficulties as were just raised with Aronson's model. A clear disconfirmation of an expectation does not result in dissonance arousal, except under very special circumstances. In addition to the comments we have already made about this issue, an example provided by Bramel shows how awkward the expectation—disconfirmation interpretation becomes when applied to certain accomplished research. The example is this: Bramel assumes that a person who makes a decision expects to decide rationally, which seems to be a fair assumption. But then, when discrepant information is encountered, the person's expectation of himself as rational is disconfirmed— according to Bramel. This is difficult to understand. We would think that to be rational in decision making is to select the best course of action, and encountering a negative consequence is not equivalent to discovering irrationality. But more important, the disconfirmation-of-expectation reasoning implies that dissonance will be greatest when undesirable consequences are unanticipated, and this is simply not the case.

Bramel's second origin of dissonance is behavior that implies incompetence or immorality. Conceptually, this source of dissonance is independent of deviations from expantancy, for a person's immoral actions might arouse dissonance whether or not he expects those actions. This source of dissonance seems relatively straightforward and easy to implement, but how does it fit with other theoretical thinking and research?

If immoral acts arouse dissonance even if the person expects himself to act in such ways, it is difficult to understand where the dissonance originates. Returning to Aronson's remarks, why should an immoral act create dissonance if the person views himself as immoral and has every expectation of acting that way? We fail to understand where dissonance arises if not from cognitions that are in some way contradictory.

There is a more general way to state this criticism. We see no advantage in qualifying the theory such that some specified class of behaviors must be treated as dissonance arousing. Certainly any behavior, no matter what its description, can be consistent with what a person knows about himself or about the environment, provided the person and/or environment happen to manifest features consonant with the behavior. In short, situations and people can always be arranged in research so that a given instance of behavior is completely consonant with relevant, salient cognitions.

Feelings of Social Rejection

Following his dichotomization of sources of dissonance, Bramel wonders what the two sources have in common. Although the reader might well expect him to conclude "dissonance," the answer is by no means so simple. It is suggested instead that the common psychological element is a feeling of social rejection. Evidently people feel rejected both when their expectancies are disconfirmed and when they behave with immorality or incompetence. Bramel proceeds to note that this concept broadens the theory, for he proposes that dissonance is actually the experience of social rejection no matter how this feeling comes about. There is, of course, no necessity that the social rejection be explicit. It is simply the case that some kinds of behaviors, especially those involving deviations from expectations, or incompetence—immorality, call up feelings of rejection as a result of earlier conditioning.

Where does this revision take us? We might try substituting the construct "social rejection" for "dissonance," but that does not add anything to the theory. The concept of social rejection does not carry with it a revision of the theoretical structure of dissonance theory, and for this reason it is hard to understand why the new term would be of any value.

There is a more general point to be made in the context of Bramel's imputation of social rejection into the dissonant organism. It is doubtful that anyone who uses dissonance theory would claim that his dissonance-arousing procedures result in a pure state of psychological dissonance to the exclusion of all other states. Coexisting may be social rejection feelings, frustration, numerous emotions, elation, depression, or almost any psychological state describable. The purpose of characterizing a theory in terms of one psychological construct rather than another is that the theoretical structure fits easily around that concept. Ideally the variables of the theory (i.e., theoretical structure) and its concept have a close, perhaps almost intuitive fit, and to the extent that they do not, an alternative psychological term then becomes appropriate. For example, if the variables associated with dissonance theory were "anticipation of danger," "degree of trauma," and "physiological arousal," the term "dissonance" might well be supplanted by "fear" or "anxiety." But at this stage of theorizing very little is to be gained by replacing the familiar term.

DISSONANCE FROM SUBJECTIVE HYPOTHESES

A modification of dissonance theory developed by Irle (1975) also deals with disconfirmations, but the analysis is considerably different from those of Aronson or Bramel. Aronson deals with expectancies about the self, and with the dissonance resulting when those expectancies are disconfirmed. For example, one cognitive element would be "I am skillful," and the disconfirming element would be "I have blundered in some instance." With Irle's approach a hypothesis *about* the self need not be disconfirmed in order for there to be dissonance.

The idea basic to this new framework is that the individual holds "subjective" Hypotheses (H_s) about the relationship between two cognitive elements. A person might have a hypothesis about the relationship between a particular intelligence test and his own native intelligence. In one case the hypothesis might be nothing more than that the test should reflect accurately one's own positive self-conception. Alternatively, the same individual might hold the hypothesis that the test will not necessarily manifest his innately given high intelligence, due to the test's invalidity. Dissonance is created to the degree that the person's subjective hypothesis is confronted by contrary evidence. In short, dissonance results when a hypothesis *of* the self (about any set of cognitions) is disconfirmed, whereas Aronson's conception deals with hypotheses *about* the self.

Such an approach has clear advantages from the standpoint of a more precise specification of the roots of specific instances of dissonance arousal. A naive application of the original theory might simply hold that dissonance occurs when a person who thinks himself to be intelligent receives a low score on an IQ test. But if the individual held the hypothesis that a high innate IQ did not always imply high test scores, perhaps because of his feelings about the futility of intelligence testing, there should be no dissonance. Irle's approach emphasizes the individual as an active agent who holds specific hypotheses about the way cognitions should fit together, whereas the original theory has characteristically been interpreted such that pairs of cognitions are viewed by the investigator as mutually dissonant (or consonant) independent of the perspectives and hypotheses of the person experiencing dissonance.

Another central feature of Irle's statement is a renewed emphasis on the concept of resistance to change. As we have pointed out repeatedly, this concept is the primary, perhaps sole factor differentiating dissonance theory from alternative cognitive balance formulations. It is this emphasis that moves research relevant to Irle's theory in such directions as the study by Götz–Marchand *et al.* (1974), discussed in Chapter 8.

In general the theory does not take issue with Festinger's (1957) formulation, but the central feature (subjective hypotheses) has led the framework toward a certain realm of application—namely paradigms in which personal hypotheses are explicitly disconfirmed. For example, a study by Frey, Irle, and Kumpf (1975) is mentioned by Irle as illustrative of how his notion would be put to a test. The experiment involved building different strengths of hypotheses in subjects about the occurrence of certain visual patterns. Disconfirming evidence was presented once subjects had established hypotheses, and one of the central measures of response to dissonance was the extent to which subjects changed their hypotheses. Without going into detail, it can be said simply that subjects' hypotheses were changed (weakened, or lowered) in order to account for the disconfirming evidence. Irle proposes that this hypothesis changing serves an immunizing function, in that the hypothesis is altered to the point where it can incorporate evidence that originally would have been disconfirming.

Given that this reformulation is about personal hypotheses, and that suitable paradigms for its testing are likely to be similar to the Frey *et al.* (1975) experiment, we should make a comment about the range of applicability of the reformulation. Evidently the notion cannot be applied to the surprise consequences research we have examined in Chapter 4. The reason is simple. If dissonance (this reformulation) is aroused by negating a person's hypothesis, and if strong disconfirmations of hypotheses often consist in surprises, then the dissonance resulting from a *fait accompli* should indeed be substantial. But such is not the case, as witnessed in Chapter 4. Irle's reformulation addresses problems, or paradigms, somewhat divergent from those we have examined in Chapters 3 and 4 (i.e., when foreseeability is required as an antecedent of dissonance arousal). Probably his statement can most readily be applied when an individual has some specific hypothesis about the relationship between two cognitions and the hypothesis is disconfirmed by an outside agent. This implies direct applicability to paradigms such as that just mentioned (Frey *et al.*, 1975), the Götz–Marchand *et al.* (1974) procedure, and certainly the performance– expectancy paradigm. These are, in fact, paradigms to which Irle gives much of his attention in his 1975 volume.

As a final note we might comment on the dependent measure of the above mentioned Frey *et al.* (1975) study. Rather than clinging to their earlier hypotheses in the face of disconfirming evidence, the subjects "immunized" their hypotheses by shifting them in a direction that would accomodate the evidence. What this must mean, given Irle's emphasis on the resistance-to-change concept, is that a hypothesis is resistant to change only in the sense of its not being wholly discarded: It is simply altered to fit new evidence. This leaves open the question of whether the hypothesis, or the disconfirming evidence is ultimately more resistant to change. The conception of the individual as being prepared to adapt to changing evidence is a provocative departure from the original theory, and although Irle's notion is at its beginning stages, it seems entirely likely that this dependent measure characterizes a direction to be taken in future relevant research.

BALANCE THEORIES

The present section is a consideration of theories that are in many ways parallel to dissonance theory, both in terms of chronology and basic theoretical underpinnings. As such, these other theories are certainly not derivations from or modifications of dissonance theory, but we discuss these balance formulations here because their historical development shares a common element with the theory central to this volume.

Cognitive dissonance is regarded by Festinger (1957) as a motivational state because it has behavioral properties in common with other motivational states, especially the so-called homeostatic drives. When homeostatic drives are aroused, the organism engages in behavior that is directed to reducing drive tension. Cognitive dissonance is included among a psychologist's inventory of drives or motives because its arousal elicits behavior that is directed to returning the organism to a state in which the drive is at a lower level of arousal or is entirely quiescent. Motivational states, in general, have other properties than these drive-reducing ones, and we have seen evidence of this in Chapter 6 (energizing effects of dissonance).

In considering the relationship of dissonance theory to other theories of balance or incongruity, a major issue concerns the motivational one: Just what pushes the organism to reduce inconsistency between the various cognitions or between cognitions and behavior? This question has to do with the kinds of pressures that set the process of resolution going, that make for tension which must be reduced by various paths or balanced states.

Most incongruity theorists conceive of the need to reduce inconsistency as a general motive; this, therefore, accounts for its drive value. Even such a physiological determinist as Hebb (1955) can speak of the "immediate drive value of cognitive processes without intermediary [p. 252]." Although he relates such processes to "basic motives," he does discuss the feedback from cortical functioning that "makes intelligible the equating of anxiety aroused by threat of pain and the anxiety aroused by cognitive processes related to idea of the self [p.

251].'' For cognitive theorists, the specification of the discrepancy-reduction notion as a drive is even more explicit.

Heider (1958), for example, takes the most classical Gestalt position on this matter, locating the idea of incongruity in the stimulus field. For him, imbalance is completely encapsulated in the stimulus field and thus inconsistency is motivating in itself. For Heider, as for Jordan (1953), who states this in terms of pragnanz, there is no reason whatsoever to make any assumptions about underlying motives. In attempting to explain the development and stabilization of interpersonal perceptions, Heider stresses the fact that the sentiment (or affect) characterizing one's response toward some object will tend toward a balanced relation with a person having some relationship to that object. A simple consequence of a person experiencing an unstable interpersonal cognition is that there will be further cognitive work attempted by the person until changes occur that make the cognition balanced and therefore stable. Osgood (1960, p. 345) characterizes Heider's theory as one in which "if a person likes another person, and desires a certain object X, it is fitting (i.e., "balanced") that he strive to be with the other person and acquire the object, that he assumes the other person also likes him, and that the object is of value intrinsically, that he assume the other person also finds the object desirable, and so forth." States of imbalance might be created when P, for example, finds that the O he admires does not like X the way he does. Such a state of imbalance produces stress and tension, and it is these stresses that generate cognitive change. In effect, Heider (1958) assumes a preference for balanced states, and in so doing he adopts a position widely accepted by Gestaltists that people need to organize their experience as meaningfully as possible and that the dynamics of such a need are not motivational ones but stimulus field dynamics.

Both Osgood (1960) and Festinger (1957) speak of cognitive inconsistencies as motives analagous to other drive states like hunger, thirst, sex, and anxiety, though they are purely cognitive in origin. Osgood, Suci, and Tannenbaum (1957) equate "cognitive elements" with the meaning of signs and claim that congruity exists when the evaluative meaning of interacting signs are equally polarized or intense, either in the same or opposite evaluative directions. In the process of cognizing these signs, any incongruity that exists because of differences in polarization must be resolved, and therefore cognitive changes ensue.

Festinger's (1957) view is that cognitive dissonance is a need that has much the same motivating characteristics as other needs. He assumes that the simultaneous existence of cognitions that in one way or another do not "fit together" (dissonance) leads to effort on the part of the person to somehow make them fit better (dissonance reduction). For Festinger (1957, p. 3), as we have seen, the existence of nonfitting cognitions is a motivating factor in its own right; in place of dissonance one could conceivably substitute other notions like "hunger," "frustration," "disequilibrium," and so forth. Cognitive elements are said to be dissonant when one implies the obverse of the other. The degree to which there are dissonant elements determines the degree to which psychological tension having drive character is said to exist, making for the stress toward cognitive modification.

It should be understood that neither of these latter theorists necessarily makes the Gestalt assumption about the tendency to maintain consistency as part of the widely operative motivation toward the elaboration and stabilization of ordered forms. In effect, they do not necessarily lean on the conventional Gestalt emphasis on unlearned autochthonous determination. All these theorists except for Heider of course, assume that the need for resolution of inconsistency has its origins and motivational dynamics in much the same processes as other needs. Thus, through child training history with its long record of trials in "conflictlike" situations resulting in the elimination of competing and incompatible responses, a state of consistency between cognitive, affective, and behavioral responses toward objects will itself become a gratifying state of affiars. In effect, it will become a stable learned motive or, as Allport (1937) puts it, an autonomous motive. Thus, an encounter with any inconsistency will be painful in itself and will activate the individual's learned responses or reorganisation toward consistency (see Hovland & Rosenberg, 1960, p. 225).

The other possible basis for the strain toward resolution of inconsistency, is, of course, in direct and deliberate social training. Most overtly in formal educational procedures, and more subtly in the demands that parents and the structured nature of the world of things make from earliest years, the child is subject to the constant requirement that he endow his responses with some consistency, with varying immediate rewards and punishments for compliance and failure. Thus, although none of the present incongruity theorists takes a position on which of these two mediational processes is responsible for motivation toward resolution of inconsistencies, either sequence is consistent with their assumption of a general motivating tendency resulting from incongruity.

It seems to us, however, that it is not too useful to speak of dissonance or incongruity reduction as a *general* motive. First of all, it simply adds to the plethora of need states postulated by psychological theorists to account for any given response tendency. We feel that psychology would benefit from an attempt to specify the conditions under which responses occur in as economical a fashion as possible without adding a new need every time some new and puzzling behavior is isolated. Secondly, the present and increasing unclarity of the motivation concept itself would seem not to encourage the addition of some new general motive to the present list. As Cofer (1959, p. 194) says, motivation apparently "has no automatic response indicators," and on the antecedent side "the rejection of homeostatic drives as sufficient to motivation also makes insufficient the deprivation operation in the control of motivation."

Furthermore, we feel that the specification of dissonance, incongruity, or imbalance as a general motive rests on a theoretical confusion between motives and motivational states. Motives themselves are generally thought of as states of chronic arousal. They refer to the "energizing of behavior and especially to the sources of energy in a particular set of responses that keep them temporarily dominant over others and account for continuity and direction in behavior" (Hebb, 1955, p. 244). Drives, or motivational states, deal with a more specific conception about the way in which this occurs; drive is a hypothesis of motivation that "makes the energy a function of a special process distinct from those stimulus–response or cognitive functions that are energized" (Hebb, 1955, p. 244). Motivational or drive states are tied to specific arousal through discrepancies between motives and their satisfaction. The point is that the discrepancies between other motives and their satisfaction result in behavior in the interests of discrepancy reduction; such behavior is not necessarily simply due to the fact that two stimuli or cognitions are "inconsistent" with one another.

In one of his major theoretical writings, Osgood appears to take this position, though he does not appear to do so explicitly in other places. In his Nebraska symposium paper, Osgood (1957) brings in the reticular formation as the physiological basis of the immediate drive value of cognitive processes, but he takes the position that when meaning is blocked because of incongruity, there is drive-producing tension largely because there has been some effect on rewards and punishments or their anticipation, with regard to a possible host of primary and social needs. In sum, it may be reward and punishment related to other needs that makes inconsistency motivating.

However, in the experimental work that has come out of his laboratory, Osgood does not deal explicitly with the idea of the blockage to the satisfactions of other needs or motives that discrepancy produces. His major focus is on semantic incongruities; on the basic dimensions of verbal meaning. In his experimental work he has tried to show that incongruities centering around inconsistencies along the dimensions of evaluation, potency and activity motivate cognitive change. Thus, inconsistency reduction takes place largely as a result of logical inconsistencies along the evaluative dimension that serves as a crucial focus for the assignment of other cognitions. When liked persons were associated with disliked objects, incongruities were assumed to have been created. Osgood and Tannenbaum (1955) and Osgood *et al.* (1957) then bring to bear their general "principle of congruity" and expect that the evaluations of the person and the object will regress in the direction of a common value; the liked person when associated with the disliked object becomes less liked and the disliked object when associated with the liked person becomes less disliked.

To return to our main concern, we feel that cognitive dissonance involves more than what Festinger has explicitly prescribed in his theoretical statement. This has to do with the sources of relevance of psychological implication. It should be apparent from the review of evidence that each experimenter generally knows intuitively just which elements are likely to be relevant and which elements are likely to be irrelevant. But what are the conditions that produce relevance independently of an experimenter's familiarity with his society? One answer to this question is *other motives*. Motives are capable of implying that certain elements should exist and that certain other elements should not exist. The cognition corresponding to smoking ("I am smoking") and the cognition corresponding to reading about lung cancer and smoking ("Smoking causes death from lung cancer") are relevant to one another because obvious motives interact, namely, "gain pleasure from smoking" and "avoid painful death," in addition to many others. As Festinger (1957) points out, the cognitions "hot weather is good for corn" and "letters take two weeks to go from New York to Paris" might become relevant if the individual who entertained these cognitions was motivated to earn money by speculating on the American corn crop at the Paris exchange. This kind of analysis has enabled us to elaborate cognitive dissonance in a way not explicitly stated by Festinger (1957) in his theory: *Cognitive dissonance is a general "motivational state" that occurs when there is some prior motive associated with the cognitions that are dissonant.* Although a dissonant relationship is defined more broadly, we are not confident that other forms of psychological implication would in fact provide the conditions necessary to the arousal of dissonance. It is true that other motives such as *n* achievement, or *n* affiliation, and so forth, can be reduced to "simpler" or more "basic" tendencies and drives, but they are not defined in a way that makes this elaboration essential to a complete explanation. Cognitive dissonance, however, must necessarily be defined in such a manner because of the *relevance* criterion.

We have implied earlier that relevance is usually determined in an a priori, common-sense fashion by the experimenter. Through his experience with the culture in which he is conducting his research, the investigator knows what behaviors, beliefs, values, and so on, have something to do with one another. The investigator will also know how these various elements relate to satisfactions or dissatisfactions of particular motives. Since relevance of cognitions is essential to the production of dissonance, only the outcomes of experiments can show that the investigator has been correct in his a priori analysis of relevance. If cognitions were not relevant, no dissonance would occur and the predicted effect of dissonance would not be obtained.

It is in this sphere that the distinctive advantage of dissonance theory with regard to the motivation of discrepancy resolution becomes apparent. In the other incongruity theories, a general residual motive is always assumed to get behavior going. This, we feel, leaves a general undifferentiated state always responsible for cognitive change or behavior and makes difficult the prediction of specific courses of resolution unless some "regression hypothesis" (Osgood *et al.,* 1957) or some "least effort principle" (Rosenberg & Abelson, 1960) is introduced. The point is that while Festinger takes the same general position and speaks of a general motive (Festinger, 1957, p. 229), the theory has a unique predictive power because of the relevance criterion and because most of the dissonance-theory experiments explicitly trade on the frustration of other motives. Thus in the gambling experiments, the choice experiments, the coercion experiments, the hunger, thirst, and avoidance experiments, and so forth, *some prior motivation* is always considered. In effect, what we are saying is that the effects of the dissonance manipulations in the various experiments are due to the commmitment on the part of the person to a behavior that has implications for the frustration of important motives. Every experiment evokes another motive whose instrumental connection to inconsistency produces drives toward the resolution of inconsistency. Basic to the arousal of dissonance appears to be the incompatibility introduced by the individual's commitment to behave in some way, presumably out of some strong motive, such as pleasing the experimenter, that frustrates another strong motive.

Dissonance theory, we have seen, is in part a theory of *postdecision* behavior, and it is the process of the decision to behave in a way that may frustrate motive satisfaction that links motivation to the resolution of inconsistencies. In any one of the experiments mentioned, the simple existence of inconsistency has not been shown to be enough to motivate behavior; in each case the person has arrived at a state of dissonance as a consequence of some prior commitment that has consequences for satisfaction of important needs.

This gap between Festinger's theoretical statement and the actual experiments that have been generated by it is reflected in Osgood's (1960, p. 349) comment that Festinger's theory fails to give explicit recognition to the need for cognitive elements to be brought into some relation with one another if they are to interact and produce cognitive modification. However, Osgood does make the same point we are making: "The implicit recognition of the need for linkage in some unit" appears in the design of dissonance experiments. Thus dissonance only occurs "when a person is forced to make a choice to behave in some way that is discrepant from his cognitions or if a prior choice that he has made has led to a situation of cognitive discrepancy." Dissonance is aroused by the process of decision that has some negative consequences for the individual and that therefore creates a discrepancy between some prior state (or the cognitions that would lead him to maintain that state) and the present behavior he engages in.

A second way in which dissonance theory is different from other models of cognitive inconsistency is in its specification of resistance to change, especially through commitment. For if we assume that a given inconsistency of cognitive elements arouses a motivational state, a problem remains about which consequences will ensue. This problem is handled in dissonance theory by appeal to the notion of differential resistance to change of the relevant cognitive elements. Those elements least resistant to change tend to be those that do in fact change in order for dissonance to be reduced. Since decisional or behavioral commitment contributes to resistance to change, commitment tends to result in the "fixing" of one of the important relevant elements. Hence, dissonance tends to be reduced by change in cognitions other than those involved in the commitment. The net result is that where dissonance is aroused in conjunction with a commitment, its effects are more limited (and specifiable) than where the incongruity has nothing to do with commitment (or other forms of resistance to change).

It is interesting to note than any one of the balance theories we have discussed could be given the same predictive power as dissonance theory simply by adding the notion of resistance to change, and perhaps also the responsibility concept discussed earlier. For example, Insko, Worchel, Folger, and Kutkus (1975) have integrated these concepts into the thinking of Heider, thereby developing a model that parallels dissonance theory with some success.

Another relevant issue here concerns the extension made by some incongruity theorists like Newcomb (1953) and especially Cartwright and Harary (1956) from interpersonal perception to interpersonal relations. The latter attempt a formal definition of balance in Heider's (1958) system in terms of the mathematical theory of linear graphs. While there may be tremendous advantages in such specification, as Osgood (1960, p. 346) points out, it causes some confusion in conceptualizing the notion of cognitive change. Cognitive dynamics, he says, transpire within the nervous systems of individuals, and the representations we make of them reflect relationships as the individual perceives them. However, it seems that Newcomb and Cartwright and Harary shift too easily from the subjective cognitive interactions within individuals to the objective issues of group structure and dynamics. While it is possible that the laws governing the resolution of incongruities within the cognitive structures of individuals can be transferred to interactions between people and within groups of people, such transformations remain to be proven and tested, and the new mediating assumptions necessary to go from one set of issues to another must be clearly specified. It is clear, however, that Festinger (1957) and Osgood (1960) are quite aware of this restriction of their systems. It is also possible that a good deal of predictive looseness enters a system that is based on the pressures to resolve incongruities between aspects of an individual cognitive structure when that system attempts to be specific with regard to interactions between individuals.

In summary, we may say that discrepancies or inconsistencies, especially as they appear in the experiments deriving from the dissonance formulation, produce a drive toward their resolution because of motive states, insofar as discrepancy has some instrumental relationship to their satisfaction or frustration.

SUMMARY

This chapter has discussed five modifications or extensions of dissonance theory. Taking them in reverse order, Irle has devised a theoretical modification which analyses dissonance in terms of disconfirmation of personal hypotheses about the compatibility of various groups of cognitions. This modification seems especially applicable to instances of dissonance in which the individual is met by unexpected consequences. However, just as in Aronson's (1968, 1969b) approach, the central problem of the preceding Chapter 4 arises: Under what circumstances is dissonance created by a surprise consequence? Bramel's (1968) recommendations for the theory have all the appearances of splintering a cohesive theory. The dichotomy of disconfirmed expectation and incompetent-immoral behaviors does little to add to the predictive power of the theory, and his stipulation that dissonance is based in social rejection offers little in the way of a tangible contribution to theoretical thinking. Aronson's suggestions regarding the self-concept can be useful in implementing the theory, especially in those areas where there is little reason to expect people to be homogeneous in whatever characteristics are relevant to dissonance arousal. However, his broader proposal that dissonance ensues when strong expectancies are violated does not coincide with the research on disconfirmed expectancies (Chapter 4). Mills' (1968) choice–certainty theory has opened an exploration of dissonance-like effects, especially selective exposure, prior to the point of commitment. The theory has generated a good deal of support, and the major question for the evidence is whether or not it is predecisional. Kiesler's model of commitment has also generated considerable evidence, and his treatment of commitment as varying in intensity is a useful and thorough-going means of approaching the concept of resistance to change. This chapter also discussed the relationship between dissonance theory and other theories of cognitive balance.

16
Alternative Explanations of Dissonance Phenomena

This chapter includes several theoretical ideas that purport to account for phenomena we have thus far examined. These ideas, unlike those of the previous chapter, are not derivations from or additions to dissonance theory, but instead, are attempted alternative accounts for "dissonance phenomena" in terms unrelated to the theory. A vast array of alternative viewpoints of dissonance-like phenomena may be found in the volume of Abelson, Aronson, McGuire, Newcomb, Rosenberg, and Tannenbaum (1968), but this chapter is considerably more focused. We shall discuss just those viewpoints that offer a relatively thoroughgoing attempt to account for several dissonance phenomena by means of alternative schemes. The most pervasive of these notions is a theory of self-perception advanced by Bem (1965), which is discussed first.

SELF-PERCEPTION THEORY

In one of his first statements of the self-perception thesis Bem (1965) proposed that cognitive dissonance experiments have their effects because of the judgmental, self-observational abilities of the subjects, rather than because of the motivational underpinnings of dissonance theory. His idea is best captured by considering an experimental situation from the standpoint of an onlooker. Suppose an observer watches someone perform an attitude-relevant behavior, such as delivering a segregationist speech before the local parent—teachers association. The observer is told nothing about the attitudes of the speaker, but he is provided with another kind of information: In one instance the speaker has been instructed by his employer and family to give the speech; in another, he issues his diatribe against integration in the absence of any apparent constraints. If asked to infer the speaker's attitude on segregation, it seems likely that a more segregationist position will be inferred when there are no pressures to deliver the talk. This conclusion can be reached on the basis of several models of person perception (Heider, 1958; Jones & Davis, 1965; Kelley, 1971). To the extent that external forces are absent, internal forces will be inferred.

Thus far, Bem's thinking does not differ significantly from that of other models of attribution to other persons. However, he has gone one step further to propose that such attributional processes are performed by the individual *on himself*. This means that the person delivering a racist talk will examine the circumstances of his behavior, and in the process of inferring an attitude of himself he will take into account environmental forces. If the forces are strong, then he loses credibility, in his own eyes, as a racist. If there are no environmental pressures, or if there are pressures to be of a liberal mind, he would then infer of himself a definite segregationist attitude. Otherwise stated, he then becomes credible in the sense that his behavior is seen by him as reflecting a definite segregationist attitude.

This analysis may sound peculiar because it seems to assume that a person doesn't even know his own attitudes. But it happens that this very assumption is necessary to Bem's thinking. Bem's argument is simply that the actor and the observer employ similar kinds of information in inferring attitudes of the actor. Neither of them has a firm conception of the actor's attitude before he behaves, but each of them uses the attribution analysis outlined above to infer attitudes from behavior. Obviously Bem's assumption of the actor's ignorance of his own attitudes opens numerous questions, but we will pursue them later. For the present we assume, with Bem, that people infer their own attitudes in a manner similar to the inference processes of observers. Where does this assumption take us?

If actors and observers are alike in their inference processes, a number of phenomena we have attributed to dissonance arousal should be predictable by passive observers. Bem's first tack in providing evidence for his thesis has been to create simulated dissonance experiments, wherein his subjects are informed about the details of the procedure of a dissonance experiment and then asked to estimate the attitude of one particular subject who is involved in the procedure.

Interpersonal Simulations

Bem's first study (1965) was a simulation of the Cohen (1962a) experiment involving Yale undergraduates (Chapter 5). Subjects were provided with background information about altercations between students and police, and it is fair to say that Bem provided a reasonable summary description of the situation existing at Yale at the time of the original experiment. The subject then learned the following:

> As part of a research project, a student member of a research team from the Institute of Human Relations at Yale selected a student at random and asked him to write a strong, forceful essay entitled, "Why the New Haven Police Actions Were Justified," an

essay which was to be unequivocally in favor of the police side of the riots. The decision to write such an essay or not was entirely up to the student, and he was told that he would be paid the sume of $.50 [$1.00] if he would be willing to do so. The student who was asked agreed to do so, and wrote such an essay [Bem, 1965, p. 203].

At this point in the procedure Bem's subjects knew only that the particular student selected by the researcher had agreed to write the essay, and that the student had been promised $.50 (or $1). Bem elected not to replicate Cohen's other conditions, which presents no problem. Given this information the subject was asked to estimate the opinion of the student writing the essay. There was no specification of whether this was to be the pre- or postessay opinion, but simply a request for the student's "actual opinion." Bem also ran a control condition, as did Cohen, in which there was no request for an essay.

The pattern of results for the original (Cohen, 1962a) and interpersonal–simulation studies are virtually identical, and in fact, the significance levels are almost the same. Returning to Bem's reasoning, there does appear to be evidence that a passive observer can reproduce results generated from actual subjects, and this is the kind of evidence that leads Bem to propose that involved subjects engage in the same attribution processes as passive observers. Applying Bem's reasoning to the original Cohen study, it would be assumed that the subject was most credible to himself in the $.50 condition, where there was little external pressure to endorse the police actions. Given slightly more pressure by the $1 treatment, subjects as self-observers would be somewhat less credible. In other words, there is progressively less basis for inferring a strong attitude as external incentives (pressures) for behavior increase.

Bem (1965) reports another interpersonal simulation, this one a carbon copy of the Brehm and Crocker (1962) hunger experiment (Chapter 10). Bem's treatment of this experiment paralleled his interpersonal simulation of Cohen's study, and again, subjects were told just about one person involved in the actual procedure: "This individual agreed to continue his participation. From this description, try to estimate how hungry this particular person must have been at the end of the first session just described" (Bem, 1965, p. 206). It will be recalled that Brehm and Crocker offered some subjects $5 for continuing their participation, and this aspect of the procedure was replicated closely by Bem. The results were also similar "to those of Brehm and Crocker": subjects offered payment were estimated to be hungrier than those not offered payment.

These two experiments put wind in the sails of Bem's self-perception analysis of dissonance phenomena. If observers can predict accurately the responses of involved subjects, it may well be that involved subjects employ exactly those same attribution processes. It may also be the case that passive observers happen to be expert dissonance theorists, but for the present we will not raise that issue. Instead, it is appropriate at this point to show what happened when several researchers examined Bem's evidence critically and attempted to control for what seemed to be a flaw in his designs.

Interpersonal Simulations: Controlling for Self-Selection

In taking a close look at Bem's interpersonal simulations, Jones, Linder, Kiesler, Zanna, and Brehm (1968) found what appeared to be an obvious and debilitating flaw in the procedures. Bem's (1965) observer subjects were told about the participation of just one actual subject in such a way that the observers could easily have concluded that many actual subjects would not have decided to proceed with the essay or with additional hours of fasting. For example, subjects in the first experiment, after learning that the police were unpopular among Yale students, found that the student who was interviewed agreed to write the essay. This raises a distinct possibility of subjects' concluding that this particular student did not have anything against the police, or at least that he did not hold the same disdain for them as other potential essay writers. For all the subject knew, most students approached by the researcher may have turned him down because of their strong feelings. It would also follow that a student offered a small monetary incentive would be likely to volunteer only if his feelings against the police were not extreme. Further, the greater the monetary incentive, the more that extremely antipolice students would lean toward volunteering for essay writing.

The previous line of reasoning was the basis for several experiments by Jones *et al.* (1968). It seemed evident that Bem's results could easily have been due to a self-selection process assumed by the observer subjects, whereby the observer would suppose that students in strong opposition to the police would not volunteer, unless the monetary incentives were sufficient. If the subject were told that a student volunteered for a $.50 incentive, he would infer a more charitable attitude toward police than if the student volunteered in response to a greater incentive. Very simply, it is quite reasonable for observer–subjects to assume that anyone can be bought if the price is right.

Jones *et al.* (1968) conducted a number of experiments that included controls for this self-selection bias. For example, in their Experiment 2 there was a straight replication of Bem's (1965) procedure in addition to two kinds of control for the bias that presumably accounted for Bem's interpersonal simulation of Cohen's experiment. Jones *et al.* (1968) created three conditions indentical to the interpersonal simulation of Bem. These were labeled the "Bem" conditions, and varied in the amount of monetary inducement reportedly offered to actual subjects (no commitment, $.50, and $1). The two kinds of control were the following:

1. First, a pair of conditions labeled "nonrandom" was run. In Bem's original procedure the student was said to have been selected at random, opening the possibility that by a simple accident of random sampling he happened to be relatively positive toward police. In the nonrandom conditions (both $.50 and $1) subjects were told that a researcher at Yale had contacted *a number* of students, and that *all of them* indicated a negative opinion toward the police.

With this knowledge it would be difficult for the subject—observer to derive his attitude estimate by the assumption of self-selection.

2. Second, there were two conditions called "complete" ($.50 and $1), in which a more substantial proportion of Cohen's original instructions was included. One element not included by Bem was the researcher's citing of numerous reasons for writing the essays. For example, the students were told that many people were concerned about the issue, the research was important, and there were even more reasons. Jones *et al.* (1968) argued that the inclusion of these more complete instructions would decrease the possibility of observer-subjects' operating on the assumptoin of self-selection.

The results of six of these conditions are shown in Table 17. In the straight replication (Bem condition) it is evident that the direction of difference between the $.50 and $1 conditions was similar to that of Bem, and it reaches significance. The contrast appears in examination of the other two conditions, in which the difference obtained by Bem tended either to reverse or disappear. Consistent with the self-selection reasoning of Jones *et al.* (1968), the effect originally obtained by Bem was found only when observer—subjects remained ignorant of the student's initial attitude. When steps were taken to make subects aware of the universally negative attitudes toward police, the negative relationship between amount of incentive and positivity of attitude toward police could not be obtained.

Before proceeding, we might note that Bem (1967) has also conducted interpersonal simulations of the Brehm and Cohen (1959b) and Festinger and Carlsmith (1959) experiments, and although the results paralleled those obtained from actual subjects, the self-selection process could easily have operated in those experiments as well as in the two summarized above. The Brehm and Cohen (1959b) experiment involved a free choice, and in order to demonstrate the impact of eliminating self-selection from the free choice interpersonal simulation, Jones *et al.* (1968) report an interpersonal simulation of the free choice study by Brehm (1956). In Bem's (1967) free-choice study the subjects were not told anything about the initial ratings of alternatives given by actual subjects, allowing the self-selection process to operate freely. That is, if an observer—subject finds that an actual subject has chosen Alternative A, he has every reason to infer that the subject was especially attracted to that alternative prior to the decision, and that he would have chosen otherwise if he was not so attracted. Jones *et al.* (1968) simply performed an interpersonal simulation of the high- and low-dissonance conditions of Brehm's (1956) experiment, taking care to inform subjects of the initial attractiveness of the alternatives. The Jones *et al.* (1968) experiment showed no dissonance reduction whatsoever, and no hint of a difference between high- and low-dissonance conditions. Again, it appears as though the self-selection bias was responsible for Bem's several successful interpersonal simulations.

TABLE 17
Mean Attitude Estimates in Experiment II

Payment	Bem	Nonrandom	Complete instruction
$ .50	4.3	3.6	3.6
$1.00	3.3	4.0	3.6

A Reply on Behalf of Self-Perception Theory

Perhaps surprisingly, the reasoning behind self-perception theory turns out to depend upon a perceived self-selection, whether on the part of the actor or the observer. In his reply to Jones *et al.* (1968), Bem (1968) elevates self-selection into a crucial component of his framework. His argument depends upon the assumption that initial attitudes are salient neither for an involved subject nor for a passive observer. When the subject of Cohen's study finds himself applauding the police actions, he presumably asks himself "What sort of person am I to write such an essay?" and concludes that he must not be terribly opposed to the police. From the standpoint of self-perception theory the subject does not distinguish between his pre- and postessay attitudes. He simply asks himself, upon behaving, what kind of person would behave in such a way, and thereby arrives at his inference of a relatively positive attitude toward the police. If he has been coerced into writing the essay (i.e., paid substantially), the inference would be more toward the negative end of the scale. Exactly the same reasoning applies to passive observers, who ask themselves, "What sort of person condones the police?" Evidently, a person would condone the police only if he liked them, especially if the incentive were only a few cents.

It will help at this point to review Bem's reasoning with respect to the Cohen study, and in doing so we might take the perspective of the involved subject. Suppose the subject discovers that he has just written the essay for an incentive of $10. In attempting to infer an attitude in order to supply the experimenter with a questionnaire response, the subject considers the conditions under which he complied. Given his knowledge of the $10 incentive, it would be hard for him to conclude that any particular attitude led him to write the essay. This is because he might have complied no matter what his feelings. Accordingly, his inference of attitude will be more antipolice than that of someone offered only $.50. The individual in the latter case has very little explanation for his behavior other than the possibility of a propolice attitude, thus he manifests compassion for the police when responding to the questionnaire.

Bem (1968) criticizes Jones *et al.* (1968) for artifically inflating the salience of initial attitudes. He argues that he has simulated, to the best of his ability, the situation as it existed for actual subjects, and that the procedures of Jones *et al.* (1968) have introduced elements into the minds of passive observers that were not in the minds of actual subjects. It is his thesis that their efforts to give observer—subjects a firm idea of initial attitudes interfered with the self-selection process that is basic to "dissonance" results.

Now the issue is one of initial attitudes. Surely a firm knowledge of initial attitudes will eliminate a conclusion based on self-selection—i.e., the conclusion that "I would write a propolice essay only if I liked police," but is it really the case that actual subjects have a minimal or nonexisting knowledge of their prior attitudes? It is Bem's thesis that the information supplied to his observers is more in keeping with actual subjects' knowledge than was the information supplied to observers by Jones and his associates. But to which of the Jones *et al.* (1968) experiments does Bem refer? His comments focus on the Jones *et al.* (1968) procedures that led to increasing the salience, for observers, of actual subjects' initial attitudes. And he may be right, in that those attitudes might have not been salient for actual subjects by the time they had carried out their essay writing. Bem suggests that writing of essays served to "swamp" the prior attitudes, this swamping being a prerequisite for obtaining dissonance-like effects.

A Reply to Self-Perception Theory: The Authenticity of Bem's Simulations

The critique of Jones *et al.* (1968) focused on procedures that raised salience of initial attitudes, and it was assumed that these procedures resulted in an artificial, less-than-authentic, replication of the procedure as it registered on the minds of actual subjects. However, Bem overlooked a pair of conditions described above (Experiment II, Jones *et al.*, 1968) in which the details supplied to observer—subjects were more complete than those supplied in his own research. It will be recalled that Bem's descriptions of the Cohen study deleted several remarks about the importance of the research, and the fact that many people were concerned about the issue. These comments, delivered to the original subjects, were inserted into the "complete" conditions of Jones *et al.* (1968), and otherwise the descriptions were equivalent to those of Bem. It may also be recalled that the effects of Cohen (1962a) (hence, those of Bem) were not reproduced in the two complete conditions.

A more recent study by Piliavin, Piliavin, Loewenton, McCauley, and Hammond (1969) was also designed to provide observer—subjects with a complete description of the actual procedure of Cohen (1962a). These authors found that Bem had neglected a number of elements, such as those listed below, each of which implies that the actual subject's attitude may have been a salient feature of Cohen's procedure:

What we really need now are some essays favoring the police side. I understand that you have very different views on the matter, but as you can see it's very interesting to know what kinds of arguments people bring up in their essays if they have very different opinions about it [Piliavin *et al.*, 1969, p. 101].

The decision to write the essay is entirely your own choice. But I *do* need your help in the study since I am a student and this is part of my research paper [p. 101].

Now that you have looked at some of the reasons for the actions of the New Haven police, we'd like to get some of your reactions to the issue; you may possibly want to look at the situation in light of this. So would you please fill out this questionnaire [p. 101].

Piliavin *et al.* (1969) patterned three conditions closely after Bem's procedure, although they were more extensive in their simulation and included a $5 condition in addition to the $1 and $.50 variations. In three other conditions, called the "Cohen" conditions, Bem's descriptions were supplemented by a considerable body of Cohen's original instructions, including the material quoted above. If Bem is correct in arguing that passive observers can best replicate the original results given complete descriptions of the original situation, it should follow that the results of Piliavin *et al.* (1969) would closely mimic those of Cohen.

The results are shown in Table 18. In the Bem replication the results are similar to his, with a significant inverse relationship between payment and attitude change. However, the Cohen conditions show no such effect.

The complete conditions of Jones *et al.* (1968) and the Cohen conditions of Piliavin *et al.* (1969) appear at face value to satisfy Bem's (1965) requirements for an interpersonal simulation. If the phenomenology of the original subject is to be reproduced for the observer–subject, what better way is there than to equate the stimulus conditions of the simulation with those of the original? Although Bem has not responded directly to these two experimental variations, it would be difficult to comprehend an argument that these tests have artificially inflated the salience of original subjects' initial attitudes. By deleting aspects of

TABLE 18
Mean Judgments of Attitudes
for Bem and Cohen Replications

Payment	Bem replication	Cohen replication
$ .50	19.5	16.0
$1.00	16.5	15.9
$5.00	15.9	16.0

the original procedure Bem evidently has artifically eliminated the salience of original attitudes.

The interpersonal simulation procedures depend upon the experimenter's skill in recreating the original stimulus conditions, and there may be an easier, and more accurate, method of informing observers about the phenomenological impact of experimental instructions. Why not turn actual subjects into observers of other subjects? In this way the comparability of the interpersonal simulation and the original procedure is guaranteed. This procedure was followed by Arrowood, Wood, and Ross (1970).

The procedure was similar to an earlier-cited effort justification experiment by Arrowood and Ross (1966; see Chapter 5 of this book). Subjects were told that they would take either one of two intelligence tests, and that one of the tests would be selected for them by random procedure. The experimenter then informed all subjects of the necessity of preparing for one of the tests (the IICT test) just in case it was randomly selected for them. Some subjects expected the preparation to entail considerable effort, and others expected to devote only minimal effort. At that point, before subjects had actually studied and before a test was selected for them to take, they were asked to estimate the probability of their taking either test. The reasoning from dissonance theory is straightforward: To reduce dissonance resulting from anticipated effort they should inflate their estimated chances of taking the IICT, and this is exactly what happened.

The interpersonal simulation part of the experiment was made possible by running subjects in large groups. Each group was composed of entirely high-effort (or low-effort) subjects, insuring that every subject knew that the procedure for every other subject in his group was the same as his own. In addition to providing his own probability estimate, each subject was given the following instructions: "Pick the person seated three seats away from you in any direction: Which of the two tests do you think *he* will write?" (Arrowood *et al.*, 1970, p. 311). Subjects were asked to estimate the likelihood of the observed subject's taking each test, and the results of this measure plus the results of the subject's self-estimate are shown in Table 19. It is evident that the effort variable had an impact only for self-estimate. Even though the subjects should have had excellent insight into the phenomenological impact of the procedure on observed subjects, their estimates for others bore no similarity to Bem's earlier replications.

The cumulative message of these several studies becomes progressively clearer. If the researcher goes out of his way to duplicate the precise conditions under which actual subjects are run, observers seem unable to reproduce the original results. There seems only one way for self-perception theory to handle this series of disconfirmations, and that is to argue that reproducing the exact instructions is not the best route to reproducing the phenomenological impact on original subjects. Bem suggests that an involved subject's initial attitude, if there is an initial attitude, becomes obscured (swamped) by the behavior he is requested to perform. Since observers do not behave overtly, as do involved subjects, observ-

TABLE 19

Percentages of Involved Subjects Who Expected
to Take the Preparation-Relevant Test and
Percentages of Observer Subjects Who Expected the
Target Person to Take the Preparation-Relevant Test

	Involved subjects	Observer subjects
High-anticipated effort	81	53
Low-anticipated effort	52	52

ers would retain a feeling for the original attitude when provided with complete descriptions of the experimental procedure. Therefore, in order to reduce the observer's awareness of initial attitudes to a level comparable to actual subjects' "swamped" awareness of initial attitudes, it becomes necessary to delete various facets of the procedure when describing it to observers. This is, of course, what Bem did, although we do not impute this chain of reasoning to him, nor do we find this chain of reasoning to be anything less than contorted. Certainly no researcher, nor anyone except the involved subject himself, would be aware of the exact phenomenological impact of the experimental procedures.

Salience of Initial Attitudes among Involved Subjects

In the preceding line of thought we have sought to show that the self-selection processes entering into Bem's interpersonal simulations are not applicable to involved subjects in dissonance-arousing situations. When observer subjects are provided with complete descriptions of the original situations, those observers are then incapable of replicating the original results, suggesting rather convincingly that the original subjects did not arrive at their "dissonance reduction" through an implicit process of self-selection reasoning.

The interpersonal simulation simply does not make a case for Bem's reinterpretation of dissonance phenomena. However, before leaving our discussion of research directed toward Bem's thesis, we will devote this short section to another facet of the self-perception theory explanation—this being the issue of salience of initial attitudes. Bem has argued that the person in a "dissonance-arousing" situation is quite unaware of a preexisting attitude, while dissonance theory depends upon such awareness in order for the dissonance to be realized. This juxtaposition of reasoning implies a possibly informative experiment: If dissonance-like phenomena can be found under conditions where subjects show no evidence of recall of initial attitudes, there may be some reason to credit Bem with a correct analysis.

Bem and McConnell (1970) conducted an experiment to test the above reasoning. This was Bem's first reported study with involved, nonobserver subjects. One week before the experimental session subjects filled out a premeasure on the issue of how much control students should exert over university course offerings. During the actual experimental session subjects were asked to write an essay taking the position that "Students should have VERY LITTLE or NO CONTROL over the kinds of courses offered by the University" (Bem & McConnell, 1970, p. 26). Precautions were taken that all subjects' initial attitudes were in disagreement with the essay. It is not clear from Bem's idea why this would be necessary, since he proposes that initial attitudes are virtually nonexistent, and his reason for this "counterattitudinal" method is that "the forced compliance paradigm requires that all subjects argue the counterattitudinal position . . ." (Bem & McConnell, 1970, p. 26). The subjects were given choice or no choice in the writing of this essay, then a further variable was introduced at the time of the measure. Half of the subjects in each condition were asked for a final opinion on the issue, while the remaining subjects were asked to restate their initial opinions before their final opinions.

The crucial results for this experiment involve the comparison between initial attitude estimates and attitude change among subjects who were asked for both final attitude and estimate of initial attitude. When this is done it is quite clear that estimates of initial attitude were brought into close proximity with the final attitude, and it is fair to say that asking subjects for their estimates of initial attitudes produced virtually the same mean values as did the request for their final attitudes. Moreover, the correlations between actual initial attitude and recall of initial attitude were significantly lower than the correlations between final attitude and recall of initial attitude.

Perhaps Bem is right. Initial attitudes do not appear to be a salient feature of the period following essay writing. But there is another *perhaps:* the experiment was ambiguous as a test of the two theories. We have discussed Brehm's study of recall (1962a; discussed in Chapter 8 of this book), which showed that selective forgetting of discrepant elements can be a response to a dissonance-arousing situation. More important, selective recall follows directly from dissonance theory, and it is not at all surprising that subjects would distort their recall of initial attitudes. To admit to oneself that his prior attitude was "wrong" or incompatible with forced-compliant behavior would only serve to prolong dissonance arousal. In fact, Bem and McConnell (1970) explicitly mention this dissonance interpretation. At best, the Bem and McConnell experiment is consistent with the self-perception approach, but the study by no means has implications for the correctness of dissonance theory. As noted by Harvey and Mills (1971), the Bem and McConnell study simply does not pose a confrontation between the two formulations.

An experiment by Shaffer (in press) may be viewed as a direct reply to the argument of Bem and McConnell. We need only discuss Shaffer's dissonance-arousing condition to make the point. Subjects were asked to compose a written essay at variance with a previously-stated opinion. Half of them were then asked for their present attitudes, while the remainder were asked to indicate their

SELF-PERCEPTION THEORY   271

earlier attitude on the relevant issue. As might be expected, statements of present attitude showed a considerable agreement with the espoused position as compared against appropriate low-dissonance control groups. Further, subjects in the dissonance-arousing condition who were asked to estimate their earlier attitudes showed a recall bias in the direction of their espoused position. This much is also predictable from dissonance theory. However, the important point is that the amount of recall error could not be accounted for entirely by the amount of actual attitude change. Subjects who were asked for their current attitudes were significantly more extreme (in the direction of the essay) than were subjects asked for recall of earlier attitudes, implying that one's current statement of attitudinal position is not the sole determinant of estimates of earlier attitudes. Evidently subjects in forced-compliance procedures do come to the situation with preexisting attitudes. Moreover, these earlier attitudes are not altogether "swamped" by the behaviors involved in creating dissonance.

There is an alternative tack. Instead of measuring salience of initial attitudes following an attitude-discrepant behavior, salience of initial attitudes could be induced artifically. The results, from Bem's perspective, should be an elimination of "dissonance" effects, since the self-selection-based inferences of subjects would not operate in the presence of information inhibiting implicit self-selection reasoning by subjects. From the perspective of dissonance theory, experimentally increased salience of initial attitudes would either increase attitude change or have no impact. No impact could easily result if initial attitudes were already salient at the time of the discrepant behavior. Therefore, in order for this kind of paradigm to cast doubt on the dissonance analysis, it would be necessary to show a *reduction* of dissonance effects as a result of increased salience.

The first of two relevant experiments was conducted by Snyder and Ebbesen (1972). Using the Bem and McConnell procedure, salience of initial attitudes was bolstered for some subjects by telling them, prior to the choice manipulation, to

... 'take a few minutes to think about and organize your thoughts and views on the issue of student control over the kinds of courses offered by the University (i.e., Should students have control? How much or how little? If students should have some control, who should have the rest? What kinds of control? Why or why not?, etc.) DO NOT PROCEED FURTHER UNTIL YOU HAVE FULLY ORGANIZED YOUR THOUGHTS ON THIS ISSUE [Snyder & Ebbesen, 1972, p. 506].

Subjects were then subjected to the choice—no choice treatment, and finally attitudes toward the student-control issue were measured. When nothing was made salient the choice—no choice variable operated as predicted, but among subjects confronted with salience instructions the choice variable had no effect whatsoever. Although these results at first glance appear to cast doubt on dissonance theory, Snyder and Ebbesen raise the possibility that the salience instructions committed subjects to their positions and rendered attitude shifts impossible. We also find this to be an ambiguity in the design. Having spent several minutes to "fully organize your thoughts," subjects' initial attitudes may have become so firmly enmeshed in relevant thoughts and previous behaviors that the resistance to change of the attitude reaches an imposing level. This being a strong possibility, we will move on to an analogous study that did not have a similar methodological problem.

Ross and Shulman (1973) also borrowed the Bem and McConnell procedure, again manipulating choice. A premeasure was taken, subjects were asked to compose essays, then a "reinstatement" manipulation was introduced. Subjects in the nonreinstatement condition proceeded to record their final attitudes, but in the reinstatement condition subjects first were asked to examine their premeasure questionnaires, record their exact premeasure attitude on a separate piece of paper, then seal that paper plus initial questionnaire in an envelope to be mailed to a bogus address. This latter part of the procedure was followed for nonreinstatement subjects, but they were not asked to examine their premeasure scores. Since the postmeasure was given immediately after examination of the premeasure, the original attitude should have been highly salient for reinstatement subjects.

The results of this study showed no effect for reinstatement, and in fact, there was a slight tendency for the choice variable to operate more strongly in the reinstatement conditions. As evidence that premeasure scores were indeed salient in the appropriate condition, Ross and Schulman asked all subjects to recall their initial attitudes immediately after final attitudes had been marked, and not surprisingly, recall was highly accurate in both the choice and no choice reinstatement conditions. The mean recall error in the choice–reinstatement condition and corresponding no-choice condition was negligible (approximately 1 point or less on a 72-point scale.) Thus, change took place as a function of choice no matter whether initial attitudes were salient or not, and this result is clearly inconsistent with an important tenet of self-perception theory.

There are two final research endeavors that address themselves to the question of salience of initial attitudes. The first of these, by Pallak, Sogin, and Cook (1974), reasoned that a person will possess a firm conception of his initial attitude to the extent that it is extreme. Granting this tenable assumption, self-perception theory would lead to the hypothesis that the greatest "dissonance" effects should be found among relatively moderate subjects. Alternatively, self-perception theory may not draw distinctions among more or less extreme subjects, but either way, there is a clear juxtaposition with dissonance theory: Certainly dissonance resulting from a forced-compliance act would be in proportion to the discrepancy of that act from the initial attitude. Thus, forces toward attitude change should be greater to the degree that initial attitudes are extreme.

There is one factor that may operate against the dissonance prediction. As noted by Pallak, Sogin, and Cook (1974) extreme subjects may be so frozen to their positions that their dissonance would not be reflected in attitude change. Instead, we might imagine that they would attempt to minimize the consequences of their actions or adopt other modes of dissonance reduction. But this only means that the research of Pallak and his associates provides a conservative test of the theory.

Without going into detail, it may be said that the results of two separate experiments were completely consistent with dissonance theory. In the first study both choice and initial extremity were varied in the familiar essay-writing paradigm, and the choice manipulation affected attitudes only among relatively extreme subjects. The more initial extremity, the more attitude change in the direction of the essay. The interaction between the two variables was of borderline significance ($p < .07$). Although this probability level might not give one complete confidence in the result, a second experiment by Pallak, Sogin, and Cook (1974) makes the same point. Among subjects who were given a cue to render initial attitudes salient, initially extreme subjects changed attitudes more than initially moderate subjects. It should also be noted that a highly similar pattern of results was obtained by Cohen et al. (1959), reported in Chapter 3.

The other research effort (Green, 1974) resembles the thinking of Pallak, Sogin, and Cook (1974), except that the paradigm involved subjects committing themselves to prolonged thirst deprivation, after Brehm (1962). By means of a thirst-inducing hot sauce some of Green's subjects were given an initial high level of thirst, while others are not. The subjects were requested to suffer through an extended 24-hr period of thirst deprivation, either for a sum of $5 or $20.

The reasoning from dissonance theory should be clear. Among subjects with an initial extreme attitude (high thirst), the commitment for a relatively low sum of money will be especially dissonance arousing. From the standpoint of self-perception theory the initial thirst level should be irrelevant, just as initial attitude extremity should not have been a consideration in the investigations of Pallak, Sogin, and Cook (1974). The results indicated an interaction between payment and initial thirst, such that the high-thirst–low-payment group showed an inordinate amount of subjective thirst minimization. The results quite obviously are completely in accord with those of Pallak and his associates.

This recent research of Pallak and his associates and of Green (1974) strikes us as impossible to account for in terms of the self-perception analysis. If one were to assume that initially extreme people know their attitudes less well than those initially moderate, the results would make sense, but such an assumption approaches unreality.

Interpersonal Simulations and Salience of Initial Attitudes:
A Summing Up

The two kinds of evidence we have examined do not leave self-perception theory as a viable interpretation of the psychological processes involved in experiments discussed throughout this book. A blatant salience of initial attitudes does not systematically reduce the dissonance-reduction processes, as self-perception theory would assume. Further, the interpersonal replication paradigm does nothing to increase the tenability of Bem's assumption that "dissonance reduction" is merely a logical conclusion drawn from self-perception. With respect to this latter point, the evidence shows that a passive observer who is provided with a *complete* description of the original situation is incapable of accurately estimating involved subjects' attitudes. It is quite likely that Bem's interpersonal simulations, based on incomplete information, found dissonance-like effects because his subjects employed an implicit self-selection reasoning. However, the experiments that included more complete descriptions imply directly that involved subjects were not dependent on such a self-selection reasoning. Accordingly, Bem's interpersonal replications, with results produced by observer–subjects' self-selection reasoning, would seem to have no bearing on the question of whether or not the psychological processes of involved subjects are in accord with his model.

By Bem's (1972) own admission the interpersonal replications are not completely essential evidence for his hypothesis. Such experiments simply illustrate his reasoning. Even though the "corrected" interpersonal replications failed to replicate, it should be noted that involved subjects may conceivably act as self-perceivers even if passive observers cannot successfully mimic the original results. But if so, what then are the crucial differences between being an involved subject and a passive observer? From the standpoint of Bem's theory the only variables of any consequence are the person's awareness of the various elements of the "dissonance-arousing" situation. Given that awareness, logical processes will lead the person to draw inferences, and there is no stipulation within self-perception theory for a difference between involved and passive subjects. If an observer were provided with exactly the same information as the involved person, and if their attention to that information were equal, they should draw similar inferences about attitudes. In several of the experiments described above, especially the Arrowood *et al.* (1970) experiment in which subjects were both involved and passive observers, the quality of information and attention to it should have been virtually identical for involved and observer–subjects. It remains a mystery why observers should encounter so much difficulty in replicating the responses of involved subjects, unless being involved has some special significance independent of amount of information available. Dissonance theory, needless to say, assumes very different psychological states in comparing involved and onlooker subjects, and has no difficulty in handling such results as those by Arrowood *et al.* (1970).

Other Dissonance Phenomena

Most of the preceding research has been oriented around Bem's reinterpretation, but there are also important questions to be asked about the generality of his reinterpretation. The interpersonal simulations have addressed themselves to a relatively small proportion of dissonance phenomena, and the purpose of this section is to try out the self-perception model in a diversity of dissonance-provoking situations. While on the topic of generality, it is only fair to note that a substantial portion of Bem's work has been largely independent of dissonance phenomena, just as much of the dissonance literature (to follow) is beyond the reach of self-perception theory. Certainly the cartoon experiment (Bem, 1965), the false-confession experiment (Bem, 1966), and the pain perception experiment (Bandler, Madaras, & Bem, 1968) address issues on a different plane from those of interest to us here.

Clarity of decision consequences. In the context of Jecker's experiment, described in detail in Chapter 8, Festinger (1964) provided a useful specification of the notion of decision in the context of dissonance theory. The experiment showed that an overt discrimination or public statement of decision is not sufficient to engage dissonance reduction. The consequences of that overt discrimination must first be clear to the person deciding. For example, if a person decides but still thinks there is a chance of receiving the rejected alternative, no dissonance reduction will be evidenced. These were the results of Jecker's study, but self-perception theory would not imply such a result. Very simply, the self-perceiving person examines his behavior to infer his attitudes, and if his decision has been to choose a given alternative, he should come to infer a favorable attitude toward the selected option even if there remains some slight chance of receiving both.

Alternative modes of dissonance reduction. One route to coping with dissonance entails no reordering of cognitive elements, but instead is an avoidance of the tension state of dissonance. The research of Pallak (1970) and Pallak *et al.* (1967) has been the most informative on this point, and the idea is perfectly consistent with the presumption of dissonance as a tension state. Self-perception theory, a model based on assumptions about man's propensity to process information rather than to experience tension states, has nothing to say about avoidance.

There are numerous other modes implied by the theory that have little place in Bem's analysis. For example, Brock and Buss (1962) found that both minimization of pain and felt obligation resulted under conditions of high dissonance, but what do these measures have to do with the inference-of-attitude-from-behavior model? Someone who elects to deliver electric shocks to a victim may infer a favorable attitude toward administering punishment, but it doesn't follow that he would minimize his estimate of the impat of the shock. Self-perception theory does not address itself to cognitive distortions of the behavior. The analysis takes the behavior as a fixed entity and proceeds to analyze causal inferences derived from behavior. The same reasoning applies to Brock and Buss' measure of perceived obligation. Felt obligation is a distortion of the conditions under which behavior was performed, not an inference drawn from behavior.

Resistance to change of cognitive elements. Early in this volume we noted that the single factor most responsible for dissonance theory's productivity is the idea of resistance-to-change of cognitions. Without this factor, dissonance theory would have approximately the same explanatory power as other balance theories. Bem's notion includes an implicit fixed factor of resistance to change in the sense that behavior is always 100% resistant, while the attitude inferred is the flexible entity. We should emphasize that he does not discuss the idea of resistance—it is simply a constant in his system.

In distinguishing the dissonance and self-perception approaches, resistance to change of cognitions becomes an issue when the behavior, or commitment, is not the most resistant element. Although these cases are infrequent in the dissonance literature, the presence of any such cases, or even the possibility of their presence, is an important consideration in evaluating the generality of the two approaches. The reader is referred to Chapter 9 for a detailed consideration of resistance to change and modes of dissonance reduction.

Surprise consequences and responsibility. As we have viewed dissonance theory, a crucial theoretical ingredient is responsibility. It appears necessary for dissonance arousal that the individual sense some causal connection between himself and a discrepant event, whether that causal connection results from foreknowledge and intention, or simply from the person's abilities, personality traits, or other components of self. The numerous experiments that failed to show dissonance reduction as a function of fait accompli consequences are consistent with Bem's approach as well as with dissonance theory. However, the concept "responsibility" is not to be found within Bem's treatment. The reasoning is simply that a person who uses the consequences of his behavior in order to infer attitudes will *not* use unanticipated consequences as a basis for inference.

If just the above-cited experiments are considered, we find complete overlap between the two theoretical ideas. But when responsibility is defined in ways other than through foreseeability (see Chapter 4) self-perception theory is of no value for explanation, for it makes no allowance for the impact of unanticipated consequences on inference of attitudes.

Dissonance as a tension state. Bem (1972) would have it that a new Zeitgeist is well under way in psychology: "There is, in short, a shift of paradigm taking place within social psychology, a shift from motivational-drive models of cognitions, behaviors, and internal states to information processing/attribution models of such phenomena [p. 43]." Although it is always tempting to be the first on the bandwagon, we find several phenomena associated with dissonance theory that make it difficult to discard the motivational roots of the theory.

1. First, dissonance reduction does not necessarily proceed immediately upon the creation of dissonant elements. As shown by Brehm (the recall experiment of Chapter 8), Brehm and Wicklund (1970), Festinger and Walster (1964), and

Walster (1964), dissonance reduction can be preceded by the *opposite* of dissonance reduction, a phenomenon labeled regret. It is difficult to view this phenomenon as a product of inferences drawn from behaviors, for a person would have no behavioral basis for such inferences. The presence of regret quite clearly implies the presence of a tension state.

2. Second, cognitive dissonance has been shown repeatedly (Chapter 6) to energize behaviors unrelated to dissonance arousal. Although these effects are not specifically predicted by the theory, they are convincing evidence that a drive state is generated through dissonance arousal.

3. Finally, a study by Zanna and Cooper (1974) demonstrates that dissonance effects do not occur when the tension state associated with dissonance arousal can be relabeled, that is, misattributed to other causes of tension. Subjects wrote a counterattitudinal essay, either under conditions of high or low choice, then a postmeasure of attitude was administered. The important part of this experiment revolved around a pill given to subjects shortly before the essay writing. In all cases the pill contained nothing but powdered milk, but it was described otherwise depending on experimental condition: In the arousal condition subjects were led to think that the pill would generate a tenseness, while in the no-information condition the experimenter noted that there would be no side effects. What should this manipulation have to do with dissonance arousal?

Choice subjects should have experienced more tension, upon committing themselves, than no-choice subjects, and Zanna and Cooper (1974) argue that this tension normally would be attributed to the discrepancy created by a high-choice counterattitudinal commitment. In short, the person operates as though his tension state has been brought about by his discrepant commitment, thus he proceeds to do something about the discrepancy. But when the cause of tension can be located in a pill the individual will be less likely to locate causality elsewhere, implying that dissonance effects will not manifest themselves. The results took exactly the form predicted, as illustrated in the first two columns of Table 20. The choice manipulation operated as expected within the no-information condition, but it had no impact whatever among arousal subjects. Zanna and Cooper also included a relaxation condition, in which the pill

TABLE 20
Mean Attitude Change in the
Dissonance-Reducing Direction

	Potential side effect of drug		
Decision Freedom	Arousal	No Information	Relaxation
High choice	3.4	9.1	13.4
Low choice	3.5	4.5	4.7

was said to have a relaxing effect. According to their reasoning, any experienced tension state should then be attributed to the discrepant act even more than in the no-information condition, for the impact of dissonance from the subject's standpoint would seem to overpower the relaxing effect of the pill. Column 3 of the table bears out this final consideration: the choice variable operates more strongly among relaxed subjects than among no-information subjects.

A conceptually similar study is reported by Drachman and Worchel (in press), using arousing visual stimuli rather than pills. Subjects were exposed during the procedure either to *Playboy Magazine* nudes (one arousing condition), pictures of war and accident victims and related themes (another arousing condition), or to innocuous interior decorating pictures. As in the Zanna–Cooper (1974) experiment, subjects were given either high or low choice in writing a counter-attitudinal essay, and the results took a highly similar pattern. Within the choice condition attitude change was significantly reduced by the arousing stimuli, no matter whether the stimuli were pleasant or noxious, whereas dissonance-reducing attitude change in the no arousal–choice condition remained high.

Using a somewhat more complicated design, Pittman (1975) obtained essentially the same effects of attributional possibilities on dissonance reduction. As in the two previously described experiments, subjects (females) were given high or low choice, in this case to engage in counterattitudinal behavior. Half of each choice group also expected to take part in an innocuous second experiment, while the other half expected to take part in a second experiment that involved electric shock. In addition, a confederate who posed as a second subject either did or did not express concern to the subject about making the counter-attitudinal statement. It was assumed by Pittman that the threat of shock would result in attribution of arousal to shock, an attribution that would lessen dissonance reducing attitude change. It was also assumed, however, that the confederate's expression of concern about making the counterattitudinal state-ment would encourage the subject to attribute her arousal to the dissonant relationship, an attribution that would maintain or increase dissonance reducing attitude change. Consistent with these expectations, the increase in attitudinal change due to high choice was eliminated by the threat of shock, and was reinstated in the shock-threat condition by the confederate's expressed concern about the attitude statement. Unexpectedly, the effect of choice on attitude change was reversed (nonsignificantly) where there was no threat of shock and the confederate expressed concern about the attitude statement. Pitman's (1975) explanation of this failure to obtain dissonance reduction effects, that subjects saw themselves as being relatively unaroused in contrast to the confederate's apparent concern, remains to be tested in future research. In general, the results of this experiment are like those of Zanna and Cooper (1974), and Drachman and Worchel (in press), and they support the idea that arousal is a necessary aspect of the dissonance reduction process.

An Untestable Theoretical Distinction?

Greenwald (1975) has devoted a considerable discussion to the Snyder and Ebbesen study, concluding that their experiment was thoroughly ambiguous as a test of dissonance versus self-perception principles. More important, he proposes that it may be impossible to discriminate successfully between predictions of the two theories in the context of areas to which they are commonly applied. With respect to the less frequent applications of dissonance theory, Greenwald allows that dissonance theory may offer some additional "noncognitive" predictions unavailable to a self-perception theorist. As he does not elaborate on this point, we have no way of knowing whether or not such studies as the Drachman–Worchel (in press) and Zanna–Cooper (1974) efforts would fall into the noncognitive class. If not, then Greenwald has overlooked some crucial evidence bearing on the controversy.

Our survey of the controversy leads to a conclusion quite divergent from that of Greenwald. It is granted that the Snyder and Ebbesen (1972) experiment might be an ambiguous test, particularly because of the socially complex nature of the operations, but various other experiments described appear to offer entirely cogent discriminations between the two approaches. The best evidence has dealt with salience or extremity of initial positions, and we find the Green (1974), Pallak, Sogin, and Cook (1974), and Ross and Shulman (1973) research impossible to understand from the perspective of self-perception theory. Nevertheless, Greenwald spells out a mode of reasoning whereby the self-perception approach might explain the absence of the salience effect in the experiment by Ross and Shulman (1973). Prior to addressing Greenwald's (1975) reasoning, we might summarize their experiment briefly.

It will be recalled that Ross and Shulman (1973) predicted that salience should, based on their reading of self-perception theory, reduce attitude change. In fact, Bem (1968) says exactly this. More generally, Bem (e.g., Bem & McConnell, 1970) has proposed that attitudes will be inferred from behavior to the extent that internal cues are weak. Such a statement implies that strengthening internal cues would inhibit attitude change following an attitude-relevant behavior. But the salience variable had no such effect, leaving the authors in the position of finding a weakness in the predictive power of Bem's self-perception notion.

Greenwald (1975) proceeds to reason, paradoxically, that Ross and Shulman (1973) could have made just the opposite prediction. The idea is as follows: Greenwald notes first that the self-perception analysis commonly predicts that attitude judgments are inferred from observed behavior only to the degree that the behavior is uncalled for in the situation. This much is incontestable. He then proposes that a behavior can be discrepant from a situational demand when a clear expression of the actor's behavior-discrepant attitude is part of the situation. With this last assumption, it then becomes possible to predict greater attitude change when the person's initial attitude is highly salient (Ross & Shulman, 1973) and also when it is extreme (Green, 1974; Pallak, Sogin, and Cook, 1974). In short, Greenwald would treat a salient, contrabehavior initial attitude on the same level as a situational obstacle such as absence of payment or physical effort.

The ironic conclusion we find here involves a clever chain of reasoning, but it entirely misses the spirit of self-perception theory. In analyzing the situational determinants of attitudes, Bem obviously does not intend for direct internal cues about those attitudes to be among the determinants. Why else would he propose that external cues must be relied upon when internal cues are weak?

The only way in which we can understand Greenwald's construction is as an attempt to show that self-perception theory can, with a stretch of the imagination, be rendered ultimately flexible. But to take Greenwald's step is totally unnecessary, given that the author of self-perception theory has already implicitly ruled out Greenwald's reasoning. It would seem to us that the research Greenwald criticizes, particularly the Ross and Shulman study, stands as a fair test of the two theories. For that matter, the research he does not cite also remains as a viable body of discriminating tests. Given that Greenwald does not systematically find fault with other than the Ross and Shulman and Snyder and Ebbesen experiments, and considering the nature of his reasoning (above), we find it hard to take his overall purpose seriously, which is to demonstrate the untestability of dissonance versus self-perception theory.

Summary

Considering the light that has been shed on the question of whether self-perception or dissonance, it is possible to offer a retrospective suggestion. Bem's theory, interpreted literally, is an idea designed to say something about people who either do not yet hold attitudes or who are not cognizant of their attitudes. As a theory of attitude development among persons with no preexisting attitudes, Bem's notion may be perfectly correct and could no doubt be developed in the direction of greater precision. But to apply his theory to instances of cognitive inconsistency has not been fruitful, for there are simply too many examples of its unsuitability in this domain.

Epilogue

Somewhat later than Bem, and evidently independently, Totman (1973) has constructed an alternative model of dissonance phenomena which he calls "An approach to cognitive dissonance theory in terms of ordinary language." Like Bem, he reasons his way to dissonance effects without the assistance of motivational constructs, and also paralleling Bem he views the person as a self-observer who finds explanations for his behaviors in behavior-relevant attitudes. However, since Bem's thesis has been considerably more elaborate as applied to the phenomena of interest here, we will not pursue Totman's ideas further.

IMPRESSION MANAGEMENT THEORY

Tedeschi, Schlenker, and Bonoma (1971) have proposed a substitute for cognitive dissonance theory that purports to subsume Bem's theory (above), Brehm's (1966) theory of psychological reactance, and Steiner's (1970) conceptualization of freedom, as well as offering a replacement for dissonance theory. We will focus just on its potential as an alternative to dissonance theory. We find this proposal to be parallel in one respect to that of Bem, for these two frameworks are the only two that ostensibly offer a complete reinterpretation of dissonance phenomena.

Why does dissonance theory need to be replaced? Tedeschi *et al.* (1971) find several shortcomings that we should summarize quickly, for these are shortcomings that they plan to correct in the context of their counterproposal. One quite serious attack is toward dissonance theory's ambiguity: "... cognitive dissonance theory does not state clearly the conditions under which the phenomena in question will be manifested; rather, it seems much more suitable for postdiction than prediction" (Tedeschi *et al.*, 1971, p. 687). Since they do not elaborate on this assault, we will move on to their second criticism: "... the mechanism by which the organism is aroused to action in order to reduce dissonance remains unexplicated by either Festinger or his followers... [p. 689]." They give Festinger credit for his assumption that a tension state is the motivational basis of dissonance phenomena, but they find the origins of such tension to be unclear. The criticism concludes on the note that an adequate theory would explain why inconsistency serves to motivate. These criticisms will be addressed below, after a look at impression management theory as it applies to dissonance phenomena.

The theory of impression management begins by characterizing people as disposed to convey an image of consistency to others. Tedeschi *et al.* (1971) assume that a person can tolerate cognitive inconsistency when by himself, but through socialization he learns to present a consistent self to others. In order to apply their notions directly to dissonance phenomena they relate modes of self-presentation to the variable of external pressure for counterattitudinal performance. We can best spell out their arguments with an example.

If someone manifests an attitude, his statement of attitude can either be the product of external pressures or of his internal state. According to impression management theory, an observer will hold a person responsible for his attitude statement only when external pressures to make a given statement are minimal. By "held responsible" we mean only that the observer would take the person's behavior, whether a check mark on a scale or counterattitudinal statement, to represent that person's inner feelings.

What happens if an observer thinks that the person is responsible neither for his initial attitude statement nor his counterattitudinal act? Tedeschi *et al.* (1971) assume that the person would not, under these conditions, change his attitude with the intent of creating an image of consistency. The reason is that the person will not think of himself as portraying an inconsistent image, since the behaviors do not represent himself. The important point here is that the person will suppose that the observer will not take a behavior performed under high-external constraint as an index of the person's true feelings. What happens when just one of the two behaviors—either the attitude statement of counter-attitudinal act—is performed without external pressure? In this case the impression-managing person will assume that the observer will infer that the person's true feelings are represented by whichever behavior was performed in the absence of pressure. The observer (in the person's eyes) will not take the constrained behavior to be representative of anything about the person's internal state. Therefore, an image of inconsistency is not created, and no cognitive work is necessary to create a consistent image. Finally, what happens when *both* behaviors are carried out in the absence of external pressure? Here there is an impression-management crisis. The observer will think that the person is manifesting inconsistent inner states, and in order to avoid creating such an impression the person will proceed to align his final attitude with the counter-attitudinal behavior. Presumably, then, when the person's postcounterattitudinal-behavior attitude comes to coincide with the nature of the act, he will have some degree of confidence that he has impressed an image of consistency upon the observer.

It should be evident that the thesis of Tedeschi *et al.* (1971) assumes only a need to impress one's consistency upon others. Their proposition assumes nothing about a drive toward internal consistency, and this allows it to predict something contrary to dissonance theory. Specifically, if a person knows that he has performed both acts without external constraint, but if he also knows that the observer imputes constraint into the situation, there will be no subsequent increased consistency for public consumption. This is simply because the observer will not view the person as manifesting two contradictory inner impulses.

Now that the theory has been described we might ask several questions of it. First we will take a look at their criticisms of dissonance theory, which evidently provide the impetus for their alternative view:

1. Their accusation that the theory is better suited for postdiction than prediction is difficult to follow. In the research we have reviewed thus far, prediction has been the rule, and experiments have typically been designed so that predictions from the theory are straightforward. Since Tedeschi *et al.* neither cite examples of this criticism nor indicate in what manner the theory fails in predictive power, we see no reason to pursue this point.

2. It is true that Festinger (1957) did not reduce the tension state of dissonance to more molecular elements in an attempt to explain why inconsistency should be motivating. It was taken as a theoretical assumption that dissonance was a tension state, just as any other drive. Tedeschi *et al.* (1971) have attempted to subsume the motivation toward cognitive consistency within a motivation to present oneself favorably, and it might therefore be concluded that they have explained the motivational basis of cognitive inconsistency. But aside from the cogency of their model, we don't see that anything is gained by substituting one motivation for another. It would now be incumbent upon them to explain why people are motivated to please others, and this would lead to a *reductio ad absurdum*. In fact, they ascribe this motivation to the socialization process which means that the motivation is acquired. No doubt it could also be said that consistency-restoration motivation is acquired in childhood, but this would add nothing to dissonance theory.

What of the application of impression management theory to dissonance phenomena? Unfortunately Tedeschi *et al.* (1971) deal only with the forced compliance paradigm, putting us in a position of having to read between the lines in order to apply their idea universally. But taking just the forced compliance extension, their reasoning does seem to fit some kinds of attitude change effects. Certainly when a person performs a behavior without undue constraint there is reason to invoke a concern about others' impressions of him. If his subsequent manifested attitude is contrary to that behavior, observers will conclude that he is hypocritical, stupid, and so forth. This would seem sufficient reason for a person's shifting his attitudes to be consistent with behaviors, and further, it does follow from their reasoning that high choice or minimal monetary inducement would feed into impression management.

If impression management theory does handle the forced compliance situation with ease, it should be possible to observe decrements in dissonance reduction (that is, impression-managing attitude change) when subjects have no reason to be concerned about appearing consistent. For example, if one experimenter requests and observes the counterattitudinal act, but is absent from and unconnected to the attitude-measurement phase of the study, there is no reason to think that the subject would be concerned with impressing any one experimenter. No one experimenter is in a position to view the subject's contradictory situation. Certainly such studies exist (e.g., Festinger & Carlsmith, 1959; Linder *et al.*, 1967; Nuttin, 1975) and there is no reason whatever to think that separation of behavior-inducement and measurement phases weakens attitude change effects.

How would impression management be applied to the free-decision paradigm? This is less than obvious, since a person does not necessarily present an inconsistent image simply by choosing. It is neither irrational nor hypocritical to choose when a choice is called for, thus it is difficult to imagine the application of impression management to this case. The same applies to selective exposure. If anything it seems as if a person would want to impress an observer with his openness and fair mindedness, rather than with a biased approach in reacting to new information.

In summary, the impression management model as applied to dissonance phenomena falls short in three respects:

1. The Tedeschi *et al.* (1971) critique of dissonance theory, which seems intended to pave the way for an alternative approach, is simply haphazard.

2. The authors have provided no rules for extending their model to phenomena other than those associated with the forced compliance paradigm. Whether this represents a difficulty in their model or their lack of interest in those other phenomena is not clear.

3. Most important: The model of impression management is testable by varying conditions that should lead to more or less concern with conveying a correct impression.

The authors have discussed no research in which the theory has been tested appropriately, although if we examine the dissonance research in which impression management should not have been a concern, dissonance effects appear anyway.

As with Bem's model, the greatest deficit of the present notion seems to be one of misapplication. Clearly the ideas of Tedeschi and his associates should enter when it is possible to specify something about the nature of the social climate surrounding a person's hypocritical or otherwise inconsistent behavior. But to assume that a complex form of social expectations and demands can account for the observed instances of dissonance reduction is going much further than is allowed by the structure of this social interaction model. When others are present in some significant respect, and when theoretical variables about their impact is known, impression management then becomes a significant consideration.

RESPONSE CONTAGION THEORY

Nuttin (1975) has written an entire monograph on the forced compliance paradigm, and in the process has developed a theoretical view that does without the cognitive character of cognitive dissonance theory. The starting point for his analysis consists of research reported in his book that finds no differential effect for proattitudinal and counterattitudinal behaviors. We should expect, of course, that only *counter*attitudinal behavior would create dissonance and produce attitude change in inverse proportion to whatever justifications are supplied. Certainly we have seen important exceptions to Nuttin's findings (e.g. Green, 1974; Pallak, Sogin, and Cook, 1974), but the important point is that Nuttin's findings prompted him to consider an alternative to the dissonance-among-cognitions approach.

The analysis begins with the usual kind of attitude-relevant behavior that we have seen in a variety of forced-compliance procedures. A person is asked to engage in some evaluative behavior, usually an advocacy, and an attitude measurement is then given shortly after. Nuttin assumes that "response contagion" takes place between these two evaluative responses (forced compliance response and attitude measure) to the degree that they are in close temporal proximity and to the degree that the first response is subject to "perturbation." This last term is the crucial one, and we should elaborate upon it.

Perturbation is the result of the individual's subjugation to unusual, bizarre, embarrassing, or disturbing stimuli. In terms of the research reported by Nuttin, perturbation is created in the forced-compliance setting by giving subjects unusually and insultingly low rewards, treating them to valuable but illegitimate exam points, subjecting them to insults and other hostile treatment, and eliciting their evaluative responses in the presence of an experimenter who wears unexpectedly erotic clothing. It is not Nuttin's argument that low rewards, sexy clothing, or any of his other stimuli simply arouse cognitive dissonance. Instead, the perturbation resulting from these unexpected or undesirable treatments are said to generate arousal, with resulting energization of whatever response is in progress. This means that the "forced-compliance" response, whether consistent or inconsistent with the person's prior history of evaluative responses, will increase in strength.

The next step is simple. To the degree that a subsequent and related evaluative response is evoked in close proximity to the "perturbed" first response, the changes in that first response will have an impact on the second. In short, there will be contagion from the first to the second, and the response we would normally call an "attitude," derived from a postmeasure, will shift in a direction consistent with the perturbed response.

This view may seem reminiscent of the drive X habit notion found in Spence (1956) or Zajonc (1965), but there is one crucial difference. Many of the responses dealt with in this analysis are not dominant in the individual's repertoire, as evidenced by his previous evaluative responses. In more familiar language, the overt response given in a counterattitudinal essay is clearly not dominant, since dominance would presumably be reflected by the premeasure of attitude, and this measure characteristically would be divergent from the later "forced-compliant" behavior. This means that Nuttin cannot easily invoke a drive X habit notion, and in recognizing this problem he has suggested that recency of a response may play a greater role than its overall dominance. However, this difficulty is not completely clarified, and the reconciliation of drive X habit theory with Nuttin's notions remains to be done.

In assessing the feasibility of Nuttin's approach we should first note that the groundwork, or impetus for his model has to some extent been attenuated. Since he found no differences between subjects who took proattitudinal stands and those who argued counterattitudinally, he assumed that the whole idea of cognitive imbalance as the source of dissonance phenomena should be called into question. But there is indeed evidence consistent with the view of inconsistent cognitions as the mediator (Green, 1974; Himmelfarb & Arazi, 1975; Pallak, Sogin, & Cook, 1974).

Independent of the original impetus for Nuttin's theorizing, what else might be said about the idea? First, it is obviously limited to the forced compliance facet of dissonance phenomena, and as such, does not make as bold claims as the self-perception approach. Dissonance theory is still required to explain other phenomena. Second, the response contagion notion demands that the attitude measure "postadvocacy evaluative response" be elicited in close proximity with the advocacy. Nuttin provides support for this notion, but we cannot take his evidence to be the final word. An examination of the research on sequential processes (Chapter 8) makes this obvious. For example, even though the relevant research is primarily within the free decision paradigm (Brehm & Wicklund, 1970; Walster, 1964), it appears as if dissonance reduction effects generally are not maximal immediately after the dissonance-arousing behavior. Third, Nuttin's model implies that "dissonance" effects in the forced compliance paradigm would be accompanied by arousal, however that might be measured. It has indeed been demonstrated that dissonance-arousing forced compliance situations have arousal-like effects (Chapter 6). Thus the conditions that make for dissonance should, in general, also be appropriate for Nuttin's model. However, and this is the fourth point, the situations created by Nuttin to energize subjects would not always fit the requirements of dissonance theory, and here we have the possiblity of extending his formulation. It is intriguing that attitude change (evaluative response) effects might be produced through the presence of any unusual, bizarre, disturbing, or embarrassing stimulus, particularly since the subject need not choose to experience these perturbations in order for their presence to have the desired impact.

STIMULUS INCONGRUITY THEORY

Kiesler (1974) has developed an extensive theoretical scheme that purports to account for dissonance phenomena, as well as effects falling within a number of other theoretical areas. The central idea is that organisms undergo arousal when confronted with incongruous stimuli (the parallel to Nuttin should be apparent), and that to "identify" or "explain" the incongruities is often to "reduce dissonance." As Kiesler's notion has yet to be elaborated in printed form, we will not elaborate upon it further at this writing.

The present chapter has examined several theoretical formulations that purport to subsume dissonance phenomena within nonbalance theory systems. The most thoroughgoing of these has been set forth by Bem, and has generated numerous research efforts oriented toward discriminating his self-perception approach from the motivational workings of dissonance theory. It is evident from the accumulated evidence that the motivational tension idea, and notion of resistance to change, are indeed necessary in treating the research reported throughout this volume. A logical model of the human mind, as portrayed in self-perception theory, does not explain the diverse phenomena we have examined.

The other formulations discussed here are somewhat more limited in scope than Bem's approach, and thus far have not generated a great deal of research. Impression management theory is untenable on various grounds as an alternative explanation. Kiesler's stimulus incongruity theory and Nuttin's response contagion theory, while having some interesting implications, are too recent to have been tested thoroughly at the time of this writing.

17
Applications

Certainly the numerous laboratory experiments we have examined have a plethora of implications for the worlds of buying and selling, politics, religion and psychotherapy. In fact, it is probably a short leap from the laboratory to the matter of dissonance reduction in naturally occurring settings. The leap seems short because the experimental research has shown that behavior, and opinions in particular, of a political or religious nature can be influenced substantially by the dissonance process. Unless naturally occurring conditions are unsuitable, in the sense of not meeting assumptions for application of the theory, there is every reason to think that dissonance phenomena should be readily observable in any context. The only real difficulty with carrying the theory into the applied or naturalistic realm has to do with the question of confounding of variables, which can be averted in the laboratory.

This chapter is devoted to an overview of applications of the theory outside of the experimental laboratory, and to research conducted by those whose purpose is other than theory testing. Among the projects we will discuss are historical analyses, observation of group phenomena, correlational studies, and experimental investigations that have been undertaken for reasons of practical import. The research of this chapter has been categorized in terms of broad areas of application, rather than with respect to amount of scientific control. Accordingly, there are a number of seemingly startling juxtapositions of well-controlled field experiments with less-than-controlled historical or political analyses. We hope that the reader will not be dismayed by these incongruous groupings of research, for methodology is not the central concern in this chapter. Of greater importance is the extent to which the theory has been taken to a number of important topic areas, and the extent to which diverse methodologies have been brought to bear on each of those areas.

MARKETING

To date the most thoroughgoing applied extensions of the theory have been in the area of marketing research, perhaps because those interested in marketing would have a special interest in creating conditions conducive to purchasing and to consumer satisfaction. Except for one investigation, all of the material cited in this section was originally published in the *Journal of Marketing Research,* an encouraging sign that dissonance is no longer the exclusive domain of social psychologists. These marketing endeavors fall neatly into three classes: free decisions, insufficient justification, and regret. Our review here encompasses what appears to be the more convincing research in this area, and for a more complete review the reader is referred to Cummings and Venkatesan (1974).

Free Decisions

The study of postdecisional spreading of alternatives by Brehm (1956) may have been a comfort for anyone in the business of marketing, for there was a definite suggestion that consumer satisfaction would take care of itself. In the absence of any special campaigns or justification for a purchase, a customer should come to like what he has chosen in proportion to the amount of dissonance present. Anderson, Taylor, and Holloway (1966) and LoSciuto and Perloff (1967) conducted near replications of the Brehm study, and the LoScuito and Perloff investigation was particularly successful in showing that postdecisional spreading is a function of initial differential attractiveness of decision alternatives. A similar experiment was carried out by Mittelstaedt (1969), although with a behavioral measure. After initially choosing between their third- and fourth-ranked (or third- and fifth-ranked) alternatives, subjects had the opportunity to choose between their third- and second-ranked alternatives. Presumably dissonance would have been greater given an initial high conflict, and consistent with this reasoning, a disproportionate number of subjects in the high-dissonance condition subsequently chose the initially chosen third-ranked item.

Finally, Cohen and Houston (1972) applied the postdecisional spreading notion to the question of whether to brush with *Colgate* or *Crest*. They reasoned that buyers who had become loyal to one of those two brands would have come to justify their preferences, and therefore would show a larger differential preference between the two brands than buyers who preferred neither brand. The results took exactly this form, but as with any correlational study a disclaimer is necessary: The differential preference between *Colgate* and *Crest* easily could have existed prior to the decision to become a *Colgate* or *Crest* fan.

Insufficient Justification:
Initial Selling Price as a Source of Dissonance

A common marketing ploy is the low introductory offer, a device designed to entice buyers to become interested. The theoretical reasoning behind this ploy is no doubt a common-sense reinforcement or incentive theory, and although a sufficiently low selling price should indeed attract customers, it may backfire as a method of instilling customer loyalty. Doob, Carlsmith, Freedman, Landauer, and Tom (1969) conducted five related field experiments to show that a low introductory offer does indeed interfere with customer loyalty.

The idea was to put a product on the shelves of two stores, varying the initial selling price. At one store the product was sold for its normal price, but that price was undercut by the second store. Reasoning from dissonance theory, a customer should experience very little dissonance when buying a product on sale, for he has almost complete monetary justification. Relative to the customer who buys the "introductory offer" item, someone who purchases the same item at the regular price should experience more dissonance and should therefore come to find the product appealing, with the end result of increased loyalty.

After one to three weeks the introductory offer was eliminated and the price was raised to a level equal to that of the second store (i.e., the normal selling price). Thus began the test phase of the experiment. With the prices at the two stores now held equal it would be possible to see whether the initial low selling price interfered with brand loyalty. The results for all five studies took a similar form. Predictably, sales were higher during the introductory offer period at the less expensive store, but as time elapsed during the test phase, buyer loyalty fell off rapidly at the store that offered the initial low price. The results followed this form for all five experiments, indicating that this effect is reliable. Considering the strength of these results it is surprising that the phenomenon has been disregarded by all of those firms and advertising agencies that promote introductory offers. Surely a low introductory offer would make sense if customer loyalty were not an issue, but in many merchandising settings it would make sense to learn a lesson from Doob *et al.* (1969) and the dissonance analysis.

Helping the Consumer through the Regret Phase

The present field experiment is unique in that the focus is not on dissonance reduction, but instead, on the debilitating effect of postdecisional regret on the customer's following through with a purchase. Donnelly and Ivancevich (1970) studied 1,827 purchasers from two automobile dealerships. Each of the customers had made an initial decision to purchase the car, and the question was how many of these buyers backed out of the purchase before the car was delivered. The authors proposed that the dissonance aroused between the time of initial decision and delivery could well be responsible for customers' revoking their decisions. Another way to state this point is in terms of regret. If immediate postdecision dissonance does result in lowered attractiveness of the chosen course of action, it seems quite likely that this changed attractiveness would then lead to attempted rescinding of the decision. Donnelly and Ivancevich attempted to reduce dissonance (hence, regret) for a number of automobile purchasers with the following technique: Within two weeks after the initial sale a salesman would call the customer to paint a favorable picture of the chosen car, and to reassure the customer of the wisdom of his decision. This technique proved definitely to be effective. A control group of buyers who received no dissonance-reducing phone calls were more likely to take back their decisions than were customers in the experimental group.

It is ironic that exactly the opposite treatment may also inhibit the appearance of regret. Rather than offering subjects consonant information, Brehm and Wicklund (1970) forced subjects to consider a negative feature of the chosen alternative, and this, too, reduced regret. Thus it may well be that either of two strategies could affect a person's rescinding of a dissonance-arousing decision.

INTERPERSONAL PERSUASION

In a book entitled *Psychological solutions to social problems,* Varela (1971) has made ingenious use of social psychological theory in solving problems of marketing, personnel, and other social questions arising within the business community of Uruguay. Much of what he has to say about dissonance theory is in the area of worker satisfaction, and he suggests that many disputes and protests among employees can be traced back to arousal of dissonance by the management. We will cite some examples to illustrate his use of the theory.

Concern about Stability

Suppose a person feels that he is secure in his employment, and then one day he arrives at work only to find that two fellow workers have been fired, without having been given a sufficient explanation. Varela (1971) proposes that this discovery will create dissonance, in that the prior cognition of job security would never imply a capricious firing of fellow employees. How is the dissonance handled? By derogating the responsible authorities, according to Varela, although this reaction seems difficult to understand as a means of dissonance reduction. No matter what the person thinks of his employers, he is still confronted with the possibility that he, too, would lose his position for no good reason. It seems more likely to us that dissonance theory would predict the derogation of those two fired employees. However, this is not Varela's only application, and the reasoning from the theory is clearer in others we will describe.

Lack of Recognition for Work Done

In this example a worker takes great pains to prepare a job, and when he presents the finished product for evaluation his supervisor criticizes it in a most picky manner. Dissonance will be aroused due to the inconsistency between self-evaluation and supervisor's reaction, and Varela (1971) indicates that one dissonance-reducing outcome will be, "With the pay I get what does he expect? [p. 68]" Evidently the supervisor's evaluation has come to be the cognition most resistant to change, and the employee looks for cognitions consonant with a mediocre performance—one of which would be low pay. Not only does the person come to think that his low pay might have led to less than sterling performance, but he also seeks social support, urging others to agree that the pay is indeed low. Varela proposes that this kind of behavior, although stemming from dissonance arousal, will often be labeled mistakenly as "agitation." The management could easily conclude that the person has infiltrated into the company in order to stir up trouble.

Exclusion from Meetings

In this instance an employee believes that he is an indispensable component of a work group, and dissonance is created when he is not invited to the group's meeting. Varela suggests that the worker will derogate the meetings, claiming them to be useless, a waste of time, and accomplishing nothing. In this example we are led to suppose that the most resistant cognition is the person's rejection, thus to minimize the value of the meetings is to create cognitive elements consonant with not attending. The process here resembles derogation of an unchosen choice alternative, but without the element of choice.

Varela's use of dissonance theory deserves some further general comment. First, it should be apparent that the previous situations are not completely parallel to the experimental work on cognitive dissonance. Most of the dissonance-provoking situations he discusses entail consequences that are largely unchosen and sometimes unexpected, although there is no way in any instance to know to what degree there might have been a prior expectation of insult, exclusion, or firing. With the worker whose finished product was derogated there was probably some degree of foreseeability, but it is less clear in other instances. In short, in Varela's applications we must be willing to assume that foreseeability is not always a prerequisite for dissonance arousal.

Second, to reiterate a previous point, we do not yet understand how dissonance is reduced by berating the management in the first example cited above. This sounds more like a provocation–aggression effect than anything stemming from dissonance processes. However, his interpretations make sense among the other instances we have cited. Certainly it could be dissonance reducing to find reasons for one's poorly evaluated performance, and low pay represents one such reason. Further, it makes particularly good sense that social support would be sought to bolster whatever consonant cognitions a worker invents. Finally, the sour grapes reaction of the worker excluded from the group meeting resembles quite closely other dissonance phenomena we have examined, although given that the person did not choose his exclusion, the dissonance analysis is not totally convincing.

Perhaps we should emphasize that Varela's central purpose is not to perform a field experiment for the benefit of dissonance theory, but instead, to bring the theory to bear on interpersonal conflict within an organization and to offer suggestions for managerial behavior. It is interesting to note that every one of the dissonance reduction modes cited by Varela involves worker hostility toward the management, or toward some part of the organization. This hostility, which might easily be labeled as unprovoked agitation, can often be understood in dissonance-theory terms, and if management officials were as perceptive as Varela, they might understand that they themselves are often the source of such "agitations."

Persuasion: Combining Dissonance with Reactance Theory

A common technique relied upon by Varela is the use of "boomerang" change in response to attempted social influence. Based on reactance theory principles (Brehm, 1966), Varela assumes that a strong attempted influence can often cause the target to disagree openly. In reactance-theory language, such disagreement represents a response to threatened freedom, in the sense that freedom of opinion or action is threatened when a person encounters strong efforts to persuade him.

An example provided by Varela (1971, pp. 90–91) involves the author's strategy for convincing a friend to seek medical attention. This example is fairly involved, and we will look just at segments of it. The reactance aspect of the overall persuasion effect consists, for example, of suggesting to the friend that his "health certainly seems to be a lot better now than when we all were first married" (Varela, 1971, p. 91). This "influence attempt," according to Varela, should cause the person to disagree openly. The reasoning is simple. The suggestion threatens the target's freedom to consider himself less than healthy, thus to reassert the freedom he disagrees.

Disagreement, of course, consists of a self-admission of being less than totally healthy. For example, the target person might counter with "I could't dream of indulging in the rough sports I used to practice ..." and "... Besides, I often feel tired and low" (Varela, 1971, p. 91).

The persuader now has the friend where he wants him. Due to reactance, the friend has made an overt verbal commitment in the form of an admission of less than perfect health. This commitment is dissonant with the individual's original assessment of himself and, argues Varela, will motivate the friend to change his private views toward agreement with that publicly expressed view. Further reactance arousal and verbal commitments ensue in this example in order to produce successive steps of change, but we have presented sufficient material to illustrate Varela's technique.

This latter application, much more than the earlier personnel relations extensions, is a clear and recognizable use of the theory. The use of these two phenomena—reactance and dissonance—in a complementary scheme is a clever and evidently viable approach.

THREE FIELD STUDIES ON CONTEMPORARY POLITICAL BELIEFS

An Appeal from a Hippie

Social comparison theory (Festinger, 1954) or even a common sense under-standing of reinforcement principles would hold that a communicator will be more effective if he is similar to his audience and is liked by his audience. We have already seen exceptions to this rule in dissonance experiments by Jones and Brehm (1967) and Kiesler and Corbin (1965), and a recent study by Cooper, Darley, and Henderson (1974) makes the point quite dramatically in the context of a door-to-door political persuasion.

In the Cooper et al. (1974) study residents of an eastern Pennsylvania com-munity were first called by a representative of a bogus institute, and asked if they would submit to a short in-person talk by a representative of the institute. The talk was to be on a current voting issue that dealt with the question of a state sales tax versus state income tax. During the telephone conversation the subject was given complete freedom to decline the interview even when the worker arrived, a procedure designed to maximize felt choice. Shortly after the telephone call a worker arrived at the subject's house, and was either conven-tional in appearance or completely "hippie," with a beard, extremely long hair, and wearing blue jeans. The worker proceeded to argue for a predesignated point of view on the tax issue, then the subject's opinion was assessed at a later date in a seemingly unrelated context.

Contrary to common sense, the hippie campaigner was more persuasive than was the conventional campaigner. We should emphasize that this result would not necessarily hold for all instances of "straight" versus unconventional com-municators, for most naturally-occurring comparisons of this kind would not have a built-in dissonance-increasing procedure. A crucial aspect of this field experiment was the element of volition created through the telephone call. Theoretically, the subject had the freedom to refuse to listen to the hippie worker once he arrived at the house, and given that the subject chose to listen, the clearest avenue of dissonance reduction entailed agreement with the position advocated. The results of this experiment are strikingly similar to the choice conditions of the Jones and Brehm (1967) study, and from that standpoint should not be seen as completely surprising.

The Foot in the Door
and Willingness to Support a Campaign

Dissonance theory implies that a substantial favor might be gained by someone by a method of successive approximations to the favor. That is, if the favor is so imposing that an outright request for it would meet with failure, the following strategy might be attempted. First, ask for a small favor. If the person complies, the decision to do so should arouse some dissonance, generating a consequent liking for the beneficiary. Then, given this increased liking, a larger request could be made, presuming that the target will now have more tolerance for a more substantial favor. This process would be repeated until the eventual favor can be requested successfully. There is a certain irony in such a procedure, for the person granting the favor gives up a great deal more in this successive approximation routine than if he grants the large favor outright. Two field experiments by Freedman and Fraser (1966) took this tack of successive approximations, and they met with success by asking for just two favors—an insignificantly small one followed by an imposing and objectionable one.

In the second experiment the following sequence of events took place. First, residents of a California community were contacted by either a representative of the "Community Committee for Traffic Safety" or the "Keep California Beautiful Committee." In the case of the traffic safety issue some of the residents were requested to place a small sticker which read "Be a safe driver" in a window of their homes. Other residents were asked to sign a petition promoting safe driving that would be sent to California's senators. There were two parallel conditions in the case where the interviewer was from the Keep California Beautiful Committee: Some residents were asked to place a small "Keep California Beautiful" sticker in their windows, and others were asked to sign a Keep-California-Beautiful petition. Finally, residents in a control condition were not contacted at all.

Reasoning from dissonance theory, we might expect the decision to post a sticker or sign a petition to arouse dissonance for at least two reasons. For one, the person may not completely agree with the position supported, and second, there could conceivably be adverse side effects such as unwanted publicity. What should the dissonance effects be? We would expect the person to come to believe more strongly in the position endorsed, but the effects might also be more general. That is, in justifying his decision, the respondent may come to see more value in taking an active part in any sort of acceptable movement or campaign.

The dependent measure was gathered approximately two weeks later, and was identical for all five conditions. A representative of "Citizens for Safe Driving" came to the door of the respondent and requested the following favor: A very large and rather poorly lettered sign was to be placed in the subject's lawn, obscuring much of the front of his house and concealing the doorway. The sign was to be there for over a week, and would leave a hole in the front lawn.

The results were tabulated in terms of percentages of subjects agreeing to submit to the rather bizarre request. Among the controls, who had not been contacted prior to the initial request, only 17% agreed to allow the sign. Taking the other four conditions as a whole, the figure was approximately 55%. Further, and somewhat surprising, there were no significant differences among the four experimental conditions, which suggests that the dissonance reduction process was not specific to a given issue or sponsor. (It will be recalled that half of the subjects were confronted with two different issues on the two occasions.) Instead, it appears as though the initial dissonance arousal generated a positive set toward acceptance of a variety of public commitments. In terms of specific cognitions, subjects may have told themselves that it is wise to become a part of the community, that they have a responsibility to support high community standards, that they believe in setting a positive example for the community, etc. Whatever the precise nature of the dissonance reduction process, it is clear that the foot-in-the-door technique is workable, and it appears to be workable by virtue of creating a more acceptable attitude toward behaviors congruent with the initial commitment.

Dissonance Created by Receipt of a Favorable Draft Lottery Number

Although cognitive dissonance experiments involving money or other rewards have typically found stronger dissonance reduction effects when incentives are low, there are special circumstances under which dissonance would be *positively* related to magnitude of incentive or reward. One example of such conditions was noted earlier in Nuttin's (1975) research, in which students received illicit examination points for their counterattitudinal performance. Even though they willingly accepted the exam points, subsequent dissonance-reducing attitude change was greater when the incentive was offered than when it was not. Nuttin assumed that this special variety of reward caused subjects to be uncomfortable, or guilty, and as a consequence they had to justify receipt of the experimenter's favor.

An analogous situation existed in the case of the 1969 American draft lottery, although no counterattitudinal performance was involved here. In that year the Selective Service System, by means of a random device, informed some draft eligible men that they would almost certainly be drafted, others that they might be drafted, and still others were assured of their safety from the draft. Notz, Staw, and Cook (1971), who studied reactions to the lottery, suggest that men who fell into the "safe" category should have experienced dissonance due to the inequitable nature of the lottery. Following the Notz et al. (1971) argument, these men in the safe category would experience dissonance because they did not earn their security through work, talent, or physical incapacity. In short, they had no good reason for possessing a status of being safe from the draft. The reasoning here is reminiscent of Adams' dissonance analysis of inequity. The authors proposed that such dissonance might be reduced by extending the same freedom (from the draft) to others, and this implies that men in the safe category would come to support vigorously a troop withdrawal from the southeastern Asian conflict. In fact, that is exactly what happened. Men who were made secure from the draft by the lottery showed substantially more positive attitudes toward U.S. troop withdrawal from the conflict than did men who fell into the unfavorable, eligible category.

Assuming that receipt of a "safe" designation did create an unpleasant feeling of inequity or undeservingness among respondents, it still remains to be explained why dissonance reduction took place. After all, receipt of a lottery number was completely beyond the respondents' control: choice was absent, and so why was there dissonance reduction? Perhaps the answer is that there was, in fact, an element of choice. Any of these previously eligible men could have elected to join the armed services, or possibly a designated substitute, but they chose instead to abide by the outcome of the lottery. Further, they obviously could have foreseen the possibility of receiving a favorable number, and it is entirely likely that they desired one. In short, to make the argument of Notz et al. (1971) complete, we may assume that the "safe" category was foreseen and in a sense chosen, accounting for any dissonance arousal that resulted from feelings of inequity or guilt.

DISCONFIRMATION OF OUTMODED AND CHERISHED BELIEFS

When a person holds a belief, whether political, religious, or scientific, dissonance is aroused upon a confrontation with incontestable evidence of the belief's invalidity. The first major investigation of belief–disconfirmations consisted of a series of observations of a religious sect, reported by Festinger, Riecken, and Schachter (1956). That sect, called the "Lake City" group, expected a series of remarkable events to save them from a divinely inspired destruction of life on earth, and when those events failed to manifest themselves a good deal of proselyting began. Members of the sect openly preached the virtues of their creed, and according to Festinger et al. (1956), such proselytizing was a mode of dissonance reduction set in motion by the dissonance resulting from a severe disconfirmation. Certainly other reactions to disconfirmation might have been expected, such as clinging to the belief more strongly or denying the disconfirming evidence, and we will see examples of some of these in investigations to be reported below.

Before moving on to describe some post-Festinger et al. (1956) investigations of belief disconfirmation, two questions should be asked about the applicability of dissonance theory. First, it has been shown in earlier chapters that dissonance processes are normally dependent on the foreseeability of the dissonance-provoking event. Did the members of Lake City anticipate the disconfirmation? In that study, and in those to follow, an element of foreseeability seems obvious once the situations are described. For example, the Lake City group was exposed repeatedly to the taunts and sarcasms of nonbelievers, almost guaranteeing that every member foresaw the possibility of disconfirmation. In the studies to be described below, which deal with religious or scientific beliefs, a similar element

is present. When the believer commits himself to belief-relevant actions, there appear to be adequate reminders that he is taking a risk of being incorrect in totally committing himself to the belief. More important, in most of these investigations we are dealing with more than just one commitment. There are repeated disconfirmations, raising the possibility that each believer has to make repeated choices to commit himself to the faith. Surely after the first disconfirmation there is good basis for understanding that the faith may go awry.

Disconfirmation of a Scientific Belief: The Phlogiston Controversy

A clear alternative to the laboratory or field study is a historical analysis of dissonance phenomena. Admittedly this is not easy, for we could seldom be sure that historical accounts of potentially dissonance-arousing events are sufficiently complete for a justifiable application of the theory. However, a unique opportunity for invoking dissonance theory retrospectively was uncovered by Verbruggen (1974).

According to Verbruggen a new scientific theory was advanced by a chemist named Lavoisier in approximately 1776, a theory that was destined to provoke dissonance arousal among a good many scientists who had previously held to another theory. This earlier and widely accepted theory was attributed to Stahl, and was a chemical theory that assumed the existence of phlogiston. The entrance of Lavoisier's system raised a good deal of conflict, for the new theory not only denied the existence of phlogiston but was also opposite to the phlogistic system in significant respects.

Verbruggen was able to obtain certain dissonance-relevant information on a number of chemists—including scientists from France, an English-speaking area, a German-speaking area, the Netherlands, and Italy. First, he calculated for each chemist what he calls the length of "positive commitment." This simply refers to the number of years, prior to the particular chemist's awareness of the antithesis between Stahl and Lavoisier, that the chemist had supported phlogistic thinking through published articles. It is assumed by Verbruggen that the dissonance created by Lavoisier's system would be greater among chemists who had longer positive commitments to the older system. This assumption may be questionable, and we will return to it below, but for the present we will grant Verbruggen's reasoning. Second, a variable called "persuasion time" was calculated. This refers to the number of years between the chemist's awareness of the antithesis and that same chemist's acceptance of Lavoisier's theory. Verbruggen is not explicit on the method by which acceptance of Lavoisier's theory was ascertained, but presumably this was inferred through each chemist's publications.

The hypothesis advanced for this group of chemists was as follows: The longer the period of positive commitment, the greater the magnitude of persuasion time. Verbruggen's (1974) reasoning presumes that a high degree of commitment makes it difficult to reduce dissonance by means of behavior change. Other dissonance-reducing maneuvers may have taken place, but the mode of behavior change (or belief change) should be manifested more readily among relatively uncommitted chemists. As a corollary, it should also be true that even the highly committed individuals may change their beliefs when the disconfirmation becomes overwhelming. That is, in the years following Lavoisier's postulate of a new system, his ideas gained both scientific support as well as the benefit of scientific opinion, and as these elements mounted it would have been progressively more difficult for a highly committed advocate of phlogistic thinking to abide by his original beliefs.

Verbruggen's (1974) results were presented in terms of rank-order correlations between time of positive commitment and time required for conversion. For the sample of scientists mentioned above, this correlation was .69, which is highly significant. Before drawing any conclusions we should note one likely confounding variable, this being the scientist's age. It is no doubt true that the chemists who were committed longer also happened to be older, and it may simply be that this older set did not live long enough to become converted. Verbruggen computed separate correlations between age and time required for conversion, and although these correlations were positive, they were significantly lower than the correlation between time of commitment and time for conversion.

If commitment time is indeed the determining factor in time taken for conversion, as Verbruggen argues, it makes sense to consider the dissonance interpretation more carefully in order to discover just what was dissonant with what. First, we might think that a scientist who has committed himself to the phlogistic system should experience dissonance when a viable, antiphlogiston framework challenges the earlier thinking. Second, what determines the degree of dissonance? Following Festinger (1957), dissonance will persist until one of the two elements gives way, which is to say that the greatest dissonance in the present historical study should have been experienced by highly committed scientists several years after the introduction of Lavoisier's system. Presumably at this point the original belief would still resist change, but at the same time public opinion and scientific research would pose a threatening challenge to the original belief. Third, it follows that a scientist would at some point become converted when the evidence became overwhelming (just as Festinger's subjects who suffered extreme losses in the 1957 gambling experiment), and predictably, the more irrevocable the original commitment, the more disconfirming evidence required before conversion.

In addition to the above results based on an international group of chemists, Verbruggen also reports a case study of just one of them—a particularly devout phlogiston defender named Delametherie. Although it was impossible to investigate each chemist in the above sample, Verbruggen managed to obtain information of other dissonance-reducing modes employed by Delametherie. Such an analysis is particularly appropriate for this individual, because he never did convert to the new system. This makes it possible to specify, a priori, the types of modes that Delametherie would have selected from to reduce dissonance. Some examples of these modes will be discussed briefly.

Avoidance of discrepant information. Given Delametherie's commitment to the phlogiston approach, he might have been expected to rush to an immediate attack. But this was not the case. It was 10 years after Lavoisier's entrance that Delametherie finally argued overtly that the two systems were opposite each other. Evidently Delametherie had been attempting, successfully or not, to avoid admission that the earlier theory had been successfully challenged.

Attempts at changing the environment. Beginning in 1786, and until his death in 1817, Delametherie tried unceasingly to persuade the scientific world of the incorrectness of Lavoisier's antiphlogiston proposal. This was done with his own experimental findings, and with the arguments of selected other chemists.

Attempts to break down the dissonance relation. Delametherie, evidently flailing out, argued in 1786 and 1787 that the antiphlogistians do not have to deny the older system, because they have a phlogiston of their own. Then, as the years progressed, he saw progressively fewer differences between the two systems, evidently reflecting his desire not to suffer the difficulties of experiencing the two systems as opposites.

Summary. Verbruggen (1974) has paved the way for what may be a ripe field of inquiry. Even within the field of psychology, including the dissonance versus incentive-theory controversy, it should be possible to examine the writings, public statements, conversions, and avoidance attempts of the proponents of mutually disagreeing systems, with an eye toward their efforts to reduce the dissonance between commitment to one system given knowledge of contrary systems. The effects he describes, particularly in his analysis of the lone, highly committed phlogiston defender, are a good sampling of the dissonance-reducing devices implied by the theory, and a similar analysis should be possible for contemporary scientists whenever individuals can be found who cling to strongly disconfirmed beliefs. One of the effects Verbruggen describes—attempts by Delametherie to change everyone's mind—brings us to the next dissonance analysis of disconfirmed beliefs.

Disconfirmation of a Religious Belief:
Prophecy Fails Again

After the manner of Festinger et al. (*When Prophecy Fails*, 1956), a series of observations was made by Hardyck and Braden (1962) on a religious group that had made elaborate preparations for a nuclear attack. The analysis was of members of the "Church of the True Word" (pseudonym), a sect associated with the Pentecostal movement. The members of the Church accepted the Bible literally, and as a integral part of their religious lives took part in speaking and interpreting of tongues, personal prophecy, and faith healing.

The event that sparked an extreme and eventually dissonance-arousing commitment was a message from one of the group's prophets, who became inspired to warn the group that it had just six months to prepare for a nuclear devastation. Upon receiving this message over 100 members packed their belongings and moved to a remote area of the southwestern part of the United States. They immediately set to work establishing new homes and constructing bomb shelters. From the book of Revelations the group had formulated a notion about impending events: They had reason to think that about one-third of the earth's population would be obliterated by warfare, and further, they expected to play a vital divinely inspired role in healing and converting survivors.

Finally the group went underground into their shelters, prompted by a prophetic message that "The Egyptians are coming." For 42 days 103 of the devout remained underground, awaiting a nuclear attack, but it was not forthcoming, and at the end of 42 days they finally emerged from the shelters, beliefs disconfirmed. To reiterate an earlier point, we might note that this disconfirmation was not a fait accompli. The attack was originally expected at approximately the time the shelters were entered, thus each successive day led to another disconfirmation. By choosing to stay in the shelter, each member was risking the possibility of being wrong. It should also be noted that there was a sufficient element of choice: Approximately 135 people originally entered the shelters, and only 103 remained for the entire period.

What happened to their beliefs upon emerging back into the sunlight? The members reinterpreted the purpose of their underground sufferings. The group discovered, by looking in retrospect at their various messages, that there had never been a clear message of an impending nuclear attack. Instead, God had used them to warn a nonvigilant world, and at the same time he was testing the members' faith. They concluded that they had passed the test and were now especially worthy in the eyes of God. At the same time they continued to believe that an attack would be forthcoming, but for some reason this did not prompt them to run back into their shelters. These are some of the dissonance-reducing devices employed by the Church of the True Word, and assuming that the commitment to 42 days underground was a highly resistant element, it makes perfectly good sense that relevant cognitions would have to be aligned with the fact of that lengthy hardship.

Hardyck and Braden were especially interested in proselyting behavior, since that was one of the more conspicuous modes of dissonance reduction in the report of Festinger et al. (1956). But this time proselyting was absent. In accounting for this difference between When Prophecy Fails and their own study, Hardyck and Braden invoke two reasonable explanations:

1. Festinger et al. indicated that a certain minimal social support is necessary before proselyting can occur. This is because some bare minimum of support is

required before the individual is able to sustain his beliefs in the face of disconfirming evidence. It also follows from the theory that too much social support would serve to minimize dissonance, and consequently eliminate proselyting, thus for proselyting to be at a maximum we would look for conditions approximating those of the *When Prophecy Fails* group. And indeed, there was not complete unanimity of opinion in this group, the group was small, but each person did have some element of support for his belief.

In contrast, support was much more readily available in the True Word group. The members had isolated themselves from the surrounding community much more so than the Lake City group, and there was almost complete unanimity of opinion. Under these conditions proselyting would seem a less likely reaction to disconfirmation, because each member had numerous other associates who agreed with him. In short, at some extreme level of already extant social support, it would be superfluous to proselyte. Further, to try to convince others is to incur doubts and criticisms, thus the relatively secure True Word member who tried to proselyte would have run the risk of increasing his dissonance.

2. A second important difference between the Lake City and True Word groups was with respect to surrounding community reaction. The Lake City faction was subject to constant torment from sarcastic newspaper columnists, reporters, editors, and others, while the True Word group received benevolent treatment within its community. If a group is already being ridiculed for its beliefs, one way to reduce dissonance would be to attempt to change the thinking of the community, but if the community voices no apparent adverse opinion there is no impetus to reduce dissonance by trying to proselyte. In short, the community under such conditions does not serve as a source of further dissonance.

Christianity as Dissonance Reduction

In a master's degree thesis written at the Hebrew University of Jerusalem, Wernik (1972) has interpreted the rise of Christianity in terms of dissonance principles. Wernik analyzes both an early Christianity, which he views as a reaction to Jesus' death, and the later development of Christianity, interpreted by him as a reaction to disconfirmations of eschatological expectations. We will examine just the first of these, which seems to be the clearest. Our summary is necessarily brief, owing to the straightforward nature of the analysis.

To begin with, Jesus' followers believed him to be a kind of superman, different from the human race in some important respects, and their commitment to this belief was highly resistant to change. The disconfirming event was simply Jesus' death. Suddenly this superman, presumed to be virtually immortal, died a mortal death. The dissonance arousal created by this apparent disconfirmation was met in the following ways, according to Wernik's analysis:

Bolstering. There was a bolstering in their preexisting beliefs about Jesus' superiority, such as an emphasizing of 1. Jesus' extraordinary and prodigious birth and childhood, 2. His recognition by God, men of excellence, and believers, and 3. Jesus' recognition of himself for what he was.

Denial. 1. The death was reinterpreted as a very special kind of death, in fact a "nondeath" that implied resurrection, appearance, and ascendence to heaven. 2. It was proclaimed that Jesus knew, predicted and chose his own death. 3. Jesus' death was for the purpose of atonement. 4. Others were to be blamed for his death. (It is not clear from Wernik's description how blaming served the function of denial.)

Transcendence. This reaction consisted of promoting Jesus as being from another world. Human concepts of birth and death are not relevant for his being.

The parallels between the perpetuation of Christianity and the reactions of the Lake City and True Word groups are striking. Given a firm commitment to a belief, particularly when a significant part of the person's life is devoted to that belief, disconfirmation is met with denial, bolstering of the preexisting belief, and proselyting. These three cases we have examined are especially suitable for the cognitive dissonance approach because the members of all three groups (Lake City, True Word, and Jesus' Followers) were highly committed to their beliefs. To change the belief would imply a radical alteration of life style, thus the easiest cognitive resolution available was the multifaceted bringing of other cognitive elements into line with original commitments. Only in our first analysis—that of the phlogiston scientists—was the commitment sufficiently revocable that an entire life style would not be disrupted by revoking the original belief, and indeed, that was the only one of these four instances in which behavior change played a significant role in lowering dissonance.

The Impact of a Legally Imposed Behavior Change on Relevant Attitudes

In offering some proposals for implementing dissonance theory in desegregation, Brehm and Cohen (1962) suggested that minimal force would be advantageous if attitudes were to change. This suggestion is entirely plausible and has been substantiated on numerous occasions in experimental research, but unfortunately, this suggestion has not been followed up by studies comparing "forced" versus "relatively nonforced" racial desegregation. In fact during earlier stages of desegregation the federal government employed a good deal of force, and this might give us reason to wonder if desegregation had any impact on attitudes due to dissonance processes. Various members of Congress have also questioned the efficacy of legally prescribed behaviors in bringing forth attitude change. For example, Senator Thurmond of South Carolina had the following comments on this question:

> I am sure that you will agree it does not take much of a prophet to foresee an act of Congress such as this now before this committee will fail to change individual attitudes, although it is conceivable that the full force of the National Government may compel substantial compliance with the letter of the law [Excerpt from the testimony of Secretary of State Dean Rusk before U.S. Senate Committee on Commerce, 88th Congress, 1st Session, hearings on S. 1732, a bill to Eliminate Discrimination in Public Accommodations Affecting Interstate Commerce, Part I, pp. 316–317, July 10, 1963].

Although it is true that the iron hand of the law does not in itself create an atmosphere of perceived freedom, free decisions are possible if we focus on the course of events that follow the passage of any new laws. Normally it is possible either to disobey, or to choose not to remain within the law's jurisdiction. A study by Muir (1967) is an excellent case in point. His focus was on the dissonance-arousing consequences of a Supreme Court ruling that banned prayer in public schools, and we will now turn to his inquiry.

Muir's (1967) investigations were of a town he calls "Midland," and his data came from interviews with individuals for whom prayer in schools was a central fact of life. These 28 respondents can be divided into three groups: the school board, superintendents, and principals. Prior to the court ruling on prayer, the community from which Muir drew his sample was generally content with the local practice of daily prayers in the classrooms. There had been occasional protests from members of the Jewish community, but otherwise the practice of schoolhouse religion—at least the recitation of the Lord's Prayer—was widely accepted. Among the subjects of Muir's interviews only four were strictly opposed to schoolhouse prayer at the time immediately preceding the court's decision. The remainder were on a continuum of archconservative (religious training is imperative) to merely tolerant of religious rites in school.

If Midland had been a controlled experiment, attitudes toward prayer in school -might have been altered effectively by placing each individual into a forced compliance situation where an antiprayer stance were called for, while fostering an atmosphere of freedom of choice. Dissonance would have thrived under these conditions, and certainly we would have expected a considerable shift away from the typical Midland favorability toward schoolhouse prayer. But the Supreme Court of the United States—not a social psychologist—created the forced compliance, and the court decision was clearly not a subtle technique inspired by dissonance theory.

On June 17, 1963 the court's decision on prayer was printed in the newspapers, perhaps with the implication that all United States school personnel would thereafter abide by the landmark decision. It would be naive to suggest that all school personnel would from that point on resign themselves to school without prayer, for there were other options that we will spell out in the course of following Muir's analysis of several individual reactions. What these options mean for our analysis is that the court's decision was indeed dissonance-arousing. Individuals who had been committed to a daily routine of public religion were now in the position of having to leave the schools or disobey the courts, and within this dilemma lies the root of the dissonance arousal. Muir's analysis classifies their reactions five ways, but we will discuss just three of these. Of particular note is Muir's sophisicated understanding of the idea of resistance to change of cognitive elements. This concept provides much of his basis for distinguishing among alternative reactions to the court decision.

The backlashers. Muir (1967) conducted extensive surveys of attitudes both before and after the court decision, and among his respondents four showed a backlash, or boomerang attitude change, such that they became even more favorable toward schoolhouse religion. Obviously a commitment to follow the court's guidelines was not, for them, the focal point around which dissonance reduction revolved. It is interesting to consider some of the individual cases through Muir's perspective. For example, three of the four evidenced a failure even to comprehend the logic of the court's decision. They simply could not provide an explanation for why the court decided the way it did. This inability (or refusal) to acknowledge the logical or legal basis for the court decision appears to be a definite first step toward eliminating cognitive elements dissonant with a commitment to prayer. Related to this was a quest for information that would depict the court as a low-caliber institution. Muir saw evidence of their seeking out social support as well as printed information in support of their beliefs about the necessity of daily public-school prayer.

Why were the original attitudes so resistant to change? Muir probed into the life style of one of the principals, a spinster, and found her existence to be predicated largely on religion. She was incapable of separating God from the learning of worldly wisdom, and her self-esteem evidently rested upon her classroom conveyance of a God theory of reality. Acceptance of the court's decision would have been a serious threat to her dignity, an assumption that would account well for her bolstering her original attitudes. Further, she was not irrevocably committed to the school system, and rather than succumb to the court's pressures she indicated that she would first leave the school system.

Resistance to change had a different locus for two other backlashers. Relative to the other school personnel they had pervading social commitments throughout the conservative Midland community, belonging to the Rotary Club and Knights of Columbus, and they also shunned social life within the school system. For them to accept the court's decision as correct would have shaken their entire social existence, thus they stuck by their prior beliefs.

All four of the backlashers reported entertaining the possibility of leaving the school system, and in fact one man did resign shortly after Muir's final interview. In summary, the backlashers were for at least two reasons irrevocably committed to prayer in schools, and their prior commitments were evidently more resistant to change than their teaching professions. However, given that resigning was not a completely viable alternative, the only course of dissonance reduction remaining was to add consonant cognitions to the most resistant element—and this, of course, implies the backlash attitude change.

The nulists. A small number of school personnel held to their original attitudes. For all of these respondents the original attitude was described by Muir (1967) as a "watered-down policy preference for merely the commonplace religious exercises [p. 88]." Given that their original attitudes were conservative we might wonder why these individuals did not join the backlashers in becoming more extreme, and Muir suggests the following. Unlike the backlashers, whose social anchor points were in the conservative Midland community, the nulists enjoyed a considerable extent of social contact with others in the school system. Considering that the school officials were more liberal than the larger community, and that contact with school officials carried exposure to the school board's decision to comply with the court, dissonance would only have been exacerbated by strengthening prior attitudes. But it still remains to be explained why they did not change their attitudes to coincide more closely with the court's decision.

Muir appears to have uncovered two factors that were at least correlated with the nulists' reactions. The first of these is that compliant attitude change was "intellectually impossible." Evidently these several members of the school system were simply not intellectually capable of employing attitude change as a means of rationalizing their continuation in the school system. This reasoning involves some assumptions beyond the core of dissonance theory, but Muir may be correct. That is, there may be individuals who are not sufficiently "cognitive" to put their behaviors and attitudes into consistent relation. The earlier chapter on focused attention and dissonance reduction is consistent with such an idea.

Second, and growing directly out of the first factor, is a denial of responsibility for the court order and its implications. According to Muir these respondents found it easier to rule out choice than to change their attitudes, thus they were observed to make claims to having no choice, and they appeared to treat the court as an undeniable, omnipotent force.

The converts. Just like the nulists, the converts kept frequent social contact with the school community. According to Muir the primary difference between nulists and converts was the intellectual capability of the latter group, which led them to accept a degree of choice in adopting or rejecting the court decision. Of course, it may not simply have been intellectual capability that led to compliant attitude change. There was also another important difference between this group and the converts: the converts were much more likely to be social isolates with respect to the Midland community. Among the converts all three principals had recently arrived at their respective schools, the superintendent went out of his way to eschew social contacts, and the board member was a newcomer to town who belonged to the black community—a community that apparently was not terribly concerned with the issue. This meant that a shift in attitude against schoolhouse prayer would not have the effect of alienating established friends. Independent of possible differences between nulists and converts in intellectual capability, this single difference of relative social isolation seems more than adequate to explain the differential attitude change.

A control group.   Muir found an uninvolved control among five headmasters of private schools in Midland. The headmasters were not employees of the government, hence were unaffected by the court decisions, but they were in many other ways comparable to the main group of respondents. Perhaps predictably, the five never saw the court decision as pertinent to the conduct of their own schools, nor did they evidence any attitude change.

Summary.   Muir's investigations and interpretations offer a prime example of the complexities of applying dissonance theory to a group of individuals who do not share a common "most resistant cognitive element." In better defined and manipulable laboratory or field settings we can more easily find conditions conducive to a homogeneous reaction to dissonance arousal, but in a situation with the complexities of the Midland case, Muir has done exactly what is necessary. The necessity is to understand for each individual what is resistant and what is not, and this inevitably leads to a study of each person's values, particularly religious and educational values, in addition to the person's social life and potential role in the postcourt decision school setting. Some of these analyses will evidence a post hoc quality, but this may also be necessary in attempting to understand fully the multitude of sources of resistance to change. Finally, we should note that Muir has grappled with a case of naturally occurring dissonance in which denial of responsibility was antecedently a likely reaction to the court's decision, and this fact certainly rendered his analysis more complex. Had each individual member chosen a course of action, with freedom from external constraint, the application of dissonance theory would have been relatively free of complications.

CLINICAL PSYCHOLOGY

One of the more evident ramifications of dissonance theory for clincial practices derives from the "insufficient justification" paradigm. If the therapist has in mind a behavior change for his patient, the person should be induced to perform that behavior under minimal constraint. Only then will the change become internalized and highly resistant to extinction. This suggestion parallels Aronson and Carlsmith's (1963) recommendation for the socialization of children. It will be recalled, in the context of their experiment of forbidden toys, that the children who were admonished least were the most likely to internalize a decision not to play with the forbidden toy.

Of the following two implementations of dissonance theory, the first illustrates the use of effort justification, while the second focuses more on the idea of free choice. The reader will find a more comprehensive discussion of how dissonance theory can be used in clinical practice in the volume by S. Brehm (in press).

Initiation into a Therapy Group

According to Goldstein, Heller, and Sechrest (1966), group psychotherapists vary considerably in the conditions they pose for entry into their therapy groups. At one extreme is the therapist who simply uses a single screening interview, and sometimes even this is neglected. At the other extreme, a patient might have to submit to (a) psychological testing, (b) an individual interview focusing on test results, (c) an interview centering on the procedures of group psychotherapy, (d) discussion of mundane matters such as extraoffice meetings, ethics, and group goals, and (e) a trial attendance during which time the candidate for therapy and the group can decide whether they want each other. Although they cite no direct supporting evidence for the operation of dissonance in a group therapy context, Goldstein *et al.* (1966) formulate a dissonance-theory hypothesis, which is one of several clinically oriented hypotheses drawn from social psychology.

> The degree of effort required of the patient-candidate to gain therapy group membership will positively influence the subsequent initial attractiveness of membership status to him if he persists in completing the required premembership tasks. At the upper limit of this relationship, a curvilinear or asymptotic pattern will emerge [Goldstein *et al.*, 1966, p. 345].

The only point at which we might elaborate on Goldstein *et al.* (1966) is with respect to their assertion of an asymptotic level beyond which additional effort will have no impact. Conceivably they are right, and they could be right for either of two reasons: If the initiation is sufficiently strenuous, it seems likely that potential members would decide against joining, and second, at some extreme level of pain and suffering additional requirements may not be felt psychologically. This latter point has little to do with dissonance theory, but is more a question of when stimuli will be noticed and acted upon. In general, their proposal seems clearly derived and workable.

A Cognitive Dissonance Approach to Psychotherapy

An intriguing approach to patients' concerns over maladaptive behaviors has been developed by Hattem (1973), whose logic and techniques we will attempt to summarize. Dissonance theory is at the base of his ideas, although we will find it necessary to note special assumptions implementing the theory in this clinical approach.

First, Hattem's characterization of what constitutes a "patient in need of help" is important. He suggests that maladaptive behaviors per se do not make for the problem, but instead, the debilitating factor is concern with those maladaptive behaviors. Many people have anxieties, hallucinations, insomnia, or depression, but this fact alone does not bring them for help or even imply that help is required. What brings a person to a therapist is self-concern over behaviors or attitudes. From this assumption it follows that elimination of maladaptive behaviors is not essential to therapy. Instead, what is necessary is removal of the worry and anxiety about behaviors.

Successful therapy also requires the patient to gain a sense of control over his behaviors. Hattem (1973) indicates that a feeling of lack of control is basic to the debilitating anxiety about behaviors. The patient who feels that he does not choose those behaviors is, of course, in a position to be anxious about them.

Given this conceptualization of a patient, Hattem's (1973) approach is to instill in the patient a feeling of control. The therapist attempts to convince the patient that the behavior, rather than being unchosen and maladaptive, was indeed chosen as the better of several alternatives. For example, an obese girl might be told that she chose obesity in order to avoid an active social life, for which she was not yet prepared. The therapist attempts to bring out all possible alternative courses the patient might have taken, and he helps the patient to conclude that the "maladaptive" one in question was selected wisely.

Prior to the initiation of this therapy the patient possesses a particular kind of cognitive consonance. According to Hattem's assumptions consonance exists between the patient's feeling that his behaviors are not adaptive and the accompanying worry or self-concern. To have a serious problem, labeled as a problem, and not to be worried about it would create dissonance. But this is exactly the dissonance that Hattem's therapist tries to create: the therapist tries to instill a feeling that there is no reason for concern. The result is cognitive dissonance between (a) the person's feeling of possessing a maladaptive behavior and (b) the cognition of a highly credible therapist's saying that self-concern about the behavior is completely unnecessary.

The resolution of this dissonance relieves the patient's problem and can take either of two forms: He can change his behavior to some alternative behavior he feels is adaptive, or he can allow himself to be persuaded that there is no basis to be concerned about the original "maladaptive" behavior. There is another alternative, less therapeutic than the first, which would be to leave the field, but the warm and credible qualities of the therapist make this final option unattractive.

We might also note that the patient who chooses a new behavior may do so in part because the therapist has instilled a feeling of control. If the therapist cannot create a feeling of control, then of course behavior change would be less likely. But this does not mean that the other mode of dissonance reduction is not still viable, for as long as the therapist can bring his patient to entertain seriously the possibility of there being no basis for worry, dissonance will be aroused and can be reduced by disclaiming self-concern over the uncontrollable behavior.

One final theoretical note is necessary: This approach definitely does not prescribe alternative behaviors to the person. Hattem is very much of a dissonance theorist on this point, for he maintains that behaviors performed under pressure from the therapist will be shortlived. The advantage of his technique seems obvious. The therapist is completely spared the myriad of complexities associated with eliminating old behaviors and shaping up new ones. Successful therapy for this approach requires only that the therapist persuasively make the subject aware of the distinct possibility that self-concern is unnecessary.

MARRIAGE, GAMBLING, AND SMOKING

Dissonance Arousal from Becoming Engaged

A correlational study by Cohen (1962c) provides an interesting exception to the similarity-breeds-liking notion of Byrne (1969). According to Cohen's derivation from dissonance theory, a couple not ideally suited for each other in various objective ways should, following the decision to marry, invent reasons for being together. Cohen located a sample of male college students who were considering becoming engaged, and just prior to a Christmas vacation he asked them a number of questions in order to ascertain what basis they had for becoming engaged to their steady girl friends. He asked them such questions as, "How much religious disagreement is there between you and your fiancee?" and "How many girls are you dating now while taking out your intended fiancee?" Presumably predecisional conflict about whether or not to become engaged would be high if the subject thought he and his girl friend were dissimilar, or if the subject were simultaneously dating other attractive females.

During the ensuing Christmas break 20 of Cohen's original subjects did become engaged. It was expected that they would experience postdecisional dissonance in proportion to their predecisional conflict. In order to test this idea the sample of 20 was split at the median on the basis of answers to the "objective reasons for becoming engaged" questionnaire, then dissonance reduction was examined as a function of that variable. Dissonance reduction was ascertained by a three-item measure, given both before and after the vacation, that measured the subject's need and devotion toward his tentative spouse. In examining change in need and devotion Cohen found a substantial increase among his high-conflict group, while the low-conflict group exhibited virtually no change whatever. The difference between groups was highly significant ($p < .001$).

While this study leaves open the possibility that the increases in love and devotion among high-conflict subjects preceded the decision, the results are at the very least consistent with dissonance theory. Cohen's findings have some definite implications for interpersonal liking and attraction. Evidently it is not safe to assume that similarity is a consistent determinant of liking, for the dissonance created after commitment to a questionable other can easily shroud the similarity-liking phenomenon. It is conceivable that similarity (or suitability) and liking would even be inversely related, given a sufficiently careful specification of dissonance-arousing conditions. This is, of course, exactly what Kiesler and his associates have accomplished in the context of liking for a larger group (Chapter 12).

Postdecision Dissonance at Post Time

Dissonance theory has a definite implication for the rationality and objectivity of the gambler. Although the gambler may weigh evidence in a perfectly objective manner prior to placing his bet, his postbet evaluations of the alternatives will be subject to the impact of postdecisional dissonance. Given that someone bets on a horse, the theory would imply an increased estimate of the probability of that horse's winning. A pair of quite similar experiments by Knox and Inkster (1968) investigated that possibility.

Their field studies were conducted at a horse-racing track, where subjects were selected among people who approached the $2 window. In the first experiment subjects were asked for the likelihood that the horse they were about to select would win, and in the second study an analogous question was asked about confidence in the to-be-chosen horse. "Postchoice" subjects were contacted immediately after having placed a bet, and were asked about the likelihood of winning (Experiment I) and confidence in winning (Experiment II). There was also a "prechoice" control group of individuals who had not yet decided. These were interviewed just before their bets were placed. The results of both experiments were strong and consistent: The group that had already placed bets was more likely to anticipate winning, and was more confident in the prospect of winning.

The results of these two studies have a broader ramification for the world of gambling in general. If a person bets on a horse or selects a strategy with the understanding that he might lose, dissonance will certainly be aroused and can be reduced through the gambler's trying to find some "extra" attraction in the chosen strategy. To the extent that there is such an increased attraction, what happens when there arises a second opportunity to select that strategy among others? Clearly the person will not be totally objective, and there will be a tendency to select the very alternative that only recently met with failure. Such a process could become circular, whereby each time the chosen strategy fails the person becomes increasingly attracted to it and each time more likely to select it. Thus a dissonance analysis provides a potential explanation for the phenomenon of compulsive betting.

Reactions to the Surgeon General's Report on Smoking and Health

Shortly after the United States Surgeon General proclaimed a causal link between cigarette smoking and cancer (January, 1964), Kassarjian and Cohen (1965) conducted an elaborate survey in Santa Monica, California, to investigate smokers' dissonance-reducing reactions to the Surgeon General's report. Both sexes were represented in the sample and were drawn randomly from the Santa Monica community.

The first result Kassarjian and Cohen note is that the cognition of being a smoker was indeed highly resistant to change. Upon hearing the news of a link between cigarettes and cancer a smoker could conceivable deal with his dissonance by changing behaviors, but this was found to be an unlikely response. Between the time of the Surgeon General's report and the time of the survey reported here, only 9% of the respondents claimed to have abandoned cigarette smoking. Another type of behavior change would be to switch to a safer cigarette, or to pipes and cigars, but such changes were almost nonexistent. For example, only 1.6% of the heavy smokers switched from cigarettes to a pipe. All of this suggests rather strongly that cigarette smoking was highly resistant to change, thus the dissonance created between being a smoker and being confronted with a government-issued medical report would have to be handled in other ways.

One of the clearest routes to eliminate dissonance would be to debunk the report, and when asked whether the cigarette—cancer link was proven, respondents answered as shown in Table 21. Note that the greater the commitment to cigarettes, the more denial of a real relationship between smoking and cancer. Since it is possible that educational level would affect a person's access to the report or his credulity with respect to a scientific report of this kind, Kassarjian and Cohen (1965) broke their subjects into educational levels, and found the same denial phenomenon within each education level.

Other modes of dealing with dissonance would include the following: to play down the importance of the issue, to overemphasize other kinds of dangers to life, and to seek out social support. For example, one item asked for subjects' agreement-disagreement with the following notion: "Lots of hazards in life— facts are not clear—many smokers live a long time—both get lung cancer" (Kassarjian and Cohen, 1965, p. 61). Over twice as many cigarette smokers as nonsmokers assented to this item. Smokers also employed such rationalizations as there being lots of other hazards in life, and that smoking is preferable to being a nervous wreck, taking pills, or excessive drinking.

All of these responses add up to a conclusion that is entirely in keeping with dissonance theory. Evidently cigarette smokers cannot easily revoke their habits, thus numerous varieties of denials and rationalizations are engaged in order to cope with dissonance. As a reminder we should note that this study was based

TABLE 21
Relationship of Smoking to Believability of Health Report

People (%) saying linkage is:	Heavy smokers	Moderate smokers	Light smokers	Pipe—cigar smokers	Non-smokers
Proven	52.2	58.3	77.0	83.8	80.4
Not proven	40.9	37.5	20.5	13.5	10.8
Don't know	6.8	4.2	2.5	2.7	8.7

just on interviews taken after the Surgeon General's report, and it is certainly possible that the responses would have been similar prior to the report. But this is the nature of a correlational study, and aside from this obvious word of caution, the findings are entirely supportive of the idea that rationalizations will be sought in proportion to the degree of dissonance.

SUMMARY

This chapter makes explicit that which was at least implicit in the experimental research we have already reviewed: dissonance theory has easy applicability to the economic, interpersonal, political, and religious issues surrounding all of us. The research examined here comprises an entire continuum of methodology, from tightly controlled field experimentation to an inferential–historical–archival approach. In the interest of illustrating the various domains of dissonance-theory application, we have disregarded methodological boundaries and instead discussed the distinct categories of marketing, interpersonal persuasion, politics and religion, disconfirmation of cherished beliefs, clinical psychology, marriage, smoking, and gambling.

There is no doubt that conceptual interpretations other than dissonance theory would be applicable to at least parts of the cases discussed here, but our purpose has not been to test the theory and attempt to eliminate alternative explanations. Rather, this chapter serves as a guide from which researchers might follow their noses, armed with such concepts as resistance to change, in analyzing complex social phenomena. By holding fast to the central tenets of the theory in their explorations, some of the investigators responsible for this applied work have met with good success in making a convincing case for the dissonance analysis, and as we have seen amply illustrated, the theory is sufficiently simple and workable that it can be introduced into a variety of complex and dynamic social settings.

18
Perspectives

The preceding chapters have shown that there is abundant evidence in support of Festinger's (1957) original statement of dissonance theory. Having cognitions that are inconsistent tends to create dissonance in a person, and as dissonance arousal increases there are increased attempts to reduce or eliminate it. The magnitude of dissonance is a direct function of the importance of the inconsistent cognitions, and in regard to any one cognition, the magnitude of dissonance is a direct function of the ratio of dissonant to consonant cognitions. In general, dissonance can be reduced by eliminating dissonant relationships between cognitions, and where more than one relationship is concerned, by reducing the ratio of dissonant to consonant cognitions. Further, because cognitions differ in their resistance to change, a person will attempt to reduce dissonance by changing those cognitions that are least resistant.

This conceptual outline led Festinger (1957) to suggest three general implications: (1) When a person chooses between attractive alternatives he experiences dissonance that can be reduced by magnifying the attractiveness of the chosen alternative and by reducing the attractiveness of the rejected alternative; (2) When a person is "forced" to engage in behavior that he would normally avoid, he experiences dissonance that can be reduced by coming to favor the behavior in which he has engaged; and (3) When a person is experiencing dissonance with regard to some issue, he will tend to seek dissonance-reducing information, and correspondingly, he will tend to avoid dissonance-increasing information. As we have seen, most of the research on dissonance theory is related to one or another of these general implications.

In some of the relatively early work on dissonance theory, Brehm and Cohen (1962) raised questions about what conditions are necessary and sufficient for the arousal of dissonance. They suggested that only cognitive inconsistencies occurring as a consequence of a volitional act would arouse dissonance. However, as we saw in Chapter 4, not all cognitive inconsistencies resulting from volitional acts arouse dissonance. Indeed, the research on this question has shown that what determines whether a cognitive inconsistency arouses dissonance is responsibility for the inconsistency. Cognitive inconsistencies for which the person feels no responsibility apparently create no dissonance.

A second point from Brehm and Cohen (1962) is that commitment is a necessary condition for the arousal of dissonance. Subsequent research by Festinger (1964) and his associates confirmed that dissonance reduction processes do not occur until the consequences of a commitment are clear. While this emphasis on commitment as a prerequisite for dissonance reduction effects may seem to be an innovation on Festinger's (1957) original statement, a careful reading of the latter indicates that the notion of commitment is encompassed by the idea of resistance to change. Committing a person to an attitudinal position or behavioral act renders the corresponding cognitions highly resistant to change. While the notion of commitment may be a heuristic device for analyzing behavior in terms of dissonance theory, the more general, accurate, and presumably more useful way to conceptualize events is in terms of the resistance to change of cognitive elements.

To summarize, the original statement of dissonance theory has been well supported by research, and the only useful modification to the theory is the stipulation of responsibility as a prerequisite for dissonance arousal. Nevertheless, while the main outlines of the theory have been supported, and the theory has been somewhat modified in line with consistent evidence bearing on the responsibility issue, a number of issues remain. It is to these issues that we now turn.

WHAT ARE THE CENTRAL THEORETICAL ISSUES?

Responsibility

Although research has taken us a considerable distance toward an elucidation of responsibility, as defined through choice and foreseeability, there remains some exploration to be done in regard to the precise nature of responsibility. In addition to choice and foreseeability as sources of responsibility, we found in Chapter 4 that a discrepant outcome resulting directly from inadequate performance was a source of dissonance arousal. This could imply that personal characteristics such as ability operate as sources of responsibility, independent of choice and foreseeability. The research on relatively chronic personal traits as sources of dissonance arousal has just begun, and it remains to be seen whether or not the responsibility concept can be broadened in this direction.

Resistance to Change and Recency of Behavioral Commitment

It is only in recent years that we have seen systematic manipulations of the resistance to change of relevant cognitions (e.g. Götz–Marchand et al., 1974; Walster et al., 1967). As was suspected long ago (Festinger, 1957), it is indeed possible to specify which of several cognitive elements will have the relatively greatest resistance. The more complex issue has to do with an assumption that has been made in most of dissonance research—namely, the assumption that cognitive work centers on a given behavioral commitment.

The first thing to be said about this behavioral commitment assumption is that it appears to work. In virtually every study we have examined the experimental subjects are asked to decide to behave in some manner, and investigators almost always find evidence of alignment of cognitions with that particular behavior. The remaining question is this: If the relevant cognitions have existed prior to the research in question, and if the subject has taken prior action relevant to those same cognitions, why should the *experimental* behavior necessarily be the cognitive element most resistant to change? To cite what may be a common occurrence, imagine a religious attitude that has existed for a number of years, certainly not in a behavioral vacuum. The individual has acted repeatedly on this attitude, and then a dissonance researcher asks him to behave in some opposite manner. Certainly dissonance is aroused, but how is it to be reduced? Could we not argue that the accumulation of preexisting proreligious behaviors provides the dominant, most resistant cognitive element? Should dissonance not be reduced through alignment of cognitions with those prior behaviors? Perhaps so, but "boomerang" attitude change is rare in the dissonance research paradigm. This leaves us with an important question to answer, which is simply this: Why is the most recent behavioral commitment the most resistant to change?

Among plausible answers are the following:

1. Perhaps that recent element is not the most resistant. Conceivably there are dissonance-reducing processes occurring that have as yet not been measured—these processes serving to align the person cognitively with his preexisting behaviors. This argument would suppose that some amount of dissonance reduction would be manifested by attitude change consistent with the recent behavior, but that there would be perhaps even a greater amount of cognitive work (unmeasured) aimed at consistency with previous behavioral commitments. The problem with such an explanation, quite obviously, is that it requires the individual to reduce dissonance in contrary directions simultaneously. As such, this account seems unlikely.

2. A second possibility is that the recent behavior is not necessarily more resistant than all previous behaviors, but that the person's focus of attention renders the recent behavior as the only salient behavior. Very simply, he may not be thinking about earlier attitude-relevant commitments, even though the attitude itself is salient. One implication for future experimentation is this: If previous behaviors could be brought into focus, and be made relatively more or less salient than the experimental behavior, we may well find dissonance reduction to take the form of attitude change in a direction opposite from the recent commitment. This is pure speculation, and should simply serve as a reminder that the question we are raising here has as yet no definite answer.

Modes of Dissonance Reduction and Focused Attention

Only recently has systematic work been accomplished on the question of whether or not various routes to dissonance reduction can be blocked from use, and whether or not there is a hydraulic relationship among the various potential routes to disssonance reduction. Indeed, it has been demonstrated that there are effective experimental means by which a person can be blocked from specified modes (Götz–Marchand *et al.*, 1974; Walster *et al.*, 1967), and that alternative modes operate together in hydraulic fashion (Götz–Marchand *et al.*). Further, in the Götz–Marchand *et al.* (1974) research there is an indication that modes may exist, latently, and will be brought into play only if the person is made cognizant of them. This is reminiscent of our discussion (above) of awareness of earlier behaviors highly resistant to change. In general, it is likely that the course of dissonance reduction proceeds as a function of the direction of attention, and although focused attention is not at this point a formal aspect of the theory, further understanding of cognitive dissonance processes will no doubt be facilitated by a careful examination of the awareness question. Although our Chapter 7 explores the relationship between awareness of dissonant elements and subsequent dissonance reduction, a more specific analysis of awareness and specific alternative modes would be a fruitful area for inquiry.

Sequential Effects

Perhaps the most important point stemming from Chapter 7 has to do with the onset of dissonance reduction. In 1964 Festinger argued that the consequences of a decision must be clear and unequivocal before the rationalization process begins, but at this stage of development a more general conclusion is in order. Certainly some of the more important dissonance paradigms we have reviewed involve no overt decision, although a dissonance analysis can proceed provided there is some specifiable cognitive element highly resistant to change. Further, the relevant cognitive elements, of which the individual is aware, must bear some definite consonant or dissonant relation to the central, highly resistant cognition. The reason seems obvious. If a person does not know whether a cognitive element is consistent or inconsistent with another relevant element, there is no definite way in which dissonance reduction can proceed. The clearest example of such ambiguity of cognitions is in the Jecker experiment, discussed in Chapter 8. When a person does not know if a given alternative is to be among the selected or rejected alternatives, he has no way of knowing whether to enhance or derogate its attractiveness relative to other alternatives.

The advantage of a decision is that it gives the investigator, and subject, some starting point for a dissonance-reduction process to operate. But a decision is not altogether necessary, as witnessed by the performance expectancy paradigm and performance feedback paradigms in general. What is required for dissonance reduction to be set in motion is the following pair of conditions: (a) some definite, highly resistant cognition around which dissonance reduction can be organized—whether this be a decision or a self-conception, and (b) a clarity regarding the relation of other relevant elements to that central cognition.

The sequential effect just discussed refers to the distinction between a phase during which dissonance reduction cannot begin, versus one in which the conditions conducive to the dissonance reduction process are present. At least two other sequential phenomena were discussed in Chapter 8. One of these was postdecisional regret, which remains in part a mystery. The reason for this is that regret does not seem to be accountable in terms of Festinger's (1964) interpretation, and at this point it may be that regret is an extradissonance phenomenon. Certainly more research is required to determine under what conditions the individual is willing to admit to an incorrect decision, or lower his attraction to the chosen alternative, or exhibit other effects that can be labeled as postdecision regret.

Another sequential phenomenon is the relative longevity of dissonance reduction phenomena. Placing the relevant research together, we find that dissonance reduction effects seem to persist to the degree that there are not external pressures operating to return those effects to a predissonance-arousal level. To summarize this argument: If the researcher deals with an attitude, or other matter, that is deeply imbedded in the subject's everyday life, there will then be postexperimental forces operating to return that attitude to its previous level. If long-term effects are desired, either of the following steps might be followed:

1. The experiment could be carried out within the context of the subject's everyday dealings with the relevant attitude. In this way he will be committing himself to a new life style with regard to the attitude in question, and such a commitment should act to alter his relationship to the preexisting forces on his attitude. For example, if a person commits himself to take issue with a prior attitude reference group, that commitment should have some lasting impact on that group's ability to pull his attitude back to its original level.

2. If the investigator changes an attitude that is in isolation, being largely irrelevant to the individual's outside existence, there should then be a minimum of forces operating to return the attitude to any previous level. The Freedman (1965c) study is a prime example. Presumably the choice objects (childrens' toys) were not encountered in their exact form outside the laboratory, thus when the subjects returned one month later to reevaluate the toys, it should not have been surprising that the earlier experimentally-created attitude would persist.

To summarize, probably the greatest existing question about sequential phenomena has to do with regret. If further research could lead to a better understanding of the antecedent conditions of regret, and of the explanatory mechanisms, we would be in a much better position to derive precise predictions for immediate postdecisional cognitive changes. As the theory presently stands, an investigator may occasionally be surprised by the absence of dissonance reduction effects due to the counterforce of regret, and these surprises will continue until the theory is clarified in this important respect. Fortunately, regret does not appear to be a direct function of the amount of dissonance arousal, which means that a manipulation of dissonance is not likely to operate in a reverse manner. Instead, regret seems to be an ever-present possibility that can generally operate against the kind of rationalization we have come to associate with the theory.

RECENT RESEARCH AND THE THEORY'S CRITICS

The Impact of Reward or Incentive in the Forced Compliance Paradigm

The most frequent and most widely-accepted criticisms of the theory have centered on one specific paradigm, originally generated by Festinger and Carlsmith (1959). The critics (e.g. Chapanis & Chapanis, 1964; Elms & Janis, 1965; Janis & Gilmore, 1965; Rosenberg, 1965) have argued that to pay a person for a counterattitudinal act is to create the potential for distrust, suspicion, "apprehension evaluation," and related states that would inhibit attitude change. These various states, it was argued, minimize attitude change for reasons other than the mere absence of dissonance. It is now more than 10 years since these criticisms, and the issue has been handled by means of a variety of carefully designed research involving variations in personal responsibility. It has especially been the research combining monetary payment and choice (Chapter 3) that has clarified the operation of monetary incentives vis-a-vis the theory, and that has provided a fair answer to the earlier critiques. These several experiments, together with recent research by Gerard and his colleagues (1974) (Chapter 3), have gone to considerable lengths to clarify the conditions under which monetary incentives create various effects, while at the same time eliminating the supposed untrusting states that were said to have existed in early dissonance work with monetary payment.

Post Hoc Analyses?

Another variety of criticism (e.g. Chapanis & Chapanis, 1964; Tedeschi *et al.*, 1971) attacked the theory on the grounds of its potential for an unacceptable flexibility. For example, pointing to the Cohen, Brehm, and Latané (1959) and Festinger (1957) experiments on gambling, Chapanis and Chapanis accused the theory of being sufficiently vague to incorporate almost any pattern of data. Without going into a detailed examination of any one paradigm, it can be said that the overwhelming body of research we have reported is simply not of the post hoc variety. The increased emphasis on responsibility as a mediator of dissonance effects has played a role in clarifying predictions in whatever paradigms that may have been ambiguous previously. For example, to the best of our knowledge there is not one instance of a study of choice, or foreseeability, coming out backwards with respect to those variables. This means, quite obviously, that an experiment incorporating such variables has virtually no potential for ambiguous prediction. The same can be said in a more specific context regarding the effort justification and free choice paradigms. Now that these two paradigms have been gradually refined, and the potential for regret has been recognized, there is little reason to be concerned about postulating post hoc explanations of backward or confusing results.

Has the Theory Been Usurped by Other Accounts of the Same Phenomena?

Perhaps the greatest attack on dissonance theory, which attempted to place many dissonance phenomena under the semantic umbrella of "self-perception" theory, originated in Bem's formulation of a judgmental or rationalistic account of dissonance phenomena. As was abundantly clear from the relevant evidence reviewed in Chapter 15, a judgmental analysis does not explain all dissonance effects, nor does the subject in a dissonance paradigm even behave in accordance with the tenets of such a judgmental model. The notion of self-perception undoubtedly has merit in a more circumscribed universe of phenomena, but as an account of the effects generated from dissonance theory it is simply unfounded—and in several instances obviously wrong.

Bem's model comes closer than any other to providing an alternative approach. The other attempts (e.g., Nuttin, 1975; Tedeschi *et al.*, 1971) are not sufficiently thoroughgoing to capture the array of derivations made from the original theory. It has become clear that one of dissonance theory's virtues lies in its generality. Although there have been a number of clever (and also less clever) suggestions for replacements, each of the attempts has fallen short on grounds of insufficient potential for broad extention.

A more specific alternative explanation issue has to do with whether or not any given body of research might be explained in terms different from dissonance theory. The answer in certain instances is no doubt "yes." But when the reader examines the conceptual replications of any one experiment it will usually be true that the specific alternative account fails to hold across a broad number of situations. In short, we are suggesting that dissonance theory's generality gives it an advantage over a number of relevant, but specific, possible explanations. Also related to this point is the theory's development. The notion of responsibility, and more particularly the concepts of foreseeability and choice, give the dissonance investigator a definite leverage that was impossible at the time the theory was first formulated. Using the evolved theory, which hinges on cognitive imbalance for which the individual is personally responsible, it seems a straightforward matter to generate predictions that have no easy or compelling alternative interpretations.

What of the Existence of Selective Exposure and Performance Expectancy Phenomena?

As of 1965 (i.e., Freedman & Sears) there was only questionable basis for the existence of selective exposure as a dissonance-reduction device. Since that time there have developed more sophisticated approaches to the problem, and in particular, investigators have discovered the necessity of ruling out "counter-selective" processes such as curiosity, intellectual honesty, and the desire to refute opposing arguments. For reasons we have discussed in Chapter 11, selective exposure as a dependent measure creates special problems in that there are a number of other processes (e.g. curiosity) that work in a contrary direction. Thus, special pains must be taken in formulating research so that clear dissonance-theory predictions can be made. Nonetheless, it may safely be said at this time that selective exposure is a viable mode of dissonance reduction.

The effect noted by Aronson and Carlsmith (1962), whereby individuals who had failed preferred to avoid further success, has proven to be a point of contention among a number of researchers. Very simply, the phenomenon was never replicated, with the exception of one of seven experiments reported by Brock et al. (1965). Finally Maracek and Mettee (1972) appear to have clarified the issue, bringing closure to what has been an active dispute ever since 1962.

Summary

It is our observation that researchers of dissonance processes have been genuinely responsive to the theory's critics. The most general and often compelling criticisms, which we have just reviewed, have been addressed through a combination of improved methodology and sensitivity to competing theoretical formulations. To the extent that these same criticisms still apply, they appear to apply only if the overall picture of accumulated research is disregarded.

THE THEORY EXTENDED

Approximately 20 years ago a person required a sense of imagination to foresee the possible extensions of the notion of cognitive dissonance. At this time there is no longer such a need for imagination. All one need do is examine the numerous existing efforts. In addition to the great body of literature devoted strictly to testing the theory, there have been numerous significant efforts to examine the workings of the theory in domains that initially may have seemed out of the realm of the theory. In this volume we have summarized extensions of the theory to (a) motivational issues, including general drive or arousal, biological drives, avoidance of failure, and expectancies about performance, (b) resistance to extinction in animals, (c) selective exposure, (d) a variety of inter-personal and group behavior, (e) personality processes that have more tradition-ally been viewed in terms associated with clinical psychology, and finally, (f) broader and more applied questions such as marketing, personnel relations, political and religious beliefs and propagandizing.

In asserting that the theory has been broadly extended and that it has been tested rigorously in many respects, we are not attempting to paint a picture of completeness. The field of cognitive dissonance seems ripe for at least two further types of activity. For one, now that the basic postulates are understood somewhat better than 20 years ago, there is an excellent basis for continuing the kind of applications illustrated in Chapter 17. Second, the nature of the theory qua theory continues to require probing, especially along the lines we have noted above. That the theory has evolved as far as it has is most gratifying for those who have worked at its development. It is a mark of a good theory, of course, that it stimulates research and further theoretical work. Judged by these stan-dards, the theory of cognitive dissonance is remarkable for its past and con-tinuing contribution to the understanding of man.

References

Abelson, R. P., Aronson, E., McGuire, W. J., Newcomb, T. M., Rosenberg, M. J., & Tannenbaum, P. H. (Eds.). *Theories of cognitive consistency: A sourcebook.* Chicago, Illinois: Rand-McNally, 1968.

Ackerman, N. W., & Jahoda, M. *Anti-Semitism and emotional disorder: A psychoanalytic interpretation.* New York: Harper, 1950.

Adams, J. S. Wage inequities in a clerical task. Unpublished study. General Electric Co., New York, 1961.

Adams, J. S. Toward an understanding of inequity. *Journal of Abnormal and Social Psychology,* 1963, 67, 422–436.

Adams, J. S. Inequity in social exchange. In L. Berkowitz (Ed.), *Advances in experimental social psychology.* Vol. 2. New York: Academic Press, 1965, Pp. 267–299.

Adams, J. S., & Freedman, S. Equity theory revisited: Comments and annotated bibliography. In L. Berkowitz (Ed.), *Advances in experimental social psychology.* New York: Academic Press, 1976. In press.

Adams, J. S., & Jacobsen, P. R. Effects of wage inequities on work quality. *Journal of Abnormal and Social Psychology,* 1964, 69, 19–25.

Adams, J. S., & Rosenbaum, W. B. The relationship of worker productivity to cognitive dissonance about wage inequities. *Journal of Applied Psychology,* 1962, 46, 161–164.

Adorno, T. W., Frenkel-Brunswick, E., Levinson, D. J., & Sanford, R. N. *The authoritarian personality.* New York: Harper & Row, 1950.

Allen, V. L. Effect of extraneous cognitive activity on dissonance reduction. *Psychological Reports,* 1965, 16, 1145–1151.

Allport, G. W. *Personality: A psychological interpretation.* New York: Holt, 1937.

Amsel, A. The role of frustrative nonreward in noncontinuous reward situations. *Psychological Bulletin,* 1958, 55, 102–119.

Amsel, A. Frustrative nonreward in partial reinforcement and discrimination learning: Some recent history and a theoretical extension. *Psychological Review,* 1962, 69, 306–328.

Amsel, A. Behavioral habituation, counterconditioning, and a general theory of persistence. In A. H. Black & W. F. Prokasy (Eds.), *Classical conditioning II: Current research and theory.* New York: Appleton-Century-Crofts, 1972. Pp. 409–426.

Amsel, A., & Roussel, J. Motivational properties of frustration: I. Effect on a running response of the addition of frustration to the motivational complex. *Journal of Experimental Psychology,* 1952, 43, 363–368.

324

Anderson, L. K., Taylor, J. R., & Holloway, R. J. The consumer and his alternatives: An experimental approach. *Journal of Marketing Research*, 1966, **3**, 62–67.

Aronson, E. The cognitive and behavioral consequences of the confirmation and disconfirmation of expectancies. Application for Research Grant submitted to the National Science Foundation. Harvard University, 1960.

Aronson, E. The effect of effort on the attactiveness of rewarded and unrewarded stimuli. *Journal of Abnormal and Social Psychology*, 1961, **63**, 375–380.

Aronson, E. Dissonance theory: Progress and problems. In R. P. Abelson, E. Aronson, W. J. McGuire, T. M. Newcomb, M. J. Rosenberg, & P. H. Tannenbaum (Eds.), *Theories of cognitive consistency: A sourcebook.* Chicago: Rand-McNally, 1968. Pp. 5–27.

Aronson, E. Some antecedents of interpersonal attraction. In W. J. Arnold & D. Levine (Eds.), *Nebraska symposium on motivation.* Lincoln, Nebraska: University of Nebraska Press, 1969. (a)

Aronson, E. The theory of cognitive dissonance: A current perspective. In L. Berkowitz (Ed.), *Advances in experimental social psychology.* Vol. 4. New York: Academic Press, 1969. Pp. 1–34. (b)

Aronson, E., & Carlsmith, J. M. Performance expectancy as a determinant of actual performance. *Journal of Abnormal and Social Psychology*, 1962, **65**, 178–182.

Aronson, E., & Carlsmith, J. M. Effect of severity of threat on the valuation of forbidden behavior. *Journal of Abnormal and Social Psychology*, 1963, **66**, 584–588.

Aronson, E., Chase, T., Helmreich, R., & Ruhnke, R. Feeling stupid and feeling "awful"— two aspects of the self-concept which mediate dissonance arousal. Unpublished manuscript, University of Texas at Austin, 1970.

Aronson, E., & Linder, D. E. Gain and loss of esteem as determinants of interpersonal attractiveness. *Journal of Experimental Social Psychology*, 1965, **1**, 156–171.

Aronson, E., & Mills, J. The effects of severity of initiation on liking for a group. *Journal of Abnormal and Social Psychology*, 1959, **59**, 177–181.

Aronson, E., Turner, J., & Carlsmith, J. M. Communicator credibility and communication discrepancy as determinants of opinion change. *Journal of Abnormal and Social Psychology*, 1963, **67**, 31–36.

Arrowood, A. J., & Ross, L. Anticipated effort and subjective probability. *Journal of Personality and Society Psychology*, 1966, **4**, 57–64.

Arrowood, A. J., Wood, L., & Ross, L. Dissonance, self-perception, and the perception of others: A study in *cognitive* cognitive dissonance. *Journal of Experimental Social Psychology*, 1970, **6**, 304–315.

Atkinson, J. W. Motivational determinants of risk-taking behavior. *Psychological Review*, 1957, **64**, 359–372.

Atkinson, J. W., & McClelland, D. C. The projective expression of needs: II. The effect of different intensities of hunger drive on thematic apperception. *Journal of Experimental Psychology*, 1948, **38**, 643–658.

Bandler, R. J., Madaras, G. R., & Bem, D. J. Self-observation as a source of pain perception. *Journal of Personality and Social Psychology*, 1968, **9**, 205–209.

Battig, W. F., Wright, J. H., & Gescheider, G. A. Reply to comments by Janet Taylor Spence. *Perceptual and Motor Skills*, 1963, **17**, 410.

Bem, D. J. An experimental analysis of self-persuasion. *Journal of Experimental Social Psychology*, 1965, **1**, 199–218.

Bem, D. J. Inducing belief in false confessions. *Journal of Personality and Social Psychology*, 1966, **3**, 707–710.

Bem, D. J. Self-perception: An alternative interpretation of cognitive dissonance phenomena. *Psychological review*, 1967, **74**, 183–200.

Bem, D. J. The epistemological status of interpersonal simulations: A reply to Jones, Linder, Kiesler, Zanna, and Brehm. *Journal of Experimental Social Psychology*, 1968, **4**, 270–274.

Bem, D. J. Self-perception theory. In L. Berkowitz (Ed.), *Advances in experimental social psychology*. New York: Academic Press, 1972. Pp. 1–62.

Bem, D. J. & McConnell, H. K. Testing the self-perception explanation of dissonance phenomena: On the salience of premanipulation attitudes. *Journal of Personality and Social Psychology*, 1970, **14**, 23–31.

Berkowitz, L. The judgmental process in personality functioning. *Psychological Review*, 1960, **67**, 130–142.

Berlyne, D. E. A decade of motivational theory. *American Scientist*, 1964, **62**, 448–453.

Bochner, S., & Insko, C. A. Communicator discrepancy, source credibility, and influence. *Journal of Personality and Social Psychology*, 1966, **4**, 614–621.

Braden, M., & Walster, E. The effect of anticipated dissonance on predecision behavior. In L. Festinger, *Conflict, decision, and dissoance*. Stanford, California: Stanford University Press, 1964. Pp. 145–151.

Bramel, D. A dissonance theory approach to defensive projection. *Journal of Abnormal and Social Psychology*, 1962, **64**, 121–129.

Bramel, D. Selection of a target for defensive projection. *Journal of Abnormal and Social Psychology*, 1963, **66**, 318–324.

Bramel, D. Dissonance, expectation, and the self. In R. P. Abelson, E. Aronson, W. J. McGuire, T. M. Newcomb, M. J. Rosenberg, & P. H. Tannenbaum (Eds.), *Theories of cognitive consistency: A sourcebook*. Chicago, Illinois: Rand-McNally, 1968, Pp. 355–365.

Brehm, J. W. Postdecision changes in the desirability of alternatives. *Journal of Abnormal and Social Psychology*, 1956, **52**, 384–389.

Brehm, J. W. Increasing cognitive dissonance by a fait-accompli. *Journal of Abnormal and Social Psychology*, 1959, **58**, 379–382.

Brehm, J. W. An experiment on recall of discrepant information. In J. W. Brehm & A. R. Cohen, *Explorations in cognitive dissonance*. New York: Wiley, 1962. Pp. 92–97. (a)

Brehm, J. W. Motivational effects of cognitive dissonance. In M. R. Jones (Ed.), *Nebraska symposium on motivation*. Lincoln, Nebraska: University of Nebraska Press, 1962. (b)

Brehm, J. W. Comment on 'Counter-norm attitudes induced by consonant versus dissonant conditions of role playing.' *Journal of Experimental Research in Personality*, 1965, **1**, 61–64.

Brehm, J. W. *A theory of psychological reactance*. New York: Academic Press, 1966.

Brehm, J. W. Some integrative effects of certain "irrational" behaviors. *Annals of the New York Academy of Sciences*, 1972, **193**, 189–193.

Brehm, J. W., & Cohen, A. R. Choice and chance relative deprivation as determinants of cognitive dissonance. *Journal of Abnormal and Social Psychology*, 1959, **58**, 383–387. (a)

Brehm, J. W., & Cohen, A. R. Reevaluation of choice alternatives as a function of their number and qualitative similarity. *Journal of Abnormal and Social Psychology*, 1959, **58**, 373–378. (b)

Brehm, J. W., & Cohen, A. R. *Explorations in cognitive dissonance*. New York: Wiley, 1962.

Brehm, J. W., & Crocker, J. C. An experiment on hunger. In J. W. Brehm & A. R. Cohen, *Explorations in cognitive dissonance*. New York: Wiley, 1962. Pp. 133–137.

Brehm, J. W., & Jones, R. A. The effect on dissonance of surprise consequences. *Journal of Experimental Social Psychology*, 1970, **6**, 420–431.

Brehm, J. W., & Leventhal, G. S. An experiment on the effect of commitment. In J. W. Brehm & A. R. Cohen, *Explorations in cognitive dissonance*. New York: Wiley, 1962. Pp. 192–198.

Brehm, J. W., & Mann, M. Effect of importance of freedom and attraction to group members on influence produced by group pressure. *Journal of Personality and Social Psychology*, 1975, **31**, 816–824.

Brehm, J. W., & Wicklund, R. A. Regret and dissonance reduction as a function of postdecision salience of dissonant information. *Journal of Personality and Social Psychology*, 1970, 14, 1–7.

Brehm, M. L., Back, K. W., & Bogdonoff, M. D. A physiological effect of cognitive dissonance under stress and deprivation. *Journal of Abnormal and Social Psychology*, 1964, 69, 303–310.

Brehm, S. S. *The application of social psychology to clinical practice.* Washington, D.C.: Hemisphere Press, in press.

Brock, T. C. Cognitive restructuring and attitude change. *Journal of Abnormal and Social Psychology*, 1962, 64, 264–271.

Brock, T. C. Effects of prior dishonesty on postdecision dissonance. *Journal of Abnormal and Social Psychology*, 1963, 66, 325–331.

Brock, T. C. Commitment to exposure as a determinant of information receptivity. *Journal of Personality and Social Psychology*, 1965, 2, 10–19.

Brock, T. C. Dissonance without awareness. In R. P. Abelson, E. Aronson, W. J. McGuire, T. M. Newcomb, M. J. Rosenberg, & P. H. Tannenbaum (Eds.), *Theories of cognitive consistency: A sourcebook.* Chicago, Illinois: Rand-McNally, 1968. Pp. 408–416.

Brock, T. C. Relative efficacy of volition and justification in arousing dissonance. *Journal of Personality*, 1968, 36, 49–66.

Brock, T. C., & Balloun, J. L. Behavioral receptivity to dissonant information. *Journal of Personality and Social Psychology*, 1967, 6, 413–428.

Brock, T. C., & Blackwood, J. E. Dissonance reduction, social comparison and modification of others' opinions. *Journal of Abnormal and Social Psychology*, 1962, 65, 319–324.

Brock, T. C., & Buss, A. H. Dissonance, aggression, and evaluation of pain. *Journal of Abnormal and Social Psychology*, 1962, 65, 197–202.

Brock, T. C., Edelman, S. K., Edwards, D. C., & Schuck, J. R. Seven studies of performance expectancy as a determinant of actual performance. *Journal of Experimental Social Psychology*, 1965, 1, 295–310.

Brock, T. C., & Grant, L. D. Dissonance, awareness, and motivation. *Journal of Abnormal and Social Psychology*, 1963, 67, 53–60.

Brown, J. S. *The motivation of behavior.* New York: McGraw-Hill, 1961.

Byrne, D. Attitudes and attraction. In L. Berkowitz (Ed.), *Advances in experimental social psychology.* New York: Academic Press, 1969. Pp. 35–89.

Byrne, D., & Clore, G. L. A reinforcement model of evaluative responses. *Personality: An International Journal*, 1970, 1, 103–128.

Canon, L. K. Self-confidence and selective exposure to information. In L. Festinger, *Conflict, decision, and dissonance.* Stanford, California: Stanford University Press, 1964. Pp. 83–95.

Carlsmith, J. M., Collins, B. E., & Helmreich, R. L. Studies in forced compliance: I. The effect of pressure for compliance on attitude change produced by face-to-face role playing and anonymous essay writing. *Journal of Personality and Social Psychology*, 1966, 4, 1–13.

Carlsmith, J. M., Ebbesen, E. B., Lepper, M. R., Zanna, M. P., Joncas, A. J., & Abelson, R. P. Dissonance reduction following forced attention to the dissonance. *Proceedings of the 77th Annual Convention of the American Psychological Association*, 1969, 4, 321–322. (Summary)

Cartwright, D., & Harary, F. Structural balance: a generalization of Heider's theory. *Psychological Review*, 1956, 63, 277–293.

Chapanis, N. P., & Chapanis, A. C. Cognitive dissonance: Five years later. *Psychological Bulletin*, 1964, 61, 1–22.

Cofer, C. N. Motivation. In *Annual review of psychology.* Stanford, California: Annual Reviews, 1959.

Cofer, C. N., & Appley, M. H. *Motivation: Theory and research*. New York: Wiley, 1964.

Cohen, A. R. Communication discrepancy and attitude change: A dissonance theory approach. *Journal of Personality*, 1959, 27, 386–396. (a)

Cohen, A. R. Some implications of self-esteem for social influence. In C. I. Hovland & I. L. Janis (Eds.), *Personality and persuasibility*. New Haven: Yale University Press, 1959. (b)

Cohen, A. R. An experiment on small rewards for discrepant compliance and attitude change. In J. W. Brehm & A. R. Cohen, *Explorations in cognitive dissonance*. New York: Wiley, 1962. Pp. 73–78. (a)

Cohen, A. R. A "forced-compliance" experiment on repeated dissonance. In J. W. Brehm & A. R. Cohen, *Explorations in cognitive dissonance*. New York: Wiley, 1962. Pp. 97–104. (b)

Cohen, A. R. A study of discrepant information in betrothal. In J. W. Brehm & A. R. Cohen, *Explorations in cognitive dissonance*. New York: Wiley, 1962. Pp. 78–81. (c)

Cohen, A. R., & Brehm, J. W. An experiment on illegitimate coercion, volition, and attitude change. In J. W. Brehm & A. R. Cohen, *Explorations in cognitive dissonance*. New York: Wiley, 1962. Pp. 206–210.

Cohen, A. R., Brehm, J. W., & Fleming, W. H. Attitude change and justification for compliance. *Journal of Abnormal and Social Psychology*, 1958, 56, 276–278.

Cohen, A. R., Brehm, J. W., & Latané, B. Choice of strategy and voluntary exposure to information under public and private conditions. *Journal of Personality*, 1959, 27, 63–73.

Cohen, A. R., Greenbaum, C. W., & Mansson, H. H. Commitment to social deprivation and verbal conditioning. *Journal of Abnormal and Social Psychology*, 1963, 67, 410–422.

Cohen, A. R., & Latané, B. An experiment on choice in commitment to counterattitudinal behavior. In J. W. Brehm & A. R. Cohen, *Explorations in cognitive dissonance*. New York: Wiley, 1962. Pp. 88–91.

Cohen, A. R., Terry, H. I., & Jones, C. B. Attitudinal effects of choice in exposure to counterpropaganda. *Journal of Abnormal and Social Psychology*, 1959, 58, 388–391.

Cohen, A. R., & Zimbardo, P. G. An experiment on avoidance motivation. In J. W. Brehm & A. R. Cohen, *Explorations in cognitive dissonance*. New York: Wiley, 1962. Pp. 143–151.

Cohen, J. B., & Houston, M. J. Cognitive consequences of brand loyalty. *Journal of Marketing Research*, 1972, 9, 97–99.

Collins, B. E., & Hoyt, M. F. Personal responsibility-for-consequences: An integration and extension of the "forced compliance" literature. *Journal of Experimental Social Psychology*, 1972, 8, 558–593.

Cooper, J. Personal responsibility and dissonance: The role of foreseen consequences. *Journal of Personality and Social Psychology*, 1971, 18, 354–363.

Cooper, J., & Brehm, J. W. Prechoice awareness of relative deprivation as a determinant of cognitive dissonance. *Journal of Experimental Social Psychology*, 1971, 7, 571–581.

Cooper, J., Darley, J. M., & Henderson, J. E. On the effectiveness of deviant- and conventional-appearing communicators: A field experiment. *Journal of Personality and Social Psychology*, 1974, 29, 752–757.

Cooper, J., & Duncan, B. L. Cognitive dissonance as a function of self-esteem and logical inconsistency. *Journal of Personality*, 1971, 39, 289–302.

Cooper, J., & Goethals, G. R. Unforeseen events and the elimination of cognitive dissonance. *Journal of Personality and Social Psychology*, 1974, 29, 441–445.

Cooper, J., & Scalise, C. J. Dissonance produced by deviations from life styles: The interaction of Jungian typology and conformity. *Journal of Personality and Social Psychology*, 1974, 29, 566–571.

Cottrell, N. B. Performance expectancy as a determinant of actual performance: A replication with a new design. *Journal of Personality and Social Psychology*, 1965, 2, 685–691.

Cottrell, N. B. Social facilitation. In C. B. McClintock (Ed.), *Experimental social psychology*. New York: Holt, Rinehart, & Winston, 1972. Pp. 185–236.

Cottrell, N. B. Rajecki, D. W., & Smith, D. U. The energizing effects of postdecision dissonance upon performance of an irrelevant task. *Journal of Social Psychology*, 1974, **93**, 81–92.

Cottrell, N. B., Rittle, R. H., & Wack, D. L. The presence of an audience and list type (competitional or noncompetitional) as joint determinants of performance in paired-associates learning. *Journal of Personality*, 1967, **35**, 425–434.

Cottrell, N. B., & Wack, D. L. Energizing effects of cognitive dissonance upon dominant and subordinate responses. *Journal of Personality and Social Psychology*, 1967, **6**, 132–138.

Crano, W. D., & Messé, L. A. When does dissonance fail? The time dimension in attitude measurement. *Journal of Personality*, 1970, **38**, 493–508.

Cummings, W. H., & Venkatesan, M. Cognitive dissonance and consumer behavior: A critical review. Iowa City, Iowa: College of Business Administration, Working Paper Series No. 74-1, 1974.

Dansereau, F., Cashman, J., & Graen, G. Instrumentality theory and equity theory as complementary approaches in predicting the relationship of leadership and turnover among managers. *Organizational Behavior and Human Performance*, 1973, **10**, 184–200.

Darley, S. A., & Cooper, J. Cognitive consequences of forced noncompliance. *Journal of Personality and Social Psychology*, 1972, **24**, 321–326.

Davidson, J. R. Cognitive familiarity and dissonance reduction. In L. Festinger, *Conflict, decision, and dissonance*. Stanford, California: Stanford University Press, 1964. Pp. 45–59.

Davis, K. E., & Jones, E. E. Changes in interpersonal perception as a means of reducing cognitive dissonance. *Journal of Abnormal and Social Psychology*, 1960, **61**, 402–410.

Deci, E. L. Effects of externally mediated rewards on intrinsic motivation. *Journal of Personality and Social Psychology*, 1971, **18**, 105–115.

Deci, E. L. Intrinsic motivation, extrinsic reinforcement, and inequity. *Journal of Personality and Social Psychology*, 1972, **22**, 113–120.

Deutsch, M., Krauss, R. M., & Rosenau, N. Dissonance or defensiveness? *Journal of Personality*, 1962, **30**, 16–28.

Donin, J. A., Surridge, C. T., & Amsel, A. Extinction following partial delay of reward with immediate continuous reward interpolated, at 24-hour intertrial intervals. *Journal of Experimental Psychology*, 1967, **74**, 50–53.

Donnelly, J. H., & Ivancevich, J. M. Postpurchase reinforcement and back-out behavior. *Journal of Marketing Research*, 1970, **7**, 399–400.

Doob, A. N., Carlsmith, J. M., Freedman, J. L., Landauer, T. K., & Tom, S. Effect of initial selling price on subsequent sales. *Journal of Personality and Social Psychology*, 1969, **11**, 345–350.

Doob, L. W. The behavior of attitudes. *Psychological Review*, 1947, **54**, 135–156.

Drachman, D., & Worchel, S. Misattribution of arousal as a means of dissonance reduction. *Sociometry*, in press.

Duffy, E. *Activation and behavior*. New York: Wiley, 1962.

Duval, S., & Wicklund, R. A. *A theory of objective self awareness*. New York: Academic Press, 1972.

Edlow, D. W., & Kiesler, C. A. Ease of denial and defensive projection. *Journal of Experimental Social Psychology*, 1966, **2**, 56–69.

Edwards, A. L. *Experimental design in psychological research*. New York: Holt, Rinehart, & Winston, 1960.

Ehrlich, D., Guttman, I., Schönbach, P., & Mills, J. Postdecision exposure to relevant information. *Journal of Abnormal and Social Psychology*, 1957, **54**, 98–102.

Elms, A. C., & Janis, I. L. Counternorm attitudes induced by consonant versus dissonant conditions of role playing. *Journal of Experimental Research in Personality*, 1965, **1**, 50–60.

Epstein, R. Effects of commitment to social isolation on children's imitative behavior. *Journal of Personality and Social Psychology*, 1968, **9**, 90–95.

Epstein, S., & Lewitt, H. Influence of hunger on the learning and recall of food selected words. *Journal of Abnormal and Social Psychology*, 1962, **64**, 130–135.

Feather, N. T. Cigarette smoking and lung cancer: A study of cognitive dissonance. *Australian Journal of Psychology*, 1962, **14**, 55–64.

Ferdinand, P. R. The effect of forced compliance on recognition. Unpublished doctoral dissertation, Purdue University, 1965.

Festinger, L. A theory of social comparison processes. *Human Relations*, 1954, 7, 117–140.

Festinger, L. *A theory of cognitive dissonance.* Evanston, Illinois: Row, Peterson, 1957.

Festinger, L. *Conflict, decision, and dissonance.* Stanford, California: Stanford University Press, 1964.

Festinger, L., & Bramel, D. The reactions of humans to cognitive dissonance. In A. Bachrach (Ed.), *The experimental foundations of clinical psychology.* New York: Basic Books, 1962.

Festinger, L., & Carlsmith, J. M. Cognitive consequences of forced compliance. *Journal of Abnormal and Social Psychology,* 1959, **58**, 203–210.

Festinger, L., Riecken, H., & Schachter, S. *When prophecy fails.* Minneapolis, Minnesota: University of Minnesota Press, 1956.

Festinger, L., & Walster, E. Postdecision regret and decision reversal. In L. Festinger, *Conflict, decision, and dissonance.* Stanford, California: Stanford University Press, 1964. Pp. 100–112.

Finn, R. H., & Lee, S. M. Salary equity: Its determination, analysis, and correlates. *Journal of Applied Psychology*, 1972, **56**, 283–292.

Firestone, I. J. Insulted and provoked: The effects of choice and provocation on hostility and aggression. In P. G. Zimbardo (Ed.), *The cognitive control of motivation.* Glenview, Illinois: Scott, Foresman, 1969. Pp. 229–250.

Freedman, J. L. Attitudinal effects of inadequate justification. *Journal of Personality*, 1963, **31**, 371–385.

Freedman, J. L. Preference for dissonant information. *Journal of Personality and Social Psychology*, 1965, **2**, 287–289.   (a)

Freedman, J. L. Confidence, utility, and selective exposure: A partial replication. *Journal of Personality and Social Psychology*, 1965, **2**, 778–780.   (b)

Freedman, J. L. Long-term behavioral effects of cognitive dissonance. *Journal of Experimental Social Psychology*, 1965, **1**, 145–155.   (c)

Freedman, J. L., & Fraser, S. C. Compliance without pressure: The foot-in-the-door technique. *Journal of Personality and Social Psychology,* 1966, **4**, 195–202.

Freedman, J. L., & Sears, D. O. Selective exposure. In L. Berkowitz (Ed.), *Advances in experimental social psychology.* Vol. 2. New York: Academic Press, 1965. Pp. 58–98.

Frey, D. Der augenblickliche stand der "forced-compliance" forschung. *Zeitschrift für Sozialpsychologie,* 1971, **2**, 323–342.

Frey, D., & Irle, M. Some conditions to produce a dissonance and an incentive effect in a 'forced-compliance' situation. *European Journal of Social Psychology*, 1972, **2**, 45–54.

Frey, D., Irle, M., & Kumpf, M. Hypothesen in kognitiver dissonanz. In M. Irle, *Lehrbuch der sozialpsychologie.* Göttingen, Federal Republic of Germany: Hogrefe, 1975. Pp. 343–346.

Fromkin, H. L. Reinforcement and effort expenditure: Predictions of "reinforcement theory" versus predictions of dissonance theory. *Journal of Personality and Social Psychology*, 1968, **9**, 347–352.

330

Gailon, A. K., & Watts, W. A. The time of measurement parameter in studies of dissonance reduction. *Journal of Personality*, 1967, **35**, 521–534.

Gerard, H. B. Deviation, conformity, and commitment. In I. D. Steiner & M. Fishbein (Eds.), *Current studies in social psychology*. New York: Holt, Rinehart, & Winston, 1965. Pp. 263–277.

Gerard, H. B. Choice difficulty, dissonance, and the decision sequence. *Journal of Personality*, 1967, **35**, 91–108.

Gerard, H. B., Blevans, S. A., & Malcolm, T. Self-evaluation and the evaluation of choice alternatives. *Journal of Personality*, 1964, **32**, 395–410.

Gerard, H. B., Conolley, E. S., & Wilhelmy, R. A. Compliance, justification, and cognitive change. In L. Berkowitz (Ed.), *Advances in experimental social psychology*. Vol. 7. New York: Academic Press, 1974. Pp. 217–247.

Gerard, H. B., del Valle, J., Olivos, R., Rodriguez, A., Sanchez–Sosa, J., Thatcher, M., & Zadny, J. Choice, timing of reward and attitude change. Unpublished manuscript, University of California, Los Angeles, 1971.

Gerard, H. B., & Mathewson, G. C. The effects of severity of initiation on liking for a group: A replication. *Journal of Experimental Social Psychology*, 1966, **2**, 278–287.

Glass, D. C. Changes in liking as a means of reducing cognitive discrepancies between self-esteem and agression. *Journal of Personality*, 1964, **32**, 531–549.

Glass, D. C. Theories of consistency and the study of personality. In E. F. Borgatta & W. W. Lambert (Eds.), *Handbook of personality theory and research*. Chicago, Illinois: Rand McNally, 1968. Pp. 788–854. (a)

Glass, D. C. Individual differences and the resolution of cognitive inconsistencies. In R. P. Abelson, E. Aronson, W. J. McGuire, T. M. Newcomb, M. J. Rosenberg, & P. H. Tannenbaum (Eds.), *Theories of cognitive consistency: A sourcebook*. Chicago, Illinois: Rand-McNally, 1968. Pp. 615–623. (b)

Glass, D. C., Canavan, D., & Schiavo, S. Achievement motivation, dissonance, and defensiveness. *Journal of Personality*, 1968, **36**, 474–492.

Glass, D. C., & Mayhew, P. The effects of cognitive processes on skin conductance reactivity to an aversive film. *Psychonomic Science*, 1969, **16**, 72–74.

Goethals, G. R., & Cooper, J. Role of intention and postbehavioral consequence in the arousal of cognitive dissonance. *Journal of Personality and Social Psychology*, 1972, **23**, 293–301.

Goldstein, A. P., Heller, K., & Sechrest, L. B. *Psychotherapy and the psychology of behavior change*. New York: Wiley, 1966.

Goodrich, K. P. Performance in different segments of an instrumental response chain as a function of reinforcement schedule. *Journal of Experimental Psychology*, 1959, **57**, 57–63.

Gordon, A., & Glass, D. C. Choice ambiguity, dissonance, and defensiveness. *Journal of Personality*, 1970, **38**, 264–272.

Götz–Marchand, B., Götz, J., & Irle, M. Preference of dissonance reduction modes as a function of their order, familiarity and reversibility. *European Journal of Social Psychology*, 1974, **4**, 201–228.

Green, D. Dissonance and self-perception analyses of "forced compliance": When two theories make competing predictions. *Journal of Personality and Social Psychology*, 1974, **29**, 819–828.

Greenbaum, C. W. Effect of situational and personality variables on improvisation and attitude change. *Journal of Personality and Social Psychology*, 1966, **4**, 260–269.

Greenbaum, C. W., Cohn, A., & Krauss, R. M. Choice, negative information, and attractiveness of tasks. *Journal of Personality*, 1965, **33**, 46–59.

Greenbaum, C. W., & Zemach, M. Role playing and change of attitude toward the police after a campus riot: Effects of situational demand and justification. *Human Relations,* 1972, **25,** 87–99.

Greenwald, A. G. On the inconclusiveness of "crucial" cognitive tests of dissonance versus self-perception theories. *Journal of Experimental Social Psychology,* in press.

Grinker, J. Cognitive control of classical eyelid conditioning. In P. G. Zimbardo (Ed.), *The cognitive control of motivation.* Glenview, Illinois: Scott, Foresman, 1969. Pp. 126–135.

Hardyck, J. A., & Braden, M. Prophecy fails again: A report of a failure to replicate. *Journal of Abnormal and Social Psychology,* 1962, **65,** 136–141.

Hare, A. P. *Handbook of small group research.* New York: Free Press of Glencoe, 1962.

Harvey, J., & Mills, J. Effect of an opportunity to revoke a counterattitudinal action upon attitude change. *Journal of Personality and Social Psychology,* 1971, **18,** 201–209.

Harvey, O. J. Some situation and cognitive determinants of dissonance resolution. *Journal of Personality and Social Psychology,* 1965, **1,** 349–354.

Hattem, J. V. A cognitive dissonance approach to psychotherapy. Unpublished manuscript, Los Angeles, California: Los Angeles County—University of Southern California Medical Center, Adult Psychiatric Outpatient Clinic, 1973.

Hebb, D. O. Drives and the C. N. S. *Psychological Review,* 1955, **62,** 243–254.

Heider, F. *The psychology of interpersonal relations.* New York: Wiley, 1958.

Helmreich, R. L. Attitudinal effects of stress and justification: A replication and extension. *Journal of Experimental Social Psychology,* 1968, **4,** 153–161.

Helson, H. *Adaptation-level theory.* New York: Harper & Row, 1964.

Hilgard, E. R. Levels of awareness: Second thoughts on some of William James' ideas. In R. B. MacLeod (Ed.), *William James: Unfinished business.* Washington, D.C.: American Psychological Association, 1969.

Himmelfarb, S., & Arazi, D. Choice and source attractiveness in exposure to discrepant messages. *Journal of Experimental Social Psychology,* in press.

Hochgürtel, G., Frey, D., & Götz, J. Die attraktivität von aufgaben in abhängigkeit von der belohnungshöhe und dem zeitpunkt der bekanntgabe der belohnung. *Zeitschrift für Sozialpsychologie,* 1973, **4,** 231–241.

Holmes, J. G., & Strickland, L. H. Choice freedom and confirmation of incentive expectancy as determinants of attitude change. *Journal of Personality and Social Psychology,* 1970, **14,** 39–45.

Homans, G. C. Status among clerical workers. *Human Organization* 1953, **12,** 5–10.

Hovland, C. I., & Rosenberg, M. J. (Eds.), *Attitude organization and change.* New Haven, Conneticut: Yale University Press, 1960.

Hoyt, M. F., Henley, M. D., & Collins, B. E. Studies in forced compliance: Confluence of choice and consequence on attitude change. *Journal of Personality and Social Psychology,* 1972, **23,** 205–210.

Humphreys, L. G. The effect of random alternation of reinforcement on the acquisition and extinction of conditioned eyelid reactions. *Journal of Experimental Psychology,* 1939, **25,** 141–158.

Insko, C. A., Worchel, S., Folger, R., & Kutkus, A. A balance theory interpretation of dissonance. *Psychological Review,* 1975, **82,** 169–183.

Insko, C. A., Worchel, S., Songer, E., & Arnold, S. E. Effort, objective self-awareness, choice, and dissonance. *Journal of Personality and Social Psychology,* 1973, **28,** 262–269.

Irle, M. *Lehrbuch der sozialpsychologie.* Göttingen, Federal Republic of Germay: Hogrefe, 1975.

Janis, I. L., & Field, P. B. A behavioral assessment of persuasibility: Consistency of individual differences. In C. I. Hovland & I. L. Janis (Eds.), *Personality and persuasibility.* New Haven: Yale University Press, 1959. Pp. 29–54.

Janis, I. L., & Gilmore, J. B. The influence of incentive conditions on the success of role

332

playing in modifying attitudes. *Journal of Personality and Social Psychology*, 1965, **1**, 17–27.

Janis, I. L., Kaye, D., & Kirschner, P. Facilitating effects of "eating while reading" on responsiveness to persuasive communications. *Journal of Personality and Social Psychology*, 1965, **1**, 181–186.

Jecker, J. D. The cognitive effects of conflict and dissonance. In L. Festinger, *Conflict, decision, and dissonance.* Stanford, California: Stanford University Press, 1964. Pp. 21–30.

Jecker, J. D. Conflict and dissonance: A time of decision. In R. P. Abelson, E. Aronson, W. J. McGuire, T. M. Newcomb, M. J. Rosenberg, & P. H. Tannenbaum (Eds.), *Theories of cognitive consistency: A sourcebook.* Chicago, Illinois: Rand-McNally, 1968. Pp. 571–576.

Jellison, J. M., & Mills, J. Effect of public commitment upon opinions. *Journal of Experimental Social Psychology*, 1969, **5**, 340–346.

Jenkins, H. M. Resistance to extinction when partial reinforcement is followed by regular reinforcement. *Journal of Experimental Psychology*, 1962, **64**, 441–450.

Jones, E. E., & Davis, K. E. From acts to dispositions: The attribution process in person perception. In L. Berkowitz (Ed.), *Advances in experimental social psychology.* New York: Academic Press, 1965.

Jones, E. E., & Gerard, H. B. *Foundations of social psychology.* New York: Wiley, 1967.

Jones, R. A., & Brehm, J. W. Attitudinal effects of communicator attractiveness when one chooses to listen. *Journal of Personality and Social Psychology*, 1967, **6**, 64–70.

Jones, R. A., Linder, D. E., Kiesler, C. A., Zanna, M. P., & Brehm, J. W. Internal states or external stimuli: Observers' attitude judgments and the dissonance theory–self-persuasion controversy. *Journal of Experimental Social Psychology*, 1968, **4**, 247–269.

Jordan, N. Behavioral forces that are a function of attitudes and of cognitive organization.*Human Relations*, 1953, **6**, 273–287.

Jordan, N. The mythology of the nonobvious–autism or fact? *Contemporary Psychology*, 1964, **9**, 140–142.

Kassarjian, H. H., & Cohen, J. B. Cognitive dissonance and consumer behavior. *California Management Review*, 1965, **8**, 55–64.

Katz, E. On reopening the question of selectivity in exposure to mass communications. In R. P. Abelson, E. Aronson, W. J. McGuire, T. M. Newcomb, M. J. Rosenberg, & P. H. Tannenbaum (Eds.), *Theories of cognitive consistency: A sourcebook.* Chicago, Illinois: Rand-McNally, 1968. Pp. 788–796.

Kelley, H. H. *Attribution in social interaction.* New York: General Learning Press, 1971.

Kiesler, C. A. *The psychology of commitment.* New York: Academic Press, 1971.

Kiesler, C. A. A motivational theory of stimulus incongruity, with applications for such phenomena as dissonance and self-attribution. Paper presented at the annual meeting of the Midwestern Psychological Association, Chicago, Illinois, 1974.

Kiesler, C. A., & Corbin, L. Commitment, attraction, and conformity. *Journal of Personality and Social Psychology*, 1965, **2**, 890–895.

Kiesler, C. A., & DeSalvo, J. The group as an influencing agent in a forced compliance paradigm. *Journal of Experimental Social Psychology*, 1967, **3**, 160–171.

Kiesler, C. A., Pallak, M. S., & Kanouse, D. E. Interaction of commitment and dissonance. *Journal of Personality and Social Psychology*, 1968, **8**, 331–338.

Kiesler, C. A., Zanna, M. P., & DeSalvo, J. Deviation and conformity: Opinion change as a function of commitment, attraction, and presence of a deviate. *Journal of Personality and Social Psychology*, 1966, **3**, 458–467.

Knight, K. E. effect of effort on behavioral rigidity in a Luchins Water Jar Task. *Journal of Abnormal and Social Psychology*, 1963, **66**, 190–192.

Knox, R. E., & Inkster, J. A. Postdecision dissonance at post time. *Journal of Personality and Social Psychology*, 1968, 8, 319–323.

Kruglanski, A. W., Alon, S., & Lewis, T. Retrospective misattribution and task enjoyment. *Journal of Experimental Social Psychology*, 1972, 8 493–501.

Lawrence, D. H., & Festinger, L. *Deterrents and reinforcement.* Stanford, California: Stanford University Press, 1962.

Lepper, M. R., Greene, D., & Nisbett, R. E. Undermining children's intrinsic interest with extrinsic reward. *Journal of Personality and Social Psychology*, 1973, 28, 129–137.

Lepper, M. R., Zanna, M. P., & Abelson, R. P. Cognitive irreversibility in a dissonance reduction situation. *Journal of Personality and Social Psychology*, 1970, 16, 191–198.

Lewin, K. *Field theory in social science.* New York: Harper, 1951.

Lewis, M. Effect of effort on value: An exploratory study of children. *Child Development*, 1964, 35, 1337–1342. (a)

Lewis, M. Some nondecremental effects of effort. *Journal of Comparative Physiological Psychology*, 1964, 57, 367–372. (b)

Linder, D. E., Cooper, J., & Jones, E. E. Decision freedom as a determinant of the role of incentive magnitude in attitude change. *Journal of Personality and Social Psychology*, 1967, 6, 245–254.

Linder, D. E., Cooper, J., & Wicklund, R. A. Preexposure persuasion as a result of commitment to preexposure effort. *Journal of Experimental Social Psychology*, 1968, 4, 470–482.

Linder, D. E., & Crane, K. A. Reactance theory analysis of predecisional cognitive processes. *Journal of Personality and Social Psychology*, 1970, 15, 258–264.

Linder, D. E., & Worchel, S. Opinion change as a result of effortfully drawing a counterattitudinal conclusion. *Journal of Experimental Social Psychology*, 1970, 6, 432–448.

Linder, D. E., Wortman, C. B., & Brehm, J. W. Temporal changes in predecision preferences among choice alternatives. *Journal of Personality and Social Psychology*, 1971, 19, 282–284.

Lombardo, J. P., Libkuman, T. M., & Weiss, R. F. The energizing effects of disagreement-induced drive. *Journal of Research in Personality,* 1972, 6, 133–141.

LoSciuto, L., & Perloff, R. Influence of product preference on dissonance reduction. *Journal of Marketing Research*, 1967, 4, 286–290.

Lott, A. J., Aponte, J. F., Lott, B. E., & McGinley, W. H. The effect of delayed reward on the development of positive attitudes toward persons. *Journal of Experimental Social Psychology*, 1969, 5, 101–113.

Lott, A. J., & Lott, B. E. The power of liking: Consequences of interpersonal attitudes derived from a liberalized view of secondary reinforcement. In L. Berkowitz (Ed.), *Advances in experimental social psychology.* New York: Academic Press, 1972. Pp. 109–148.

Lowin, A. Approach and avoidance as alternate modes of selective exposure to information. *Journal of Personality and Social Psychology*, 1967, 6, 1–9.

Lowin, A. Further evidence for an approach–avoidance interpretation of selective exposure. *Journal of Experimental Social Psychology*, 1969, 5, 265–271.

Lowin, A., & Epstein, G. F. Does expectancy determine performance? *Journal of Experimental Social Psychology*, 1965, 1, 248–255.

Malewski, A. The influence of positive and negative self-evaluation on postdecisional dissonance. *Polish Sociological Bulletin,* 1962, No. 3–4, 39–49.

Malmo, R. B. Activation: A neurophysiological dimension. *Psychological Review*, 1959, 66, 367–386.

Mann, L., Janis, I. L., & Chaplin, R. Effects of anticipation of forthcoming information on predecisional processes. *Journal of Personality and Social Psychology*, 1969, 11, 10–16.

334

Mansson, H. H. The relation of dissonance reduction to cognitive, perceptual, consummatory, and learning measures of thirst. In P. G. Zimbardo (Ed.), *The cognitive control of motivation*. Glenview, Illinois: Scott, Foresman, 1969. Pp. 78–97.

Marecek, J., & Mettee, D. R. Avoidance of continued success as a function of self-esteem, level of esteem certainty, and responsibility for success. *Journal of Personality and Social Psychology*, 1972, **22**, 98–107.

McGuire, W. J. The current status of cognitive consistency theories. In S. Feldman (Ed.), *Cognitive consistency: Motivational antecedents and behavioral consequents*. New York: Academic Press, 1966, Pp. 1–46.

Mettee, D. R. Rejection of unexpected success as a function of the negative consequences of accepting success. *Journal of Personality and Social Psychology*, 1971, **17**, 332–341.

Miller, G. R., & Rokeach, M. Individual differences and tolerance for inconsistency. In R. P. Abelson, E. Aronson, W. J. McGuire, T. M. Newcomb, M. J. Rosenberg, & P. H. Tannenbaum (Eds.), *Theories of cognitive consistency: A sourcebook*. Chicago, Illinois: Rand-McNally, 1968. Pp. 624–632.

Miller, N. As time goes by. In R. P. Abelson, E. Aronson, W. J. McGuire, T. M. Newcomb, M. J. Rosenberg, & P. H. Tannenbaum (Eds.), *Theories of cognitive consistency: A sourcebook*. Chicago, Illinois: Rand-McNally, 1968. Pp. 589–598.

Miller, N. E. Theory and experiment relating psychoanalytic displacement to stimulus–response generalization. *Journal of Abnormal and Social Psychology*, 1948, **43**, 155–178.

Miller, N. E. Liberalization of basic S–R concepts: Extensions to conflict behavior, motivation, and social learning. In S. Koch (Ed.), *Psychology: The study of science*. Vol. 2. New York: McGraw Hill, 1959.

Mills, J. Avoidance of dissonant information. *Journal of Personality and Social Psychology*, 1965, **2**, 589–593. (a)

Mills, J. Effect of certainty about a decision upon postdecision exposure to consonant and dissonant information. *Journal of Personality and Social Psychology*, 1965, **2**, 749–752.- (b)

Mills, J. The effect of certainty on exposure to information prior to commitment. *Journal of Experimental Social Psychology*, 1965, **1**, 348–355. (c)

Mills, J. Interest in supporting and discrepant information. In R. P. Abelson, E. Aronson, W. J. McGuire, T. M. Newcomb, M. J. Rosenberg, & P. H. Tannenbaum (Eds.), *Theories of cognitive consistency: A sourcebook*. Chicago, Illinois: Rand-McNally, 1968. Pp. 771–776.

Mills, J., Aronson, E., & Robinson, H. Selectivity in exposure to information. *Journal of Abnormal and Social Psychology*, 1959, **59**, 250–253.

Mills, J., & Jellison, J. M. Avoidance of discrepant information prior to commitment. *Journal of Personality and Social Psychology*, 1968, **8**, 59–62.

Mills, J., & O'Neal, E. Anticipated choice, attention, and the halo effect. *Psychonomic Science*, 1971, **22**, 231–233.

Mills, J., & Ross, A. Effects of commitment and certainty upon interest in supporting information. *Journal of Abnormal and Social Psychology*, 1964, **68**, 552–555.

Mischel, W., Grusec, J., & Masters, J. C. Effects of expected delay time on the subjective value of rewards and punishments. *Journal of Personality and Social Psychology*, 1969, **11**, 363–373.

Mittelstaedt, R. A dissonance approach to repeat purchasing behavior. *Journal of Marketing Research*, 1969, **6**, 444–446.

Mowrer, O. H. Cognitive dissonance or counterconditioning?–A reappraisal of certain behavioral "paradoxes." *Psychological Record*, 1963, **133**, 197–211.

Muir, W. K. *Prayer in the public schools*. Chicago, Illinois: The University of Chicago Press, 1967.

Nash, M. C. An experimental test of the Michels–Helson theory of judgment. *American Journal of Psychology,* 1950, **63**, 214–220.

Nel, E., Helmreich, R., & Aronson, E. Opinion change in the advocate as a function of the persuasibility of his audience: A clarification of the meaning of dissonance. *Journal of Personality and Social Psychology,* 1969, **12**, 117–124.

Newcomb, T. M. An approach to the study of communicative acts. *Psychological Review,* 1953, **60**, 393–404.

Notz, W. W., Staw, B. M., & Cook, T. D. Attitude toward troop withdrawal from Indochina as a function of draft number: Dissonance or self-interest? *Journal of Personality and Social Psychology,* 1971, **20**, 118–126.

Nuttin, J. M., Jr. *The illusion of attitude change: Towards a response contagion theory of persuasion.* London: Academic Press, 1975.

O'Neal, E. Influence of future choice importance and arousal upon the halo effect. *Journal of Personality and Social Psychology,* 1971, **19**, 334–340.

O'Neal, E., & Mills, J. The influence of anticipated choice on the halo effect. *Journal of Experimental Social Psychology,* 1969, **5**, 347–351.

Osgood, C. E. Motivational dynamics of language behavior. In *Nebraska symposium on motivation.* Lincoln, Nebraska: University of Nebraska Press, 1957.

Osgood, C. E. Cognitive dynamics in the conduct of human affairs. *Public Opinion Quarterly,* 1960, **24**, 341–365.

Osgood, C. E., Suci, G. J., & Tannenbaum, P. H. *The measurement of meaning.* Urbana, Illinois: University of Illinois Press, 1957.

Osgood, C. E., & Tannenbaum, P. H. The principle of congruity in the prediction of attitude change. *Psychological Review,* 1955, **62**, 42–55.

Ostrom, T. M. Physical effort and attitude change. Paper presented at the meeting of the American Psychological Association, New York, 1966.

Pallak, M. S. Effects of expected shock and relevant or irrelevant dissonance on incidental retention. *Journal of Personality and Social Psychology,* 1970, **14**, 271–280.

Pallak, M. S., & Andrews, J. The effects of expected shock and expected payment on incidental retention. *Psychonomic Science,* 1970, **18**, 323–325.

Pallak, M. S., Brock, T. C., & Kiesler, C. A. Dissonance arousal and task performance in an incidental verbal learning paradigm. *Journal of Personality and Social Psychology,* 1967, **7**, 11–20.

Pallak, M. S., & Pittman, T. S. General motivational effects of dissonance arousal. *Journal of Personality and Social Psychology,* 1972, **21**, 349–358.

Pallak, M. S., Sogin, S. R., & Cook, D. Dissonance and self-perception: Attitude change and belief inference for actors and observers. Unpublished manuscript, University of Iowa, 1974.

Pallak, M. S., Sogin, S. R., & Van Zante, A. Bad decisions: Effect of volition, locus of causality, and negative consequences on attitude change. *Journal of Personality and Social Psychology,* 1974, **30**, 217–227.

Patchen, M. Study of work and life satisfaction, Report No. 2: Absences and attitudes toward work experience. Institute for Social Research, Ann Arbor, Michigan, 1959.

Paul, I. H. Impressions of personality, authoritarianism, and the *fait accompli* effect. *Journal of Abnormal and Social Psychology,* 1956, **53**, 338–344.

Pepitone, A., McCauley, C., & Hammond, P. Change in attractiveness of forbidden toys as a function of severity of threat. *Journal of Experimental Social Psychology,* 1967, **3**, 221–229.

Piliavin, J. A., Piliavin, I. M., Loewenton, E. P., McCauley, C. & Hammond, P. On observers' reproductions of dissonance effects: The right answers for the wrong reasons? *Journal of Personality and Social Psychology,* 1969, **13**, 98–106.

336

Pittman, T. S. Attribution of arousal as a mediator in dissonance reduction. *Journal of Experimental Social Psychology*, 1975, **11**, 53–63.

Rabbie, J. M., Brehm, J. W., & Cohen, A. R. Verbalization and reactions to cognitive dissonance. *Journal of Personality*, 1959, **27**, 407–417.

Rahman, S. M. Attractiveness of goal objects as a function of dissonance reduction. Unpublished doctoral dissertation, Duke University, 1962.

Rhine, R. J. Some problems in dissonance theory research on information selectivity. *Psychological Bulletin*, 1967, **68**, 21–28. (a)

Rhine, R. J. The 1964 presidential election and curves of information seeking and avoiding. *Journal of Personality and Social Psychology*, 1967, **5**, 416–423. (b)

Rosen, S. Postdecision affinity for incompatible information. *Journal of Abnormal and Social Psychology*, 1961, **63**, 188–190.

Rosenberg, M. J. Cognitive structure and attitudinal affect. *Journal of Abnormal and Social Psychology*, 1956, **53**, 367–372.

Rosenberg, M. J. An analysis of affective-cognitive consistency. In M. J. Rosenberg, C. I. Hovland, W. J. McGuire, R. P. Abelson, & J. W. Brehm (Eds.), *Attitude organization and change*. New Haven: Yale University Press, 1960. Pp. 15–64.

Rosenberg, M. J. When dissonance fails: On eliminating evaluation apprehension from attitude measurement. *Journal of Personality and Social Psychology*, 1965, **1**, 28–42.

Rosenberg, M. J. The experimental parable of inauthenticity: Consequences of counterattitudinal performance. In J. S. Antrobus (Ed.), *Cognition and affect*. Boston, Massachusetts: Little, Brown, 1970. Pp. 179–201.

Rosenberg, M. J., & Abelson, R. P. An analysis of cognitive balancing. In C. I. Hovland & M. J. Rosenberg (Eds.), *Attitude organization and change*. New Haven, Connecticut: Yale University Press, 1960.

Rosnow, R. L., Gitter, A. G., & Holz, R. F. Some determinants of postdecisional information perferences. Unpublished manuscript, 1968.

Ross, M., & Shulman, R. F. Increasing the salience of initial attitudes: Dissonance versus self-perception theory. *Journal of Personality and Social Psychology*, 1973, **28**, 138–144.

Schachter, S., & Singer, J. E. Cognitive, social and physiological determinants of emotional state. *Psychological Review*, 1962, **69**, 379–399.

Schlachet, P. J. The effect of dissonance arousal on the recall of failure stimuli. *Journal of Personality*, 1965, **33**, 443–461.

Schopler, J., & Bateson, N. A dependence interpretation of the effects of a severe initiation. *Journal of Personality*, 1962, **30**, 633–649.

Sears, D. O. Biased indoctrination and selectivity of exposure to new information. *Sociometry*, 1965, **28**, 363–376.

Sears, D. O. The paradox of de facto selective exposure without preferences for supportive information. In R. P. Abelson, E. Aronson, W. J. McGuire, T. M. Newcomb, M. J. Rosenberg, & P. H. Tannenbaum (Eds.), *Theories of cognitive consistency: A sourcebook*. Chicago, Illinois: Rand-McNally, 1968. Pp. 777–787.

Sensenig, J. Self-exposure to information as a function of decision certainty and direction of information. Unpublished doctoral dissertation, Duke University, 1969.

Shaffer, D. R. Some effects of consonant and dissonant attitudinal advocacy on initial attitude salience and attitude change. *Journal of Personality and Social Psychology*, in press.

Shaffer, D. R., & Hendrick, C. Effects of actual effort and anticipated effort on task enhancement. *Journal of Experimental Social Psychology*, 1971, **7**, 435–447.

Shaffer, D. R., & Hendrick, C. Dogmatism and tolerance for ambiguity as determinants of differential reactions to cognitive inconsistency. *Journal of Personality and Social Psychology*, 1974, **29**, 601–608.

Shaffer, D. R., Hendrick, C., Regula, C. R., & Freconna, J. Interactive effects of ambiguity tolerance and task effort on dissonance reduction. *Journal of Personality*, 1973, **41**, 224–233.

Sherman, S. J. Effects of choice and incentive on attitude change in a discrepant behavior situation. *Journal of Personality and Social Psychology*, 1970, **15**, 245–252. (a)

Sherman, S. J. Attitudinal effects of unforeseen consequences. *Journal of Personality and Social Psychology*, 1970, **16**, 510–519. (b)

Silverman, I., & Marcantonio, C. Demand characteristics versus dissonance-reduction as determinants of failure-seeking behavior. *Journal of Personality and Social Psychology*, 1965, **2**, 882–884.

Smith, E. E. The power of dissonance techniques to change attitudes. *Public Opinion Quarterly*, 1961, **25**, 626–639.

Snyder, M., & Ebbesen, E. B. Dissonance awareness: A test of dissonance theory versus self-perception theory. *Journal of Experimental Social Psychology*, 1972, 8, 502–517.

Sogin, S. R., & Pallak, M. S. Responsibility, bad decisions, and attitude change: Volition, foreseeability, and locus of causality for negative consequences. Unpublished manuscript, University of Iowa, 1974.

Spence, D. P., & Ehrenberg, B. Effects of oral deprivation on responses to subliminal and supraliminal verbal food stimuli. *Journal of Abnormal and Social Psychology*, 1964, **69**, 10–18.

Spence, J. T. Further comments on "Performance on a motor task as related to MAS scores." *Perceptual and Motor Skills*, 1963, **17**, 564.

Spence, K. W. *Behavior theory and conditioning.* New Haven: Yale University Press, 1956.

Spence, K. W., Farber, I. E., & McFann, H. H. The relation of anxiety (drive) level to performance in competitional and noncompetitional paired-associates learning. *Journal of Experimental Psychology*, 1956, **52**, 296–305.

Spence, K. W., & Goldstein, H. Eyelid conditioning performance as a function of emotion-producing instructions. *Journal of Experimental Psychology*, 1961, **62**, 291–294.

Staats, A. W. Social behaviorism and human motivation: Principles of the attitude-reinforcer-discriminative system. In A. G. Greenwald, T. C. Brock, & T. M. Ostrom (Eds.), *Psychological foundations of attitudes.* New York: Academic Press, 1968. Pp. 33–66.

Steiner, I. D. Responses to inconsistency. In R. P. Abelson, E. Aronson, W. J. McGuire, T. M. Newcomb, M. J. Rosenberg, & P. H. Tannenbaum (Eds.), *Theories of cognitive consistency: A sourcebook.* Chicago, Illinois: Rand-McNally, 1968. Pp. 641–647.

Steiner, I. D. Perceived freedom. In L. Berkowitz (Ed.), *Advances in experimental social psychology.* New York: Academic Press, 1970.

Steiner, I. D., & Rogers, E. D. Alternative responses to dissonance. *Journal of Abnormal and Social Psychology*, 1963, **66**, 128–136.

Stevens, S. S. On the psychophysical law. *Psychological Review,* 1957, **63**, 153–181.

Stroop, J. R. Studies of interference in serial verbal reactions. *Journal of Experimental Psychology*, 1935, **18**, 643–662.

Tedeschi, J. T., Schlenker, B. R., & Bonoma, T. V. Cognitive dissonance: Private ratiocination or public spectacle? *American Psychologist,* 1971, **26**, 685–695.

Theios, J. The partial reinforcement effect sustained through blocks of continuous reinforcement. *Journal of Experimental Psychology*, 1962, **64**, 1–6.

Thibaut, J. An experimental study of the cohesiveness of underprivileged groups. *Human Relations,* 1950, **3**, 251–278.

Thibaut, J., & Ross, M. Commitment and experience as determinants of assimilation and contrast. *Journal of Personality and Social Psychology*, 1969, **13**, 322–329.

Totman, R. An approach to cognitive dissonance theory in terms of ordinary language. *Journal for the Theory of Social Behavior,* 1973, **3**, 215–238.

338

Turner, E. A., & Wright, J. Effects of severity of threat and perceived availability on the attractiveness of objects. *Journal of Personality and Social Psychology*, 1965, 2, 128–132.

Varela, J. A. *Psychological solutions to social problems.* New York: Academic Press, 1971.

Verbruggen, F. *Looking out for Leon Festinger in the 18th century.* Ghent, Belgium: Communication and Cognition (Faculteit Letteren en Wijsbegeerte, R.U.G., University of Ghent), 1974.

Walster, E. The temporal sequence of postdecision processes. In L. Festinger, *Conflict, decision, and dissonance.* Stanford, California: Stanford University Press, 1964. Pp. 112–128.

Walster, E., & Berscheid, E. The effects of time on cognitive consistency. In R. P. Abelson, E. Aronson, W. J. McGuire, T. M. Newcomb, M. J. Rosenberg, & P. H. Tannenbaum (Eds.), *Theories of cognitive consistency: A sourcebook.* Chicago, Illinois: Rand-McNally, 1968. Pp. 599–608.

Walster, E., Berscheid, E., & Barclay, A. M. A determinant of preference among modes of dissonance reduction. *Journal of Personality and Social Psychology*, 1967, 7, 211–216.

Walster, E., Berscheid, E., & Walster, G. W. New directions in equity research. *Journal of Personality and Social Psychology*, 1973, 25, 151–176.

Ward, W. D., Sandvold, K. D. Performance expectancy as a determinant of actual performance: A partial replication. *Journal of Abnormal and Social Psychology*, 1963, 67, 293–295.

Waterman, C. K. The facilitating and interfering effects of cognitive dissonance on simple and complex paired associates learning tasks. *Journal of Experimental Social Psychology*, 1969, 5, 31–42.

Watts, W. A. Commitment under conditions of risk. *Journal of Personality and Social Psychology*, 1966, 3, 507–515.

Webb, W. B., & Goodman, I. J. Activating role of an irrelevant drive in absence of the relevant drive. *Psychological Reports*, 1958, 4, 235–238.

Weick, K. E. Reduction of cognitive dissonance through task enhancement and effort expenditure. *Journal of Abnormal and Social Psychology*, 1964, 68, 533–539.

Weick, K. E., Prestholdt, P. Realignment of discrepant reinforcement value. *Journal of Personality and Social Psychology*, 1968, 8, 180–187.

Weiss, R. F., & Miller, F. G. The drive theory of social facilitation. *Psychological Review*, 1971, 78, 44–57.

Wernick, U. Cognitive dissonance and its solution: The application of a psychological model to the status of Christology in New Testament Scripture. Unpublished Master's thesis (Hebrew), Department of Psychology, The Hebrew University of Jerusalem, 1972.

Wicklund, R. A. Prechoice preference reversal as a result of threat to decision freedom. *Journal of Personality and Social Psychology*, 1970, 14, 8–17.

Wicklund, R. A., Cooper, J., & Linder, D. E. Effects of expected effort on attitude change prior to exposure. *Journal of Experimental Social Psychology*, 1967, 3, 416–428.

Wicklund, R. A., & Duval, S. Opinion change and performance facilitation as a result of objective self-awareness. *Journal of Experimental Social Psychology*, 1971, 7, 319–342.

Wilson, P. R., & Russell, P. N. Modification of psychophysical judgments as a method of reducing dissonance. *Journal of Personality and Social Psychology*, 1966, 3, 710–712.

Wolitzky, D. L. Cognitive control and cognitive dissonance. *Journal of Personality and Social Psychology*, 1967, 5, 486–490.

Worchel, S., & Arnold, S. E. The effect of combined arousal states on attitude change. *Journal of Experimental Social Psychology*, 1974, 10, 549–560.

Worchel, S., & Brand, J. Role of responsibility and violated expectancy in the arousal of dissonance. *Journal of Personality and Social Psychology*, 1972, 22, 87–97.

Wortman, C. B. Some determinants of perceived control. *Journal of Personality and Social Psychology*, 1975, 31, 282–294.

Yaryan, R., & Festinger, L. Preparatory action and belief in the probable occurrence of future events. *Journal of Abnormal and Social Psychology*, 1961, **63**, 603–606.

Zajonc, R. B. Social facilitation. *Science*, 1965, **149**, 269–274.

Zanna, M. P. The effect of distraction on resolving cognitive dilemmas. Paper presented at the annual meeting of the American Psychological Association, Chicago, 1975.

Zanna, M. P., & Cooper, J. Dissonance and the pill: An attribution approach to studying the arousal properties of dissonance. *Journal of Personality and Social Psychology*, 1974, **29**, 703–709.

Zanna, M. P., Lepper, M. R., & Abelson, R. P. Attentional mechanisms in children's devaluation of a forbidden activity in a forced-compliance situation. *Journal of Personality and Social Psychology*, 1973, **28**, 355–359.

Zeigarnik, B. Über das behalten von erledigten und unerledigten handlungen. *Psychologische Forschung*, 1927, **9**, 1–85.

Zimbardo, P. G. Involvement and communication discrepancy as determinants of opinion conformity. *Journal of Abnormal and Social Psychology*, 1960, **60**, 86–94.

Zimbardo, P. G. The effect of effort and improvisation on self-persuasion produced by role playing. *Journal of Experimental Social Psychology*, 1965, **1**, 103–120.

Zimbardo, P. G. (Ed.). *The cognitive control of motivation*. Glenview, Illinois: Scott, Foresman, 1969.

Zimbardo, P. G., Cohen, A. R., Weisenberg, M., Dworkin, L., & Firestone, I. The control of experimental pain. In P. G. Zimbardo (Ed.), *The cognitive control of motivation*. Glenview, Illinois: Scott, Foresman, 1969. Pp. 100–125.

Zimbardo, P. G., Weisenberg, M., Firestone, I. J., & Levy, B. Communicator effectiveness in producing public conformity and private attitude change. *Journal of Personality*, 1965, **33**, 233–255.

Author Index

Numbers in *italics* refer to pages on which the complete references are listed.

A

Abelson, R. P., 55, 56, 57, 59, 101, 102, 120, 121, 122, 222, 256, 260, *323, 326, 333, 336, 339*
Ackerman, N. W., 205, *323*
Adams, J. S., 89, 211, 212, 213, 214, 215, 216, *323*
Adorno, T. W., 230, *323*
Allen, V. L., 102, 104, *323*
Allport, G. W., 254, *323*
Alon, S., 61, 65, 67, 69, 214, *333*
Amsel, A., 162, 165, 166, 167, 168, *323, 328*
Anderson, L. K., 289, *324*
Andrews, J., 93, *335*
Aponte, J. F., 30, 31, *333*
Appley, M. H., 86, *327*
Arazi, D., 49, 286, *331*
Arnold, S. E., 95, 104, 222, *331, 338*
Aronson, E., 17, 55, 63, 65, 66, 69, 81, 82, 84, 101, 117, 132, 155, 156, 157, 160, 162, 178, 188, 191, 193, 214, 225, 245, 246, 247, 259, 260, 307, 321, *323, 324, 334, 335*
Arrowood, A. J., 78, 79, 268, 274, *324*
Atkinson, J. W., 146, 153, *324*

B

Back, K. W., 143, 144, 147, *326*
Balloun, J. L., 186, 187, 188, 189, *326*

Bandler, R. J., 275, *324*
Barclay, A. M., 131, 132, 134, 238, 315, 317, *338*
Bateson, N., 81, *336*
Battig, W. F., 87, *324*
Bem, D. J., 260, 261, 262, 263, 264, 265, 267, 269, 270, 274, 275, 276, 279, *324, 325*
Berkowitz, L., 208, 209, *325*
Berlyne, D. E., 86, *325*
Berscheid, E., 58, 131, 132, 134, 216, 218, 238, 315, 317, *338*
Blackwood, J. E., 78, *326*
Blevans, S. A., 225, 226, 227, *330*
Bochner, S., 132, *325*
Bogdonoff, M. D., 143, 144, 147, *326*
Bonoma, T. V., 281, 282, 283, 284, 319, 320, *337*
Braden, M., 138, 300, *325, 331*
Bramel, D., 132, 201, 202, 205, 206, 219, 248, *325, 329*
Brand, J., 62, 63, 67, 70, 154, *338*
Brehm, J. W., 6, 7, 9, 13, 35, 36, 38, 39, 48, 53, 55, 56, 58, 59, 60, 67, 68, 76, 78, 83, 84, 101, 110, 114, 116, 120, 122, 132, 133, 140, 141, 143, 144, 145, 146, 147, 171, 180, 183, 187, 188, 189, 191, 192, 221, 222, 223, 245, 262, 263, 264, 265, 266, 267, 270, 273, 276, 281, 286, 289, 291, 293, 294, 303, 314, 315, 319, *325, 327, 332, 333, 336*
Brehm, M. L., 143, 144, 147, *326*

341

Subject Index